I MAY BE SOME TIME

edited by the same author

THE CHATTO BOOK OF CABBAGES AND KINGS:
Lists in Literature
THE CHATTO BOOK OF THE DEVIL
CULTURAL BABBAGE:
Technology, Time and Invention
(with Jenny Uglow)

I May Be Some Time
Ice and the English Imagination

Francis Spufford

St. Martin's Press
New York

ISBN 0-312-17442-X

Library of Congress Cataloging-in-Publication Data to be found at
the Library of Congress

First published in 1996 by Faber and Faber Limited
First St. Martin's edition: November, 1997
10 9 8 7 6 5 4 3 2 1

for Jessica

Contents

Illustrations

We'd rather have the iceberg than the ship,
although it meant the end of travel.
                                        Elizabeth Bishop

A Different History for the Poles

We had better begin with the question asked by every reader of the standard accounts of the great expeditions, the urgent question that floats irresistibly to the surface of one's mind as the contrast grows stronger and stronger between the safe, sensible surroundings in which one is reading, and the scenes that are being described. It works like a charm, always. One is sitting down somewhere in the warm – perhaps it is sunny, perhaps it is a dark evening of a temperate winter and the radiators are on – and whatever one's attitude, whatever the scepticism one applies to the boyish, adventurous text in one's hands, into one's mind come potent pictures of a place that is definitively elsewhere, so far away in fact that one would call it unimaginable if one were not at that moment imagining it at full force. Perhaps the place is a howling trough between two huge waves of the Antarctic Ocean, where a twelve-foot open boat encrusted with ice and containing five men, one of whom has gone mad and won't move, looks as if it is about to founder. Perhaps the place is the foot of a cliff in the dark, so cold and still that the breath of the travellers crystallises and falls to the snow in showers, so cold that their clothes will freeze at impossible angles if they do not keep their limbs moving. Perhaps the place is the South Pole itself, an abomination of desolation, a perfect nullity of a landscape, where a party of people are standing in a formal group, one pulling a string attached to a camera shutter. One is there in imagination as one reads, but with the possibility of instant withdrawal; one feels for the human figures at the centre of the scene, but one is not exactly in sympathy with them, though it is through their eyes that one is seeing. Their presence is as astonishing as their astonishing surroundings, something to be wondered at. And one asks, of course, everyone asks, *why?* Why did they do these insane things?

Another scene, not famous, not potent, requiring to be searched for. The beige and cream, rattan and mosquito netting of the Base Hospital, Delhi, in February 1910; despite the best efforts of the staff, a little dust spangling the strong Indian sunlight that projects in blocks and bars through chinks in the shuttered windows. The light's like something solid. Sitting up in bed in his pyjamas, Captain Laurence Edward Grace Oates of the Inniskilling Dragoons, who will be staggering out into a blizzard in two years' time, is writing a letter to his mother on paper tiger-striped by sun and shade. 'Do not let the above address frighten you, I have merely drifted in here after eating a bad tin of fish on manoeuvres . . .' Scratch, scratch goes Oates' pen, which he holds like a schoolboy. He has just heard that he has almost certainly been accepted for Scott's expedition to the Antarctic. 'Points in favour of going. It will help me professionally as in the army if they want a man to wash labels off bottles they would sooner employ a man who had been to the North Pole than one who had only got as far as the Mile End Road. The job is most suitable to my tastes. Scott is almost certain to get to the Pole and it is something to say you were with the first party. The climate is very healthy although inclined to be cold . . .'

But then explorers are notoriously bad at saying *why*. Or perhaps they are notoriously good at avoiding giving a satisfactory answer. They laugh at themselves, they deplore the sensationalising of their expeditions, they say it all made sense at the time, they write books filled with practical detail which make readers ask *why* again. They decline to answer in terms that match a question arising as this one does. Maybe then the question is impossible, less of a real question than a gesture that a reader must make. It may be that no answer is really expected, that the question does all it is intended to do by registering astonishment, and signalling the difference between sensible us and mad them.

Sometimes that difference seems so wide that the histories of Antarctic exploration by the British in 'the heroic age' might as well be myths. Although it is easy to list and date the major expeditions – Scott's *Discovery* expedition, 1901–4; Shackleton in *Nimrod*, 1907–9; Scott in *Terra Nova*, 1910–13; Shackleton in *Endurance*, 1914–16 –

they can seem to shed their identifying marks of period as we read about them. The guy ropes tying them to their time snap, and they float free, into a strange region of uncalendared events. The explorers still have Edwardian moustaches, Edwardian attitudes, Edwardian pasts in the cavalry or the Navy, but they appear to possess these things as purely personal characteristics, out of time and out of society, in a world peopled only by themselves. What's more, that world – at least as we experience it through print – is at times even structured like the world of myth, of legend, of moral tales. As it is often told, the story of Scott's last expedition divides cleanly into three parts. What more natural, when woodcutters always have three sons, when the third key always opens the secret box? The story begins with a perilous journey: the expedition ship *Terra Nova*, terribly overladen, flying the burgee of the Royal Yacht Club because it is too unseaworthy to carry the White Ensign, fights its way down through the mountainous waves of the Roaring Forties, almost sinking, until it reaches the shelter of the true South, where pack-ice calms the sea. Then there is the period of preparation, of loin-girding, of feats of arms: the explorers work in their hut by the hiss of gas-lamps through the long darkness of the Antarctic winter, readying equipment and sallying out on preparatory journeys. Finally there comes the climax, the resolution of the quest: the march on the pole, with the focus always narrowing as the supporting parties drop away, mounting to the magnified gestures and conclusive speeches of the disaster. This pattern is as satisfying as it always is. No tree decorates the bleakness of the landscapes, but the story clearly takes place on the traditional terrain of the magic wood, from which – this time – the trail of breadcrumbs does not lead the travellers back to safety.

Perhaps this is why the stories have survived, why they have the power to cross the decades and still *work* for people very remote from the dead explorers. It is not at all certain that we would like them, if we were able to meet them off the page, away from the clinching immediacy of myth. There's a passage in *Our Mutual Friend* where Dickens describes a group of Thames watermen fishing a body out of the river. They despise Rogue Riderhood, the apparent corpse, but they try to revive him. 'No one has the least regard for the man: with them all, he has been an object of avoidance, suspicion, and aversion; but the spark of life within him is curiously separable from himself now, and they have a deep interest in it, probably because it is life, and they are living and must die . . .' We probably do not find ourselves repelled by the explorers. On the other hand it is not necessarily because we feel much personal affinity with them that we are drawn in so intensely. The deep interest of those who are living and must die is the permanent source for the effectiveness of myth. We die along with Scott and Oates and the others on the return from the pole; then we find that we have survived the experience. So it touches fundamentals.

And the stories do survive; Scott's story in particular survives. Like any successful myth, it provides a skeleton ready to be dressed over and over in the different flesh different decades feel to be appropriate. It has changed many times over in the course of its transmission from 1913 to the present. In the postwar anomie of the 1920s, Apsley Cherry-Garrard published his memoir of the expedition, *The Worst Journey in the World*, as a lament for 'an age in geological time, so many hundreds of years ago, when we were artistic Christians'; already the decade-long gap, the geological shift represented by the First World War, was a presence in the story, a source of astringency and sorrow. The 1930s saw the expedition's concern with natural history fashioned into something congruent with *Tarka the Otter*, and rambling in shorts. The 1948 film *Scott of the Antarctic*, with John Mills as Scott, shaped it as a postwar fable of class integration, apt for the austerity era. The myth had a quiescent period in the 1950s and 1960s, when it held a secure if shrunken position as a perfectly typical subject for a Ladybird book for children. But it metamorphosed, rather than died, on the publication of Roland Huntford's debunking biography *Scott and Amundsen* in 1979. It survived even Huntford's devastating evidence of blundering. Even if you allow that the reverses on the homeward journey from the South Pole that killed Scott's party were mostly his own fault, rather than tragic bad luck, still they occupy the place in this kind of story reserved for inevitabilities, whatever their cause; they come in as downward turns of events that seem almost stipulated by the story's structure; while at the same time as you feel the approaching deaths to be inevitable, the perpetual present tense in which the story happens every time keeps hope helplessly alive. Nor was the debunked version any less open to new cultural colouring. Huntford denounced Scott from the New Right, as an example of the sclerotic official personality; the playwright Trevor Griffiths, adapting Huntford's book as a TV drama, attacked Scott from the Left as a representative of privilege and the Establishment bested by a rather democratic, workmanlike set of Scandinavians.

It would be perfectly possible, in other words, to assemble a history of all the things that the Scott myth has meant in Britain in the twentieth century. But if we want to understand why, and how, real, historical Edwardian men participated in the Antarctic adventure, we need to know what *they* thought their exploring meant. Myths, Roland Barthes pointed out, are a special kind of 'sign' in that they are not constructed from whole cloth, but from a set of elements that are already packed with meaning and association. As well as beginning a history, Scott's expeditions – and Shackleton's – consummated and effectively ended a much older tradition of British polar activity. We need to ask what that history, beginning a century and more before Scott sailed in 1901, did to load meaning into the ways of seeing, ways of being brave, and ways of being in company that later became the elements of myth.

First stumbling block: most of them knew nothing about polar exploration when they set out to do it. The English were uniquely unprepared for the job. Other nationalities, less friendly to amateurism, chose experts who, for example, knew what skis were before they travelled to the polar regions. 'I may as well confess at once', wrote Robert Falcon Scott in *The Voyage of the 'Discovery'*, 'that I had no predilection for Polar exploration . . .' Consequently, when he had the encounter in Buckingham Palace Road with Sir Clements Markham, President of the Royal Geographical Society, that led to his being offered the leadership of an expedition sponsored by the RGS, he was hardly able to be influenced by the history of exploration up till then. Having accepted, wishing to seize the kind of chance to distinguish himself that the peacetime Navy was unlikely to offer, he then read up on the achievements of previous explorers: Cook and Franklin, Ross and Nansen, Bellingshausen and the rest. He gave himself a technical education in the subject.

And polar history, as it is usually written, is technical history. It recounts a sequence of expeditions. There is a degree of variety in the chosen starting point – does it begin with the semi-legendary classical navigator who first saw the sea turn stiff with cold, or with the Elizabethan venturers in search of the North-East Passage to China? or even with the narratives and origin-stories of the Eskimos? – but a great constancy of focus and emphasis thereafter. The different explorers form a chain of discovery. They map the fringes of the world, learn the proper techniques of ice-navigation and sledge-travel. Their achievement is measured easily by the distance they leave untravelled to the two poles: a sort of geographical determinism informs this history, causing judgements of failure and success to spring from, not hindsight, but an eerily perfect rationality. Gradually, gradually, the lines on the map representing the different expeditions – sometimes coloured, sometimes broken into different combinations of dots and dashes, making an urgent polar morse – push towards the goal.

But there is a second kind of polar history, largely uncharted; an intangible history of assumptions, responses to landscape, cultural fascinations, aesthetic attraction to the cold regions. It comes into view in a passage of a memoir of her famous brother written by Grace Scott, in which she tries to reconstruct the range of his motives for accepting Markham's offer.

RFS had no urge towards snow, ice, or that kind of adventure, but he did realise that such an expedition could give the leader great interests and expansion of life with new experiences; a fact that was immediately apparent when the appointment came, for at once he came into contact with men of the big world, all sorts of experiences and interests. In addition, he felt in himself keenly the call of the vast empty spaces; silence; the beauty of untrodden snow; liberty of thought and action; the wonder of the snow and seeming infinitude of its uninhabited regions whose secrets man had not then pierced, and the hoped-for conquest of raging elements.

Grace Scott clearly did not think this was a surprising thing to write. She evidently saw no contradiction between Scott having 'no urge' towards exploration, and his feeling 'keenly' this very specific appetite for the romance of snow. Some part of the tone of the last sentence may derive from the hindsight with which she wrote her memoir, the posthumous glory of 'RFS' colouring her presentation of his early life; yet she is, after all, making a fundamentally un-glorious point. Scott was not destined to be an explorer. His recruitment resulted, at least in some measure, from accident. He was not connected, by ancestry, by vocation, or by early influence, with the practical history of exploration. His 'additional' feelings, then, so strangely developed, so full a little agenda of romantic responses to the prospect of snowy places, represent a sensitivity of another kind. If he possessed them without an active 'urge', it seems unlikely that they were in a strict sense personal feelings. Grace Scott seems confident that she is naming well-known, indeed conventional stimuli to feeling when she mentions '*the* call of the vast empty spaces', '*the* beauty of untrodden snow' (my italics). If she had thought there were any chance of them not being recognised, she would not have said 'the'. We see here, I think, the accepted influence of polar material on the collective imagination at the turn of the century.

A history of this second kind – an imaginative history of polar exploration – would have to explain where Scott's feelings came from, how they got there and how they got to be too obvious to require comment or to elicit surprise. It would need a genealogy different from the simple chronological chain of events recorded by the first sort. It would require demonstrating, not that knowledge grew, or that one impression was succeeded by another, but that the means existed to make of the data of polar discovery a stuff of conventional imagination. While it is easy to uncover particular nineteenth-century manifestations of imaginative interest in polar matters – like, for example, the huge Arctic diorama created in the Vauxhall pleasure gardens in the summer of 1852, to give the public a topical thrill at the height of the search for the missing explorer Sir John Franklin – it is far harder to trace a line of influence on from them. 'Influence' is necessarily impalpable. But by the same token, it does not have to be proved that (for example) Scott was himself aware of particular books, plays, or fashionable enthusiasms, so long as the styles of feeling they gave currency to survived, and flourished, without marks of origin, in the repertoire of the obvious.

This book is an attempt to construct an outline of such a history. Implicit in it is the assumption that ideas lose their form when they decay, yet do not necessarily lose their place in the mentality of an age. They turn to imaginative compost. Complex reasoning lives on, perhaps, as a couple of self-evident maxims. A taste it took a book to establish, and many more to justify, becomes the single word 'attractive' in a tourist guide. Schools of thought, life's-works, artistic endeavours, all find their ultimate destination in a habit of vision scarcely worth discussion. So each chapter is intended to correspond to a particular area of unattributed, unexamined thought in the minds of those who, like Oates in Delhi, could perhaps scarcely say why exploration 'is most suitable to my tastes'. Each chapter is an archaeology of one aspect of the hazy love affair between the ice and the English. As Apsley Cherry-Garrard said of a book by a fellow veteran about the life of penguins, 'It is all quite true': except that in the next-to-last section of the final chapter, which pieces back together the story of Scott, I had to describe events for which there can be by definition no written evidence. That section is pure invention.

Before going into the thick detail of exploration's imaginative history, let me give one instance of it – an unusual one, because it allows the passage of a single, very powerful imaginative impression to be traced the whole way from the obscurity of a factual appendix, to the collective consciousness of an age, via a famous novel. This particular contribution to polar sensibility has to do with seabirds; or at least it did in the beginning, in the first decades of the nineteenth century. The British whale-fishery off Greenland was then reaching the peak of its productivity. At the same time the Admiralty, largely at the suggestion of an activist Secretary, Sir John Barrow, who had served as an apprentice on a whaler as a boy, was starting to use the manpower left spare after the Napoleonic wars to mount naval expeditions to the Arctic. Between whaling captains with a bent for natural philosophy, like the remarkable William Scoresby of Whitby, and the naturalists carried northward by the Navy, some surprising information began to accumulate about the wildlife of the Arctic. Nothing much lived on land. 'The antiseptical property of frost is rather remarkable,' wrote

Scoresby. The cold that killed bacteria would kill most other forms of life. His account of Spitzbergen, *faute de mieux*, deals mostly with the island's geology. However, he points out, 'though the soil of the whole of this remote country does not produce vegetables suitable or sufficient for the nourishment of a single human being, yet its coasts and adjacent seas have afforded riches and independence to thousands'. (His comments on the sciences of life reveal Scoresby at his most business-like. He reserved his passionate enthusiasm for the study of ice-formation, and the earth's magnetic field.) Almost the entire ecology of the Arctic was marine, and there was so *much* of it, species upon species of fish, uncountable billions of one-celled creatures for the fish to feed on – and birds. For the first time, this biological skew – an essential feature of the polar landscape – was given systematic scrutiny. Though the naval expeditions showed a great appetite for shooting and eating their discoveries, the reports published after each returned usually included an ornithological appendix. In 1821, a 'Memoir on the Birds of Greenland', by Captain Sabine, appeared at the back of Edward Parry's *Journal of a Voyage for the Discovery of the North-West Passage*.

Sabine's work found an avid reader in Thomas Bewick, the engraver and natural historian. Bewick's *History of British Birds* included a large number of migrants, birds that only visited Britain en route from somewhere to somewhere else. Using Sabine he could establish, to take one case, that the gull-billed tern (place of breeding unknown) was probably the same bird as Greenland's glaucous gull, and the empire of knowledge expanded its boundaries a trifle. But he also took from his reading of Sabine's practical text a vivid visual idea of the Arctic; and here the details of the glaucous gull's beak-size fall away into insignificance beside Bewick's evident fascination with the peculiarity of a place where teeming wings co-existed with utter emptiness. In a way the Arctic represented the nemesis of ornithology. At some especial spot in its cold expanses lay breeding-grounds apparently out of reach for ever, a dreadful thought but a striking one to a man as mindful of Providence as Bewick.

Bewick carefully explained the thinking behind his *History* in a preface to its sixth edition (it was extraordinarily popular). 'When I first undertook my labours in Natural History, my strongest motive was to lead the minds of youth to the study of that delightful pursuit, the surest foundation on which Religion and Morality can efficiently be implanted in the heart, as being the unerring and unalterable book of the Deity.' He had set out to create, in fact, an improving children's book. Probably the reason that children actually liked it so much was the obvious delight Bewick himself had felt at his subject; and, 'the more readily to allure their pliable . . . attention to the Great Truths of Creation', he had filled it with small woodcuts, some accurate pictures of birds, others '*Tale*-pieces of gaiety and humour'. It was thus with an audience very different from Sabine's in mind that he put his perception of the strangeness of the Arctic into words, striking a consciously attractive note of grandeur. For reasons that will shortly become clear, reasons connected with the next stage in the process of transmission and adaptation, it is worth quoting Bewick at length. He is moving on from a quick survey of the bird-life of what might be called the Near North:

Other parts of the World – the bleak shores of Lapland, Siberia, Spitzbergen, Nova Zembla, Iceland, Greenland, &c with the vast sweep of the Arctic Zone, are also enlivened in their seasons by swarms of sea-fowl, which range the intervening open parts of the seas to the shoreless frozen ocean. There a barrier is put to further enquiry, beyond which the prying eye of man must not look, and there his imagination only must take the view, to supply the place of reality. In these forlorn regions of unknowable dreary space, this reservoir of frost and snow, where firm fields of ice, the accumulation of centuries of winters, glazed in Alpine heights above heights, surround the pole, and concentre the multiplied rigours of extreme cold; even here, so far as human intelligence has been able to penetrate, there appears to subsist an abundance of animals, in the air, and in the waters: and, perhaps, it may not be carrying conjecture too far to suppose that every region of the earth, air, and water, however ungenial the clime appears to us, is replete with animals, suited, each kind, to the place assigned to it.

Certain it is, however, that the deeps of the frozen zone are the great receptacle whence the finny tribes issue, in so wonderful a profusion, to re-stock all the watery world of the northern hemisphere; and that this immense icy protruberance of the globe, this gathering together, this hoard of congealed waters, is periodically diminished by the influence of the unsetting summer's sun, whose rays being perpetually, though obliquely, shed, during that season, on the widely extended rim of the frozen continent, gradually dissolve its margin, which is thus crumbled into innumerable floating isles, that are driven southward to replenish the seas of warmer climates.

Amidst these drifts of ice, and following this widely spreading current, teeming with life, the whole host of sea-fowl find in the waters an inexhaustible supply of food: for the great movement, the immense southward migration of fishes is then begun, and shoal after shoal, probably as the removal of their dark ice canopy unveils them to the sun, are invited forth, and, guided by its light and heat, pour forward in thousands of myriads, in multitudes which set all calculation at defiance. The flocks of sea-birds, for their numbers, baffle the power of figures; but the swarms of fishes, as if engendered in the clouds, and showered down like the rain, are multiplied in an incomprehensible degree: they may indeed be called infinite, if infinity were applicable to any thing created.

About twenty-five years after *British Birds* first appeared, when it was an established classic and an ornament to any educated household, the many real children who had read it were joined by a fictional child. Hidden behind the curtain of a window-seat in the breakfast-room, the young Jane Eyre picks it up because it is 'stored with pictures', and hopes to find something in it that will carry her away from her misery in the household of her Aunt Reed. She does not read the opening pages as Bewick intended: she does not feel the intended awe at the great beneficent design by which the polar ice-cap supplies the world with fish, nor respond with enthusiasm to the suggestion that, in the eyes of God, every clime has a certain genial usefulness, whether we perceive it or not. She scarcely even notices that she is being told about seabirds. Her attention is caught only by the core of Bewick's perception of the Arctic, which feeds a mood he certainly did not anticipate, and his pictures, whose 'gaiety' and 'humour' elude her completely.

I returned to my book – Bewick's *History of British Birds*: the letterpress thereof I cared little for, generally speaking; and yet there were certain introductory pages that, child as I was, I could not pass quite as a blank. They were those which treat of the haunts of sea-fowl; of 'the solitary rocks and promontories' by them only inhabited; of the coast of Norway, studded with

isles from its southern extremity, the Lindeness, or Naze, to the North Cape
. . . Nor could I pass unnoticed the suggestion of the bleak shores of Lapland,
Siberia, Spitzbergen, Nova Zembla, Iceland, Greenland, with 'the vast sweep
of the Arctic Zone, and those forlorn regions of dreary space – that reservoir
of frost and snow, where firm fields of ice, the accumulation of centuries of
winters, glazed in Alpine heights above heights, surround the pole, and
concentre the multiplied rigours of extreme cold'. Of these death-white
regions I formed an idea of my own: shadowy, like all the half-comprehended
notions that float dim through children's brains, but strangely impressive.
The words in these introductory pages connected themselves with the
succeeding vignettes, and gave significance to the rock standing up alone in a
sea of billow and spray; to the broken boat stranded on a desolate coast; to the
cold and ghastly moon glancing through bars at a wreck just sinking. Each
picture told a story; mysterious often to my undeveloped understanding and
imperfect feelings, yet ever profoundly interesting . . . With Bewick on my
knee, I was then happy: happy at least in my own way. I feared nothing but
interruption, and that came too soon.

Where are we now? Not sailing up the Denmark Strait, off the coast
of Greenland, with a telescope in one hand and a fowling-gun in the
other, set upon scientific taxidermy; nor in the geographical limbo of
Bewick's prose, where, without being there, we may examine the
northern zone of the globe and see divine schemes and reliable
functions, mysteries and details. We are indoors, sitting between the
window and the curtain, between the 'raw twilight' of an English
winter evening and a house that is chilly too, though physically well
heated. Perhaps this seems obvious, but it makes something different
of the North Pole to bring it into a domestic interior. For Bewick
'imagination' had had to replace real scrutiny; now the Arctic has
become voluntarily imaginative, a picture in the mind, purely internal.
It is close at hand – '*these* death-white regions', in here, not '*those* . . .
regions', away at a far distance – and available for contrast and
metaphor as it was not when Sabine and Bewick gave it a geographical
location.

One critic of the novel, interested in the ice and fire that figure so
often in Jane's descriptions of herself, has commented that the striking
sentence Brontë quotes from Bewick is written 'not [in] the language

of geography but of romance and fantasy'. This surely confuses Bewick with the use made of him in *Jane Eyre*: a justifiable confusion, perhaps, since Charlotte Brontë does not re-write Bewick, and hardly even seems to gloss him. But it might be better to say that she does not need to re-write him. The circumstances of Jane's reading, and the kind of reading that it is, already change the import of the quotation completely. Jane, as she tells us, takes from Bewick 'an idea of [her] own', born of a 'half-comprehension' which amounts to no simple misunderstanding. It typifies, rather, a form of perception which belongs distinctly to the novel, that home of uncertainty and filtered truths. From being the language of pious geography, albeit heightened and intensified, Bewick's words *become* here the language of romance and fantasy.

Psychological fantasy, moreover, of the most obviously compensatory kind, serving the needs of the child, relieving the pressure of actuality on her. It even makes her happy, 'at least in my own way' – a rather alarming contentment. Each of Bewick's phrases has an application to Jane's situation. She is forlorn, she is in dreary space herself. Centuries of time are not in prospect; but time does pass for her without the promise of change, made limitless by lack of hope, and by a child's inability to see beyond present misery. She knows about 'multiplied rigours', and all her perceptions are 'concentred' (a word used repeatedly by Coleridge in his self-investigations) in a miserable isolation. But the most important part of Bewick's evocation of the pole – and the reason that it offers an arctic satisfaction to her – must be the cold, the extreme cold.

Heat and cold probably provide the oldest metaphors for emotion that exist. Charlotte Brontë is not original in her use of them, though she does so with a romantic violence that it is rare to find within a Victorian sensibility; and it is not usually little girls whose inner life is thought to warrant imagery of scorching and freezing. Jane's constricted life moves, however, between emotional dangers that Brontë can best illustrate with fire and ice. 'A ridge of lighted heath, alive, glancing, devouring, would have been a great emblem of my mind when I accused and menaced Mrs Reed,' thinks Jane two chapters later; 'the same ridge, black and blasted after the flames are dead, would have represented as meetly my subsequent condition, when half an hour's silence and reflection had shown me the madness of my conduct, and the dreariness of my hated and hating position.' The polar imagery does not receive the same explicit rebuttal, but Jane's satisfaction in the imagined cold contains its own warning.

Jane has been ejected from the drawing-room, where Mrs Reed and her own children are gathered in a family circle, presumably around the warmth of a fire. By finding a refuge in a cold deeper than the one imposed upon her, in rigours worse than her rigorous rejection, she makes imagination outbid actuality. Better absolute zero, runs the dangerous logic of her position, than fears renewed again and again; better ice imagined in solitude, cold enough to freeze all feeling, than feeling sensitive to slights in hostile company. Jane's consolation in ice is definitely morbid – Bewick had not coloured 'death-white' the wastes that supported such surprising life. Like the blazing heath that consumes itself, the glazed ice provides an injurious satisfaction. One may perceive a certain rightness in imagining oneself as something so extreme – in committing the self to an absolute – but the ice too is a 'great emblem' of a state of mind it cannot be safe to continue in. Here, unexpectedly, lies the continuity between Bewick and Brontë that might seem to be utterly absent. What is transmitted down the line from Sabine to *Jane Eyre* is a thought about the relation of the poles to life. Sabine simply records bird-life. Bewick wonders at the generosity of nature that allows life to exist abundantly in desolation. Brontë, abandoning the marvel of the glaucous gull, points to the life that the pole can have in a desolate mind, integrating it, not into an ecosystem, but into the systems of images by which a person helps or harms herself. She shows, like Sabine and Bewick, that the Arctic has a place in the world of life; she conveys, enormously changed, the same astonishment that the polar wastes are connected to life we recognise.

Charlotte Brontë did not invent the use of the poles as a metaphor of this kind. Medical discourse, for example, had given heat and cold permanent seats in the human anatomy, and figured some states of mind as results of hot or cold disorders of the system. The early travellers, to take the question from a completely different angle, had, too, almost all anthropomorphised the ice, seeing its bleakness as a kind of geographical misery afflicting the extreme ends of the earth. But Jane Eyre's brief imaginative sojourn at the North Pole is both a fuller, more elaborated expression of the possibilities of the metaphor, and an influential exploitation of it in the form – the novel – from which readers would most readily expect to take information about the human soul, and the unexpected shapes into which it might mould itself.

Scott's men had *Jane Eyre* in the Antarctic with them in 1910–13, as part of a useful cabinet library of classics donated by a sympathiser. It was not a favourite book. They were much more enthusiastic when they found, 'encased in ice' at a previous expedition's hut, 'an incomplete copy of Stanley Weyman's *My Lady Rotha*; it was carefully thawed out and read by everybody, and the excitement was increased by the fact that the end of the book was missing' (Cherry-Garrard). That does not matter, when the fame of the novel ensured that its heroine's dangers and exhilarations permanently modified the nineteenth century's conception of 'romance and fantasy'. Many metaphors, many fragmentary perceptions informed the explorers' attitudes to their labours. But among them, buried when the work was successful, revived when it was not, was a consistent conviction of the perversity of being where they were, a sense, worthy of Charlotte Brontë, that their presence might be dangerous to themselves, and not just physically. The explorers moved through landscapes conventionally used to signify psychological extremes.

Lieutenant Edward Evans, afterwards Admiral Evans, was invalided home from the Antarctic in late 1911 aboard the expedition ship *Terra Nova*, returning with it a year later to find Scott dead. He organised the final departure, and described it in his *South with Scott*:

Early on 26th January [1913] we left these inhospitable coasts, and those who were on deck watched the familiar, rocky, snow-capped shores fast disappearing from view. We had been happy there before disaster overtook our Expedition, but now we were glad to leave, and some of us must have realised that these ice-girt rocks and mountains were not meant for human beings to associate their lives with.

Yet they had: an association prepared for, warned against, prefigured, and underwritten by many histories of feeling.

TWO

The Sublime

These days the air of Dublin is saturated by the smells of brewing
stout, which always seem in some distinctive way *brown*. In the hard
wet January of 1746, on the other hand, the brewery had not yet begun
to dominate the atmosphere, while through the centre of the elegant
capital ran the visible brown of the river Liffey, a quivering tan-
coloured streak of water, tense and whirling in its dark stone runnel.
The Liffey was in spate, loaded with the mud of the counties
upstream. An angry rain slanted into its surface. From the window of
his father's house on Arran Quay – beside the Four Courts on the
north bank – the young Edmund Burke watched the muscular waters
swell; they rose and rose, pushing over the northern lip of the river in
jets and billows, then spreading swiftly out to fill straight streets and
inundate classical squares. Buildings became islands; waves broke on
street corners; around pillars and through arches the dirty flood
surged to and fro. The elements had come to town.

Burke was sixteen, the son of a successful attorney and an
unconverted Catholic lady. For about a year and a half already he had
been a student at Trinity College, but he was trying his best to keep
up a friendship with the son of his old schoolmaster at the Ballitore
Academy in the country. Every week, if he could manage it, he wrote
to Richard Shackleton with news of the city, of his studies, of mutual
friends. In the letters he paraded his growing intellectual powers, and,
inevitably, for all Burke's nostalgia for his school persona – he had
been the wittily serious one, the grave young joker – strains arose
now and then between the two boys. Shackleton perhaps disliked
being his friend's audience. It was not quite sufficient for Burke to
dispatch amiable flights of dog-Latin and mock-Greek; papering over
the gap that separated him from Shackleton did not quite work. In

the long run the friendship was doomed to sink into a distant mutual respect, with Burke bringing his wife to call at Ballitore in order to show her the scenes of his youth, and Shackleton treasuring his early intimacy with the great orator and legislator. Indeed Shackleton probably preserved the letters as literary relics, knowing, as the years passed, that they would be valuable as a record of Burke's embryonic thinking. On 25 January 1746, however, they had just had a minor bust-up. Burke, looking around for a peace-offering, pressed the remarkable deluge outdoors into service. 'I received your favour,' he wrote,

the product of ill humour yet will I endeavour to answer it the best I can, though everything around conspires to excite in me a contrary disposition; the melancholy gloom of the day, the whistling winds, and the hoarse rumbling of the swollen Liffey, with the flood, which even where I write, lays close siege to our whole street, not permitting any to go in or out to supply us with the necessaries of life; yet the joy of conversing with my friend can dispel the cloudiness of the day, lull the winds, and stop the rapid passage of the flood. How happy was the time when we could mutually interchange our thoughts, and pour the friendly sentiments of our hearts without obstruction, from our lips, unindebted to the pen and unimpeded by the post!

No one perhaps has seen such a flood here as we have now. The Quay wall which before our door is about [illegible] feet high is scarce discernible, serving only as a mark to show us where the bank once bounded the Liffey. Our cellars are drowned, not as before, for that was but a trifle to this, for now the water comes up to the first floor of the house, threatening us every minute with rising a great deal higher, the consequence of which would infallibly be the fall of the house: and to add to our misfortune, the inhabitants of the other Quay, secured by their situation, deride the poor prisoners; while from our doors and windows we watch the rise and fall of the waters as carefully as the Egyptians do the Nile, but for different reasons.

It gives me pleasure to see nature in these great though terrible scenes. It fills the mind with grand ideas, and turns the soul in upon herself. This together with the sedentary life I lead, forced some reflections on me which perhaps otherwise would not have occurred.

I considered how little man is, yet in his mind, how great! He is Lord and Master of all things, yet scarce can command anything. He is given a freedom of his will, but wherefore? Was it but to torment and perplex him the more?

How little avails the freedom, if the objects he is to act upon be not as much disposed to obey as he is to command?

– and Burke, very much the precocious savant, continued with a series of reflections on the weakness of man and the greatness of God.

If Burke had not, some ten years later, become the author of *A Philosophical Enquiry into the Origin of our Ideas of the Sublime and Beautiful*, this youthful letter would not be particularly interesting. But the future scrutineer of the sublime, bounding happily forward into philosophy while still sharing with Shackleton a fondness for puns in dog-Latin, had in fact put his finger on the essential components of the treatise he would later write.

What have Dublin floods to do with Edwardian exploration? Why is the sublime relevant to the poles? Because in the sublime – an eighteenth-century idea transformed by Romanticism and diffused into the perceptions of the Victorians – is to be found a popular, and highly influential, attempt to think through the pleasures afforded by sights that were (like the Liffey flood) 'great though terrible'. Like the Liffey, the sublime was an uncontrolled category of perception that roared through and around the tidy certainties of art and experience. It provided a name for a whole heterogeneous group of sensations that all, in their different ways, seemed to go *beyond* the rules and systems that were supposed to govern taste. In the first half of the eighteenth century, the sublime meant a rush of noble emotion; you felt it when a play, or a poem, or a human action, displayed qualities so admirable that it became irrelevant to ask whether whatever-it-was had been well expressed, or neatly bundled into a couplet of verse. From the 1750s to the 1790s, partly because of Burke, it more often meant a sensation of wonder mixed with fear, a pleasurable encounter with forbidding landscape or the darker passions. Among the Romantic poets, sublimity labelled the most elevated moments in the transactions between Nature and the human soul; while for the German philosopher Kant, increasingly important in England at the beginning of the nineteenth century, human reason generated the sublime as it reached for absolute ideas beyond the grasp of the senses. Yet even these disgraceful summaries of complicated positions only hint at the wealth of different sublimes. Over the period, besides the 'natural sublime', there were a negative, a positive, a mathematical, an ethical, a psychological, a religious, an egotistical, a rhetorical, an aesthetic, and a dynamic sublime – to name only some. Some were codified by systematic thinkers, others condensed onto the page by novelists from a vapour of current assumptions and public preferences. Others still were carried in from tree-nurseries by landscape gardeners, and patted down with trowels. The sublime was, you might say, a growth area. All these sublimes agreed, however, in putting forward for consideration something distinctly pleasurable, but definitely un-beautiful. Beauty tended to be thought of as regular, tender, soothing, polished; and the forceful sensations of the sublime were none of these. The sublime was greater, and when one felt sublime sensations one's attention seemed to be at a greater stretch. In a way both intimidating and flattering, one seemed to become larger oneself when contemplating a sublime object. 'This is why,' wrote the classical aesthetician Longinus, a great favourite of the eighteenth century, 'by a sort of natural impulse, we admire not the small streams, useful and pellucid though they be, but the Nile, the Danube or the Rhine, and still more the Ocean.' The Liffey, at least when it was at its winter worst, clearly qualified for a place as well.

But Burke had written, *It fills the mind with grand ideas, and turns the soul in upon herself.* This was not really a contradiction, though as the eighteenth century wore on, a great deal of attention was paid to the finer points of response to the sublime; to the question of whether sublimity lay in the mind or in the object looked at, and whether (so to speak) the sublime opened you up or closed you down. By *mind* Burke meant the conscious part of a person that knows and understands things. By *soul* he meant the centre of one's self – the part whose workings are much harder to fathom, and which only sometimes is fully aware that it exists. When one saw a river in flood, its size and might provoked ideas in the mind, and also reminded the soul of its own greatness, its own turbulent existence. Naturally, a sublime sight made one look inwards, as well as outwards. In that respect it was a selfish pleasure. Indeed one could only feel sublime *if* one was so absorbed in the wash and thrust of the Liffey, and in what it seemed to tell one about one's self, that one was prepared to forget the other aspects of the moment. Downstairs the river had invaded the drawing-room, perhaps. It had drowned the sideboards and was slapping against the prints. It reached just high enough, maybe, to catch at the dangling base of the chandelier, and was tweaking it to and fro at random, causing a peculiar groaning in the ceiling of that room, which was the floor you were standing on upstairs. To enjoy any of this required one to forget (or at any rate ignore) the havoc that would have to be dealt with later: the ruined plaster, the warped furniture, the silted carpets.

One index of the Liffey's sublimity was its power to reverse the usual order of things. Instead of flowing where it belonged, it burst in elsewhere. Instead of obeying, as Burke put it in his religious reflection on the flood, it rebelled, and temporarily over-mastered the citizens who were accustomed to using it for trade and transport. Accordingly, one popular theme in writing that set out to be sublime was just this sort of reversal, just this sort of counter-attack on the everyday scheme of the world. And here, without very much subtlety or psychological ambition, is the first point of connection between the sublime and the poles, for one of the things that could be reversed to sublime effect was the order of the seasons. Snow and ice were, in their proper place, natural things: the proper decoration of winter, as hot suns and haywains were the proper decoration of summer. But suppose that snow were to invade another season as peremptorily as the Liffey invaded the streets of Dublin, with a cold white menace instead of a brown wet one. That was a sublime idea, to be sure. Think of snow choking the lilies and the wild flowers in a May meadow! Think of featureless snow cloaking the brown face of August! In poetry it was relatively easy to arrange such an unlikely outbreak of seasonal disorder; and when Thomson, the author of *The Seasons*, wrote encouragingly to his disciple Mallet about the latter's long poem *The Excursion*, he singled out for particular praise the part where Mallet expressed a wish

> . . . to invert the year
> And bring wild Winter into summer's place
> Or spread brown Night and tempest o'er the morn.

'This is Poetry,' trumpeted Thomson, 'this is arousing fancy – enthusiasm – rapturous terror.'

One did not need, however, to be quite so wholesale, or so fanciful, to achieve the effect. Eighteenth-century technology provided a practical way to bring a little bit of winter into summer. Some wealthy families were building, in a shady corner of their grounds, an ice-house. This igloo-shaped early version of a refrigerator would be constructed with a double skin of stone or brick for insulation, and half sunk into the earth. While riding through your woodland on a summer's day, you might come across its hemispherical bobble, and know that deep inside, packed between layers of hay, the blocks of ice your servants had harvested from the river months ago were still unmelted. You stepped through its multiple doors from natural heat into a profound artificial chill. The ice-house made it possible to have ice in your summer drinks, and to preserve, if you wished, delicate seasonal fruits from decay. Both were exotic treats, of course; too few plinking glasses of hock can have been served for them to lose their wonder. The poet Anna Letitia Barbauld composed a lyric in praise of a frozen peach, its rigid flesh and frost-starred bloom; here, in a witty paradox, were summer and winter fused together, small enough to hold in your hand, and, though destined for a fruit compote, still administering a little shock of the sublime.

Likewise Anna Seward, 'the Swan of Lichfield', the rising star of poetry in the 1780s, imagined Captain Cook, in her 'Elegy' to him, leaving behind

> . . . imperial London's gorgeous plains,
> Where, rob'd in thousand tints, bright Pleasure reigns;
> In cups of summer-ice her nectar pours,
> And twines, 'mid wintry snows, her roseate bow'rs . . .

Seward's icy-summery image of London was quite cunningly chosen, for she then led the reader out from it to disruptions of the natural order that were far more strenuous – that were sublime without being urbane at all. Her elegy followed Cook on a poetic recapitulation of his famous Second Voyage to the South Seas. Two parts of that voyage had particularly appealed to the public imagination. His landfall on

'Otaheite', or Tahiti, had seemed to reveal an unfallen Eden in the tropics, where summer lasted for ever and graceful sensuality reigned. The other high-point had been Cook's stubborn circumnavigation of the South Pole, amid enormous icebergs and unforgiving storms. Seward made Tahiti exemplify the 'roseate bow'rs' of nature, and the Antarctic represent the quintessence of 'wintry snows', disentangling the elements of her first little paradox, and pointing her readers' attention to the sublime reversals laid on around the world by different climates. Tahiti itself perhaps was more floral than tremendous (more beautiful than sublime); but Cook's swift journey from its heat to the polar cold delivered a thrill comparable to the idea of a blizzard in July. Stronger indeed, because here real geography proved that it could surpass the *outré* feats of the imagination. Here was another way of inverting the seasons. And then there was the delightful contradiction between the northern and southern hemispheres to be considered. Winter did happen in the Antipodes at the exact time when summer reached its height at home. Snow in July was normal in Patagonia and Tierra del Fuego. Though it was true one could not exactly bring this snow home to scandalise a basking vicarage lawn, nothing prevented the sublimity-seeking mind from dreaming globally, and holding side by side in the fancy the local warmth and the distant frost.

Once invented, that particular sublime possibility persisted. Take a passage from the young Charles Darwin's *Journal of Researches*, published in 1839 and more often known as *The Voyage of the Beagle*. From December 1832 to June 1834 HMS *Beagle* had doubled backwards and forwards along the South Atlantic coast of South America, surveying coastlines and recording observations on flora and fauna. Among the more obvious excitements – such as the anthropologically fascinating return of 'Jemmy Button', 'York Minster' and other Tierra del Fuegians snatched from their country on an earlier voyage – Darwin became interested in the peculiar climatic imbalance between the hemispheres. In the lower half of the world, the tropics continued much further to the south than the corresponding zone on the other side of the Equator did to the north. Then there was a comparatively thin region of temperate weather, and below that a sudden transition to sub-polar cold, much sooner than in the north. At the latitude of 54° south one would find oneself in the deep-frozen interior of South Georgia. 54° north, by contrast, put one amidst the comfortable hotels of Harrogate, in the West Riding of Yorkshire, where glaciers were scarce. Chapter 11 of Darwin's book considered the geological and zoological implications of this contrast, and in his conclusion to the chapter he summarised the difference of the hemispheres. His purpose was scientific, his literary flourishes incidental, but he wrote:

I will recapitulate the principal facts with regard to the climate, ice-action, and organic productions of the southern hemisphere transposing the places in imagination to Europe, with which we are so much better acquainted. Then, near Lisbon, the commonest sea-shells . . . would have a tropical character. In the southern provinces of France, magnificent forests, intwined with arborescent grasses and with the trees loaded with parasitical plants, would hide the face of the land. The puma and the jaguar would haunt the Pyrenees . . . Even as far north as central Denmark, humming-birds would be seen fluttering about delicate flowers, and parrots feeding amidst the evergreen woods . . . Nevertheless, on some islands only 360 miles northward of our new Cape Horn in Denmark, a carcass buried in the soil . . . would be preserved perpetually frozen. If some bold navigator attempted to penetrate northward of these islands, he would run a thousand dangers amidst gigantic icebergs, on some of which he would see great blocks of rock borne far away from their original site. Another island of large size, in the latitude of southern Scotland, but twice as far to the west, would be 'almost wholly covered in everlasting snow', and would have each bay terminated by ice-cliffs, whence great masses would be yearly detached: this island would boast only of a little moss, grass, and burnet, and a titlark would be its only land inhabitant. From our new Cape Horn in Denmark, a chain of mountains scarcely half the height of the Alps, would run in a straight line due southward; and on its western flank every deep creek of the sea, or fiord, would end in 'bold and astonishing glaciers'. These lonely channels would frequently reverberate with the falls of ice, and so often would great waves rush along their coast; numerous icebergs, some as tall as cathedrals . . . would be stranded on the outlying islets; at intervals violent earthquakes would shoot prodigious masses into the waters below. Lastly, some Missionaries attempting to penetrate a long arm of the sea, would behold the not lofty surrounding mountains, sending down their many grand icy streams to the sea-coast, and their progress in the boats would be checked by the innumerable floating icebergs, some small and some great; and this would have occurred on our twenty-second of June, and where the Lake of Geneva is now spread out!

As Darwin names each familiar feature of Europe, he abolishes it. 'In the latitude of southern Scotland' he places his island, but Scotland is not there. Flat Denmark becomes the rocky arrow-head of a continent. Provence metamorphoses into the Amazon, northern France presumably vanishes altogether; and where England was, there is only an expanse of salt sea. Real architecture has disappeared, leaving the accidentally 'architectural' forms of nature in its stead. The metaphorical 'cathedrals' of icebergs substitute for Chartres and Canterbury. Darwin declines to specify what peoples (if any) inhabit his transformed geography, the only human figures being the 'Missionaries', a solitary group posed in a landscape better to travel through than to live in. The parallels with Patagonia are, of course, diligent; and this is why it is a little difficult to know how to take the sweeping abolitions and transformations of the passage. One cannot tell whether he is just transposing the details of the picture –those boats, for example, in which the *Beagle*'s shore-parties were certainly getting around – in order to be faithful and complete, or whether he is consciously embroidering the striking effects of the geographical reversal. He clearly knows, at any rate, that the effect created *is* striking. Whether or not he would call it 'sublime', he is aware of the shivery majesty involved in dispensing with whole nations and land-masses. He too brings the winter home to disrupt the shires, so thoroughly (because the operation presents itself to his imagination as a scientific *jeu d'esprit*) that home ceases to exist.

This short section of the *Journal* recalls the 'scientific romances' that later Victorians began to tell around the idea of catastrophe. With advances in geology, meteorology and climate studies they were able to dress fantasies of apocalyptic destruction in scientific clothes – to invent new delicious ways for their world to end. Now the *coup de grâce* would be delivered to Western civilisation by a rise in sea-levels, by a close pass from a comet, by a return of the Ice Age. For maximum chilling effect, these romances would be written as pseudo-documentaries, exploiting the pitiless neutrality of scientific language. They tended to be strong on precise dates and measurements. As Darwin had reported which sea-shells would flourish in a tropical Lisbon, but omitted the fate of the Portuguese, they would report the height of the tidal wave that drowned Bristol, or the amazing brightness (in candle-power-per-square-inch, probably) of the 'solar rays' that reduced London to a blistered heath. Of course, there would be a cast of wretched survivors to chronicle the dreadful events, and perhaps to make a stalwart stand against the inevitable, but it was generally left to the reader to infer the horrors visited upon the uncharacterised remainder of the population from the cool statistics the authors provided, or from distant reports of cannibalism in Manchester. That was the way the readers liked it, with the emphasis on the destruction, not the pity of it all.

There was an affinity between these stories and the equally popular romances in which the French landed and put Gravesend to the sword. Whatever force of nature the author chose, it invaded; it overwhelmed the familiar with a logic against which no appeal was possible. Often, though not always, the destruction conformed silently to the old rules of the sublime, and snow was certainly represented among the chosen agents of catastrophe. Richard Jeffries' *After London* (1885) was eventually published with a curious ecological catastrophe at its opening, in which a demoralised humanity is simply displaced by the tireless growth of plants. Grass eats the roads; hedges converge on the centre of cornfields. Jeffries, however, had flirted with a snowy catastrophe first, before deciding that a green doom would better suit his gifts for pastoral. In his draft of 'The Great Snow' he humbles the metropolis with a three-week blizzard. 'Where now', asks a mad preacher of the ragged mob hunting for fuel and food, 'Where now is your mighty city that defied nature and despised the conquered elements – where now is your pride when so simple and contemptible an agent as a few flakes of snow can utterly destroy it? Where are your steam-engine, your telegraphs, and your printing-press – all powerless and against what – only a little snow! Of what use is your Bank Reserve of £20,000,000 sterling against the soft noiseless snow!' The fragment ends two sentences later. It is already evident, however, that

Jeffries in no sense intends a religious moral to be drawn from the chastising of London's worldly achievements. His snow has smothered the spiritual symbols of the capital as much as the icons of financial or technological order. Like Darwin's recasting of Europe, like the Dublin flood, it both erases familiar signs and substitutes an intractable landscape of its own.

On the 29th the gale moderated, but meantime snow had fallen unceasingly, and it had now reached a uniform depth of ten feet. With slight variations it continued at this depth but the drifts of course were of enormous height. The National Gallery was wholly hidden under a mound of snow. The dome of St Paul's was alone visible, rising up like the roof of a huge Esquimoux hut. The great gilt cross on the top had been torn off by the violence of the wind.

One of the items in Grace Scott's list of her brother's motives for exploring, it will be remembered, was 'the hoped-for conquest of raging elements'. An inherited taste for the sublime does indeed partly illuminate this, for if, without the tangible assistances of civilisation (stock exchanges, telegraphs, cathedrals), as the man-hauling explorers were, they nonetheless conquered the polar snows, it argued for a strength of soul, a purely internal strength in man that could equal the worst of the elements: and this suggested a profoundly satisfying, profoundly *positive* interpretation of the 'natural impulse' by which Longinus had said that humans prefer to think of all that is greatest and grandest in nature. We like to think of the 'Ocean' because it tells us how big we are. We like to go exploring because it proves we are as big as what we conquer. Yet beside and against this triumphant aspect of the case must be set – however the information is to be valued – a cultural context which sometimes took the opposite view. The romances of catastrophe nourished another version of the sublime, a dreamed-of conquest *by* raging elements. Look, that flood has wonderfully wrecked my house: look, those snows had wonderfully undone our explorers. Now one could say, truthfully, that the available sublime of defeat only sharpened the edge of the sublime of success, when success was attained. Or one could assign the interest in sublime defeat entirely to the vulturous commentators in the press, whose loving attention to the details of Scott's death in Antarctica struck many of the expedition's survivors as morbid. But a style of feeling, which is what the sublime had become to the Edwardians, endlessly diffusing and recondensing, cannot be neatly divided. It seems arbitrary, as well, to parcel out the different bits of a style of feeling like the sublime to different participants in the cultural drama of exploration, a bit for the actors and a bit for the beholders.

What are we to make, then, of the demonstrably mixed feelings on both sides, the obvious grief of the audience that consumed the newsmen's florid memorials to the dead, and the grieving readiness with which the surviving explorers did accept a sublime rationale for the tragedy? Everyone who read Scott's diaries, as they became available, wished for the safety of the doomed party that they thought they had come to know. A biographer recorded the odd hope he experienced, each time he re-read the documents, that *this time* things might turn out differently, *this time* they might make it home. Empathy was vital to the response of the audience. Equally, a perverse and marginal satisfaction can be detected in the behaviour of the survivors, not at all a satisfaction that the polar party died, but that they should have made their undesired end so magnificently, so much in accordance with the principles of sublime defeat that the survivors could raise as their appropriate epitaph the grimly glorious last line of Tennyson's 'Ulysses': *To strive, to seek, to find, and not to yield.* It will not do to tidy away this ambivalence. Common sense might say that tragedies are sad, and no-one wants them to happen, but common sense tells only partial truths. The whole existence of something called the sublime, devoted to spectacles of grandeur and terror, testifies that our appetite for tragedies somehow hides an odd species of enjoyment.

Here we can usefully return to the flood, and the philosophy, of the young Edmund Burke. On the far bank of the Liffey, Burke had noticed, the Dubliners not affected by the flood – 'secured by their situation' – would 'deride the poor prisoners' opposite. When later he came to write his *Enquiry* it seems probable that he remembered the deriders. In the eighteenth century, the problem of people enjoying other people's suffering tended to be considered in relation to tragic drama. Again, common sense asserted that an audience only enjoyed the sufferings of tragic characters because they knew that they were fictitious; a real blinding (Gloucester in *King Lear*) or a real mass-murder (the last scenes of *Hamlet*) would arouse pity or revulsion instead. Burke differed, in a famous comparison of the relative drawing-powers of an execution and a tragedy. No matter how noble the play, the theatre would empty if the audience were told that a 'State criminal' were about to be hanged for treason in the square outside. 'I am convinced we have a degree of delight, and that no small one, in the real misfortunes and pains of others.' To some extent, Burke formed his view on a traditionally cynical opinion of human nature, the sort that can be found in every era and culture and frequently supports a conservative political philosophy. ('How pleasant it is', Confucius is supposed to have said, 'to see an old friend fall from a roof-top.') But he was ambitious to discover 'the rationale of our passions', and, if he thought people responded to plays and reality in much the same way, he did not attribute the unpleasant pleasure of watching suffering to straightforward sadism, or anything like it. 'I believe,' he wrote,

that this notion of our having a simple pain in the reality, yet a delight in the representation, arises from hence, that we do not sufficiently distinguish what we would by no means choose to do, from what we would be eager enough to see if it were once done. We delight in seeing things which, so far from doing, our heartiest wishes would be to see redressed.

Interestingly, in view of the disaster Richard Jeffries imagined a century and a half later, Burke took the destruction of London 'by a conflagration or an earthquake' as an illustration of his point: unwished for, the 'fatal accident' would still bring 'numbers from all parts' to admire the ruins. His careful sentences fit, remarkably well, the terms on which Victorian readers might allow themselves to enjoy catastrophe. I think they also illuminate, for the first but not the last time, the psychology of the Edwardian audience for polar feats. The newspaper readers of 1913 'would by no means choose' to have Scott's party die, but they were 'eager enough to see' – with the eager eyes of imagination, assisted by the gentlemen of the press – the grand details of the deaths, once they had happened. Hundreds of thousands made a mental tour of the scene, the tiny tent pitched on the Great Ice

Barrier that contained no warmth, little light, and three dead bodies, arranged on their polar bier. (Wilson had his hands clasped on his chest, like a statue of a medieval crusader.) Hundreds of thousands no doubt wished heartily, while they browsed over the reported ruins, that the deaths could be redressed; and perhaps dreamed, like the biographer, of a happier ending that no effort of theirs could ensure.

By the end of the eighteenth century the pictures that the Romantics, and others, were painting of the psyche used a palette of passions far richer than Burke's scanty duo of pain and pleasure. However, and for reasons that largely had to do with his religious conception of the human faculties, Burke had granted a role to *instinct* that was lost in the more subtle understandings of the mind that came after. Burke, in fact, had developed an anomalous, embryonic, Georgian version of the unconscious, which he thought of as a sort of physical system underlying the will, probably placed there by a benign providence as a counterbalance to humanity's erring ways.

I am afraid it is a practice much too common, in inquiries of this nature, to attribute the cause of feelings which merely arise from the mechanical structure of our bodies, or from the natural frame and constitution of our minds, to certain conclusions of the reasoning faculty on the objects presented to us; for I should imagine that the influence of reason, in producing our passions, is nothing near so extensive as it is commonly believed.

Burke talked about instinct in an unwieldy mechanical vocabulary drawn from current science, full of collisions between spheres *à la* Newton, and laws of attraction and repulsion. He used it, though, to avoid having to moralise his findings about painful delight; God, at some further remove from the action, was taking care that the appetite for the sublime was working for the good. Consequently, Burke managed to investigate some of the murkier and potentially dangerous aspects of the sublime without pushing them away from himself, without labelling them as culpable. They belonged in the ordinary mind. Until Freud's determined re-integration of the destructive urges into our model of the psyche at the beginning of this century, Burke was one of the few people to consider the relationship of pain to 'delight' without consigning it to the weird fringes of psychology, to the realm of the abnormal.

He happened to be writing, at the same time, about vastness and darkness, difficulty and sublime effort, all recognisable components of the polar scene. So it is unexpected, it is tricky to evaluate, but it is not an accident that – for example – Burke's comments on optics should also seem to read like a prescient description of the frustrations of man-hauling a sledge through sticky, irregular snow.

Whoever has remarked the different effects of some strong exercise, and some little piddling action, will understand why a teasing fretful employment, which at once wearies and weakens the body, should have nothing great; these sorts of impulses, which are rather teasing than painful, by continually and suddenly altering their tenor and direction, prevent that full tension, that species of uniform labour, which is allied to strong pain, and causes the sublime . . .

Burke means the exercise of looking: you can substitute the exercise of pulling. Burke means the impulses of coloured light that strike the eye: you can substitute the varying backward tugs by a dead weight on a leather harness, as the runners clog and ease, clog and ease. In either case, 'greatness', exhilaration, obeys certain physical rules; and only when these are satisfied does the wig-wearing eighteenth-century observer gaze with relish upon a waterfall, or the canvas-muffled Edwardian swoosh confidently forward through the snow.

The most important of Burke's rules for the sublime was that the person gaining the terrible delight should not be too close to the object of terror, whatever it was. There had to be some distance between, or the observer would be overcome with a reasonable fear that the sublime spectacle might actually overwhelm them, and be left in no state to entertain any aesthetic satisfactions. Pure unmodified fear, he knew, churned the guts, loosened the bowels, was aesthetically null. The difficulty lay in defining what distance would be required, and unsympathetic critics found it easy to pick apart his vagueness on this crucial point. So far as they were concerned, he was simply saying that if you stood back a bit, fear was magically metamorphosed into its opposite. And since he had brought up 'distance' as a criterion, he ought to be able to say exactly what he meant – so just how far away did you have to be? A mile? An inch? A rod, pole, or perch?

Burke's rule of distance was, wrote Richard Payne Knight in 1805, 'a stout instance of confusion even with every allowance that can be made for the ardour of youth in an Hibernian philosopher of five and twenty'. But for all the questions it begged, Burke's rule of distance was more than an Irish joke. Those who judged it only on its most literal level – and who laughed at the tape-measure his sublime seemed to require – judged only part of it. Yes, his 'distance' could be purely spatial: and the width of the Liffey, after all, had proved to be a sufficient separation from the flood for the other Dubliners to jeer. But it could also be, more searchingly, the distance between souls in civil society, separated by divergent interests and individual wants. No matter what laws tied people together, no matter how much the common good was supposed to guide the actions of humanity, it was also true that every individual was alone; and hungry for satisfaction. Separate atoms of society, each person looked across a gulf at his neighbour.

Burke constructed two little trios of terms, to explain the different principles that governed humans when they were isolated, and when they were acting in unison. On the one hand, the sensation of *pain* went together with the passion of *self-preservation*, and had *sublimity* as the aesthetic conseqence. On the other, *pleasure* belonged with the passion for *society*, and produced *beauty*. The first, atavistic set – which would not change however society was constituted – was more urgent, and therefore more powerful, than the second. So, when danger pressed sufficiently hard on a person, in fact or in imagination, the overriding drive to self-preservation came into play. (If Burke had lived in the twentieth century, and had had biological training, he might have called it the fight-or-flight reflex, which accelerates the heartbeat in seconds and pumps adrenalin into the system.) But supposing that something interposed itself, whether it was the width of the Liffey, or the danger being a fictional danger in the thrilling pages of a novel, or the danger only affecting the body of one's neighbour, and shielded one from it, then a rush of relief – a 'delight' – filled the mind with all the force of self-preservation itself. In one place

Burke called it a 'sort of delightful horror, a sort of tranquillity tinged with terror; which, as it belongs to self-preservation, is one of the strongest of all the passions'.

Although the risk of harm had passed, wrote Burke, the mind remained transfixed. It was as little able to resume its ordinary state as if annihilation really threatened it. The mind went on behaving, without danger, like a mouse caught in the gaze of a snake, or a rabbit hypnotised by the oncoming headlights. It could not be thoughtful: 'the mind is so entirely filled with its object, that it cannot entertain any other, nor . . . reason on that object that employs it.' His point was that this soul-swamping feeling also drove out for a time one's ability to sympathise with other people who had been directly affected by the danger. A tranquil jeering remained, or a tranquil enjoyment at others' suffering, which for the moment looked like a fascinating, arresting spectacle; a spectacle glimpsed from a position of security by an observer still under the influence of fear.

Impatient, the Regency aesthete Richard Payne Knight mocked again.

If . . . [Burke] had walked up St James's street without his breeches, it would have occasioned great and universal *astonishment*; and if he had, at the same time, carried a loaded blunderbuss in his hands, the astonishment would have been mixed with no small portion of *terror*: but I do not believe that the united effects of these two powerful passions would have produced any sentiment or sensation approaching to the sublime, even in the breasts of those who had the strongest sense of self-preservation, and the quickest sensibility of danger.

The interesting thing is that, as Knight clearly calculated, it *is* easier to recognise ordinary human reactions in this offhand bit of satire than in Burke's schemes and categorisations. It does not really answer Knight's comic attack, from this point of view, to point out that even Burke armed to the teeth in his underwear *could* be sublime, given the right circumstances. (What about King Lear raving in his wreath of flowers, one might ask. What about one of the madder Roman emperors, with blood on his hands and a dear little bunch of violets behind his ear?) Burke has the moral imagination necessary to perceive that people *sometimes* do not behave in accordance with common sense, and then the intellectual grasp required to slot the strange phenomena of the sublime back among the ordinary properties of the psyche; but his exposition of his findings is much too analytical, much too reductive in fact, to carry the same straightforward conviction as a joke. As philosophy, as pure thought, Burke's sublime of terror does not offer a model that can be applied direct to the complicated behaviour of real people without distorting it badly. It lacks nuance, the touch of experience.

Yet Burke's sublime was taken up, not by other philosophers, but by consumers of aesthetic theory, predominantly women, who used the sublime in its horrifying mode to shape their poems and their Gothic novels. Though they certainly read and digested Burke's *Enquiry*, they did not much engage with it as a system of thought. Their interest lay in what they could make of it, what it could enable them to do; they ate their way with gusto through Burke's menu of sublime effects, his famous recommendations of 'vastness', 'obscurity', and 'privation'. They learned that the visual impact of a description could be enormously strengthened by a little judicious blurring and obscuring. Show only a part of a ruined tower – wrap the rest in a rolling black mist – and the imagination, deprived of a definite scale, would enlarge the tower into an unbounded Piranesian fantasy, with shady battlements and labyrinthine dungeons extending far into the unspecified distance. They were also interested in his assertion that human compassion came and went when powerful stimuli played upon it, just as in a thrilling novel, when whole scenes of *Sturm und Drang* and clifftop violence required the reader to forget to be sympathetic for a while, and to enjoy, enjoy.

But one would expect, maybe, considering Burke's clumsiness as an observer of human behaviour, that they would have modified his ideas to fit their own purposes, moulding them around character and manners. One would expect, in other words, that they refined his formulas to suit the sensitivities of fiction. On the whole they did not. Mrs Radcliffe's *Romance of the Forest*, for example, continually threw her heroine into situations in which her feelings might just as well be direct quotations from Burke. 'The partial gleams thrown across the fabric seemed to make its desolation more solemn, while the obscurity of the greater part of the pile heightened its sublimity, and led fancy on to scenes of horror. Adeline, who had hitherto remained in silence, now uttered an exclamation of mingled admiration and fear. A kind of pleasing dread thrilled her bosom, and filled all her soul.'

Accordingly these female authors have often been represented as uncritical thrill-seekers, messing around with a philosophy they evidently did not understand, because they did not seek to transform it. One standard history of the sublime, published in the 1930s, groups them all together in a chapter at the end, like a sort of comic appendix to the serious business of aesthetics. In fact their use of Burke has another kind of revealing subtlety. Though the Gothic, and fashionable sublime poetry, do not find a flexible language that makes Burke's conclusions over into credible psychology, they do reach deep into the question of what is at stake, psychologically, in the terrible sublime, for readers and writers far more real and probable than Burke's cardboard Observers ever were.

Their adventurousness lay in what they brought the sublime to mean. The writers themselves pointed out explicitly how much the sublime meant to them as women. For one thing it provided an alternative to the classical learning that they were not usually in a position to acquire, an alternative ballast of theory for literature. More importantly, it allowed them to re-present and to re-figure the opposition between passivity and activity – and by extension the opposition between male and female itself. The heroines of Gothic novels are shown as extravagantly vulnerable. Their bodies, prone to sudden faints, always in frantic motion across ominous landscapes, are zones of innocence on which multiple threats converge, whether in the form of tempests or seducers or mad machinations. Apparently their plots demonstrate the traditional weakness of women; but, written for a female readership, these novels actually invert the rather conservative assumptions that had governed Burke's thinking. Burke believed that it was the 'social' passion of beauty which dignified the relations between men and women, and one could only feel beauty in connection with what could not possibly be frightening. Clearly, 'one' was a man. Meanwhile, a feeling of the sublime could only be inspired by what was stronger than oneself.

In effect he asserted that there was a gender boundary between the sublime and the beautiful. The critic Terry Eagleton suggests that both Burke's beautiful and his sublime were therefore aesthetics of subordination, deeply hierarchical modes of feeling. The beautiful described women's subjection to men, the sublime men's subjection to more powerful men or to great natural forces. Women were limited to feeling beauty, whereas men could feel both, because even the most downtrodden man, sublimely suppressed by every other man in creation, would still have some delicate female dependant to be superior to. On this reading, Burke can be said to have aestheticised sexual politics. He took the existing state of things – the current roles of men and women – and gave them an aesthetic garnish, a rationale for them in prettiness and profundity.

If Eagleton is broadly right, then the women writers' use of the sublime begins to look rather different. Their swathings of sublime experience might have amounted to a rebellious choice of the aesthetic reserved for men, the bigger aesthetic, the tougher aesthetic. By writing heroines exposed to extraordinary dangers – however passively those dangers had to be borne – the Gothic novelists offered their readers the lion's share of Burke's system, rather than the sweetly acquiescent portion. They proposed that it was more exciting to be grandly overmastered – and sometimes to exercise grand mastery oneself, for there was some flexibility in the heroines' adventures – than to spend one's life with bell-jars, dried flowers and good girls' stories.

When one read a Gothic novel, one could not view events entirely through the eyes of Adelina or Letitia, or Sophronisba, or whatever she happened to be called. She functioned more as the hook of the plot, the tag that kept one's interests bound close to the course of the story. To enjoy her constant peril and her breathless escapes, one needed to keep at least one foot of identification in the camp of the villain(s). Their wickedness, their schemes, kept things moving. They, not she, possessed the active if disgraceful passions; they, not she, were harmonised with the titanic thunderstorms and lighting effects of the natural sublime. Because the author had laid claim on one's behalf to the power of the sublime, one revelled in the power of the villains over a heroine ostensibly like oneself, though a careful vagueness – equivalent perhaps to Burke's 'distance' – prevented one from encountering too closely a plain, and therefore repulsive, desire to commit a rape or carry out an infanticide. (When a book breached this important rule, as Lewis' *The Monk* did, it was judged nasty rather than exciting.) The Gothic novel, then, invited one to identify with what was stronger than oneself, and indeed with what was bent on menacing one's self. Relocating the condition of 'distance' in the area of imaginative discretion, the authors, without necessarily having any philosophical intentions at all, made a notable shift in the sublime's terms of reference. Previously, one had to be assured of safety oneself in order to feel the sublime. Now, so long as the danger conformed to the sublime pattern of dangers, and so long also as the threat presented itself sufficiently cloudily not to call into play one's specific objections to being hurt in a specific way, one could apparently continue to feel the sublimity *of the threat* while being threatened oneself. This may not sound like much of an innovation, since here the necessary vagueness of the threat tended to mean that it was after all imaginary. But this extra degree of approach to the sources of sublimity – this fractional admission of it into the defended castle of subjectivity – can be read as providing just the additional looseness that was lacking in Burke's tight formulations, to make the sublime informative about the mixed desires of those who approached real danger. The sublime needed to be able to speak to the behaviour of those actually threatened. With this in mind, in addition to the sublime (but partial) light thrown on the admiration of the polar audiences, we can see something here that fits the psyches of the explorers themselves, confronted by, sometimes conquered by, a terrain stronger than them.

There is a famous photograph by Scott's cameraman Herbert Ponting (on the cover of this book): one of the permanently established images for Scott's attempt on the South Pole, although it shows the Barne Glacier some eight hundred miles away from it. Taken from the frozen sea-ice at the foot of the glacier, with Ponting standing far enough back to register the glacier top on his plate, along with a slender slice of night sky, it shows the whole height of the ice-cliff, a chasmed and variegated surface whose texture shows up as a tissue of minutely distinguished photographic greys. Right at the bottom, some way out from the glacier foot, there is a man hitched to a sledge. He is tiny: and on close examination he proves not even to be real, but a silhouette inked onto the print, posed there to give an indication of scale, like the small coin placed next to the champion pumpkin, his six-odd feet of height giving the measure for the glacier's hundreds. Then one realises that in the lucid, melodramatic theatre of Ponting's imagination, he is being measured against it in a further sense. The glacier's imperturbable grandeur is being compared to this emblematic man's smallness. To gain the pole, for which this rampart of ice is standing in so aptly, the actions of the small figure will have to be of comparable size with the object that opposes him, that stands behind him. The picture dramatises a struggle which will be based upon the difference of size between men and landscape. It sets the men up, of course, for a heroic victory (Ponting took the photograph before the polar attempt began) but it explained beautifully, in retrospect, the nature of their heroic defeat. Hence its iconic status. It is a sublime image, of course. The glacier is already sublime, sublime in and of itself. Like a perpetual flood, upreared and then frozen into place, the glacier asserts a huge, swallowing indifference to the efforts of travellers. They have their chance to be sublime by taking up the fight against its power – a graphically unequal battle. In Ponting's photograph, the ice becomes authoritative.

The Dublin deluge had impressed the young Burke because what had obeyed, did so no longer. Among the snows beneath the eightieth parallel, as between the covers of a Gothic novel, the sublime of power held sway. Like a Gothic villain (who ought not to have had the power to plot and manipulate, but did) the Antarctic landscape (which 'ought' to have admitted men to its fastnesses, but did not) in some sense took the initiative away from the heroes. Its sublime authority could not be gainsaid; and the explorers responded by identifying themselves with its sublimity, glorying in the place even as it thwarted or even hurt them. The critical vagueness of the Gothic seems to apply: the pains of exploration presented themselves without the unveiled brutality of a rape. Rather, the gentle implacability of the cold seems to have dignified the explorers' defeats. It chilled and deadened the surface of the body, rather than penetrating or wounding it. It was a worthily impersonal adversary, whose force could be acknowledged without the shattering effect of submission to a human rival.

In the course of his *Enquiry* Burke examined natural disasters, human tyrannies, and overwhelmingly bright lights: never ice-caps. He put his view of the sublime of power most succintly in connection with wild predators.

Look at a man, or at any other animal of prodigious strength, and what is your idea before reflection? Is it that this strength will be subservient to you, to your ease, to your pleasure, to your interest, in any sense? No: the emotion you feel is, lest the enormous strength should be employed to the purposes of rapine and destruction . . . We have continually about us animals of a strength that is considerable, but not pernicious. Amongst them we never look for the sublime; it comes upon us in the gloomy forest, and in the howling wilderness, in the form of the lion, the tiger, the panther, or rhinoceros. Whenever strength is only useful, and employed for our benefit or our pleasure, then it is never sublime; for nothing can act agreeably to us, that does not act in conformity to our will; but, to act agreeably to our will, it must be subject to us, and therefore can never be the cause of a grand and commanding conception.

For panthers etc, read the white wolf of the blizzards – not a denizen of the 'howling wilderness', but the wilderness itself, snapping hungrily at the heels of stragglers. Burke states the 'delight' of being overpowered, once again, with a summary simplicity that challenges belief. Perhaps that is why Richard Payne Knight issued yet another irritated common-sense rebuttal in *Principles of Taste*, fifty years after the *Enquiry*. 'Fear is the most humiliating and depressing of passions; and, when a person is under its influence, it is as unnatural for him to join in any sentiments of exultation with that which inspires it, as it would be for a man to share in the triumph or the feast of the lion, of which he was himself the victim and the prey.' Knight cannot imagine that one could feel anything but fear when standing next to – say – Nero, and a justified contempt afterwards, when safe from him. He cannot imagine that one could feel anything when on an ice-cap but anxiety and bodily cold, and a just unmixed pride in accomplishment when one returned triumphant. He denied any drift at all towards identification with the power that overmasters one. Without any special system of explanation, Knight's contemporary Hazlitt knew otherwise. Perhaps it only took a darker outlook. Hazlitt was discussing the 'right-royal' bias of poetry, in an essay on *Coriolanus* which deals with the intoxicating rhetoric of power. He observed, and his example was exactly the same as Knight's: 'A lion hunting a flock of sheep or a herd of wild asses is a more poetical object than they; and we even take part with the lordly beast, because our vanity or some other feeling makes us disposed to place ourselves in the situation of the strongest party.' Hazlitt recognised, and scowled at, the trick aesthetics plays on common sense, under the influence of that 'other feeling'.

However common sense denied it, however unsafe or unstraight-forward its excitements were, the sublime remained a heady influence on the way the conventional English saw themselves as they set about doing dangerous things. It persisted through the nineteenth century; it was, in the Edwardian imagination, old and familiar and worn by long usage.

On the other hand, common sense sometimes said the necessary thing. If the line between sublime fear and plain fright was hair-thin on occasion, and hard to pick out, then common sense could ram a useful wedge between the two phenomena. C. J. Sullivan was a blacksmith on HMS *Erebus*. He wrote up a diary of the British Antarctic Expedition of 1839–43 for his shipmate James Savage, who only joined the expedition on its return journey to England. Sullivan wanted to give his friend an idea of what they had seen; and he wanted to do so, moreover, in the language that he had presumably heard the officers using. There were quiet times of amazement to record:

Beholding with Silent Surprize the great and wonderful works of nature in this position we had an opportunity to discern the barrier in its Splendid position. Then i wished I was an artist or draughtsman instead of a blacksmith and armourer . . . We Set a Side all thoughts of mount Erebus and Victoria Land to bear in mind the more Immaginative thoughts of this rare Phenomena that was lost to human view. In Gone by Ages.

More often, though, Sullivan was surrounded by continuous sublimity, by giant waves and storms he did his best to convey. He caught the look of things far better when he made his metaphors himself ('a Steem engine in a large factory') than when he laid the conventional phrases of aesthetic appreciation end to end, but he enjoyed the vocabulary of the sublime. The vocabulary, but not always the experience. 'I not being bread to the Sea what i have heard and Read concerning the maratine Life presented no adequate idea of those Sublime Effects which the rageing of the Elements produced.' One night a hurricane blew HMS *Erebus* and HMS *Terror* broadside against berg after berg, and Sullivan rebelled against aesthetics. 'It was awfully grand two grand for Stout hearted Sailors . . .'

THREE

News from Nowhere

While the theory of the sublime was teaching travellers and spectators alike how to see frozen wastes, real information about them had begun to accumulate in the public mind.

On 17 January 1775, a Tuesday, in the weary final phase of his Second Voyage, Captain Cook discovered the island of South Georgia, a long spine of mountains rising from the south polar seas. Though Cook's crew had brought the ship in from the east, from one of the terminal islands around Cape Horn, they approached their new discovery from the north-west, because only on the western side does the central range trend at all gently down to the sea. The east, too, is a sailor's nightmare, a continuous lee shore that gives a sailing ship little room to manoeuvre: only at the west is there shelter from the prevailing winds. There the first of a series of fjords broke the inhospitable coastline, with sandy beaches among the more usual ice-cliffs. Cook drew in to the shore in a ship's boat, meaning to sound out the anchorage before risking the ship itself, which after three years in the deep southern latitudes was in no state to sustain any unnecessary accidents. He found deep water, and no reefs. Even within the bay his thirty-four-fathom line did not touch bottom. Some spots looked promising, but as Cook got a close view of the South Georgian scenery, he changed his mind about anchoring. 'I did not think it worth my while to go and examine these places,' he wrote, 'for it did not seem probable that any one would ever be benefited by the discovery.' Instead he made his reconnoitre into his whole visit, and went straight ahead with the quickest possible version of the expected ceremony. 'I landed in three different places, displayed our colours, and took possession of the country in his Majesty's name, under a discharge of small arms.'

There are something over two thousand square miles of South Georgia, almost all either glaciated or precipitous. Cook saw the rising ground around 'Possession Bay' glazed in all directions. He felt no desire to investigate further. 'The inner parts of the country were not less savage and horrible' than the coast. 'The wild rocks raised their lofty summits, till they were lost in the clouds, and the valleys lay covered with everlasting snow. Not a tree was to be seen, nor a shrub big enough to make a toothpick. The only vegetation we met with, was a coarse strong-bladed grass growing in tufts, wild burnet, a plant like moss, which sprang from the rocks.' Cook was no ironist, but it is clear he thought South Georgia one of the more useless presents that could be given a monarch, or a nation; the naming of it not likely to challenge recognition beside the other two Georgias in the world, the cotton-growing American colony and the ancient kingdom in the Caucasus. Unlike the bits of Polynesia which Cook had claimed for the Crown on his First Voyage, and the other bits he would claim on his Third, this island had no population to watch as he hauled the Union flag up and directly down again, no hostile Maoris or complaisant Tahitians it might serve policy to come to an understanding with. South Georgia was not on the way to anywhere. It had no wood useful for re-equipping a ship, even with toothpicks, let alone masts. It grew nothing fresh that seamen could be fed to stave off scurvy. Taking possession of it was a courtly, almost abstract gesture, especially since Cook, like many later first-time visitors to new parts of the polar regions, saw no reason why European sailors should ever come back. South Georgia was now known: stretches of its coast were plotted accurately on a map: nothing would follow from these additions to human knowledge.

Cook could be said to have discovered, besides the physical fact of the island, one of the characteristic absurdities that resulted when governments tried to carve up polar territory – when states met snow. Signs and symbols of authority (like a flag, like a pistol volley) which referred to organisations of *people*, were carried where they no longer referred to anything. These days anyone can participate in the same fiction by collecting the postage stamps issued for the different national zones of the Antarctic. Printed in Europe or Latin America or

Australasia, never used except by scientists and soldiers posted (in a realer sense) to Antarctic bases, the coloured commemorative sets still look nice in an album. They are the trimmings of a sovereignty that only exists in trimmings. But the absurdity is not always an innocent one. The same feeling of politics conducted in a vacuum marked the moment in 1982 when, a few fjords along from Possession Bay, the party of scrap-merchants arrived to declare a symbolic Argentine presence, and set off an absurdist war. Though Britain and Argentina fighting for the Falklands, said Jorge Luis Borges, were 'like two bald men fighting over a comb', the uselessness of the prize did not prevent the clash of sovereignties.

The question of use was much in Cook's mind as he sailed away from South Georgia in 1775, arranging in his Journal his 'Heads of what has been done in the Voyage', and drawing some careful conclusions from the experience of the previous three years. He had fulfilled his commission from the Admiralty, but the major geographical achievement of the voyage was a negative one. Straight through the areas in which some held that the forests, cities, and unknown civilisations of a Great Southern Continent were supposed to lie, Cook had sailed on empty seas. He had circumnavigated the South Pole twice and set a record for the furthest south a ship had ever gone, thereby proving there were no temperate lands left to discover. Although he had never sighted the coast of Antarctica itself, he did believe there was a polar landmass. The shapes of the icebergs he saw suggested that they had formed at a land's edge, and by a fine chain of reasoning, Cook correctly deduced not only the extent of the continent he hadn't seen, but also the two great indentations in it made by the Ross and Weddell ice shelves. The character of South Georgia, the South Sandwich Islands, and the other polar outliers Cook had come across hinted at the likely character of any continent.

Lands doomed by Nature to perpetual frigidness; never to feel the warmth of the sun's rays; whose horrible and savage aspect I have not words to describe. Such are the lands we have discovered; what then may we expect those to be, which lie still further to the South? For we may reasonably suppose that we have seen the best, as lying most to the North. If any one should have resolution and perseverance to clear up this point by proceeding further than I have done, I shall not envy him the honour of the discovery; but I will be bold to say, that the world will not be benefited by it.

This is the refreshing voice of eighteenth-century good sense, not wholly immune to the aesthetic appeal of the 'savage and horrible', yet decided in its preference for islands that satisfied a more useful curiosity. Cook, deeply interested in the wildlife and the material culture of the South Pacific, scrutinised the seabirds of the Antarctic only to tell if they testified to land near by. He saw himself replacing the speculative geography of the Great Southern Continent with real geography: the act of substituting truth for fiction had value, but the places he had truly discovered did not. More important than the details of South Georgia, in his calculation of achievement, were the lessons learned aboard that other seamen could turn to account. He had tested different preserved vegetables and fruit juices on his crew, and he could tell the Admiralty which worked best against scurvy. And he had also shown you could restock a ship with fresh water when far from land, by heaving aboard pieces of iceberg. Only the first wash off them was tainted by salt.

As it happened Cook was wrong twice over about the uselessness of the far South, despite his unexceptionable reasoning. Wrong, first, in thinking no-one would be back, or would conceivably find a benefit even in South Georgia's fjords. Within a few decades South Georgia and its like stopped being impossibly far away. Its position and its (meagre) resources became useful knowledge to the whalers of the Southern Fishery, British and American, who chased the sperm and right whales gradually further and further south. Ships from Nantucket and New Bedford and Mystic Seaport visited frequently, in polar terms. Changes in whaling technology later in the nineteenth century then made it sensible to establish shore stations there, bases where the Anglo-Norwegian companies involved could melt down blubber and ship it away while the hunting vessels themselves cruised on uninterrupted. At the height of its prosperity, South Georgia supported about seven hundred human residents. When Ernest Shackleton and his companions crossed the Allardyce Range in 1916, ending the last desperate stage of their journey from the Weddell Sea by open boat, it was these people that they saw. They looked down on the sheds, chimneys, wharves of Stromness. After two years stranded in the *Endurance* the first human sound they heard that they had not made themselves was a factory whistle; and the manager summoned to deal with the trio of filthy travellers who eventually staggered into the settlement had to be called from his office desk, where he was having an ordinary working day. At the time of the heroic expeditions, Antarctica had an industry on its doorstep.

But this chapter concerns the other aspect of Cook's error, a way in which he was more immediately mistaken (for no-one did return for many years, while this use for his polar findings required no ship, no travel, and no capital invested). Cook's travels were taken up by the public, as data for imagination. His account of his Second Voyage was handed to others to see through the press, because he sailed once more in 1776; and his death on a Hawaiian beach – the fatal result of being mistaken for the god Lono – gave the Third Voyage a martyrdom for a conclusion. He became a bestseller. The plain style he apologised for ('the Public must not expect from me the elegance of a fine writer') gave his readers something like a guarantee that the extraordinary things he related were reliable. A part of his appeal, as well, must have lain in the room he allowed for his plain reports to be embroidered on. The Tahitian episodes were the most popular, enabling paradisial reveries throughout the home counties, but the polar passages had their fans too, starting perhaps with Sir John Pringle, who grew quite excited when discoursing to the Royal Society on Cook's use of ice for watering the ship. 'Here was indeed a *wonder of the deep*! I may call it indeed the *Romance of his Voyage*! Those very shoals, fields, and floating mountains of ice, among which he steered his perilous course and which presented such terrifying prospects of destruction; those, I say, were the very means of his support . . .' Anna Seward's elegy on Cook, mentioned in the last chapter, included careful footnotes to Cook's own words, in case anyone should think that her choice of epithets was less than strictly justified. 'Furling the *iron sails with numbed hands,/Firm on the deck the great Adventurer stands' runs one couplet, directing the reader to: '*Furling the iron sails. – "Our

sails and rigging were so frozen, that they seemed plates of iron." '
With this dotting of fact, did it matter that Seward had Cook led
through the iced-up seas by a Goddess 'deck'd with vermeil youth and
beamy grace'? Or that, in the couplet above, Cook seemed able to
reach the rigging without leaving the quarterdeck? And Cook's reports
from the Antarctic were not only transformed into bad art. Coleridge's
wide reading of travel books to enrich 'The Ancient Mariner' is
famous; the ice, mast-high, that floated by, as green as emerald, was
probably fused together from Cook's and other descriptions, along
with the characteristic noises made by floes; although it is pleasant to
find in Cook's narration a totally unconscious rebuttal of the Romantic
priorities Coleridge would impose on polar material twenty years later.
Coleridge's ancient mariner breached the sacred bonds of nature when
he killed the innocent albatross. Cook's real mariners were hungrier.
'The next day, having several hours calm, we put a boat in the water,
and shot some albatrosses and peterels, which, at this time, were
highly acceptable.'

Judged as a place, tested by Cook's criteria of utility, South Georgia
offered vanishingly small returns on effort expended. In Seward's and
Coleridge's adaptations of Cook, though, a polar island was hardly a
place at all: more a scene, a location of the imagination, which it might
boost imagination to remember from time to time did correspond to a
spot in the ocean, far away over the curve of the earth. And indeed the
imaginative impact of polar exploration over the century that followed
lay in something other than it being simply news from a far country –
a country colder and in some respects weirder than others, but still a
piece of the variegated fabric of elsewhere, served bit by bit in travel
writing, and gradually revealing its details under the gas-lighting of
attention. Polar exploration had a special place in the heart; which is
another way of saying that its representations gained a life of their own
in the culture. It came to belong, via the public means of books and
cartoons and conversations, to the inner worlds of fancy and
imagination in England – to the visions of clairvoyantes, the reveries
of famous novelists, and the love letters of explorers' wives. It became
a subject for debate, a resource for metaphor and slang, and a powerful
mobiliser of emotion. All these are signs that a domain had been found

for it *in here* as well as *out there*. Bringing the icy regions home imaginatively involved the finding of all sorts of unexpected contiguities between polar, and private, life. We have already seen that the nasty pleasure of the sublime could be produced by overlaying foreign cold on English scenes, and other such links abounded. By no means all, though, were devoted to a tingling disruption of the domestic realm. Often the point was that the subject of the poles somehow confirmed and satisfied an idea of what was closest at hand. Armchair travel to the far North – an increasingly popular pursuit – may have taken people out of themselves, but it must also have done the opposite; or exploration would not have spoken, as it did, to people's identities, where they lived, at home.

Cook's voyages did just this, and an irresistible image for the warm reception given to cold places can be found in the pantomime Covent Garden Theatre mounted in 1785. *Omai, or A Trip Round the World* was a monumentally silly tribute to the man. In it the Tahitian prince Omai – Cook had brought a real Tahitian named Omai to England, and introduced him to George III – woos and weds the British nymph Londina, and an idyllically imperial time is had by all. A chorus of 'Kamtschatkan natives' sing a winter song:

> When the North Wind whistles we dance to the note,
>> We quiver
>>> And we quaff,
>> We shiver
>>> And we laugh
> At the chrystal beard that hangs from the goat.

But the plot and the lyrics were not the play's strong points. Covent Garden paid the author £40; they paid three times as much to have *Omai* designed by the brilliant Philip de Loutherbourg, who could turn almost anything into a theatrical spectacle. As well as working for Garrick and Sheridan, de Loutherbourg had invented a three-dimensional miniature panorama he called an Eidophusikon, and on it presented shipwrecks, Niagara, moonrise in Japan, and 'SATAN arraying his TROOPS on the BANKS of the FIERY LAKE'. He studied the drawings made by Cook's official artists. It was not difficult for him to bring an iceberg onto the stage in *Omai* (Part II, scene iii). The stage direction merely says, with negligent authority: '*Harlequin* having lost *Londina* and *Maid*, changes the whole Habitation to . . . A dreary *Ice Island*, where the Parties encounter a Variety of Dangers . . .' Whether de Loutherbourg used a revolving stage, or slid the iceberg from the wings on hidden castors, nobody recorded. But a harlequinade went polar, and London, in a fetching frock, gambolled upon the ice. Once admitted to public view that iceberg, so obviously made of lath and white papier-mâché, floated preposterously on through the nineteenth century, its bulky outline visible in surprising places, its little wheels squeaking.

FOUR

Damn the North Pole!

First exploration had to be defined. English familiarity with the qualities of polar landscape followed a rising curve – until at the end of the nineteenth century, for example, the igloo was a universally understood icon of polar living. (In children's encyclopedias of 1900 Eskimos waved outside igloos, as Red Indians saluted the reader from teepees and Japanese displayed houses built of paper.) A prosperous England's voracity for trade did some of the work of familiarisation. The poles were of course brought home in a very literal sense, as objects, among the flood of objects from around the world. It is no more surprising to reflect that the Victorians had the Arctic represented in their underwear (in the form of corset-stiffening whalebone from the Northern Fishery), than that their houses might contain samples of Malay gutta-percha, Indian inlaid wood, or an elephant's foot umbrella-stand from Africa – though it *is* a slight shock to discover that London's streetlights were entirely powered by whale-oil before the invention of coal-gas. But the poles had also to become the setting for familiar actions; the idea of an expedition had to take root, with its repertoire of behaviour.

For this reason, it is important to see the change brought about in perceptions by the Admiralty's decision to push polar exploration by the Navy after Waterloo. Sir John Barrow, the Admiralty Secretary, who as a boy had gone whaling (and written a poem about the Arctic modelled on 'Winter' in Thomson's *Seasons*), sent out expeditions in surplus warships. They kindled the interest on a mass scale that his own experience had fired privately, in himself. Barrow had an integrated plan which called for multiple efforts along the different avenues of approach to the Arctic. 1817 was a hot year in the far North, clearing large areas of ice; there was intense activity. But to three voyages made before 1822 in particular – by John Ross, William Parry, and John Franklin – can be traced many of the themes which would dominate later response to exploration. The experience of this period originated alike many of the practices (some disastrous) that would shape the British record at the poles, and the ways in which it was thought of. Certain incidents from the three journeys immediately revealed their imaginative potency, recurring repeatedly in commentaries. Ross, for example, sent to probe the Canadian Arctic from the Atlantic side in 1818, met a tribe of Eskimo on the north coast of Hudson Bay. These people showed a wonderfully satisfying ice-bound innocence of Europeans: they took the sailing ships for creatures with wings, they protested that Ross could not possibly have come from the south since only ice lay in that direction, and, faced with glass skylights, asked what kind of ice that was. The encounter, 'which' – wrote Ross – 'never can be forgotten by those who witnessed and enjoyed it', established an instant tradition for future meetings, and set a pattern of imaginative expectations. Parry, a rather critical second-in-command to Ross on that occasion, had his first chance the next year. He was strikingly more successful in covering the miles of ice-choked sea: he also invented a style for ships that overwintered in the Arctic. While the darkness grew, and the thermometer dropped, the crews of his *Hecla* and *Fury* did calisthenics, danced to a barrel-organ, read a shipboard newspaper, and watched amateur theatricals. As well as being adopted by the Admiralty as a standard morale-boosting ploy, this image of tenacious jollity proved irresistible to the public. Strangely snug, paradoxically homely, it seemingly made parlour games a way of defying the elements. Meanwhile the land component of Barrow's plans required a journey by foot and canoe northward across Canada towards the Arctic coast. Lieutenant Franklin, in charge, brought back a darker, yet equally compelling image of exploration, crucial in fixing the courage of the enterprise in the public mind. During their overland return, Franklin and his three naval companions had starved, suffered, and all only just escaped dying at the hands of a French-Canadian guide who turned murderous. One did die, Midshipman Hood; but he had been reading *Bickersteth's Scripture Help* at the moment of his untimely end, and the thought of such fidelity-unto-death, combined with unflinching descriptions of the rotten reindeer intestines, shoe leather, and lichen that the party ate, imprinted themselves on readers of the expedition narrative. Franklin helped start the perception of polar exploration as an activity both physical and moral, dreadful and inspiring. Reading the account thirty-five years afterwards, when in the polar *cause célèbre* of the century Franklin had vanished on a new expedition to the Canadian Arctic, Dickens felt himself 'filled with a sort of sacred joy'.

These were foundations for the future. Most important, however, in signalling that an imaginative era had opened, was the nature of the task that had been decided on by John Barrow of the Admiralty. All the expeditions he orchestrated were seeking out, from different directions, the North-West Passage – the theoretical sea connection between the Atlantic and the Pacific. Since it was already clear that the strait, if it existed, must be at too high a latitude to be easily navigated, hardly any trading advantage could be gained by the nation that contrived to penetrate it. The mission was therefore one of geographical discovery for its own sake. Unlike Captain Cook, Parry and Ross and Franklin were not heard commenting on the uselessness of their finds, and their voyages could be seen, depending on your point of view, as either gratuitous or pure. Not that the voyagers had yet developed the genteel Victorian distaste for money as a motive, it needs saying. Schooled in the Napoleonic wars, when prize-money was the great incentive for naval victories, these sailors were far franker than their later counterparts about the close relationship between glory and booty. They wanted the cash bonus the Admiralty offered for a successful expedition. Parry was quite happy to see his crew cheered up by contributions to his *North Georgia Gazette* like the nonsense verse that began, 'The moon, resplendent orb, shines bright I ween,/Its brilliance is just like our soup-tureen', and ended

> Fired with fresh ardour, and with bold intent,
> Our minds shall, like our prows, be westward bent,
> Until Pacific's waves pour forth sweet sounds,
> Chiming to us like – *Twenty thousand pounds!*

But however loudly the cash-registers chimed in the minds of hopeful sailors, the embracing of discovery as an end in itself gave exploration a distinct imaginative status, backed by the apparatus of official publicity. Returned officers of polar expeditions could expect to see their narratives accepted by prestigious publishers; there was regular coverage of expeditions in the serious reviews, including condensed extracts of those narratives; and explorers, who had perhaps set off grateful for a full-pay posting in the shrunken peace-time Navy, found themselves celebrities when they docked in England.

Doors opened for them into new social worlds: London society, the literary scene, the kind of clubs to which a hero might be admitted where a simple Navy man might not. The Navy was, anyway, in the process of gentrifying. Though it remained a distinct caste among the other subtle castes of genteel English life, it was shedding the rough-and-ready image of the eighteenth century, along with the social mobility that meant naval officers were not always fit for drawing-rooms. The Arctic captains were themselves of the generation that would cease to speak of money in public. And drawing-rooms received them. John Franklin, a dour if kindly Lincolnshire provincial, found himself taken up by literati and socialites. If it had not been for the Arctic, he would never have become engaged to his first wife, Eleanor Porden, for she ran a salon, and had been elected to the Institut de France at sixteen on the strength of her scientific poem 'The Veils'. By the time of his disappearance in the '40s, many threads of family and acquaintance wove him to the bookish, cultivated part of the Establishment. He was a well-connected man, with Tennyson for a nephew-in-law. (He had not been impressed, however, at their first encounter, when the poet sprawled full-length across three chairs and smoked a cheroot. 'Uncle Franklin rather indignant', noted his niece Catherine in her diary.) The social success of the explorers contributed to the imaginative visibility of exploration. People from the world of the arts who had not particularly noticed the polar coverage in the journals, or paid much attention to the increasing presence of polar books on John Murray's excellent list, might find themselves sharing a mantelpiece with an explorer at a party; and the Arctic made a social entrance into their minds. Questions could be

asked. What *is* an iceberg like, sir? Is it true that some are a most
beautiful blue? Even those fastidious types who let a person's standing
determine the mental houseroom they gave a subject might now,
seeing an explorer deep in conversation with the unimpeachable Lady
L——, discover that exploration was rude and barbarous only in an
exciting way. One might go over oneself. One might permit oneself to
be thrilled. I understand you *ate your boots*, Captain: how remarkable.

The explorers were also talked about. We have a reflection of that
talk in the occasional and satirical verse of the period, the kind of
writing that records the surface of a moment. Byron – an expert out of
his own experience in the ways of instant fame – made a swift polar
allusion in his 'Vision of Judgement' of 1822. The poem was a
rejoinder to unctuous official visions of the soul of George III flying
straight to heaven, and Byron subverts the solemn celestial setting by
being frivolously contemporary. Hot news from the Arctic had a
natural place among the other topical bric-à-brac. St Michael is just
issuing forth to do battle with Satan over possession of the baffled king
('for by many stories,/and true, we learn the Angels all are Tories'),
when a flash from the hinges of the pearly gates

> Flung over space an universal hue
> Of many-coloured flame, until its tinges
> Reached even our speck of earth, and made a new
> Aurora borealis spread its fringes
> O'er the North Pole; the same seen, when ice-bound,
> By Captain Parry's crew, in 'Melville's Sound'.

A few years later, someone asked Coleridge for a verse autograph.
Installing his porridgy West Country name in a line offered him a
small verbal challenge. Remembering the buzz in the newspapers,
remembering perhaps the walking tour he had made in the Hartz
Mountains in 1799 with William Parry's two younger brothers, he
wrote:

> Parry seeks out the polar ridge;
> Rhymes seeks S. T. Coleridge.

There at least the fragment stops in the respectable volume of

Coleridge's *Collected Works*. In fact the doggerel impulse produced
two more lines, utterly unpolar:

– Fit to grace a lady's album,
Or to wipe her baby's small bum.

Becoming public property had its disadvantages. Explorers'
reputations ceased to be decided entirely professionally. Details of the
success or failure of individual expeditions were amplified into public
arguments over the rival merits of different commanders, conducted
by fascinated partisan factions whose sole experience of exploration
came through the pages of *Blackwood's Edinburgh Magazine* or the
Quarterly Review. It was now possible to be an enthusiast of polar
exploration as an activity, rather than as a source for information about
meteorology, or zoology, or the earth's magnetic field. And along with
the abstracting of exploration from practical benefits there came an
increasing interest in that ultimate abstraction, the North Pole,
although none of the expeditions at this stage was aimed towards it.
Cook had won respect for the navigational skill required to reach the
high southern latitudes he did, but it was now that the meticulous
absorption began in achieving a Farthest North, measured by a
creeping progress up through the seventies of Arctic latitude to 80°
north, 81°, 82°, 83° . . . The North-West Passage had, in fact, its own
intangible magic as an idea, in the shape of a connection to the series of
Elizabethan voyagers who had first searched for it, and who offered a
national tradition of endurance and sea-doggery the nineteenth-
century English were eager to claim. But the North Pole outbid it – as
an end to the round earth, as an intelligible terminus of effort. Nor
need the North Pole refer exclusively to the exact spot on the map at
90° N. The whole Arctic regions were spoken of, familiarly, as 'the
North Pole'. Where had Parry, Ross, and Franklin been? To the North
Pole. 'I was very happy, keeping up every body's spirits at the North
Pole,' says the comical cook of the North-West Passage expedition in
Wilkie Collins' later melodrama *The Frozen Deep*.

For every enthusiast, there was naturally somebody to point out the
absurdity of growing excited over an artificial point, a geographical
construction. Sydney Smith did so gently, with the Scots philosopher

Leslie, an idolater of the North Pole who had been persecuting Smith's colleague Francis Jeffrey, the editor of the *Edinburgh Review*, with talk of it. As Leslie raised the subject for the umpteenth time, Jeffrey's patience snapped. 'Oh, damn the North Pole!' he shouted, and (he was on horseback) galloped away. The task of soothing Leslie's ruffled feelings fell to Smith, clergyman, diner-out, and wit so effective that tragic actresses had to be removed from his presence in convulsions of laughter. 'My dear fellow, never mind,' he breathed, all sympathy. 'No one cares what Jeffrey says; he is a privileged person; he respects nothing, absolutely nothing. Why, you will scarcely credit it, but, strictly between ourselves, it is not more than a week ago that I heard him speak disrespectfully of the Equator!'

Smith made delicate, conversational comedy out of Leslie's fixation. His joke was a sort of *reductio ad absurdam*. If you can revere a geographical concept, you must also be able to slander one; since we all know that a libel on the Equator is absurd, an admiration for the North Pole must be too. However light his tone (reflected Sydney Smith about his Edinburgh writings) he prided himself that he always made sound sense, and this wordplay with Leslie can be counted as part of the same mission to restore minds distempered by enthusiasm to everyday balance. A now-forgotten controversy over church governance would bring a reminder from Smith to the high-minded that they lived 'not in the abstract, timeless, nameless, placeless land of the philosophers, but . . . in the porter-brewing, cotton-spinning, tallow-melting kingdom of Great Britain': and what had that to do with wild ideas? Constitutionally sensible, he was not likely to understand the attraction of the North Pole.

More derisive, yet better attuned to the irrationality they attacked, were the satirical prints that greeted the return of the early Arctic expeditions. One in particular, by Cruikshank, catches the crowd hysteria aroused by the expeditions, and the willingness to think of polar features as real, recoverable objects. *Landing the Treasures, or Results of the Polar Expedition!!!* shows the triumphal march up Whitehall of a naval party who have all, without exception, had their noses frostbitten off. The officer leading wears a paper nose, for dignity. They have huskies with them, shrunk down to spaniel size, and a block of granite; and the sailors carry scientific specimens that burlesque the real trophies secured for the British Museum. Among other things there is 'RED SNOW for the B.M.', there is a dull-looking bird marked '—? Sabini' skewered on the end of a bayonet, there are 'WORMS found in the Intestines of a Seal by a Volunteer'. A John Bull type in the foreground comments dourly that the country has enough gulls, dogs etc 'without going to the North Pole for them'. But the principal prizes, which are also the ones exciting the spectators, have nothing to do with this sorry collection. The sailors are staggering under the weight of Ursa Major, drawn as a polar bear with the seven stars of the constellation shining on its side ('It's a good thing I've lost my nose,' remarks the sailor acting porter for the rump), and Jack Frost brings up the rear of the procession, holding a narwhal's horn. Leaping, cavorting onlookers cry: 'I see Jack Frost! I see Jack Frost!! Huzza! with the North Pole in his hand!! Huzza!' And: 'Huzza! they have got *Ursa Major* – as I live! Huzza!!' And: 'I see it! I see it! The North Pole by Jupiter!! I'll cling to it like a *leech*. Huzza! Huzza!!'

Cruikshank's print satirises two things: the inutility of exploration, which brings home such tawdry curiosities at the cost of so many noses, and the ignorance of the crowd, which believes that stars and poles might be portable. (The latter attack, on credulity, is taken up with an additional racial slur in a less distinguished cartoon of 1824. An Irish mother dances for joy as a letter from her sailor son is read aloud to her. 'The North Pole – be der powers Pats fortins made anney how – och murdther he's found the North Pole and der boy's *bringing it home with him* – what'll *Capt Parry* be sayin to that?') Look a little closer at the Cruikshank and the disenchantment reveals itself as total. Ursa Major is only a badly cured animal stuck with stars like gilt studded on gingerbread; the ivory 'North Pole', reads its label in minuscule writing, is to be 'used in Common, as a walking-stick'; while Jack Frost himself, despite his bristling frosted hair and his powder-puff loincloth, is probably just an Eskimo. 'If they kill the dogs & stuff 'em! what will they do with Jack Frost?' asks a sailor at the extreme end of the procession. 'Cut his throat, & stuff him also . . . I supposes,' replies another.

It is to be presumed that Cruikshank's crowd would line the street with equal alacrity to see any other exhibition of oddities. The site of the satire is London, and it functions to record one parade among many that decorated the urban scene. Life in the capital was notorious, as the eye of satire saw matters, for momentary prodigies and temporary witless crazes. But Cruikshank nonetheless proves himself acute at observing the balance of elements that sustained this particular excitement. For one thing, the observers shout huzza on the rooftops because the 'North Pole' has been brought home, because it has entered Whitehall and London can see it, digest it, claim it. Home is the frame within which the North Pole makes sense as a prodigy of nature, even if all geographical sense is thereby abandoned. Then, there is the way that the actual productions of the polar regions – even the red snow refers to an actual discovery by Ross, of an area where a cherry-coloured lichen dyed a snowfield – are outweighed by the romance of them, as represented by the Great Bear and the intangible treasure of 90° N. At the root of an excitement structured like this must lie a perception of the polar regions as essentially blank, a space so devoid of anything except worms and gulls and curious snow that its potential for being discovered becomes its defining characteristic. The last two stars of Ursa Major, incidentally, point the way to the North Pole's celestial companion, Polaris.

Interestingly, therefore, this kind of excitement about the Arctic is in agreement – in a peculiar, ultimate sense – with the common-sense refusal to be excited. By preferring the symbols of polar-ness over anything more material, the enthusiast implicitly agrees with the satirist that the physical features of the place are not worth getting worked up about; there is not enough there to make a practical motive for excitement. The difference between them turns on their view of motives that are not practical.

Of course, the Arctic is not blank, or featureless, or uninhabited. There may have been less tangible incentive to explore it than there was for other areas (although whaling tended to follow exploration in the Arctic, as trade followed the flag elsewhere around the nineteenth-century globe); the expeditions nevertheless returned a mass of data from their encounters with a landscape rich in its own peculiar properties. The Arctic demanded swift attention to the behaviour of the ice that so dominated its scenery. It can even be argued that the success and failure of different British expeditions of the period reflects the degrees to which they were, and were not, imaginatively captured by a vision of the Arctic as bleak, blank, hostile. Those explorers least able to perceive the Arctic as it was – indifferent rather than harsh, full rather than empty, a problematic dwelling space rather than a moral playground – were also least likely to survive there.

But the perception of Arctic emptiness also allowed much more wild and florid ideas of the region, for blank space, like blank paper, can be scribbled over with the wishes of the onlooker. There was a steady thread of fantasy concerning the poles in the nineteenth century, ranging from tall stories to mad geographical theories: and this is leaving aside the deliberately fanciful use of the frozen North in children's stories and fables. The kind of fantasy I mean involved real belief, even if only in the form of a con-trick, or a transparent delusion. It is as if the acknowledged status of the North Pole (and the South) as points both known and unreachable, real and not, allowed ideas to attach themselves to them that were likewise half-respectable, half-real, half-baked. 'I try in vain to be persuaded that the pole is the seat of frost and desolation,' says the narrator of Mary Shelley's *Frankenstein*, which she wrote between 1816 and 1817, before the return of the Admiralty's explorers, and framed with a polar sub-plot; 'it ever presents itself to my imagination as the region of beauty and delight.' He means no paradox. On the very first page of the novel Robert Walton, who will meet Victor Frankenstein and his hideous creature out on the ice-floes of the polar sea once his chartered ship has set sail, is confiding to his sceptical sister back in England his adherence to the notion of a literal polar paradise. Of gentle birth, yet only half-educated, he has filled his mind with the travel narratives and geographical speculations which 'composed the whole of our good Uncle Thomas' library'. The temporary difficulties of the ice behind him, he expects to set sail across placid waters, and claim fabulous continents. Though at this date the uncertainty of the evidence about the polar regions gave some genuine credibility to arguments for an open polar sea, neither evidence nor experience plays any part in Walton's quest. The pole that fascinates him is a pure book-learnt construction of the imagination; he feels only impatience at its actual ice and cold as he encounters them; it is, precisely, a space cleared on the map for him to fill with daydreams of discovery.

Walton's story is only the outer rind of *Frankenstein*, a frame for the central narrative. But as Walton listens to the long history of flight and terror told by the emaciated fugitive he has taken aboard, the parallels grow between Victor Frankenstein's irresponsible dream of creating life, and Walton's own polar reverie. Walton's story reproduces Frankenstein's in miniature. Both men are devotees of what has been called 'Promethean science', the period's heady sense that the powers of nature might be appropriated for humanity, as the titan Prometheus stole the fire of the gods. The later popularity of *Frankenstein* has left a wholly Gothic image of this, strong on lightning bolts and fizzing retorts; but a truer reflection of the contemporary excitement can be seen in – for example – Coleridge's remark that he went to Humphry Davy's scientific lectures in order to 'replenish my stock of metaphors'. Promethean science was poetic, hubristic, consciously marvellous. At its centre there figured a daring, definitively *male* experimenter, a Columbus of intellect, who might steer to shores of unsuspected knowledge – or assemble a patchwork monster from the spoils of the graveyard. And Victor Frankenstein himself recognises the common nature of their projects. It is the reason he imparts the cautionary tale of his life to Walton. 'One man's life or death were but a small price to pay' (Walton is saying)

for the acquirement of the knowledge which I sought, for the dominion which I should acquire and transmit over the elemental foes of our race. As I spoke, a dark gloom spread over my listener's countenance . . . at length he spoke, in broken accents: 'Unhappy man! Do you share my madness? Have you drunk also of the intoxicating draught? Hear me; let me reveal my tale, and you will dash the cup from your lips!'

The penalty for Victor's madness is death: ultimately his own, and the monster's, but first those of his wife, relations, and best friend. Walton's fate is a less lethal one. After a mutiny among his crew, and a graphic demonstration that the North is ice to its heart, we see him turning his ship around at the end of the novel, presumably to return, chastened yet unscathed, to England. Mary Shelley means more, however, than that those who dare too much are punished. She does not so much rebut the claims of Promethean science as pursue its consequences, organising the events of Victor's downfall as persistent failures to provide for the scientific discoveries he fathers; and she tests the elated language he and Walton have in common for solipsism and irresponsibility. Their gender is important. Both men fail to ground their raptures in an emotional intelligence associated throughout the novel with women; in Walton's case, with his sensible sister, whose reservations about his enthusiasm for the pole, though never appearing in the text, make up the unheard position against which he tries to justify himself. She possesses the warmth of a home, and the literal children so scarce in a novel filled with monstrous births, and the metaphorical offspring of the mind. He, aiming for an imaginary oasis at the pole, inherits only a waste of cold.

And here the reader has to ask whether the cold that Walton gets isn't really the fulfilment of his desires, for all his protestations. It was a cold northern breeze in St Petersburg on the first page of the book that ruffled his imagination: 'Inspired by this wind of promise, my daydreams become more fervent and more vivid.' It was the polar part of 'The Ancient Mariner', he confesses at one point, that settled his childhood 'attachment to, my passionate enthusiasm for, the danger-ous mysteries of the ocean'. And when Coleridge's 'ice, mast-high' *does* 'come drifting by/As green as emerald' about his ship, it seems the rightful landscape for his fantasies, the proper realisation of cold and detached enthusiasm. (Mary Shelley found the material for her Arctic in Coleridge, in a library book about Siberia, and in Percy Shelley's paeans to the Alps, which they were visiting together when she first conceived *Frankenstein*.) Walton perhaps gets what he did not know he wanted. He is made to inhabit, and to shiver in, a physical corollary to his thinking. Poetic justice.

If the pack-ice is primarily conceived as the climactic setting to the battle between Victor and the monster – if Walton is really only an extra in the main drama of the book – he learns at least, from the scenes he witnesses, what the meaning of the place he has sought out actually is. Victor, weighing in to help Walton stem the mutiny, delivers a chilling kind of encouragement to the sailors: 'This ice is not made of such stuff as your hearts may be; it is mutable, and cannot withstand you if you say that it shall not.' Here is the Arctic consequence of a philosophy based on disembodied willpower: it proves to be an enemy to the human body, an invitation to beat the Arctic by out-freezing it, and abandoning the change and flow – the *mutability* – of emotions. Then the monster, at the last, looking down at Victor's corpse, his revenge completed, announces that he will complete the voyage Walton is abandoning: 'I shall quit your vessel on the ice-raft which brought me thither and shall seek the most northern extremity of the globe; I shall collect my funeral pile and consume to ashes this miserable frame, that its remains may afford no light to any curious and unhallowed wretch who may create such another as I have been. I shall die.' The monster has named the only possible use for the North Pole that Mary Shelley is willing to endorse: it is for abnegation, expiation, death.

Frankenstein exploits a number of devices which will become commonplaces in the imaginative rendering of the poles. There is the use of polar cold as a metaphor for human coldness, culminating in a complete, deathly departure from emotion at the North Pole. There is the contrast between ranging male explorers and stable women awaiting their return. Criticism of exploration would often suggest that science is no adequate motive for risking lives; indeed, that the demand it seems to make for Arctic sacrifices reveals a monstrous dimension to science. 'There is something frightful, inexorable, inhuman', wrote a reviewer in *Blackwood's Magazine* in 1855,

in prosecuting researches, which are mere researches, after such a costly fashion . . . and when we hear of the martyrs of science, whether they perish among the arctic snow or on the sands of the desert, we begin to think of science herself as of a placid Juggernaut, a Moloch with benevolent pretensions, winning, by some weird magic, and throwing away with all the calmness of an abstract and impersonal principle, those generous lives, born to disregard their own interest and comfort, which might have saved a kingdom or helped a world.

Arguments from utility, and appeals to common sense, would always tell against polar ventures. But in another sense *Frankenstein* was quite untypical of the century's responses to the poles, for all Mary Shelley's brilliant success at casting Romantic and Gothic views of ice and darkness into permanent, nightmare images. All those recurring staples of writing about the poles, present elsewhere in stories, songs, and dramas, tended, elsewhere, to appear in balance with one another. The waiting women matched the adventuring men, and confirmed their bravery; the dark of the poles evoked the light of home. The stark pyrotechnics of the aurora recalled water-colour English fruits and flowers: 'Farewell to mossy vale, and sapphire sky', began a student poem of 1852 on 'The Arctic Regions', farewell to

> Green earth, and golden wood, and silver waves,
> The lily, and the zephyr, and the rose!

All were largely taken as complementary pairings, structured into an imaginative economy of exploration, its rightful and reassuring context. Mary Shelley did something rarer. She damned the North Pole by anatomising the attractions of emptiness to a particular male sensibility, Romantic, self-driven, and ever willing to exceed the limits of the human body; she damned it, without falling silent as common sense did before an enthusiasm that readily confessed its unreason-ableness. Perhaps this happened because she was quietly dissenting, in *Frankenstein*, from a state of mind that was domestically all too familiar to her, in the person of her husband, whose idealisms also brooked no thought of consequences. For her the pole was one of a number of symbols for destructive abstraction; and she incorporated it to chill the fancy, not to develop a topic of the times.

Her jagged-edged, uncomfortable novel stands apart from those slightly later works, and habits, of the imagination which took their starting point from the public spectacle of exploration. Mary Shelley in middle age would seem to observers to become a somewhat starchy early Victorian, her dissent from Romantic wilfulness blending into the respectability of the times; Mary Shelley at nineteen, the author of *Frankenstein*, was surrounded by a small wild world of private exaltations and private crises. It is worth remembering that Robert Walton is effectively alone in his confrontation with the Arctic: the proper poetic predicament for a Romantic soul. The Russian-speaking crew do not count as company; and no trace can be seen of exploration as the intensely social experience which would soon be familiar from the captains' reports. Party hats and amateur theatricals? Hardly. Even the loopiest polar fantasia tended to re-create the feel of exploration, as it could be garnered from available sources, in order to underpin the excesses that followed.

And certainly no other exercise in geographical fantasy ended, like *Frankenstein*, in demolishing the polar arcadia it proposed, and restoring endless ice. No other brought in the belief essential to fantasy as a subject for dissection; instead it was insisted on, played with, encouraged, primped, and sometimes adhered to with maniacal vigour. Polar emptiness, for the fantasists, remained a promising thing. There is something more than slightly polar about the chart presented by the Bellman in the century's favourite piece of radical nonsense, 'The Hunting of the Snark':

> 'Other maps are such shapes, with their islands and capes!
>   But we've got our brave Captain to thank'
> (So the crew would protest) 'that he's bought us the best –
>   A perfect and absolute blank!'

On this count, the polar regions would of course make the best destination of all: a place where place itself would be almost abolished, with its shapes and its particularities. (Undescribed and indescribable, the North Pole can be claimed as an obvious Snark.) But even the crew of this least constrained of voyages collided to a degree with harsh physical fact, for when Lewis Carroll lands them to begin the hunt, 'at first sight the crew were not pleased with the view,/Which consisted of chasms and crags'. Such disenchanting moments could easily be avoided in a purely imaginary Arctic, despite reports that chasms and crags played quite a large part in the boreal landscape. Polar fantasists would also have parted company with the Butcher, the Beaver, and the Broker on a second point. They might be ditching the inconvenient facts about the Arctic, but they could not forego its essential Arctic-ness.

'What's the good of Mercator's North Poles and Equators,
　　Tropics, Zones and Meridian Lines?'
So the Bellman would cry: and the crew would reply
　　'They are merely conventional signs!'

The absurdity of lines and zones on blankness was crucial. The
blanker the map, the more cherishable were the conventional signs.
They were the hook on which the fantasy hung. Conventional signs
were very important indeed.

Take, for example, the case of John Cleves Symmes.

Symmes was born in New Jersey to an old settler family in modest
circumstances. Largely self-educated, he joined the American infantry
in 1802, and fought against the British in the war of 1812. It seems
likely that he picked up some skill in surveying and military geometry.
Not long after the peace, he resigned his commission (though the
courtesy title of 'Captain Symmes' which he continued to use gave
him a misleadingly nautical air) and retired to St Louis on the
Mississippi. A friendly witness described him as 'of middle stature,
and tolerably proportioned; with scarcely any thing in his exterior to
characterize the secret operations of his mind, except an abstraction,
which, from attentive inspection, is found seated on a slightly
contracted brow; and the glances of a bright blue eye, that often
seems fixed on something beyond immediate surrounding objects'.
Symmes' eye fixed on something that could not have been further
distant from the streets of St Louis. There, far from any sea, let alone
from the polar regions, he began to issue geographical pamphlets at
his own expense: they expounded a novel theory of the earth which,
like his own appearance, made up for an unremarkable outside by
hinting at secrets within. In 1819 he moved to Cincinnati, but the
series continued. The seventh pamphlet was an 'Arctic Memoir',
Symmes being a devoted reader of polar narratives and the Arctic
having a special place in his geographical scheme. From 1820, he also
lectured around Kentucky and Ohio. The audiences filled the halls he
booked, though his voice was untrained and his manner peculiar;
though his arguments were 'presented in confused array, and clothed
in homely phraseology'. He lacked the temperament to be any sort of

showman. People came to marvel at the earnest zeal with which he believed his own theory. They also came, it is true, just to laugh. But he did win disciples. For the purposes of demonstration, he had a large wooden globe on the stage at his lectures, specially constructed and intricately marked. Symmes' pointer would go up, down, around, and eventually inside. The globe was hollow, with countersunk holes at the top and bottom – as Symmes believed the earth to be.

'Symmes' hole!' was a common American jeer at anything quackish or fake throughout the 1820s and 1830s, and the theory would not have had the currency it did if it had not been easy to grasp Symmes' outrageous central claim, but detailed summary is hard. This is because the theory, of its nature, changed continually, veering this way and that to stave off attacks or to appropriate some new bit of 'evidence'. In the hands of Symmes' followers, some of whom were surprisingly eminent, the pattern was a wavering advance-and-retreat, from the fullblown Symmesian idea of a hollow and *habitable* inner world, to a modest fallback argument for an ice-free polar ocean. (The poles were supposed to be ringed by a northern and southern 'icy hoop' – both duly inscribed on the wooden model.) Symmesian claims could be curbed to suit the scepticism of the hearer, and of course not all hearers were automatically sceptical. Symmes' application to the US Senate in 1822 for a polar expedition to test his propositions received twenty-five yes votes. Such hedging, however, was foreign to Symmes' own absorption in proof and counterproof. In his hands the theory just grew. From a simple one-shell earth he progressed to an arrangement of seven nested spheres, each pierced at the poles, each – he calculated, sketching planes and angles – receiving enough sunlight to support life. (Though the air deep inside might be rather unhealthy.) And then it was reasonable to assume that every other planet in the solar system was contrived in the same way. It finally became necessary for him to refute Newton's law of universal gravitation, since a planet like a Chinese toy ought not to attract us to its surface with the force it does, if gravity is proportional to a planet's mass. He had not succeeded in doing so by the time he died, in 1829.

The intellectual background to Symmes' claims was not, itself, utterly unrespectable. There had been a flow of reasonable speculation about the polar ice-caps for some time, and though Symmes was already a little late with his contribution, the geographical data was still patchy. Science theorised in the absence of sophisticated knowledge about currents, climate, and polar ecology. In particular, it was not yet clear just how the sea-ice that clogged the Arctic was formed. If, as one school argued, only a shoreline could birth the great bergs, then a landless central Arctic Ocean – correctly deduced from the common patterning of the Siberian and North American coasts – might well be free of ice. This was wrong, but reasonable.

It would be a mistake to think that people found Symmes' holes and hollownesses ridiculous because they could be absolutely certain he was wrong. As well as for *what* he said, he condemned himself as much for the *way* he said it. What identified his doctrine immediately as pseudo-science – and invited the ridicule of a continent to drop on his earnest head – was an attitude to proof, and a tone of voice. It is strange to read the Symmesians now, because their characteristic procedures and modes of assertion are so familiar from current paperback madness. Like Erich von Daniken, like the other believers in ancient astronauts and Aztec high-tech, Symmes could be said to have known quite a lot about his subject. He collected facts. He kept up religiously with explorers' reports. As a late defender of his reputation said, he amassed many 'detached instances' from different fields of inquiry, here a puzzling remark by an Eskimo, there a surprising bit of behaviour by the common herring. But his instances were, exactly, detached: detached from the contexts that made sense of them, and wilfully re-arranged. Since the notion of probability had no place in his thinking, he compounded one improbable interpretation with another, and another, and another, to produce one mighty improbability. Throughout, he entirely misunderstood the nature of scientific method – which is not a game of assertions, but a way of refining probabilities. Symmes never grasped that you were required to show likelihood before a theory was taken seriously; you had to demonstrate the congruency of polar holes with everything already known. Instead he assumed you only had to prove your theory was not impossible, and it then became the responsibility of others to disprove if they could. To his continuing bafflement, nobody bothered to. He was waiting for an answer which did not come.

And all this could be heard in his voice, his 'peculiar manner'. There was a shoddy enthusiasm, a fascination with the details of his own inventions which far overran the perfunctory and muddled attempts at justification. There was endless reference to the work yet to be done – to the further magnificent elaborations the theory demanded – for it is an axiom of pseudo-science that the final substantiation, before which the learned will quail, is always located elsewhere. Not far away, to be sure, gentlemen, but always just outside the scope of our attention at this moment. There was an evasive waving of large words, and a corresponding delight in minutiae. There was an underlying void of meaning. Unlike other lecturers, Symmes had nothing, no thing, to report: no descriptions of sights seen, no records of experiments, only the single subject of his theory. In a sense he did not intend, he was on thin ice.

Symmes was single-minded. He had at least the disinterestedness which is one part of the scientific temperament. Whether lecturing, or lobbying Congress, his sole concern was the vindication of his theory; and he did not, unworldly man, grow indignant at the cat-calls raining down on him from the cheap seats of his rented theatres. Nor did he stray into fantasies about the silence of the scientific establishment. He wanted acceptance: scientific acceptance for a 'scientific' proposition. But his followers were not so chaste. They did speculate, with resentment and petulance, about the vested interests which must be blocking the new truth; they did make accusations, see hidden influences at work, and offer overtly unscientific commentary. From Cincinnati, in 1826, James McBride published *Symmes's Theory of Concentric Spheres: Demonstrating that the Earth is Hollow, Habitable Within, and Widely Open About the Poles*. Half-sceptical, as was characteristic of the secondary Symmesian literature, McBride's book nonetheless exhibits the state of mind of those contemporaries who *wanted* to believe Symmes. McBride's unscientific defences of Symmes are, in fact, statements of the imaginative attractions of the theory, hints why it might have flourished briefly in the wider worlds of culture and opinion while it failed to in the world of science.

One set of reasons for backing Symmes was rooted in his followers' perception of their place and time, and most of all in their perception of themselves as marginal. Cincinnati in the 1820s was still a Western frontier town. It thrived, it was very willing to assert an American identity, yet it was conscious of being at the fringes of a country itself still at the distant edge of the European cultural mainstream. The breakthrough of an American school of writing lay ten years in the future; most books, from novels to scientific treatises, were imports. In the same decade as McBride picked up his pen, great offence was being caused to Cincinnati by Fanny Trollope's *Domestic Manners of the Americans*. On the basis of her experience as a failed emigrant to their city, Mrs Trollope told readers that America was a cultural wasteland, a hellhole of spittoons and public swearing. McBride therefore nominated Symmes as a homegrown scientific genius on the unspoken grounds that America needed one. The title-page of McBride's anonymous text said it was by 'a Citizen of the United States', and the pages that follow are full of anxious national pride. It was plain to him why Symmes' theory met so much resistance.

I apprehend that we only lack confidence in our own abilities, to perfect and explain many things not dreamed of by the ancient philosophers. We are inclined rather to undervalue our own efforts; and, like our former opinions on manufacturing subjects, think we can never appear to advantage, unless dressed in a coat of foreign manufacture. It appears to savour of the doctrine, that no new opinion or proposition can merit attention or be adopted, unless it come from a European source. Had the proposition of concentric spheres, or a hollow globe, been made by an English or French philosopher, instead of a native of the United States, I very much question, whether so large a share of ridicule would have been attached to its author and adherents.

Besides giving a kick in the pants to European snobs if it proved true, there was something of profoundly American appeal in Symmes' idea that limitless new territories awaited discovery beneath the earth's crust. Promising another New World (McBride uses the phrase), he promised a repeat of the discovery of the Americas. Anyone who ventured successfully through the hole would be a new Columbus.

The founding myth of the United States would be, so to speak, confirmed by repetition.

Indeed, in scope and influence Symmesianism was an almost entirely American madness. But if we turn to the attitude it involved towards specifically polar matters, we are on psychological terrain of no particular nationality, back among the absurdly appealing signs of latitude and longitude. Like his master, McBride was of course familiar with the narrative of Ross' expedition; inevitably, he offered a Symmesian gloss on the famous meeting with the Eskimos. The Symmes hypothesis, you might say, redoubled the romance and mystery of the encounter:

The Indians discovered by Captain Ross, on the coast of Baffin's Bay, in the summer of 1818, in latitude seventy-five degrees fifty-five minutes north, when interrogated from whence they came, pointed to the north, where, according to their account, there were 'plenty of people;' that it was a warmer country; and that there was much water there. And when Captain Ross informed them that he came from the contrary direction, pointing to the south, they replied, 'that could not be, because there was nothing but ice in that direction.' Consequently, these people must live in a country not composed of ice; for it appears they deem such an one uninhabitable. Hence we must infer, if the relation given by Captain Ross be correct, that, north of where they then were, the climate becomes more mild, and is habitable; a change, the cause of which is not easily accounted for on the old philosophic principles.

Not only are the Eskimos marvellously isolated; they are now wandering inhabitants of another world. Not only has their life a topsy-turvy orientation by the standard of our own; it now turns out to signal a revolutionary change in the meaning of north and south, cold and warm. Wait, though. By opting to make the Eskimos players in a lurid Symmesian romance, has not McBride actually abolished the romance Ross and his crew found in them? They were seen, in Ross' account, to be people so different from ourselves that they took ice for the norm and the glass of a binnacle for a weird aberration. Their strangeness lay in them being at home in the polar landscape, and the confusion about north and south meant that they judged the whole world, marvellously, by their knowledge of their own snowy hunting-runs, an isolated microcosm in which more open water for seal-catching happened to lie to the north, not the south. McBride's Eskimos judge a 'country composed of ice' to be 'uninhabitable', so they are like us after all. Instead of witnessing to a different relationship between people and polar landscape, they only tell us that the ice is an obstacle. For a romance of human strangeness, McBride substitutes a geographical Big Secret, to which the Eskimos are incidental clues. The feeling of the encounter – all the dumbshow communication and the contagious laughter – gives way to an overriding appetite for large, crude wonders. The palate formed by the Symmesian fantasy proves unable to taste subtle flavours: the flavours, that is, of those things actually present in the scene Ross described.

But then, in a theory springing from a sort of geometrical fascination, produced by tinkering with oddments of signs and geographical symbols, it is only natural that information challenging the ideal emptiness of the poles should be displaced. McBride must refuse a reality to the place Symmes selected for its abstraction. Conspiracy theory being the handmaiden of pseudo-science, McBride casts his refusal to believe in the real conditions of polar exploration in the form of a paranoid insinuation about the British.

Ross and Parry have visited the arctic regions; and Parry now is out on his third voyage, as though there were some hidden mystery there, which the English government is anxious to develope. It is not likely that they would have fitted out, and dispatched four successive expeditions, merely to view Ice-bergs and Esquimaux Indians. As for the discovery of a north-west passage to the East Indies, that cannot be their sole object, as the continent of America has been explored by land to seventy-two degrees of north latitude; and, according to the old theory, beyond that latitude the seas are so encumbered with ice as to render their navigation extremely difficult, if not impracticable; from which, I am induced to believe, that they have discovered something in those regions which indicates a state of things different from that heretofore believed to exist.

Merely to view Ice-bergs and Esquimaux Indians: such disappointment behind those words. Symmesian theory confesses a terrible sense of the insufficiency of the world as it has been reported to be. It only makes sense to be hungry for a newer New World, through a hole in the poles, if it feels as if the present world, New and Old, from Peking to Ohio, has been exhausted; exhausted at least of the chance to be Columbus, and shape the sum of things anew. The idea that the world is worn out is a much older one; it flourished when the globe was dated by biblical chronology, and the educated agreed that God's creation must be on its last legs, 4004 BC being a long time ago. But here we see it surfacing in a quite different context, with a different meaning: as a callow impatience with the lack of mystery in everyday life, as a species of ennui in an era of scurrying expansion. Exciting news might be pouring in, but it was the wrong type of news, too concrete, too paltry. Unbearable, therefore, to think that the polar regions, the beckoning and blank polar regions, might be furnished like everywhere else just with flora and fauna and funny foreign customs. Only in some cultures, and at some times, was this a likely feeling. Here it is the detachment of English-speaking North America from the dense hubbub of Europe and Asia – from any proximate experience of abroad – that gives the impatient sense of a fully known world its particular form. But England too could be sufficiently isolated, by an imperious lack of interest in the doings of outsiders; and in any case an individual's angle of vision on the world is involved. It took an individual inattentiveness to feel this summary scorn for the rich world close at hand, and to invest what is far-off with proportionally lavish hopes. Introverts, adolescent boys, and fantasists were particularly prone to the feeling – and perhaps a substantial segment of the armchair fans of polar exploration, although not many of them hoped for Symmesian revelations. Symmes hoped to abolish polar ice, but for some people the ice itself was enough of a mystery, enough unlike the disappointing warm world. Ever and again, without the overtly foolish paraphernalia of holes and hollows, a shadow of this impatience will figure in excitement about the poles: a faint deadness of response to whatever is less stark than ice and darkness. Squint at the explorers' accounts, and you could make the details you disliked, at least, blur and vanish.

It was impatience with the actual that an anonymous satire of 1820

picked up on. 'Captain Adam Seaborn', the hero of *Symzonia*, has a
rampant case of the disease. On the opening page he explains why he
'projected a voyage of discovery, to a new and untried world', and why
he expected to succeed:

I flattered myself that I should open the way to new fields for the enterprise of
my fellow-citizens, supply new sources of wealth, fresh food for curiosity, and
additional means of enjoyment; objects of vast importance, since the resources
of the known world have been exhausted by research, its wealth monopolized,
its wonders of curiosity explored, its every thing investigated and understood!

The state of the civilized world, and the growing evidence of the
perfectibility of the human mind, seemed to indicate the necessity of a more
extended sphere of action. Discontent and uneasiness were every where
apparent. The faculties of man had begun to dwindle for want of scope, and
the happiness of society required new and more copious contributions.

I reasoned with myself as follows: A bountiful Providence provides food for
the appetite which it creates; therefore the desire of mankind for a greater
world to bustle in, manifested by their dissatisfactions with the one which
they possess, is sufficient evidence that the means of gratification are
provided.

The author's finger is firmly on the wish-fulfilment behind the
Symmes scheme. What Captain Seaborn wants, Captain Seaborn
must get, simply by virtue of wanting it. He 'reasons' into being a
paradise of solipsism, where nature, and even the internal construction of the earth, exist to 'gratify' our needs. A dream of endless
expansibility produces – endless expansion.

Stingingly accurate about Symmesian self-deception, *Symzonia* has
nonetheless been mistaken at times for pro-Symmes propaganda.
(One twentieth-century critic assigns its writing to John Cleves
himself, crediting him with a sense of the ridiculous he certainly never
possessed.) The only tribute *Symzonia* pays Symmes is a very
American admiration for the author of an audacious hoax. But in the
ambiguous position hoaxing occupies, somewhere between plain truth
and straightforward lying, lies the cause of the error. *Symzonia* is a
hoax too, with the outward look of an honest travelogue. Dashed off
with journalistic speed, as it must have been, it was not just produced
to pop the Symmesian bubble with a satirical pin, but quite as much

because the hollow earth made for a good story. Indeed the primary appeal of the theory, after a while, was to writers and romancers, who did not have to find the idea true to develop its possibilities. Symmes' theory sounds like pulp fiction, cared as little for consistency as pulp fiction: real pulp fiction followed, until at last the only place the Captain's lifework endured was in the three-cent-a-line imagination of Edgar Rice Burroughs. *His* Hollow Earth was a canister full of steaming jungles and teeming native cities, where men were men and women wore little. You did not go there for scientific argument. Eighty years earlier, however, *Symzonia* took *Gulliver's Travels* as its model, and tried to make the 'Internals' Seaborn meets on the inside of the world beings of perfect virtue like Swift's Houyhnhnms. Like the rational horses, they were supposed to show up the defects of humanity, as represented by the traveller encountering them; like Lemuel Gulliver, Adam Seaborn is booted out of paradise. This was too much for the talents of *Symzonia*'s author, who only succeeded, witness the confused critics, in building a decent tall story. Of course, it is quite in the Swiftian tradition for readers to remember the tiny people, the huge people, or the 'Internal' people, and forget the satire.

But *Symzonia* gave the Internals a characteristic which seems to have caught the eye of a much more distinguished author, himself interested in Symmes and the poles. It makes them white, pure white, as white as the polar snows that Symmesian geography abolishes. It displaces the absent ice onto their hair and skins. When Seaborn, having sailed through the Antarctic hole and found his way to their island, encounters them for the first time, he recalls Ross' meeting with the Eskimos, whom he rightly surmises are the swarthy outcasts of Internal society. The Eskimos tugged their noses and shouted their astonishment; the Internals, he reasons, follow a civilised version of the same code. He advances, therefore, plucking his proboscis in the most refined manner imaginable, and is rewarded with the attention of an Internal, who

walked round, and surveyed my person with eager curiosity. I did the like by him, and had abundant cause; for the sootiest African does not differ more from us in darkness of skin and grossness of features, than this man did from

73

me in fairness of complexion and delicacy of form . . . I shoved up the sleeve of my coat, to show them, by the inside of my arm, (which was always excluded from the sun,) that I was a white man. I am considered fair for an American, and my skin was always in my own country thought to be one of the finest and whitest. But when one of the internals placed his arm, always exposed to the weather, by the side of mine, the difference was truly mortifying. I was not a white man, compared to him.

Sixteen years after the publication of *Symzonia*, down in the slave state of Virginia where it was worse than mortifying not to be white, a pale young man became editor of the *Southern Literary Messenger*. Across Edgar Allan Poe's desk for comment and review came Symmesian literature, for his editorship coincided with the preparations for the first United States Exploring Expedition to the far South, and a charismatic Symmesian by the name of Jeremiah Reynolds was contending for command of it. Poe wrote trenchantly in Reynolds' support; and, without subscribing to the theory himself, suffused a group of his own stories with a dilute Symmesianism. He, as much as Symmes or McBride, was shaped by the provinciality of his America, though in a very different fashion. He was the product (Edmund Wilson has written) of the lonely genteel houses of the period; of nervousness secluded from the world by long baize drapes; of tea-parties among lumpen mahogany furniture which might look, at twilight, like crouching animals. Where the Symmesians were prosaic, Poe was Gothic. If their ideas were a fascination of his – among his other interests, in decapitation and the reform of prosody – it was not because he felt the attraction of overturning geography with Yankee motherwit. They conceived space differently. The Symmesians wanted new space to be Columbus in, and for the poles to open on fresh expanses. Never do they seem to have realised the claustrophobic potential of a hollow earth. To Poe on the other hand the space of the poles, beyond the curtains, beyond the familiar confines of Richmond, Va., was always a mental space, an inward territory. There, far away and very close within his own skull, impulses to violent action could play out against a backdrop of private blankness. One of these concerned race. Cued, perhaps, by *Symzonia*, he recast the dark and light of polar terrain into skin colours, and made the Antarctic the scene for a Virginian fantasy of race-war and racial degradation.

Like *Symzonia*, Poe's *Narrative of Arthur Gordon Pym of Nantucket* poses briefly as an authentic document. Pym is supposed to have allowed Mr Poe of the *Messenger* to ghost-write his memoirs. In this case, though, the pretence is not given away by satirical digs in the text at 'the capacious mind' of 'that profound philosopher, John Cleve Symmes' (*sic*). The highly wrought, highly patterned terror of the book instead warns the reader that the Narrative has sailed into unreal polar waters. Ice hardly features: the sea grows blisteringly hot, and at 83° S the much-shipwrecked Pym and his companions discover an island of savages. The rock here is black, the sand is black, the birds, plants, and animals are all matte, absolute, midnight black. So of course are the people, from their skins inward to their hearts. (Even their teeth are coal-shaded.) They are treacherous and cruel, the worst Virginian fears about rebelling nigrahs personified; and Poe, for good measure, improvises a biblical curse on them, for their name, in dog-Hebrew, means dark. But once Pym has escaped the murderous fate visited on his shipmates, and fled the island in a stolen canoe, he sails southward on milky waves. Now the birds are 'pallid', blanched ash falls from the sky, and whiteness wins the war of colour, a supernatural white more potent by far than the ink-puddle behind. The pole approaches; a cataract, possibly Symmesian, opens in the albino ocean; Poe cuts short the log of Arthur Pym before the canoe can whirl down to depths unknown. But just before the vertiginous plunge, and the calculated sundering of the narrative, 'there arose in our pathway a shrouded human figure, very far larger in its proportions than any dweller among men. And the hue of the skin of the figure was of the perfect whiteness of the snow.'

Who the figure is, and what it portends, remain mysterious. (Jules Verne was to offer a solution of sorts later in the century. Too intoxicated with volts and amps and Big Science to leave well enough alone, he proposed that the looming shape glimpsed by Monsieur Pym was – *a giant magnet*. Poe would not have been flattered by this assault on his deliberate indistinctness.) Racial overtones apart, though, the presentation of the pole in the *Narrative* recalls its treatment in Poe's two other stories with a polar theme. The shrouded Aryan angel was not his only version of the mystery at the world's end. In 'Hans Pfaall' an aeronaut on his way to the moon has time to look down at the North Pole from a height of 7254 miles. The ice-cap, he sees, 'terminates, at the Pole itself, in a circular centre, sharply defined, whose . . . dusky hue, varying in intensity, was at all times darker than any other spot upon the visible hemisphere, and occasionally deepened into the most absolute darkness'. And in his very first story, 'Manuscript Found in a Bottle', the lost voyager whose last message the story is signs off with his vessel in the grip of an Antarctic whirlpool, its enormous sides ever steepening. 'It is evident that we are hurrying onward to some exciting knowledge – some never to be imparted secret, whose attainment is destruction. Perhaps this current leads to the South Pole itself.' Whirlpool, cataract, and circular sink-hole are all tributes to Symmes; and it should be remembered that one advantage of the theory for story-tellers is that it provides for there to be *something* at the poles, some climactic *thing* commensurate with the finality of the poles, rather than an expanse of ice significant only by geographical convention. You notice, though, that the holes Poe imagines suck at the traveller as Symmes' do not. They exert a lethal downwards pull. They compel surrender rather than inviting a new Columbus to probe them boldly. They may well close behind the unresisting bodies of the sailors they have captured. They are, so to speak, holes with teeth. At the same time, Poe is not interested in what may lie beyond these menacing thresholds. His imagination hovers on the brink itself, exploring the sensation of a limitless fall – the moment when the attraction of the drop becomes irresistible, and the traveller is gone, the flash of a waving white limb lost in a limitless rush of foam. His holes promise a delicious dissolution, sex and death fused, not transit to Symzonia.

In one way, Poe's refusal of the part of the Symmes theory dealing with the lands beyond the holes was of a piece with the caution of the later Symmesians. While Poe looked on from Richmond, Jeremiah Reynolds was romancing the Congress of the United States. His seductive *Address on the Subject of a Surveying and Exploring Expedition* carefully foreswore hollow globes and concentric spheres:

Reynolds claimed only that there was a reasonable chance of an open polar sea. He even went out of his way to quash the idea that the British had any secret motive for their Arctic endeavours. 'We answer that the question, *cui bono?* should never be put in affairs of this kind.' The spice of adventure was furnished by thrilling anecdotes about the bravery of American seamen in the South Seas. 'Dropping his spade, [Mr Jones] sprang over and through the astonished savages, with an impetuosity not to be resisted . . .'

But Poe's selectivity, when the suitcase of Symmesian wonders was opened for his inspection, really shows that he placed himself at a decisive distance from the pseudo-scientific tradition, with its literalism, and the deadening touch that turned everything it envisaged into Cincinnati. His sense of an annihilating nature that draws in the body does not belong to Symmesian romance; it stems from Poe's eccentric adherence to Romantic ideas of what it was to be a body amidst the natural world. The apparatus of Poe's polar stories may have been Symmesian, but the feeling was not. If Romantic reverence for the otherness of nature most often, in his work, curdled into terror, still the body was at the centre of attention – breathing, sensing, intimating mortality. We come now to a separate strand in the imagining of the poles: their minor use in Romantic writing. Few places could be more *other* than the Arctic or Antarctic. Nature there wore a cold face, according to the explorers' reports; a disinheriting countenance towards those who, in temperate lands, thought they had a compact with her. All the mild metamorphoses of winds and trees were absent there, yet wonders abounded. Auroras played, frost crystals scintillated, the sun quit its predictable passage across the sky and did strange things. This was a feast of phenomena sure to draw minds interested in perception and sensation; and it accorded, in a curious way, with inquiries into imagination, for here was a place where nature behaved like fantasy. Accuracy about polar conditions was not required, but by the same token neither were Symmes' holes, nor any especial rewriting of the ice. The true subject remained the consciousness of the observer. The fact that Poe, delirious on his deathbed in a New York hospital in 1849, was heard to shout 'Reynolds! Reynolds!', never surfacing again to explain his calls for

Symmes' protégé, has allowed his biographers to speculate that deep inside his head, Poe may then have been feeling himself passing helpless over the lip of a polar maelstrom, a traveller reaching the last of the space within the skull, whirling away. But the name of a man whom Poe had probably never met face to face, was only a sign for the long-imagined, now-arrived sensation.

FIVE

The Powers of Frost and Air

As the returning crews of those first expeditions to the Arctic after the Napoleonic wars fanned out homeward from Portsmouth or Chatham, they told the news of their sojourns in the ice; it percolated at second and then at third hand across the country. John Keats added a polar item, in December 1818, to one of the compendious, reflective letters he sent to his brother and sister-in-law in America. It had reached him by word of mouth. His friend Benjamin Robert Haydon, would-be reformer of British art, had called at the house in North London. And this, presumably fined down by Haydon to the anecdotes that interested *him*, before he even told Keats, was the story Keats in turn chose to remember and pass on:

Haydon was here yesterday – he amused us much by speaking of young Hop[p]ner who went with Captn Ross on a voyage of discovery to the Poles – The Ship was sometimes entirely surrounded with vast mountains and crags of ice and in a few Minutes not a particle was to be seen all round the Horizon. Once they met with so vast a Mass that th[e]y gave themselves over for lost; their last recourse was in meeting it with the Bowspit, which they did, and split it asunder and glided through it as it parted for a great distance – one Mile an[d] more Their eyes were so fatigued with the eternal dazzle and whiteness that they lay down on their backs on deck to relieve their sight on the blue Sky. Hop[p]ner describes his dreadful weriness at the continual day – the sun ever moving in a circle round above their heads – so pressing upon him that he could not rid himself of the sensation even in the dark Hold of the Ship – The Esquimaux are de[s]cribed as the most wretched of Beings – they float from their Summer to their winter residences and back again like white Bears on the ice floats – They seem never to have washed, and so when their features move, the red skin shows beneath the cracking peal of dirt. They had no notion of any inhabitants in the World but themselves. The sailors who had not seen a Star for some time, when they came again southwards, on the hailing of the first revision, of one all ran upon deck with feelings of the most joyful nature.

Some elements here are absolutely standard – the fixed points by which Ross' expedition 'to the Poles' were remembered. Those familiar Eskimos, sure till Ross' arrival that they were alone 'in the World', were too striking to lose. But otherwise it is notable how very much Hoppner's account has been filtered. Between them, the painter of sublime historical scenes and the poet of sensuous exactitude have organised the heterogeneously curious matter recounted by Hoppner, with his licence to hold forth, around two ideas: mobility, and light. The ice that hems the ship at one moment has withdrawn over the horizon at the next; the solid mass that later binds it in cracks suddenly open, and smooth motion succeeds stasis. The ship 'glides', the ice 'parts' like lips. The dirt on Eskimo faces, too, cracks with movement, while the owners of the faces make a stately, passive progress back and forth, making a vehicle out of the indifferent motion of the ice-floes, which Keats (or Haydon) has misheard as 'ice floats'. Their other, visual, preoccupation has brought into prominence a series of contrasted colours. Blue sky, dazzling whiteness, dark in the hold, red skin. Furthermore, the strain of seeing foregrounds it: an awful excess of white makes looking at blue a deliberate act of relief, while darkness becomes an unattainable luxury, and the restoration of dark and light in the usual proportions (a star's pinprick of light on a black night sky) is an occasion of joy. The kind of problematic looking represented by snow-blindness *would* interest the two of them. Both men's work was predicated on the flow of information from the eye – which told Haydon about the sheen of the cuirass on some British hero, and Keats about the bloom on the skin of a nectarine, and which had here imposed a 'sensation' of the path of the sun on Hoppner to such a degree that he still felt it even when he was not directly seeing it. It seems quite natural that George and Georgiana Keats were next told, after Hoppner's story, that 'Haydon's eyes will not [s]uffer him to proceed with his picture – his Physician tells him he must remain two months more, inactive.'

If these were topics that interested you, there was plenty in the explorers' accounts to hold your attention. The British expeditions would sail, like the whaling fleet, towards the end of spring, and cross the North Atlantic to the Davis Strait between Greenland and Labrador in order to arrive as the ice on the Strait, and on Baffin Bay beyond it, began to break up for the summer. Darkness had just abolished itself at these latitudes, and the Arctic was beginning to display its summer characteristics. After sailing up the string of Danish settlements on the west coast of Greenland, with the final opportunities they offered for buying supplies and posting letters, they would attempt to negotiate a way across to the North American side of the channel, through the banded ice-fields that were floating south. The summer pack was in a state of dangerous dissolution – large bergs fissuring into smaller, sheet-ice rupturing, the whole process occasionally going into temporary reverse upon a sudden drop in temperature – which nonetheless allowed passage as the impacted solidity of the winter ice did not. Once across without being 'nipped' (caught and crushed), an area of more open water was reached, where the whalers cruised and killed for the remainder of the season. The expedition ships continued north and west, searching the sounds and inlets on the western coast of the Bay for an access to the Canadian Arctic archipelago – to Boothia Felix, North Georgia, Melville Island. With the glaciers calving their huge offspring along the coasts, and the sea-ice in motion all around them, bobbing, capsizing, re-forming, carved into sculpture by the perpetual sun, the Arctic deployed its full panoply of optical distortions; so that the ship sometimes floated at the centre of a depthless white globe of mist, was sometimes reflected upside down in the air off the bow, was assailed by phantom shapes of all descriptions, refractions of the already peculiar ice and peaks at the horizons. The sun could multiply in the sky, so that as many as six wheeled about the zenith, and as it shone through ice and glowed through snow, it distributed coloured spectra beside which a rainbow was dowdy. But somewhere about here, if the expedition plan called for a second year of travel, or if the luck had been bad, autumn captured the ship, and the violent fluidity of the ice slowed, thickened, and ceased. The ship froze in. The dazzling light faded to universal grey, then to black. With the temperature tens of Fahrenheit below zero, movement vanished from the world, and the colour which had withdrawn from the world reappeared only in the remote curtains of the aurora, presiding over silent darkness.

The winter's coming enforced a different strain on the eye. Instead of longing for a respite from dazzle, it longed for change and variety – for a fraction, indeed, of the dazzle that had oppressed it before. 'Not an object was to be seen', *Blackwood's Magazine* quoted Parry as saying,

on which the eye could long rest with pleasure, unless when directed to the spot where the ships lay, and where our little colony was planted. The smoke which there issued from the several fires, affording a certain indication of the presence of man, gave a partial cheerfulness to this part of the prospect; and the sound of voices, which, during the cold weather, could be heard at a much greater distance than usual, served now and then to break the silence which reigned around us, a silence far different from that peaceable composure, which characterizes the landscape of a cultivated country; it was the death-like stillness of the most dreary desolation, and the total absence of animated existence. Such, indeed, was the want of objects to afford relief to the eye, or amusement to the mind, that a stone of more than usual size, appearing above the snow in the direction in which we were going, immediately became a mark, on which our eyes were unconsciously fixed, and towards which we mechanically advanced.

However miserable these optical effects were to experience, they fascinated those who heard them described. Captain Parry returned, the same *Blackwood's* article observed, with 'incidents to tell of a romantic and unusual character'; and the report of the northern lights, 'generally of a yellow colour, sometimes green, but rarely red', made the writer 'long to know if they were visible the whole day – and what were their various forms, and motions, and transparency'.

Motion and light were intimately linked, then, in the polar scene. In the arrested blank of winter, both retreated over the rim of the world to tread out the faint steps of the 'Merry Dancers' – as the aurora was known in the north of Scotland. In the mobile phase of the polar year, it was the dynamic transformations of the ice that actually created colour. Apart from Ross' red snow, nothing in the polar regions possessed much colouring of its own; but the crystalline surfaces of the snow, and the translucency of the bergs, and the ice particles suspended in the atmosphere, were all refractive mediums for the abundant light. A red front door in England, or a blue child's brick, look red and blue because, of the rays from the sun which fall on them, only the red and the blue wavelengths are not absorbed by the particular molecules on the surface of the paint. Frozen water molecules do not do this. The angle at which incident light shines on them – through them – determines the wavelength of the light that travels on from them to an observing eye; and blue became green, yellow became red, ultramarine shaded over into the profoundest colour of the sky, in a dazzling *mélange* of wavelengths, because the angles of the light were being changed over and over by the forces that moved the summer ice; in so resistless and titanic a process that it was as if the observers were watching speeded-up geology at work. Where two sheets of ice collided a mountain range arose, in an afternoon instead of an aeon, with attendant *son et lumière* – growls, roars, and a dazzling display of colour around the new summits. This was summer, chaos to winter's stasis. And in neither of the two states was the grand movement of the landscape like the movements made by live creatures, nor the colours like the deliberate, settled colouring of familiar objects. Life had to get out of the way of these processes, or survive amidst them. So how was the human body to be situated there, in actuality or in imagination?

Imagination had a certain advantage. It could mould and reshape the terms on which the human body was present. A year after the composition of 'The Ancient Mariner', Coleridge had visited Germany. January 1799 found him skating on a frozen lake near Ratzeburg; or at any rate, being pulled along on an 'ice-stool' by two skaters, 'faster than most horses can gallop'. A German winter produced effects like those of a polar summer, a brilliant splintering of the spectrum. 'O my God!' he wrote to his wife,

what sublime scenery I have beheld . . . the Mist broke in the middle; and at last stood as the waters of the red Sea are said to have done when the Israelites passed – & between these two walls of Mist the Sunlight *burnt* upon the Ice in a strait *Road* of golden Fire, all across the lake – intolerably bright, & the walls of Mist partaking of the light in a multitude of colours. – About a month ago the vehemence of the wind had shattered the Ice – part of it, quite smattered, was driven to shore & had frozen anew; this was of a deep blue & represented an agitated sea – the water, that ran up between the great Islands of Ice, shone of a yellow green (it was at sunset) and all the scattered islands of *smooth* ice were *blood*; intensely bright *Blood*: on some of the largest Islands the Fishermen were pulling out their immense nets thro' the Holes made in the Ice for this purpose, & the Fishermen, the net-poles, & the huge nets made a part of the Glory!

The 'thunders and howling of the breaking ice', he added in a later revision of the passage, were sublimer still, 'absolutely suspending the power of comparison, and more utterly absorbing the mind's self-consciousness in it's total attention to the object working upon it'. Seeing the light, and hearing the turmoil, of this miniature equivalent of a frozen sea, Coleridge attained a moment of absolute focus, all other thoughts suspended by the object of perception. It is not recorded whether the helpful students who gave his galloping chair its motive-power were able to feel the same. But he was to go further when contemplating the winter aspect of the frozen ocean. He had no comparable bodily experience to draw on now, but he needed none; he approached the zero December of the Arctic through a thought about the reality and unreality of 'objects' in a poet's mind. The suggestive minimum of information necessary for him to sustain an imagined presence in the North came from his reading of David Crantz's *History of Greenland*, and from his long-held interest in Lapland. Maybe too from gleanings in Ross and Parry, for it was probably in 1819 (the dating is uncertain) that a much wearier and less ebullient Coleridge opened his extraordinary mind on the subject to an unknown correspondent:

from my very childhood I have been accustomed to *abstract* and as it were to unrealize whatever of more than common interest my eyes dwelt on; and then by a sort of transfusion and transmission of my consciousness to identify myself with the Object – and I have often thought, within the last five or six years, that if ever I should feel once again the genial warmth and stir of the poetic impulse, and refer to my own experiences, I should venture on a yet stranger & wilder Allegory than of yore – that I would *allegorize* myself, as a Rock with it's summit just raised above the surface of some Bay or Strait in the Arctic Sea,

While yet the stern and solitary Night
Brook'd no alternate Sway –

all around me fixed and firm, methought as my own Substance, and near me lofty Masses, that might have seemed to 'hold the Moon and Stars in fee' and often in such wild play with meteoric lights, or with the quiet shine from above which they made rebound in sparkles or disband in off-shoots and splinters and iridescent Needle-shafts of keenest Glitter, that it was a pride and a place of healing to lie, as in an Apostle's Shadow, within the Eclipse and deep substance-seeming Gloom of 'these dread Ambassadors from Earth to Heaven, Great Hierarchs'! and tho' obscured yet to think myself obscured by consubstantial Forms, based in the same Foundation as my own. I grieved not to serve them – yea, lovingly and with gladsomeness I abased myself in their presence: for they are my Brothers, I said, and the Mastery is their's by right of elder birth and by right of the mightier strivings of the hidden Fire that uplifted them above me.

Now Coleridge *is* the frozen sea, or a humble 'Rock' in it at any rate. He resolves the relationship between the human consciousness and the natural world by *being* the natural world, incorporating himself into it – or, of course, by incorporating it into himself, because this rapt and placid scene is all 'Allegory', an extended metaphor for the place in nature he would ideally like to occupy. Those presences that ring and overshadow his rock – it hardly matters if they are stone or ice – are nature's senior forms, the governing spirits of its calm unity with itself. He would like to worship them in stillness. If nature was an angelic order, they would be its archangels. And nature almost is, here: Coleridge's continual homages to 'substance', which glance back at the paradox of imagining substance out of nothing, also point forward to the religious meanings of the word. In the Christian Creed, God the Son is 'of one substance with the Father'. In the communion service the bread becomes 'consubstantial' with the body of God: matter and spirit become one. Here, Coleridge's body, transfused into the rock, becomes the same substance as the frozen Arctic, as 'fixed and firm' as it is. Yet there is healing, rather than terror, in the magical shadowed arena of his vision. It is a place to be at peace, under the 'quiet shine' of the heavens, and it raises no alarms over the loss of identity, sees no challenge in the difference between flesh and ice. Coleridge could not be farther from saying, as Victor Frankenstein did in print that same year, 'This ice is not made of such stuff as your hearts may be . . .' The battle is unbegun, wholly side-stepped. (Coleridge senses no peculiarity in the 'genial warmth' of poetry enabling an allegory of ice.) Coleridge reads the impassability of winter ice as a benign impassivity, and, where the Arctic travellers saw lifelessness, sees the solid sea endowed with a calm life that precedes all the particular forms of life. Before grass, before humming-birds, before the whole helter-skelter variety of things that swim and creep and move, lies this dream of Arctic rest.

Meanwhile, in the actual Arctic, Parry's officers took their daily winter walk along the frozen foreshore, swathed in mufflers, and tried to stave off the tedium of the noontime twilight with desultory conversation about hunting in Hampshire; about promotion; about the damnably slow passing of the days. Aboard the *Hecla* and the *Fury* the seamen stood watches as if the ships were in ordinary motion, and enjoyed (or endured) the round of entertainments designed to occupy their minds and keep them active. The theatre, the newspaper; the dancing, the grog; the comic songs, the diary-writing; the lectures, the music; the pep-talks, the polishing of brasswork; the theatre, the newspaper. In the newspaper, the poet who had compared the moon to a soup-tureen did his best to deflate the other phenomena of the winter night. 'The stars shine dimly, and seem scatter'd thin,/Just like the bristles seen on ——'s chin.' Ice accumulated on the rigging, and wherever breath condensed below decks on an unheated surface a thickening glaze developed. The cold attacked fingers and faces; deck duties became a matter of purgatorial scurrying. Food on the other hand was plentiful, and the Navy issue of lime juice could keep scurvy at bay for a year or so, although Parry's sailors would have been healthier taking their vitamins from fresh game, just as furs would have been better insulation than regulation wool. They celebrated Christmas, they celebrated Valentine's Day –

Cupid! Fond of unity
Our Boreal community
Defies you with impunity;
Your arrows and your bow

– and most of all, in spring 1820, 'On Thursday last, about noon, after an absence of three months', they celebrated the return of 'Viscount Sol, Lord Caloric' to the sky; an event noted, naturally, in the social column of the *North Georgia Gazette*. The reappearance of daylight at the end of winter, like the reappearance of night at the end of summer, promised that bodily normality would be restored. Endurance had led to victory, and the battle was (for the moment) over.

Battle, siege, conquest, attack, defence: all these military metaphors for the relation between the body and the Arctic environment were frequent in polar writing, not only in the opening stages of British exploration, but right through into the twentieth century as well. Figuring the Arctic as hostile, they are the obvious response to the otherness of its light and motion when the actual bodies of actual sailors were coping with the place. Perhaps you had, like Coleridge, to be visiting the Arctic winter without the liability of a body to feel any urge towards peaceful communion with its phenomena? Yet Arctic experience and the Romantic imagination mingled as the century went on. The poetry that proposed the Romantic tie between the body and the natural world was too influential in the culture not to touch the minds of actual explorers; and not every Romantic writer experienced the poles from a bedroom in Camden Town. We need to turn to the later, diffused phase of Romantic thinking that shaped Poe, to find the Romantic engagement with ice continuing. We need to consider someone like Dr Elisha Kent Kane, whose *Personal Narrative* of the American First Grinnell Expedition in 1856 records the endless metamorphoses of the polar air in summer. Parlour whimsy of a mid-Victorian kind makes his writing cute, but his mode of attention is implicitly Romantic.

6 PM. Refraction again! There is a black globe floating in the air, about $3°$ north of the sun. What it is you can not tell. Is it a bird or a balloon? Presently comes a sort of shimmering about its circumference, and on a sudden it

changes its shape. Now you see plainly what it is. It is a grand piano, and nothing else. Too quick this time! You had hardly named it, before it was an anvil – an anvil large enough for Mulciber and his Cyclops to beat out the loadstone of the poles. You have not quite got it adjusted to your satisfaction, before your anvil itself is changing; it contracts itself centrewise, and rounds itself endwise, and, *presto*, it has made itself duplicate – a pair of colossal dumb-bells. A moment! and it is the black globe again.

'Necromantic juggle', Kane calls the looping and blobbing of forms on the horizon, as if the eye were under the casual control of an enchanter. Icebergs strike him as 'impassive', and nature-mysticism (semi-serious) is not far away, for he is one of the few travellers to feel that architectural analogies cannot fix a berg descriptively. 'There was something about them so slumberous and so pure, so massive yet so evanescent, so majestic in their cheerless beauty, without, after all, any of the salient points which give character to description, that they seemed to me the material for a dream, rather than things to be definitely painted in words.' Or, far grimmer than Kane, and far more exercised by questions of perception, there was a New England author who had served on whale-ships of the Southern Fishery, and who in the 1840s was transmuting that experience – including the polar metal in that complex alloy – into a permanent epic of whaling. Because the whale that Ahab pursues in *Moby-Dick* (1851) is a dreadful white, Herman Melville included a great chapter on the manifold meanings of whiteness: white's sacredness, white's horror, white's blankness. The whites of polar summer, as seen with shivers from between the fo'c'sle and the blubber hooks, have their place here. Melville summoned for a witness

the sailor, beholding the scenery of the Antarctic seas; where at times, by some infernal trick of legerdemain in the powers of frost and air, he, shivering and half shipwrecked, instead of rainbows speaking hope and solace to his misery, views what seems a boundless church-yard grinning upon him with its lean ice monuments and splintered crosses.

The 'powers of frost and air' do not refuse to speak – nature is not a dumb opponent to the body. It is a conjurer, whose revelations come as tricks, the quickness of the air deceiving the eye; and the magic shows the body a white destination for it.

Among the myriad voices that throng *Moby-Dick*, Coleridge's is audible. Melville was, so to speak, in conversation with him. He could not, of course, have read the letter quoted above (which was not collected in print until 1911); but he knew 'The Ancient Mariner' before he set sail himself, and the magic of the poem, both innocent and deathly, was a touchstone he carried to the southern seas where Coleridge had never gone, except in dreams. *Moby-Dick* even contains an albatross, remembered by the narrator Ishmael from a voyage preceding the fated cruise of the *Pequod*. The incident may well be autobiographical, Melville's spokesman in the novel also speaking, in this case, for the author's memory. But the passage is intensely, romantically artful. Since Ishmael did not know that the huge white bird he saw *was* an albatross until afterwards – the sailors called it a 'goney' – he credits the reverence he feels for the creature to its own qualities of repose and innocence. Coleridge, in effect, has only given a true significance to it. 'Bethink thee of the albatross: whence cometh those clouds of spiritual wonderment and pale dread, in which that phantom sails in all imaginations? Not Coleridge first threw that spell; but God's great, unflattering laureate, Nature.' An extended footnote tells the whole story, and here Melville comes close to sharing Coleridge's polar reverie, detecting in the bird a chance to shed the busyness of living in favour of a wondering awe. Not the darkness of the polar night now, but the no-colour colouring of the polar snows does the work of blessing. Angels and archangels are at hand.

I remember the first albatross I ever saw. It was during a prolonged gale, in waters hard upon the Antarctic seas. From my forenoon watch below, I ascended to the overclouded deck; and there, dashed upon the main hatches, I saw a regal, feathery thing of unspotted whiteness, and with a hooked, Roman bill sublime. At intervals, it arched forth its vast archangel wings, as if to embrace some holy ark. Wondrous flutterings and throbbings shook it. Though bodily unharmed, it uttered cries, as some king's ghost in supernatural distress. Through its inexpressible, strange eyes, methought I peeped to secrets which took hold of God. As Abraham before the angels, I bowed myself; the white thing was so white, its wings so wide, and in those for ever exiled waters, I had lost the miserable warping memories of traditions and of towns. Long I gazed at that prodigy of plumage. I cannot tell, can only hint, the things that darted through me then.

The urge to bow down and worship is the same, but I think Melville strikes a new note too, the note of Romantic alarm. The nobility of the bird is not in doubt, but it is unclear whether this may be, for Ishmael *as a man*, a scene of temptation. The rejection of human society, implicit in Coleridge, has grown explicit in the reference to 'miserable warping . . . traditions' which Ishmael has lost; he threatens to lose more as he gazes into the windows of the albatross' eyes; and Ishmael, after all, is corporeally present on the 'exiled seas' around the southern pole. What metamorphosis is actually offered him? More than all this, though, there is the question of nature's – especially polar nature's – suitability as a resting place for the surrendering soul. This thing that baffles the senses and conjures imaginary graveyards may be worse than indifferent towards the specks of humanity that travel in it. Melville's description of the shivering sailor suggests so. *Moby-Dick* as a whole is concerned with a relation between man and the natural world which can drive a man mad, who lets himself be goaded by the impersonal sublimity that surrounds him. As Ahab, set on a foolhardy defiance of that nature, says, 'Great pains, small gains for those who ask the world to solve them; it cannot solve itself.'

Coleridge's icy solution seems out of reach. And Melville, furthermore, intuits something terrible from the way the light behaves in the other polar season; in the summer of radiance and movement, deceptive colour and optical conjuring. It is the example of the snows that drives home the conclusion of Ishmael's meditation on whiteness. Extraordinary though the occasion is, Melville here summons, and names, a far commoner Romantic response to the polar scene than Coleridge's peaceful migration into ice: *horror vacui*, the terror of emptiness. If blue and green in the bergs prove only to be refractions caused by movement – angles, not angels, at work – and if, at the ends of the earth, it is so plain the flooding light only conjures appearances from null white substance, does that not lead the mind to see that all colour is artificial? Red doors in England and New England, as much as red tints at the poles, lose their qualities in darkness. The poles alert us to a general falsity. If colour retreats so completely from the polar seas in winter, does that not demonstrate that all along there was a void behind the summer appearance of things? Then the splendour of nature was illusory – laid on like paint, appliqué like a thin material in embroidery, a trick played to prevent us seeing blank white where blank white is really universal. And the terror of white (white snows, white whale) lies in the reminder it gives that nature is a mask. 'All visible objects, man,' says fanatic Ahab, 'are but as pasteboard masks.' This is Ishmael, grappling whiteness:

Is it that by its indefiniteness it shadows forth the heartless voids and immensities of the universe, and thus stabs us from behind with the thought of annihilation, when beholding the milky way? Or is it, that as in essence whiteness is not so much a colour as the visible absence of colour, and at the same time the concrete of all colours; is it for these reasons that there is such a dumb blankness, full of meaning, in a wide landscape of snows – a colourless, all-colour of atheism from which we shrink? And when we consider that other theory of the natural philosophers, that all other earthly hues – every stately or lovely emblazoning – the sweet tinges of sunset skies and woods; yea, and the gilded velvets of butterflies, and the butterfly cheeks of young girls; all these are but subtle deceits, not actually inherent in substances, but only laid on from without; so that all deified Nature absolutely paints like the harlot, whose allurements cover nothing but the charnel-house within; and when we proceed further, and consider that the mystical cosmetic which produces every one of her hues, the great principle of light, for ever remains white or colourless in itself, and if operating without medium upon matter, would touch all objects, even tulips and roses, with its own blank tinge – pondering all this, the palsied universe lies before us like a leper; and like wilful travellers in Lapland, who refuse to wear coloured and colouring glasses upon their eyes, so the wretched infidel gazes himself blind at the monumental white shroud that wraps all the prospect round him.

Coleridge had hoped, famously, to be nature's child. Melville allowed that, at best, we might be nature's step-children, linked to her magnificence but in no easy sense her heirs; at worst, as Ishmael puts it, humankind are her orphans, left alone to manage the deceits and violent indifferences of a world from which a parent's love had disappeared, if it had ever been there. On the grounds of this attention of his to alienation, Melville is sometimes claimed as a 'modern' writer, but he never denied the spiritual power that held itself withdrawn behind the mask. He still wrote within the framework of Romanticism, and *Moby-Dick* is a book of frustration. Still seeking the union with nature which nature denied, still agonised by the polar glimpses of an 'atheistical' blank world, Ishmael cannot feel the indifference he finds around him.

Nature mattered more, not less, to the nineteenth century as it discovered that, by porter-brewing and tallow-melting, by smelting steel and massacring whales, it could reshape the natural world to an unprecedented degree. Nature had the importance attached to a *contested* subject, a subject whose disputed meaning was vital in Victorians' debates about themselves. They wanted to know to what extent they were created, and to what extent they created themselves; they wanted to know, exactly, their position in life, and among life; they wanted to visit places where nature resisted industrialism and the human hand, whether these were nice spots for a Sunday picnic, or the poles. The most prominent challenge to comfortable views of the natural order would come from Victorian biology. Darwinism would offer it as a rule of nature, rather than a shocking violation, that nature was indifferent to the outcome of the individual life. But Darwinism, and the new sciences in general, also offered a chance to settle humanity's place in nature on a new footing. Dealing in separable patterns of evidence, not in the assault of phenomena on the eye, they would let observers see a new sort of unity in nature, if not a kindly one. Dr Kane, for example, the American explorer who called the polar refractions a 'necromantic juggle', also burrowed geologically at what he saw. The mountains around Disko Bay in Greenland might attract Romantic superlatives from him; they also reminded the scientist in him of 'the Hindoo Ghauts, as I had seen them about Kandalah; they had the same monumental structure, the same *plateau*-formed summit, the same sublime ravines. How strangely this crust we wander over asserts its identity through all the disguises of climate!' To know the crust beneath you follows the same morphological laws everywhere is a special kind of reassurance, for it turns the guises of a juggling tricksy nature into penetrable disguises. Lift off the robe of snow, where the powers of frost and air reign, and you find the same rocky bone-structure that hides elsewhere under a robe of jungle, a robe of forest, a robe of sand. Yet, as Kane's record of grand pianos floating in the polar sky testifies, the *feeling* remained of being in a vortex of phenomena. Likewise Romantic vocabulary, and Romantic hopes and horrors, remained important ways of negotiating the perceptual maze of the polar regions. They helped; they answered to the experience of light and motion, dark and stillness. They described the shock of finding nature other than you thought it was.

The gallant, diminutive Frenchman Joseph René Bellot sailed as a volunteer on two of Lady Franklin's expeditions in search of her lost husband. On the second one, on 18 August 1853, he fell through a crack in an ice-floe and vanished. He had liked the absurd variety of shapes the ice had shown him: camels, he said, with riders wearing burnouses, obelisks, pyramids . . . He had met Dr Kane at an Arctic rendezvous for the search-ships, and enjoyed a conversation with him about de Tocqueville. But when fog closed the perspectives about the ship, and the world turned to creeping whiteness, he told his diary:

I cannot find words enough to say of these icebergs, for which I panted so long at the peak of my feverish admiration . . . Nature no longer feels her heart beat in the slumber of the north; she is like the pitiless machinery which cuts off the arm which is caught between the cogs of the wheels . . . Moral nature seems to have abdicated, and nothing remains but a chaos without a purpose.

SIX

Lady Jane's Lament

Bellot had been a favourite with Lady Jane Franklin and her niece and companion Sophy Cracroft: the beau ideal of an explorer, almost, with his diffidence and his wit and his youthful good looks. When he died – when he 'shared the fate and glory' of Franklin himself, as his memorial in Greenwich puts it – the two ladies wore mourning. While he was alive, and winning golden notices for his willingness to serve in another nation's tragic cause, they took pleasure in his dancing and his charm, his sensitivity and his letters. Only, as befitted Lady Jane's status as a national monument of fidelity, and Miss Cracroft's as assistant-in-chief at Franklin's shrine, they registered their appreciation through other women's reactions to him. At a ball in Orkney before his first departure, 'I fancy the young ladies here rather worry him,' Sophy Cracroft told her mother in a letter; 'the other evening, he was at a party & for the enlightenment of Stromness society actually danced the Schottische with Miss Hamilton.' But they were assured of his devotion. 'Our parting with our dear little French friend was really painful – he sobbed like a child as he took leave of my Aunt. It was some time before he got courage to say a word. We are really *very* fond of him – his sweetness & simplicity & earnestness are most endearing.' Bellot had two copies of his daguerrotype printed, one for his mother, and one for Lady Jane. Eventually she was calling him her 'French son', and he was signing himself in letters to her 'with every filial and affectionate feeling'. Somehow it was his smallness that made him such a pet, made his daguerrotype 'such a pretty picture'. 'Our dear little French friend'; 'poor little Bellot'; 'like a child'. He had a toy handsomeness that allowed the ladies to feel a comfortably parental attraction to him, or perhaps to see him through the glass of nursery rhymes like the one that ran *I had a little husband, no bigger than my thumb* . . . Nor, at a little over five feet tall, did he possess a small man's self-assertion. 'He is certainly a most amiable being,' wrote Sophy Cracroft of their last meeting with him, '& free from that common, almost invariable characteristic of little people, touchiness.'

No doubt the loss of her 'French son' in 1853 punctuated Lady Franklin's long inconclusive wait for news of her missing husband with a sudden additional grief. Sir John sailed on his last expedition in 1845, and final proof of what had happened to him and his crew was not obtained until the return of the *Fox* in the summer of 1859, although it was clear by 1854 that he must be dead. Lady Jane's limbo ended, and she decisively became a widow, when the information at last arrived that Franklin had died in 1847. She had in fact been so for all but two of the fourteen years of suspense. But more can be learned from her enthusiasm over Bellot, about the ways in which exploration appealed to Victorian women. This most famous polar spouse was at the centre of a public spectacle of mourning. For the newspaper-reading public, of almost every social class, she was a living illustration of the costs, and the nobility, of the polar enterprise. Notables queued up to meet her on her constant travels to promote the search expeditions. Less genteel people sang the popular ballad about her, 'Lady Jane's Lament':

> My Franklin dear long has been gone,
> To explore the northern seas,
> I wonder if my faithful John,
> Is still battling with the breeze;
> Or if e'er he will return again,
> To these fond arms once more
> To heal the wounds of dearest Jane,
> Whose heart is griev'd full sore.
> My Franklyn dear, though long thy stay,
> Yet still my prayer shall be,
> That Providence may choose a way,
> To guide thee safe to me.

She personified female virtues that Victorian England revered; moreover, she personified a role for women who were involved, through their menfolk, in polar exploration. Her attitudes – from her special position – towards men like Bellot and her husband suggest a widespread pattern of female imagining, shaped by mid-Victorian assumptions about what women were, and shaping in turn the mid-Victorian picture of the ice.

The rules of the game had been established by evangelical religion. Beginning at the end of the eighteenth century, later spreading out to permeate the Victorian middle classes with its moral assumptions, this mode of piety offered a special moral function to the family. Though it made the husband 'the head of the wife', as recommended by St Paul, it made the marriage an enterprise of common moral seriousness. Though it circumscribed female behaviour within the bounds of decency and propriety, it also aimed to reform male behaviour. It encouraged men to observe the same standards of virtue when out in the world that they (supposedly) practised in the domestic sphere. The paterfamilias, leading servants and children through their prayers among the antimacassars, was supposed to preserve that moral character as he moved among his employees during the working day. The scope for hypocrisy and male secrecy was enormous, but the power of the ideal, for those men high-minded enough to take it seriously, was such that conscience and domesticity came to overlap. And the standard of male behaviour was therefore fashioned to some extent by female expectations. In effect, as embodiments of virtue, and even as judges of it, women gained a theoretical access to – a moral say in – the activities that the same religious outlook reserved for men.

Polar exploration was by definition an exclusively male enterprise; yet many of the most prominent English men to travel north paid lip-service to the evangelical ideal, or indeed actually tried to practise it. One was Sir John Franklin, strict Sabbatarian by upbringing, waited for so loyally by Lady Jane: although his first marriage had worked out differently, for his first wife, Eleanor Porden, to whom we shall return later, proved interestingly resistant to the female role he had in mind for her. Another was William Edward Parry; and we have the diary that his young wife, Isabella Parry, kept in the months before his second departure on expedition.

Isabella Stanley was twenty-four in October 1826 when she married

Parry. She enjoyed the beginning of her new life immensely. As Edward's wife she was able, for the first time, to evade the critical glances cast by her mother, a dry formidable bluestocking who had once been Gibbon's confidante. Eighteenth-century irony did not suit Isabella who was, by contrast, both earnest and silly. She experienced marriage as a wonderful enlargement of her freedom: 'they are all very nice here & let me do just what I like without minding it or making any observations', she told her diary. And she and Edward accorded well with each other. They were sexually happy ('love and affection, of a kind deep and tender such as one has never felt before', she wrote to a friend) and they shared an enthusiastic piety, aristocratic yet low-church. Edward, of course, took the senior spiritual position in the relationship. Several times Isabella refers happily to his 'example' and his 'teaching'. But they both fell to their knees to receive instruction from on high. Praying together and churchgoing together were important parts of the intimacy of the marriage. As the date Edward would leave approached, they told each other that, spiritually, they would not be parted. 'This is the last Sunday we shall spend together. The next he Sails & for the last time we have been to church together, though every Sunday which returns we shall be together in heart & spirit. – We shall pray together to the same Being & feel that we are indeed with one another . . .' On their next-to-last evening, Edward presented her with a Bible, 'That Book which alone can give consolation in sorrow'. (He also gave her his recently drawn tooth to keep, while she lent him her pet dog Fido for company on the polar voyage. They were partners in gush.) Despite Isabella's miscarriage in early January 1827, the pair were too essentially contented, and Isabella was too emotionally inexperienced, for the parting to be a real cause of sorrow. No premonition of tragedy clouded the occasion, no apprehension of possible widowhood really weighed Isabella down – and Parry, in fact, returned safe and sound. But the role of steadfastly enduring wife was enjoined upon Isabella by their faith, and she accepted the part with innocent alacrity, acting out the new sensation of loss in her diary *prospectively*, before the *Hecla* actually weighed anchor. Parry had to be away for two days on expedition business in the week preceding the official starting date. Writing on Sunday, expecting to see him again on Tuesday, she recorded 'The utter lonlyness of it [*sic*]. The feeling of desolation.' Finding there is a pattern of behaviour she is expected to follow, Isabella tries it out, touchingly and comically, as if it were the right thing to wear. When Edward goes for good, the diary falls silent with a flourish. (A literal flourish, drawn with a pen on a page.) Then, presumably, as the months went by, Isabella's education in the more prosaic sadness of absence began.

But before he left Parry had taken steps to show his profession to the woman who was going to wait for him. He did not just want to show it off, or to make sure that his spouse understood what exploration entailed. (Though some Arcticisms did rub off on her: she swore that *she* would never complain about household poverty, the way her aunt did, 'even if we should be obliged to live upon Pemmican or Whale . . .') He intended to assure her that, far from their scarcely established home, he would remain the man she knew. He would undertake his command in the same spirit as he had undertaken the marriage, exercising the same virtues on the quarter-deck as in the bedroom, the breakfast-room, and the family pew. Therefore, while the *Hecla* was outfitting in the January of 1827, the two of them lived aboard for a week, and when, a month later, Edward's duties took him to a court-martial in Deptford, Isabella went too to spend a further four days in his cabin. The *Hecla* had now become a familiar setting for Isabella. 'I am now quite at home there, & find it answers all my ideas of what it must be, to belong to a ship,' she wrote. With an uncanny sense of occasion, the temperature plummeted on this second visit, the Thames emulating the Arctic. 'The River was frozen up & I had a Specimen of the Heclas natural life & heard the ice grate along the side of the Ship.'

It was not quite the expedition's natural life: officers and crew were clearly on their best behaviour. But, 'made much of by Sailors', sat with companionably in the mornings by the lieutenants and midshipmen when Parry was busy, solemnly offered a sample of the seamen's pudding at the farewell dinner on board, Isabella gained the impression Parry had hoped for. She liked the first lieutenant Mr Ross 'excessively, there is so much spirit & eagerness about him & his

Whole heart & Soul are in the present expedition'; while as for the crew – 'a finer set of Men I never saw. It is indeed a comfort to think that his companions are such men, one may feel sure they will follow him in everything & are truly to be trusted.' At the same time as Isabella was reassured, straightforwardly, of Parry's safety in such trustworthy company, she had the moral temper of the ship demonstrated to her. The atmosphere of the *Hecla* of course reflected on its commander, whose responsibility it was to foster the appropriate mood. Since Parry's subordinates seemed to feel about him as she did – his health was drunk 'with one universal feeling' – shipboard life squared wonderfully with home life, at least in Isabella Parry's brief experience of it.

On Parry's part as well, it is worth saying, the show of shipboard kindliness was wholly in earnest. His voyages were noted for their high moral tone, even if naval swearing did resume once Isabella had been rowed ashore. Parry would be remembered as one of the activist reformers of naval manners; a captain dedicated to effecting the shift away from drink, sodomy, and the lash (or *rum, bum, and concertina*, in the more cheerful formulation), rather than a member of the larger group of officers who were merely carried along by the change in attitudes. Religion made him conceive of his office as paternal, almost pastoral. He was supposed, he thought, to exercise moral supervision over the men, and to deliver a fatherly blend of advice and reassurance to them. One of the plays he mounted over the Arctic winters contained a special scene designed to convince the men that *their* wives were calmly and faithfully awaiting their return. And Parry felt, too. An attraction, to women, of the evangelical style in men was the value it placed on the testimony of the heart: evangelical men spoke out their feelings, at least the creditable ones, with a comparative lack of restraint. At 82° 45' north – the farthest point the 1827 expedition attained – Parry raised his glass of the grog in a celebratory toast to the King. 'Mrs Parry!' proposed Lieutenant Ross in return. Tears came to the Captain's eyes, and he immediately wrote Isabella a letter to tell her so.

Isabella Parry learned, then, that the domestic sphere she inhabited and the polar sphere that Edward ventured into were morally congruent. The same standards applied in both places. She learned that she would be accompanying her husband spiritually throughout the journey – nestling in his conscience – and that her moral approval was important to him. (Whether she could have withheld it is a different question.) But for Isabella the focus of the whole thing was Edward's character: the fact that he was to exercise his patriarchal leadership, his virtues, and so on, in the particular activity of polar exploration, was largely incidental to her. 'How little I ever thought with what intense interest I should think of the Hecla,' she wrote. Her intense interest in the fate of an expedition ship arose because of the accident of her husband's presence aboard. Edward's chance career as an explorer happened to open for her inspection this one of the spheres of action available to active, manly men. The reason that her experience does not stand as isolated and individual lies in the gradual characterisation of exploration itself as a moral activity. This was the route by which thousands of women who were not involved through their menfolk in the polar voyages, but who *were* readers of magazines and books increasingly tailored to family audiences, had the world of ice revealed to them – were invited into it, indeed, as a domain suitable for the female imagination, and for the angelic probity assumed to belong to righteous wives and daughters.

In 1846, in retirement, Sir John Barrow of the Admiralty, prime mover of the British exploration effort, published a popular digest of the expedition narratives. What struck him as worth advertising were the moral accomplishments of the explorers – the way the officers

whether employed by sea or on shore, exhibited the most able and splendid examples of perseverance under difficulties, of endurance under afflictions, and resignation under every kind of distress. I thought it due to them . . . to publish a small and readable volume, containing the essence of the large and expensive official accounts, in order to make the merits of these brave fellows – officers and men – more generally and extensively known.

Publishers were quickly latching onto exploration as a source of uplifting, as well as entertaining, copy. By the time that Dickens founded *Household Words* in 1850, meaning it to fill a gap in the market for high-quality family fiction and non-fiction, the poles were firmly established in the repertoire of improving subjects. He published thirteen substantial polar pieces of one kind and another during the magazine's lifetime. At the height of the Franklin search in 1853, his contributor Morley reached the heights of exaggeration with an article that played the purity of exploration, now a commonplace, for all it was worth.

For three hundred years the Arctic seas have now been visited by European sailors; their narratives supply some of the finest modern instances of human energy and daring, bent on a noble undertaking, and associated constantly with kindness, generosity, and simple piety. The history of Arctic enterprise is stainless as the Arctic snows, clean to the core as an ice mountain.

He ended: 'Let us be glad . . . that we have one unspotted place upon this globe of ours; a Pole that, as it fetches truth out of a needle, so surely also gets all that is right-headed and right-hearted from the sailor whom the needle guides.' The piece was called 'Unspotted Snow', Morley taking the whiteness that had appalled Ishmael as the simplest possible metaphor for all that was light, white, and bright in human conduct.

It needs to be said immediately that these commendatory pictures of polar exploration, designed for an audience of women, were *not true*; that is, that they were necessarily unlike the experience of exploration, however palpably sincere Morley and Barrow and their like may have been, however much captains like Parry intended to make their voyages measure up to the ideal. No cynicism is required here. The difference involved is the difference between a record, as ambiguous and as moulded by the conflict of viewpoints as records always are, and a deliberately cultivated myth, which imposes a storylike sense and a storylike uniformity upon the matter of voyages. The 'large, expensive' official accounts dealt with the aims and methods of the expeditions, judging failure and success against the sealed instructions a captain had carried away from the Admiralty offices. Those considerations have been withdrawn from the moralising summaries. Moral achievement and high feeling, once incidental, now take centre stage, becoming the story. It does not do, reading Barrow's encomium, to ask the purpose for which the Arctic sailors endured what they endured, or what they were resigned to, or to what end they persevered. Either the value of exploration was taken quite for granted, or the geographical and scientific aims were moralised in their turn – so that the gallant mariners were seen to serve truth as well as goodness, a nebulous truth which made the mapping of a cape be of self-explanatory benefit to humanity. Men did these things; men, again, composed these partial portraits, tailored to their estimate of women's understanding. Yet many women welcomed the spectacle of male heroism that resulted, and refrained, with pleasure, from the questions that would have spoilt the picture. They were willing to barter the suspension of disbelief for satisfactions unsuspected, perhaps, by the popularisers. From the authorised standpoint of a moral arbiter, you could witness a semi-fictional parade of heroic masculinity. Highly particular things are asked of heroes: escape from the niggles that attend upon character in actuality, behaviour so consistent it can be taken as read, complete transparency of motives. In the real world, ignorance of a man's behaviour once out of sight posed a real danger to women. It was a Victorian woman's pressing task to assess the likely conduct of men, almost always working from far too little information – trying to imagine the whole man accurately from the slice of himself that was revealed in the female space of the drawing-room. Was a brother, a father, a future landlord dependable? Most of all, for it would determine the course of her life, was a potential husband as admirable as he seemed? Debt, disaster, and domestic violence were the extreme penalties for a failure of accurate perception, but a bad decision threatened all the milder miseries of loneliness and incompatibility too, a lifetime's worth of them. Hence the importance, to women, of the evangelical compact between husbands and wives. Hence one primary attraction of imagining – as spectators, as readers, relieved briefly of the real business of life – heroes who came, so to speak, under guarantee. The storylike simplicity of the polar voyages, as recounted for the family readership, was the point. In the wilderness of ice, men were shown as moral pin-ups; you could indulge yourself by dwelling on their axiomatic 'right-heartedness'. Despite the chuckles of men over the susceptibility of women to ideal brawny explorers, it need not have been imaginary romantic roles that the polar heroes were called on to play. Heroes can be good fathers, responsive brothers, spiritual exemplars. The first strength of these heroes was that they were able to be known – accessible from home, because they apparently inhabited a comparable moral terrain.

And the masculinity of the explorers seemed also to be of a special kind. More than the masculinity involved in war, more than the masculinity deployed in business (though both could be garlanded with morality), it appeared to fit the sensibilities women were trained to possess. It was built, judging by descriptions like Barrow's, around a set of virtues conventionally recommended to women. Endurance, perseverance, resignation: all three were excellent things for every Christian soul to aim for, but all three, more particularly, formed part of the equipment with which a virtuous *woman* was expected to face the tribulations of her state. Though the promoters of the image of exploration as 'clean' may only have intended to point up its universal acceptability, their moralism opened a door to imaginative identification. Endurance, perseverance, and resignation were likely to fall within the real experience of all but the luckiest women; for, with a beautiful circularity guaranteed by the notion of separate spheres for men and women, women needed to exercise just those virtues to survive with good humour or self-esteem the dependent place reserved for them. Now it seemed explorers had to, as well; that the travails which so assuredly made men of them also, in a sense, made them women; which produced a sort of sympathetic equivalence between mariners surviving the huge indifference and overmastering cold of the Arctic, and the travails of a lonely governess amidst a chilly household. It meant that Arctic heroism, strangely, was relevant heroism, with the natural environment of the poles compelling men to wait, suffer, and be patient, in the same way as the human environment compelled women. In the half-realised form in which the Arctic reached households, an iceberg might stand for the cold bulk of more familiar obstacles. And the imagined Arctic – visited differently by women who knew for certain, unlike male daydreamers, that they could never see it in fact – offered an ennobling translation of everyday struggles. You could envisage yourself making a pilgrim's progress across that thin ice, past that giant danger, through a landscape that crackled and froze.

Here began a continuing tradition by which women otherwise sceptical of heroic masculine agendas granted exploration an exceptional sympathy, seeing, in the thwarted attempts to 'conquer' the ice, men learning what women knew. Men fighting other men in wars might wrestle sympathetically with loneliness and fear, but men confronting an implacable environment which was, by definition, stronger than them, might grow to experience the female variety of grace under pressure, for which 'resignation' was an inaccurate word, though a reliable pointer. It did not mean surrender; it was more a species of self-preservation in the face of circumstances that could not be changed, a deliberate decision to inhabit the impossible situation on one's own terms, rather than flailing uselessly against it. Explorers seemed to have grasped it who, for example, chose to care for each other *in extremis* rather than seizing the last minimal chance for survival. The importance of the co-operative virtues in exploring was significant: like women in households, feeling the tug of demands from many directions at once, the explorers appeared to have to manage their crises in company, paying as much attention to the psychological needs of their companions as to the outward tasks of cooking and sledging.

Wonder at the bizarre gratuitousness of exploration was, of course, not absent. It seemed peculiar that men should travel to the ends of the earth to re-create, for mortal stakes, an everyday plight. Yet this was, so to speak, a vaccinating dose of disbelief; it rendered some part of the sympathetic female audience proof against the mounting evidence of bungling by the British heroes as the decades of the nineteenth and then the twentieth centuries passed, for interest in the poles of this kind has survived up to the present. The news that Scott, like Franklin before him, probably died of incompetence does not affect an attraction to his story which centres on his bearing in the face of death. Maybe it even strengthens the attraction in some ways. Our muddles and mistakes are, after all, universal components of the traps we find ourselves in. We know now that the 'bad luck' Scott blamed his party's fate on, he largely made himself; but this matters less, to the

American writer and feminist Ursula Le Guin in a recent essay, than his estimable refusal to personify the Antarctic environment as his enemy. We took necessary chances, and failed, he said instead. Scott doomed his companions, then covered his tracks with rhetoric: but in Le Guin's eyes he recognised at least the nature of his position, a recognition (however circuitous) of the human situation in the face of things as they are, and his heroism therefore persists, to her. Likewise, to take another present-day example of unlikely sympathy, Doris Lessing has written at length about her troubled admiration for Scott's expedition. Wondering and appalled over the Edwardian class divisions the expedition worked so hard to maintain (officers sleeping at one end of a blubber-streaked hole in the snow, men at the other), she finds herself still moved by the devoted tenderness these foolish men nonetheless showed to each other. Both Le Guin and Lessing first read about Scott's expedition as girls, and write about it as adults of very changed experience and convictions in order to account to themselves for their continued emotional assent to the story. What remains, when critical intelligence and historical sense have pared away the absurdities, is their feeling for the explorers' response to the catastrophe. As a child in the 1940s, steeped in natural history, and discovering Scott at the same age as Le Guin and Lessing, my mother took the story as a moral challenge. Exploration appeared to call for immediately comprehensible qualities. Though girls and women were required to show courage without the snow, the ice, the circumstances sanctioning male heroism, the thread of likeness was there. 'I wondered if I was brave enough to be an explorer.'

But, in the mid-nineteenth century, these parallels between women and male explorers did not necessarily work against the grain of accepted gender roles. Indeed the idea of men and women making parallel 'journeys' was a commonplace. In a mobile time, with many men departing for America, or Canada, or India, or Australia, or to patrol the oceans the British liked to think of as their own, wives and daughters, sisters and sweethearts, were expected to trace the absent man's route on the map; and, while their hearts went with the beloved, to turn his absence to their own moral benefit. Such women, in fact and in fiction, 'travelled' through moral territory. It made an excellent plot-device for a novel, whether the novel chiefly followed the man's adventures, or the waiting woman's. Romance was delayed, as romance must be in fiction, and happiness had the conclusive shape of a return from the sea, when it would prove that the two journeys arrived at the same place, at the same time. A sensitive male hero – or a man groomed into sensitivity by the events of his journey – might well acknowledge that the woman had borne the greater burden. A friend suggests to Dickens' Martin Chuzzlewit (1844), broken to perceptiveness by his failed emigration to a feverish American swamp, that he 'ventured a good deal for a young lady's love'. 'I begin to be far from clear upon it,' Martin replies:

You may depend upon it she is very unhappy. She has sacrificed her peace of mind; she has endangered her interests very much; she can't run away from those who are jealous of her, and opposed to her, as I have done. She has to endure, Mark: to endure without the possibility of action, poor girl! I begin to think she has more to bear than ever I have had. Upon my soul I do!

Yet a moral homage like this never disturbed the primacy of the male voyage, of which the female voyage was the echo, or the primacy of the male decision to travel, of which female endurance was the consequence. Indeed it confirmed the different destinies of men and women, which could unite on the ground of mutual sympathy. Polar exploration was a special kind of male travel. Again, though, at the back of the imaginative possibilities it offered to women, there usually lay firm notions of what men and women were: the evangelical notions, only confirmed by women's discovery of a womanly strain in the explorers' behaviour. Only with clear moral meanings for 'masculine' and 'feminine' did it make sense for women to shadow the literal journeys of men by making metaphorical journeys over the same terrain.

And not every woman who was interested in the poles wanted to endorse these sweetly complementary ideas of gender, or enjoyed imagining the evangelical style of male heroism. Take, for an eccentric example, the young – the very young – Charlotte Brontë, reading back issues of *Blackwood's Magazine* with her sisters in Haworth Parsonage in 1829. Outside that house, said Elizabeth Gaskell later, 'the sinuous hills seemed to girdle the world like the great Norse serpent, and for my part I don't know if they don't stretch to the North Pole'. Inside, in the numbers of 'the most able periodical there is' for November 1820 and June 1821, the Brontë children had an account of Parry's overwintering.

It contained elements that one can guess must have appealed to them. Indeed in retrospect some of what the Blackwood's journalist praised as 'incidents of a romantic and unusual nature' look glaringly Brontë-esque; like the macabre story of the frozen hand.

One of the sailors, who had ventured beyond his companions in search of rein-deer, returned to the ship with all his fingers frost-bitten, from carrying his musket too long. When the fingers were plunged into cold water, ice formed on its surface, and this continued to be the case for half an hour afterwards, as often as the fingers were plunged into it. The sailor lost five of his fingers.

The part of us that should be most warm and living, the part of us integral to writing and gesturing, the part of us we extend towards other bodies for a clasp of reciprocal warmth, has turned spectacularly unlike itself. With Gothic violence, what ought to be warmed by water now crusts water over, thicks it with cold. The hand has been disembodied, and not only because in the end the sailor lost the fingers which behaved so strangely. Bodies that will not be governed figure largely in the adult Brontës' novels. More especially, this moment of Arctic horror recalls the one in *Wuthering Heights* when Lockwood, reaching through a broken window to still the tapping branch of a tree, finds instead that he holds 'the fingers of a little, ice-cold hand!' – which refuses to release him, though he rubs the wrist of the ghostly hand over and over against the edge of the glass.

Charlotte's mind too would be stocked for her adult writing career with polar scenes and images. Besides the opening scene of *Jane Eyre*, glassy with the ice-upon-ice of Bewick's vision of the Arctic, there would be the 'poles' of the breakfast table in *Villette*, where Lucy Snowe (first christened Lucy Frost by her author) sat at a cold distance from her hot little suitor. But we can also reconstruct, tenuously, her first reaction at the age of thirteen to Parry; and an interesting refusal of him as a hero by her Byronic sensibilities. The

Blackwood's articles made enough impression on the girls to find a place in that year's other new entertainment. Their father had brought a box of lead soldiers home from Leeds, food, like the stack of magazines, for his children's voracious minds; and again, like the magazines, exotic messengers from afar to their isolated lives. When the box was opened, Charlotte wrote, they each snatched one soldier for their own. 'Emily's was a grave-looking fellow. We called him "Gravey". Anne's was a queer little thing, very much like herself. He was called "Waiting Boy".' But after reading *Blackwood's*, Emily's soldier became 'Parry' and Anne's 'Ross': polar heroes who better matched Charlotte's 'Duke of Wellington' and Branwell's 'Bonaparte'.

Or who did on the face of it. The soldiers were less important as physical playthings than as characters in the 'Glass Town' fantasies played out by the children in their own miniature journals. Here Parry, Ross, Bonaparte, and a whole phalanx of the Wellington family took on a life independent of their namesakes, fighting, founding cities in a mythic Africa, and frequently undergoing sudden reversals of fortune as the children conducted tiny coups against each other. Here too Charlotte's heroes contrasted violently with Emily and Anne's staider creations. She disliked their Parry and their Ross, chiefly no doubt because of the qualities her sisters had loaded on them; yet she may well have detected the source of her repugnance in the account of the exploring originals in *Blackwood's*. Can she have picked up the bland flavour of Parry's piety from the magazine? It is not impossible, for the attack she eventually mounted on the Glass Town Parry catches, to an amazing degree, the character of the real man. She is refusing, at any rate, a coercive benevolence and a tidy moralism which the real Parry was proud of exemplifying. In the *Young Men's Magazine* (circulation: one) for October 1830, she sent her hero Lord Charles Wellesley, rakish and sinuously undependable, over the border into the fief governed by the explorer. 'Parry's Land' sounds highly polar, but Wellesley

was immediately struck by the changed aspect of everything. Instead of tall, strong muscular men going about seeking whom they may devour, with guns on their shoulders or in their hands, I saw none but shiftless milk-and-water-beings, in clean, blue linen jackets and white aprons. All the houses were ranged in formal rows. They contained four rooms, each with a little garden in front. No proud castle or splendid palace towers insultingly over the cottages around . . . Every inch of ground was enclosed with stone walls . . . Rivers rushed not with foam and thunder through meads and mountains, but glided canal-like along, walled on each side that no sportive child might therein find a watery grave . . .

Charlotte was being prophetic. In life, the real Parry would spend the years after his retirement from the Navy founding workhouses in the county of Norfolk. It was, he thought, a worthy religious task. There the paupers of Norfolk *would* be ranged in formal rows, be dressed in seemly uniforms and, of course, be protected from the reign of impulse: from the temptations to devouring, disorder, and dirt which so assailed the poor. Charlotte preferred, for a vehicle of fantasy and self-projection, a man who'd descend like a wolf on this very trim fold. (Lord Charles rectifies the shameful safety of children in Parry's Land by sportively beating an imaginary child of Parry's around the head with a poker.) The combination of attraction and identification was important. Wellesley, after all, *was* her, as well as being an object of adolescent desire out of the box of imagining; and when, as an adult novelist, she wrote romantic heroes, she gave them both the cruel streak and the ability to imagine a comparable inner life in a woman. Wellesley survives, immensely refined, a red tile laid among the mosaic pieces of women's lives, in a Mr Rochester who enjoys verbal combat with Jane Eyre – and even in peppery Paul Emmanuel of *Villette*, utterly devoid of Wellesley's satanic good looks, yet the only person to perceive that Lucy Snowe is, herself, a creature of impulse. The attractive men are those who reckon with the anger and the desire of women, those able to sustain a spirited encounter with fiery qualities in women far removed from resignation. Already, with this demand for mutual recognition, we are a world away from the pious payment of moral homage to women – from the presentation of some male activities as fit stuff for the female imagination. The household at Haworth into which the polar news came was a straitened, cramping place, but the fancies the children entertained about the remote world outside were not segregated, sweetly, by gender. Charlotte grew interested in the Arctic on her own account, declining to direct her interest through admiration for Parry: that milksop.

Evading the evangelical constraints was a more painfully personal task for Eleanor Porden. It involved negotiation, not with a tin soldier, but the very solid figure of her intended husband, John Franklin. She had no difficulties with his conception of his own role as explorer: it was that suffering performance in the snows of Canada, after all, which had distinguished him in her eyes, and she took a sophisticated pleasure in teasing him about his polar fame. 'Pray am I to condole with you or congratulate you on the snow?' she asked, when London froze in January 1823, as if his experience had made him the custodian of all things cold and frosty. A little later, feeling neglected, she sent him a letter of comic reproach which appropriated his Arctic vocabulary, skilfully and wittily, as Isabella Parry could never have done with her beloved's earnest explanations.

Most Faithless Saxon,

After sitting whole days with my arms folded, my legs crossed and my feet on the fender, devising excuses for your absence; after building castles in the air; and discovering them to be but frost work; drawing your portrait in the fire, and demolishing it with the poker; or cutting it out in paper, and blowing it away with my sighs, I arrive at one conclusion – that I am utterly forsaken. Think not that I expect to melt you, for had you not been hardened by three polar winters, you must now be like my tears, and like every thing else in this great town, completely frozen. No – every spark of hope is completely extinguished in my bosom, therefore, as willows are rather out of season – and my garters withal rather the worse for wear – as the Serpentine is frozen over and even the Thames at Waterloo Bridge nearly inaccessible from icebergs – as daggers and poison are too melodramatic; and opening a vein too surgical and unsentimental; and as razors and pistols are somewhat masculine resources and moreover commonplace; I beg to know your pleasure as to the disposal of myself.

The disconsolate
Monimia.

Nota Bene: I would bury myself in the snow, but fear to be turned into spermaceti before you would hear of my fate. What think you of swallowing fire? It has but one prototype and would be a comfortable death this weather!

She imported his Arctic into the midst of her London (and into an extended joke about suicide that prefigures Dorothy Parker's famous 'Guns aren't lawful;/Nooses give') with conscious aplomb. She knew her powers. Even the apparently nonsensical business of the 'spermaceti' conceals a playful aptness. Being buried in snow would not transmogrify you into the valuable contents of a sperm whale's cranial cavity, but it would turn your body hard, white, and waxy: exactly like the expensive candles spermaceti was chiefly used to manufacture. For her grand finale, Eleanor dispatched Franklin a valentine, that February, which claimed to come from a Coppermine River Indian woman named Green Stockings. His book, *A Journey to the Shores of the Polar Sea*, would only be published later that spring, but Eleanor had already read Franklin's brief description of the real Green Stockings in manuscript – and smiled, perhaps, at his tone. He had been stolid and slightly contemptuous, put distinctly on the defensive by his encounter with the sexual manners of the Arctic natives:

I may remark that the daughter, whom we designated Green-stockings from her dress, is considered by her tribe to be a great beauty . . . The young lady . . . has already been an object of contest between her countrymen, and although under sixteen years of age, has belonged successively to two husbands, and would probably have been the wife of many more, if her mother had not required her services as a nurse.

Now Eleanor made the story over into a romantic farrago, converting Green Stockings into Franklin's polar true-love, who has pined away since his heartless departure for the warm south. Besides the way the valentine verses administered a flirtatious prod to Franklin's gravitas, Green Stockings, as a purely notional rival to Eleanor, did very nicely to signal Eleanor's understanding of the genuine rival claim on Franklin's attention posed by the Arctic. She knew he would be going back, and look: she would write down the call of the place for him herself, translated into harmless female frippery. 'Return!' begged Green Stockings,

Return! and the ice shall be swept from thy path,
 I shall breathe out my spells o'er the land and the sea;
Return! and the tempest shall pause in his wrath,
 Nor the winds nor the waves dare be rebels to thee!
Spread thy canvas once more, keep the Pole-star before thee,
'Tis constancy's type, and the beacon of glory;
By the lake, by the mountain, the forest and river,
In the wilds of the north, I am thine, and for ever!

She complimented him, too, by ascribing him the character he wanted to have: constant, persistent, faithful, serious in his calling, the very model of a 'blue-light' naval captain. This was the evangelical ideal of manhood once more; and she liked it on him, she liked the way he wore it. The problem lay, after her displays of acceptance, in what he expected of her.

She knew her verbal nimbleness baffled him. (In letters she called him 'dear Wanderer', 'Most Faithless Saxon', 'Most Magnanimous Harry the Fourth'. All Franklin could manage, after much persuasion, was 'My dear Eleanor, as it is your pleasure to be addressed by this title, I obey . . .') But she had thought he liked it; that, as she was excited to have acquired an earnest polar hero, quite unlike the circulating talkers of literary London, so he enjoyed the affection, even if he did not entirely understand it, of a metropolitan creature prepared to mention her garters on paper, who knew everybody, and who took the arts seriously. He had certainly given every sign that those were his feelings. Suddenly, in March 1823, Franklin announced that he would find it improper for the name of anyone 'connected' to him – for example, by marriage – to appear in the public prints. Since Eleanor regularly published poetry (her latest work was the epic 'Richard Coeur de Lion'), Franklin was requiring her, in effect, to abandon her writing. Evangelical friends had prompted him, one of whom was a woman; friends from before his social lionising, who found it morally inadequate for Franklin and Eleanor to gaze with satisfaction on their mutually exotic assumptions. Eleanor should quit those worldly vanities unsuitable for a woman – and be an explorer's wife.

Franklin's demand gave the gamble Eleanor was taking by marrying him an alarming new complexion. Unlike Isabella Parry, Eleanor Porden could not expect marriage to hold out the prospect of enlarged freedom. She already went where she liked, and said what she cared to, 'without any body minding it'. The father who had educated her, and encouraged her interests in literature and science, was now dead, leaving her moneyed and, for the moment, as mistress of her own destiny. She was presently responsible to herself for the propriety of her behaviour. This rare independence – reserved for tenacious widows and strong-minded brotherless daughters – was an anomaly in the society of the time, though slightly more likely to arise in the professional classes Eleanor belonged to. Eleanor nonetheless had been prepared to exchange it, for marriage to a man she had supposed was attracted to the very qualities of mind in her that made her independent life possible. Now Franklin proposed that she quit her occupation and surrender her moral judgement to him; he invited her to live exclusively through him and through his occupation. For a woman without the experience of moving in a wider sphere this might have been a tempting proposition, with its offer of a role in the public life of a distinguished man. Franklin had not noticed that Eleanor was otherwise placed, any more it seems than he had understood the difference between her taking pleasure in his distinction (she did), and devoting herself vicariously to it. Eleanor enlightened him. Risky though it was for a woman to negotiate a marriage unsupported by the counsel of relatives, it also meant that she was in a position to withdraw from her own arrangements without unbearable family ructions. In a long, tough letter – probably the most considered letter she ever wrote – she refused to marry him under his new terms. Some of the reasons she gave were deft patriarchal alibis. She said, for instance, that she was obliged to write in order to edit her father's literary remains, and a daughter's duty to a father took priority over a wife's to a husband. But most of her arguments were uncompromising: explicit refusals, with the course of her life wagered on Franklin's response, to adopt the role of waiting wife, forever looking on, assured that the chance to follow Franklin in spirit to the clean poles would be a noble substitute for everything else.

'When I requested my sister to mention to you that I expected the full indulgence of my literary pursuits, both as to writing or publication, I certainly considered that I was asking no favour, claiming no concession.' Before his friends had made him try to take his future wife in hand, he had after all admired her writing, profusely. 'From all this I should undoubtedly have concluded, that if on your return from a Polar, or any other Expedition, I had presented to you . . . these works . . . I should have brought you an acceptable offering. Imagine then, – (but I believe you will not imagine,) the pain which your answer gave me . . .' And she linked her poems with the Arctic disappearances he planned, in what amounted to a claim of moral equality. If she was willing to endure his departures, she was due an equivalent endurance from him:

One word too on the subject of your Expedition. Whatever your objections may be, and I pretend not to guess them, you must feel that nothing which I might publish could possibly give you one tenth part of the uneasiness which the Expedition must necessarily cost me, but I know that you ought to undertake it, and therefore you should find me the last person in the world that would endeavour to detain you. It is indeed my most earnest hope that you would never suffer a consideration for me to influence your mind for a moment on any such occasion; but why should you wish to deprive me of the only employment that could really interest me in your absence?

To his credit, Franklin capitulated. Eleanor's ultimatum overcame the advice of the evangelical friends. Perhaps he was swayed by her strong suggestion that a sensible man does not rob his beloved of the liveliness he first loved in her; nor a decent one steal her occupation, when she accepts so straightforwardly an occupation on his part which might give a much more conventional woman pause. The alliance, or misalliance, proceeded. After a further row over the propriety of receiving visitors from outside the family on the Sabbath (necessary, if you keep a salon), they were publicly engaged in May, and married the same August. A child, also named Eleanor, was born in the summer of 1824. Apparently they were happy. But Franklin was still to have it demonstrated to him that Eleanor had meant exactly what she said; her understanding of the contract she had entered was strict.

Childbirth caused her a lingering illness, eventually diagnosed as recurrent tuberculosis, and by January 1825 she had grown extremely weak. Franklin was supposed to sail the next month for the Arctic; in a sudden volte-face of priorities, he told her he would delay the expedition. She refused to let him. To have him linger at the bedside on her account would count as 'detaining' him, she thought – would be allowing piety to interfere with independence. Under compulsion, Franklin did sail in February. And Eleanor did not, as it turned out, wait for him in any style, approved or otherwise. Instead, incommunicado in the Arctic, Franklin waited for news of his wife for the duration of the expedition, finding when he returned that he had been a widower since 22 February 1825, five days after his departure.

The role that Eleanor declined, Lady Jane accepted. Not that Jane Griffin was a doormat or a dormouse. However little equipped Franklin had been to comprehend Eleanor's difficulties, he remained attracted to women whose minds moved faster than his, whose company threw him into unaccustomed areas of judgement and feeling. They represented perhaps a modest Other, a stimulatingly foreign mental landscape he could not cope with very well if the woman in question, like Eleanor, pressed her points or was given to insistence. Once again, when Franklin remarried in November 1828, he attached himself to somebody of sharp temperament and metropolitan experience. A friend of Eleanor Porden's, Jane Griffin knew the D'Israelis and Maria Edgeworth; could lobby successfully on behalf of her favoured candidate for a professorship; had her bumps felt by a famous phrenologist; possessed an insatiable appetite for travel. Her first encounters with explorers came at the dinner-parties in the early 1820s which marked the Arctic officers' entrance into polite society, and Miss Griffin even joked with Captain Ross over her own suitability as Arctic material: 'he asked me if I would accompany him – I accepted the invitation with alacrity, & he told me that I came 6th upon his list, for that he meant to take 12 young ladies with him'. Her cast of mind was strongly critical, and she inclined towards dissection in the word-portraits she drew of her large acquaintance. One source of rueful dissatisfaction in her marriage would be the constant bland benevolence with which Sir John reported other people's doings in *his* letters. 'You describe every body alike as being so amiable and agreeable, that I cannot tell one from the other,' she wrote; she would have preferred, in the words she used to reprove a polar captain in the 1850s, that he 'seek out the *faults* & not the virtues only'.

Yet she had personal reasons for falling in with the definition of wedlock which offered a man's wife a securely vicarious place in his life: experience through him, ambition through him. Marrying Franklin at the age of thirty-eight, with an impressive social circle and journeys around Europe behind her, she nonetheless lacked Eleanor's sense of precious, precarious autonomy. Her anxieties ran the other way. It alarmed her that her travels, and her evident resourcefulness in the face of Abroad, might call attention to her as a freak, one of those sports of nature who crossed gender boundaries by too easily crossing geographical ones. She had no intention of giving up travelling (indeed she took advantage of Franklin's next command, in the Mediterranean, to see Egypt, Palestine, Greece, and Turkey) but she wanted it set firmly in place, authorised by gender rules. Much more than a disguise or an alibi – a gloss of passivity on an active passion – was involved, though under the licence of marriage she would, as things turned out, exercise great practical freedom. She wanted to set a sure bodily distance between herself and unwomanliness; by making a declaration of utter loyalty to a man, to secure herself a physical presence feminine beyond all ambiguity. 'I feel nothing but something like shame', she wrote after five years of married life,

of being thought a *strong bodied*, as well as strong minded person, bold, masculine, independent, almost every thing in short that I most dislike . . . I hope I shall never be talked of as one of your bold, clever, energetic women, fit for anything. I am no doubt possessed of great energy and ardour, but I would rather hide than show it. It is perpetually combated and restrained by physical weakness and infirmities, and is combined, though many people are not aware of this, with an *intense* degree of constitutional shyness and timidity, and an excessive susceptibility of ridicule . . .

Marriage therefore offered a transformation of her embarrassingly assertive qualities: it transposed them into a safe key. As she dissolved her own interests into Franklin's, she gained a proper vehicle for her energy. And she welcomed the implications for her own identity. Although her route to wifely compliance had been an eccentric one, quite unconnected to the narrow certainties of Franklin's religion, she embraced the tenets of devotion to his character, his achievements, his strong body. 'My personal vanities and egoistic sensibilities have been absorbed in you ever since I married,' she told him, 'and I feel no satisfaction in any sense of superiority, such as you sometimes attribute to me, but the greatest joy and purest delight in all that *you* possess over me.' Unlike an Isabella Parry, complying without conscious reflection to her guide and teacher, Lady Jane would will compliance. Always she occupied her role decisively. She deliberately forewent the customary legal arrangements that guarded a woman's dowry, so that her money became Franklin's outright on their wedding day.

The difference between Franklin's first and second wives partly indicates a difference of eras. Born, in fact, four years earlier than her predecessor, Jane Franklin arrived at her legendary status in a changed climate. The persona she had willed into existence suited the temperament of the mid-nineteenth century. By the time of her fame, she inhabited a social world that was dizzying its inhabitants by the speed with which it dissolved inheritance after inheritance from the past. Modern times meant unprecedented wealth, unprecedented social mobility – and unprecedented pressure on the private sphere of family and marriage to compensate for these public insecurities. The bourgeois family was to be a fortress against the heartless reign of cash and commodities in the outer world. Ideally, home was supposed to re-create in little the warmth and loyalty and good humour that the Victorians imagined society had had before modern political economy stripped it away. Merry England had gone: all the more important to have merry times around the hearth. Home too, of course, was really a concept in flux. But the intense anxiety that it *should* be stable and safe produced heroes and heroines of private life, when a famous family was threatened by spectacular catastrophe – such as the paterfamilias vanishing in the frozen North. This sort of thing the newspapers boosted into common knowledge, endorsing the story with their coverage of it, just as they enthusiastically covered other threats to the family, like aristocratic divorce cases, or the suburban wife-murders that now began to take on their classic form, with poison administered behind closed doors on quiet streets. And the anxious elevation of the family had also encouraged an anxious insistence as to how the vital securities of private life should be talked and thought about. The comfortable classes had needed secure meanings for words like 'father' and 'mother', 'husband' and 'wife'. In effect they had found them in the evangelical vision of male and female roles. Eleanor Porden, defying John Franklin in the 1820s, had been able to name his ideas of marriage as 'your prejudices, for so I must be permitted to call them . . .' By the 1850s, they were prejudices no longer: they were the mainstream convictions that defined the proper stuff of lives; and the language that had once been special to the pious had become a nervous common discourse.

Lady Jane also entered Franklin's life at a point in his middle age when both exploration and Eleanor Porden appeared to be receding behind him. After his sojourn on the Mediterranean station, he served as Governor of Tasmania into the early 1840s, more than a trifle out of his depth where the politics of convict settlement were concerned, but on the surface of it an ornament to the colonial service with a fine polar past. In Hobart he maintained a keen interest in the magnetic observatory, and acted host at the governor's mansion to the younger Ross, when the first British Antarctic Expedition passed through. Lady Jane was his hostess: expert, amiable, in full ladylike command of naval protocol, feuding on his behalf behind the scenes. To her his exploring was a dormant component of his reputation, rather than a present occupation. Despite her advice early on that he 'strive . . . to resume your chieftainship in your own peculiar department', they had never been separated by the Arctic. Indeed from her point of view, when he sailed on his last voyage in 1845, at the age of fifty-nine, it was his first such departure – agitated for by her in the face of the Admiralty's preference for a less aged officer, because the clouded departure from Tasmania made it necessary to revive his former eminence, but novel to her nevertheless. With this tenacious guardian of his interests at Franklin's elbow, he can have had little incentive to recall in much detail the shocks and challenges of his brief marriage with Eleanor. If any remnants of puzzled respect for female independence showed themselves in him, Jane quashed them lovingly. *She* was not 'superior' (the term is telling). A conventionally good man, he must have found it increasingly hard, after two decades, to preserve in memory the outline of Eleanor's real awkwardness, for which he had once been prepared to compromise his views. Family piety was a different matter. The memory of Eleanor underwent the usual fate of grains of sand that find their way into the unctuous interior of an oyster. In the course of the sea-change, her poetry was recruited into family lore as a charming accomplishment. After Franklin's death, family friends reprinted the Green Stockings valentine in a private keepsake volume for Franklin's descendants, titled – unfortunately – *A Brave Man and his Belongings*. There remained the living presence of the second Eleanor, also a difficult woman, and a thorn in her stepmother's side in the early 1850s. Ferocious injunctions to silence, and hissed reminders of her duty, were directed at her on Lady Jane's behalf by Sophy Cracroft, for she married a clergyman without much ecclesiastical leverage, and wanted to have Franklin declared dead so that her share of the estate would be released. This would have cracked beyond repair the façade that the country's polar first family presented to the world. It was essential to Lady Jane that the possibility of Franklin's survival be preserved intact in the public mind. The family's patience and loyalty to the absent man had likewise to seem axiomatic to the public: they served the very practical purpose of sustaining pressure on the government. At this stage funds were found, the Admiralty mounted search expeditions, because Franklin needed rescue. When the Admiralty finally succumbed to common sense in 1854, and removed Franklin and his crews from the roster of current personnel in the Navy List, Lady Jane mounted a sartorial protest. She abandoned the funereal black she had worn till then, and started dressing in green and pink. Everyone interpreted her complex piece of social semaphore correctly: though she had mourned his *absence* readily, she declined to mourn his *death* until evidence of it was forthcoming, which implied further efforts. From then on, the search for Franklin was to be a spiritual responsibility rather than a rescue mission. Presumably, however, Lady Jane's decision that the family's obligation to Franklin overruled the interests of the survivors made the dead hand weigh no less heavily on her stepdaughter's prospects.

As with her dress, so with the whole of Lady Jane's social being: her duty to Franklin fashioned her. She encouraged people to perceive her in relation to the missing hero, so that on meeting her they felt themselves to be in the presence of the tragedy. She was, after all, visible as the lost sailors themselves could not be. An encounter with her brought a direct tug of sympathy. By making a spectacle of herself, at dinners, in drawing-rooms, on public platforms, she kept the plight of Franklin in sight, and therefore in mind; her present body testifying to the absent bodies in the Arctic, almost implying them. The successful femininity with which she did this – signalling for help with her crinoline – struck no-one as strange. The wife now spoke for the husband, now stood in for the husband, precisely because his interests were her paramount aim. In law a wife passed control of her body into her husband's keeping, and her ambitions and hopes for worldly advancement were likewise supposed to be transferred to his career. The exceptional circumstance of Franklin's disappearance allowed Lady Jane to transform this posture of wifely support into a stance of active advocacy. He wasn't there; but the marriage was preserved in her behaviour. She had the conventional relationship of wife to husband squarely behind her. Indeed, she displayed it in exemplary form. Moreover, while her presence in a room appealed to the protective instincts of admirals and mayors, millionaires and philanthropists, it would also evoke the tenderness of women, and sometimes their tears. She concentrated experiences shared by many women into a famous pattern of grief. The sight of her would pull on the webwork of feeling tying mothers to sons and sisters to brothers; it would recall the stories women told to each other about missing menfolk, mother to daughter and sister to sister. In October 1849 Lady Jane and Sophy Cracroft were in Scotland, pursuing a rumoured sighting of Franklin by a whaler that had recently returned to port. While searching for lodgings in Edinburgh, Miss Cracroft wrote to her mother, they had one more illustration of the magic effect of Lady

Jane's presence. From it they drew a point about class, though they might have drawn one about gender.

A widow woman with a nice face appeared & shewed us very handsome rooms wh. she has let for the winter after some day near the 3rd of this month. She asked more than my Aunt wished to give, tho' it was by no means much for such rooms. – My Aunt said if she wd. let her have them upon her own terms she wd. take them at once, adding 'my stay is uncertain & depends upon circumstances –' & named herself. I wish you cd. have seen the poor woman's face of joy & interest as she said 'Oh Ma'am if you are Lady Franklin I'll jist [*sic*] let you have it' & then she went on to say how happy & thankful she was to see there had been news of the Expn. 'I could have cried for joy my Lady' & she *was* fairly stopped by her tears. She went on to say that she had a daughter a teacher, who brought her the newspaper containing the intelligence & called her from the top of the house, to hear it. Another proof of the extraordinary enthusiasm manifested by *all* classes.

Usually, as in this case, Lady Jane dropped the shield of anonymity in conversations with strangers. Their knowledge of who she was protected her much better than their ignorance would have done from tactless comments on the Franklin affair, or vulgar familiarity. Knowledge of her name established rules for conversation with her; it stipulated an attitude of reverent attention to her story. When people knew her identity, and could gauge her bearing, they understood as well the terms on which she was displaying herself, and, at least in her earshot, governed their tongues. As she knew, physical notoriety was the inevitable result of having a public body. Less agreeable encounters were possible. The same month, she and Sophy found themselves trapped, incognito, in a Scottish railway compartment with three men. Before they knew it, the moment for decent disclosure had passed.

Presently the one on my right-hand (I was in a middle seat) said to the two opposite: 'What do you think of this report abt. Sir J Franklin's Expedition?' One . . . said he did not believe it . . . & talked some little time abt. it when one observed 'Lady F is in Edinburgh is she not?' The first speaker said that we had left it – that he had been invited to meet us at Lady Elliotts, but cd. not go, that he had met Capt. Elliott one day who said he was going to meet us in the Gallery of Paintings, '&' the speaker added, 'I met him afterwards with them in Princes Street.' Another asked 'did you meet Lady F' 'No' he replied 'I mean I saw her but in this way in passing. – She has a very yellow complexion.' They said some more things, but I really was in such a fever that I did not hear what they were. Can you imagine anything more unpleasant & painful?

Technically Franklin's, Lady Jane's body was no longer her own in a director way once it had been deliberately exposed to the gaze – the *male* gaze – of the curious; and although the proper responses could be cultivated in people, they could not be entirely depended upon.

Alfred Tennyson, linked to the Franklin family through his wife Emily, liked what he saw when he looked at Lady Jane. She was 'a great favourite' of his, Emily Tennyson confided to her diary, much later. 'He says she is charming, so clever yet so gentle & such a lady.' But Lady Jane was not, in fact, so very gentle. In her un-Arctic moments of leisure she already exercised, of course, the conventional influence on affairs that a lady could. (She and Sophy were engaged in promoting the emigration of marriageable young women to the colonies, which allowed the two of them to lecture captive audiences of poor people on the benefits of personal hygiene.) But by inhabiting so absolutely the authorised persona of 'a lady', by expressing her cleverness and her force of will in the ladylike mode, Lady Jane won – a familiar paradox – a freedom of action far greater than ever came to, say, Isabella Parry, the dutiful wife of a present husband, or to Eleanor Porden, who had attempted to mark off two separate zones of independence for herself and for Franklin. She won, naturally, a new reason to travel. There were captains to interview and influential ears to be bent throughout the British Isles, and in America as well; and later, after Franklin's death became a certainty, his reputation could still be furthered by her presence around the world. Towards the end of her life, she and Sophy saw Hawaii (they ate compote of pigeons with King Kamehameha IV), and then in Alaska set eyes for the first time on a piece of that Arctic which had consumed so much of her attention. Those who greeted her were glad to welcome a legend. Those who had dealt with her earlier, in the Admiralty and in government, knew that she was also a practical force to be reckoned with. In her hands the network of sympathy and sentiment she inspired became a tool of redoubtable influence. Gaining the adoration of Dickens, and through Dickens a sympathetic hearing when the Crimean War was distracting public attention; allowing Chandos Hoskyns Abrahall to dedicate his epic poem 'Arctic Enterprise' to her 'in Admiration/of/Her Patience, Perseverance, and Fortitude,/Under Trials Unexampled/in the Annals/of Her Country'; accepting the filial regard of Bellot: each contact, each successful impression made, broadened a power exerted in equally informal ways, to advance Franklin's cause. At one point it was necessary to rig the distribution of gifts off a Christmas tree so a party of visiting Americans went home pleased. With Sophy Cracroft at her side as a go-between, and when occasion required as a mouthpiece for her displeasure, she could blight or accelerate careers, bestow or withhold the sanction of her reputation. No other nineteenth-century woman raised the cash for three polar expeditions, or had her say over the appointment of captains and lieutenants. When the Admiralty seemed torpid, or reluctant to act, she pushed; when search ships were dispatched in directions she disapproved of, she launched whispering campaigns against their commanders; and when, critically, the news from the Arctic threatened the moral image of Franklin's party, she fought to preserve the ground on which the ideals of womanhood and those of polar exploration coincided.

The story of her management of the Franklin cannibalism scandal is intricate. In 1849 it had been the idea of a Dr Richard King, proponent of land-based exploration, that an overland search should be mounted towards the mouth of the Great Fish River. King was, in fact, quite right about the likely route Franklin's crews would follow if forced to abandon ship in the ice. Jane approved the plan, but disliked its source in a man who had prophesied, on Franklin's departure, that the Admiralty was dispatching him 'to form the nucleus of an iceberg'. 'Of Dr King himself I wish to say nothing,' she observed then to Sir James Ross. 'I do not desire that he shd be the person employed, but I cannot but wish that the Hudson's Bay company might receive instructions . . . to explore those parts.' Ross accordingly vetoed King's suggestion and, privately convinced the Great Fish would yield nothing, let the whole question lapse. It was four years later that an Orkney-born physician on Hudson's Bay business, Dr John Rae, did investigate the Arctic shore just there. His information was second-hand – it came from Eskimo witnesses – but shocking.

I met with Esquimaux in Pelly Bay from one of whom I learned that a party of 'white men' (Kabloonans) had perished from want of food some distance to the westward . . . Subsequently further particulars were received, and a number of articles purchased, which places the fate of a portion (if not of all) of the then survivors of Sir John Franklin's long-lost party beyond a doubt; a fate as terrible as the imagination can conceive . . .

The Eskimo informants claimed to have walked among the scattered bodies and scattered equipment of the expedition: 'From the mutilated state of many of the corpses, and the content of the kettles, it is evident that our miserable countrymen had been driven to the last resource . . .' Until then, Lady Jane had liked Dr John Rae. Bellot danced with Rae's niece in Orkney; Lady Jane took cherry brandy with Rae's impeccably dignified mother. Although his humble origins and his employment as an Arctic professional put him outside the favoured community of gentlemanly naval types, he had counted, in her eyes, as a rough diamond. Now she changed her mind about a person who would accuse her husband of the grossest bodily transgression imaginable, and changed at the same time her opinion of Rae's style of masculinity. 'Dr Rae has cut off his odious beard,' she wrote when he paid her the unavoidable courtesy call, 'but looks still very hairy and disagreeable.' At once she set the machinery in motion to refute his moral libel. And there was indeed a case for him to answer: he had, himself, not seen any of the kettles of human flesh. His story rested on the reliability of the Eskimos. There would never, in fact, be any confirming evidence of the cannibalism, while on the other hand it would emerge that accusations of man-eating were a standard name-blackening part of Inuit culture. (Cannibalism was abhorred among the northern peoples because in times of extreme dearth it might well be resorted to. It was horrible, but it was within the compass of things that happened, rather than standing for an ultimate reversal of moral standards.) But though these points were swiftly

made, the reaction to Rae was dominated by moral considerations –
by the unthinkability of his story. Many articles, letters to the press,
and pamphlets articulated a shocked refusal to believe in the scale of
moral collapse implied by Rae. If the choice lay between believing an
Eskimo, and believing in the moral fortitude of English explorers, then
the choice was easy. 'All savages are liars,' said a *Times* editorial. From
Lady Jane's point of view, it was essential to assert that Sir John's
character was sufficient refutation. Dickens, prompted, brought the
controversy to the pages of *Household Words*, and replied to Rae himself
in a mighty two-part statement of faith (liberally peppered, of course,
with blood-chilling stories of proven marine cannibalism, for the
entertainment of his readers).

In weighing the probabilities and improbabilities of the 'last resource,' the
foremost question is – not the nature of the extremity; but the nature of the
men. We submit that the memory of the lost Arctic voyagers is placed, by
reason and experience, high above the taint of this so-easily allowed
connection; and that the noble conduct and example of such men, and of
their own great leader himself, under similar endurances, belies it, and
outweighs by the weight of the whole universe the chatter of a gross handful
of uncivilised people, with a domesticity of blood and blubber.

Like Dickens, Lady Jane accepted that 'Dr Rae may be considered to
have established, by the mute but solemn testimony of the relics he has
brought home, that Sir John Franklin and his party are no more.' Like
Dickens again, she refrained from public criticism of Rae's own
character. He received restrained acknowledgement in official circles
for his undoubted efforts in the search. She did, however, attempt to
have Rae denied the Admiralty's £10,000 reward for conclusive
information upon Franklin's fate – on the grounds that the search
must continue. Her appeal to Parliament skilfully deployed the
argument of her femininity:

Though it is my humble hope and prayer that the Government of my country
will themselves complete the work they have begun, and not leave it to a weak
and helpless woman to attempt the doing that imperfectly which they
themselves can do so easily and well, yet, if need be, such is my painful
resolve, God helping me.

Though Rae collected the cash, he never received acclaim equivalent to that lavished on the authorised heroes of the search. Nor was he ever knighted, unlike them. With Lady Jane he was *persona non grata*, and she certainly never considered him for a role in her final expeditions, as at one point he had hoped. She had arranged, so far as she could, to defuse his contention, restating, against the grisly picture of degradation he drew, her husband's untarnishable masculinity, and citing its God-given complement, her devoted womanliness. (There is an echo in her appeal, I think deliberate, of Elizabeth I's Tilbury speech. When the times demanded it, and – unless the Admiralty acted – there were no men to hand, it was a moving spectacle, not an offensive one, for a frail-bodied woman to find an almost male determination within her. This was a culturally sanctioned bending of gender. 'Though I have the body of a woman, I have the heart and stomach of a man': Elizabeth I. 'If the wife is such a man, what can the husband be?': an admiring Orkney boatman, on Lady Jane.) But the best she could possibly obtain for Franklin, on the cannibalism charge, was a verdict of *not proven*; and the 'taint' Dickens had denied existed would linger until decisive information could be had, complicating immensely her final effort to secure his reputation.

For once it was clearly impossible to save Sir John, she had set her sights on vindicating him, instead, as an explorer. He must be shown to have succeeded in the task the Admiralty had set him: 'success' in navigating the North-West Passage now being carefully redefined as an impalpable goal that did not require one to return alive, or to pass on the news to the world. And as the eastern side of the Arctic archipelago was combed for signs of Franklin, the search drawing ever closer to the known regions on the western side, without turning up more than a thin trail of detritus, it began to look as if the expedition had indeed reached some spot near to the midpoint of the Passage. But in 1852 a Captain McClure of HMS *Investigator*, probing the islands and channels from the Alaskan side for the Admiralty, had himself crossed the debateable ice at the centre of the archipelago, and joined the separate maps. Though compelled soon after to abandon ship, and be rescued in his turn, McClure was awarded Parliament's £5000 prize for first discovery of the Passage. His commander Collinson gracefully acknowledged that McClure had not 'succeeded in the grand object which animated our endeavours' – finding Franklin – but the award seemed to close the competition.

Facts were not, however, the sole decisive point in interpreting the success or failure of exploration. The repeated acknowledgement of exploration's moral value had given moral judgement a say. Lady Jane had on her side the enormous force of sentiment in Franklin's favour; the case she was now making for him was an amalgam of geographical and moral considerations, cleverly balanced so that, if a sufficient minimum of geographical achievement could be shown, the debt that the nation owed to Franklin's pious sacrifice would compel it to honour him. Some of her friends were ready to assert that Franklin, not McClure, deserved the laurels for 'forging the last link' of the Passage. Those friends who dissented, like Captain Sherard Osborn, were not forgiven for years. Then the cannibalism story broke, striking at Franklin's character, and thereby weakening him exactly on the grounds she had elected for his defence. Until the matter was resolved, she would get no official support for her claim. (Here lay the weakness in Jane Franklin's deft purchase on shared values, values shared by Parliament, the Admiralty, and the nominating committees of learned societies.) Pressure was beginning to grow for a monument to Franklin, but Lady Jane delayed, unwilling for the Franklin affair to end on ambiguous terms. She would have no shadow cast upon Franklin's empty tomb, no compromising references to his 'efforts', no language restrained by unspoken suspicions. What she required was a conclusion to the search that would both dispel the cannibal taint, and provide a sufficient demonstration of discovery.

In 1859, she obtained just this. Leopold McClintock, commanding her yacht *Fox*, returned with papers from a cache at Point Victory on King William Island. They gave, marvellously, an exact date for Franklin's death: 11 June 1847. Franklin had died early enough, a good two years before the miserable remnants of his crew either did or did not take to eating each other. Whatever the truth of Rae's report, Franklin was clear of reponsibility. And he had also died late enough, when the expedition ships *Erebus* and *Terror* were already deep-frosted into their final positions in the Victoria Strait. The general rigours of the Arctic had killed the elderly Franklin: starvation had done for the rest, over the following two years. If it constituted discovering the North-West Passage to die half-way along it, on the threshold of mapped shores, Franklin had done so. An article 'by an officer of the *Fox*' presented a gratifying view of the case to the readers of the new *Cornhill Magazine*:

They all perished, and, in dying in the cause of their country, their dearest consolation must have been to feel that Englishmen would not rest until they had followed up their footsteps, and had given to the world what they could not then give – the grand result of their dreadful voyage – their Discovery of the North-West Passage. They had sailed down Peel and Victoria Straits, now appropriately named Franklin Straits, and the poor human skeletons lying upon the shores of the waters in which Dease and Simpson had sailed from the westward bore melancholy evidence of their success.

Dreadfully grand, melancholically successful. There were now, at least, grandeur and success to set against the darkness of the story.

The moral impediment removed from the way of a primarily moral gesture, the Royal Geographical Society was freed to award, and Lady Jane to accept, their Founder's Medal. And instructions could at last be given to the memorial artists. Franklin's busts and statues identified him as the Discoverer of the North-West Passage. The curious shift away from geographical criteria for success in exploration was not remarked, because the possibility of seeing it as a moral enterprise had been latent there ever since it entered the public imagination. Now, though, the representations of exploration caught up insensibly with the pursuit itself, and began to solidify into something like an English orthodoxy. This involved a little more than just the famous English reverence for disaster; it combined bodily loss with spiritual gain, conquest with abnegation. Sealed with a widow's grief, in a century much absorbed by the forms and feelings of grief, it confirmed an orthodox place for women, who might lament at the destruction of men like Franklin or Bellot in a white blur beyond the physical limits of their world, yet (so to say) within their traditional province. Lady Jane had, after all, largely achieved Franklin's vindication from *home*, operating upon the domestic perceptions and domestic reflexes which helped govern the meanings of Arctic events.

The final public ceremony in Franklin's honour remembered the pair of them exactly as Lady Jane would have wished. She died two weeks before the unveiling of his cenotaph in 1875, in Westminster Abbey, the national shrine of fame. Too ill to write the words herself, she succeeded, as ever, in inspiring the right reaction in others. He, it said, 'died . . . off Point Victory, in the Frozen Ocean, the beloved chief of the crews who perished with him in completing the discovery of the North-West Passage'; she, the erector of his monument, 'after long waiting, and sending many in search of him, herself departed, to seek and to find him in the realms of light'. There was an epitaph by Tennyson –

> Not here! the white North has thy bones; and thou
> Heroic sailor-soul,
> Art passing on thine happier voyage now
> Toward no earthly pole

– a formulation which beautifully elided material failure with the pursuit of higher goals. Sailing became pilgrimage, the pole (towards which Franklin had aimed only in the loosest sense) an emblem of the spirit's *ultima Thule*; and Franklin's actual voyage was transformed into the shadow, briefly unhappy, of the true journey. The Victorians liked to offer spiritual translations of their earthly enterprises. Here an unexceptional exercise in piety, from an expert pen, meshed three experiences of exploration. Sir John had strived; Lady Jane had waited; Tennyson, like thousands of others, had looked on, approving Jane Franklin's demeanour, sorrowfully reading aloud the *Cornhill* article to his wife, presenting young Lionel Tennyson with the improving Arctic children's book *Peter the Whaler* for a birthday present. The three now made three sides of the monument, in sombre funerary balance.

But, just as eccentric private motives had gone to form Lady Jane's formidably orthodox femininity, so gender had been involved in stranger ways in her spiritual position than were allowed to appear on the calm, marble surface. There had been a period of anguish in 1849 and 1850 when Jane Franklin and Sophy Cracroft had dabbled in clairvoyance. *Not knowing* what was happening in the Arctic had been the hardest thing to bear: hoping and praying suspendedly, without the assurance that the subject of the hopes and prayers was even alive to benefit from them. 'I wish we could see you in a glass as they do in the fairy-tales,' Jane had written in her very first letter to her departed husband, actually received by him when outbound in Orkney. For a while she changed her mind, imagining how painful it would be to see, yet be unable to alter, 'any dreadful difficulty' the ships might 'have yet to overcome'. But when the passage of time made it essential to guess at the expedition's state – when, in fact, Franklin had already died – Lady Jane resorted to the human equivalent of magic mirrors. 'There has been no attempt to look into futurity, but simply to ascertain that wh. now is by means of an extended state of vision', Sophy reassured her sister: a clouded claim to spiritual legitimacy, if an exact statement of the need. Dickens would certainly have been disturbed. When he mounted the spectacular pro-Franklin play *The Frozen Deep* at Tavistock House in 1857, he made Wilkie Collins rewrite the part of the old Scottish nurse, taking out her genuine powers of second sight. In the text that Dickens and his family performed, with cascading paper snow manufactured to the novelist's precise instructions, she appeared as a mere hysterical opportunist, coaxing fear out of the waiting womenfolk. 'The men are lost, a' lost; i' the land o' ice and snow', she croons. 'On the land o' ice and snow they shall never be found again!' Of course they *are* found again; and *The Frozen Deep*, significantly, shows the women rejecting sibylline intuitions of doom in favour of faith in their capable men. Nurse Esther stands revealed at the end as 'a Muddle-headed female . . . [who] sets up for a prophet'. Lady Jane concealed her experiments in extended vision less because of the dismissive scepticism they would arouse (she was fairly sceptical herself), than because they had this troubling association with a foolish, a hysterical femininity. And indeed it was an almost wholly female set of voices that offered her supernatural comfort. She hardly had to seek it out. On a couple of occasions she set up deliberate consultations, but otherwise she had only to open her ears to the dreams and visions of Franklin experienced by girls and women all over the country. Either their revelations figured in the newspapers, or were confided direct to her ladyship's postbag; each testifying to the entranced, uncanny moment at which the famous lost voyagers had appeared before their mind's eye; each presenting herself as an ordained intermediary, a message in a female bottle.

Some were ghoulish. Some were saccharine. Some were professionals with a knack for the telling detail, like 'E of Bolton' whose visions always observed the correct time-difference between Bolton and the Canadian Arctic. 'When the time there was nine or ten a.m. (four or five p.m. at Bolton) she wd say that such was the hour.' Some were known 'sensitives' questioned by inquisitive gentlemen: a letter to the *Manchester Guardian* reported a session with a woman 'perfectly uninstructed, and unable even to read or write' who, 'being cast into a mesmeric state' and given a map, 'puts her finger on the north-west side of Hudson's Bay'. Some were plainly crackers. 'My lady, I have took the liberty of thus a-Dressing you with a Line through whose hands I hope will forward to you this remarkable dream which I have often found too true . . . I saw in my dream 2 air Bloons a great distance off rising just like the moon – I said in my dreams to myself There's Sir J. Frankland.'

Apart from the evidence they give of the Franklin affair's place in the dream-life of British women, the psychic testimonies are remarkable as florid exercises by women in imagining the poles. Quite a number 'travelled' to the Arctic, over seas and into the jagged maze of the ice; otherwise the snow and ice appeared to them all at once, like a tableau, a sudden realisation of an Arctic scene. But the sailors themselves were naturally at the focus of the visions. It was the physical information about them – their state, their fate, their disposition on the face of the frozen ocean – that mattered most. The visions bound together the near and the far, jumping the miles in between with the speed of imagination, to deliver news of the absent male bodies, reports on limbs and frostbites and food supplies. The first clairvoyante Lady Jane and Sophy interviewed said that the explorers smelt comfortably of brandy.

The sensual solidity of the visions went along with the demand of the times for physical, corporeal reassurance about the dead and the missing. The 1850s were the decade in which spiritualism reached Britain from America. (It was invented by two sisters from New York State who could click their toe-joints at will. This unusual physical ability launched table-rapping, and the system of communication with dead relatives in which different numbers of unearthly knocks stood for 'yes' and 'no'. Later the sisters were to be scandalously linked with Dr Elisha Kane, the American searcher for Franklin: another curious connection between psychic and Arctic interests.) Lady Jane's adventures preceded by two or three years the organised arrival of the phenomenon, but the visions she sampled had a great deal in common with the later products of seances. Unlike orthodox religion, which it claimed to supplement rather than supplant, spiritualism would promise an almost embarrassingly bodily apprehension of the other world; where the churches could only say that your prayers were heard by a loving God, spiritualism could give you your dead child's hand to hold, seemingly materialised out of the air. Many of the characteristics of spiritualism were already present in the mishmash of mesmerism and Swedenborgian belief, at the end of the 1840s, that underwrote attention to the utterances of seers and clairvoyantes. In particular, spiritualism would share, and then would formalise in the role of the 'medium', the older sense that women were specially suited to spiritual communication, with their proper dominion over the sphere of grief, and their angelic function as dispensers of sympathy. A medium, leading a circle of hushed believers in a darkened room, supposedly acted as vehicle or vessel for the visiting spirits. She drew her ambiguous authority from conventional characterisations of women's bodies as passive and receptive things; yet 'through' her, distinctly assertive presences would make themselves felt, acting with unfeminine boldness. In seances, believers were touched, tickled, and occasionally slapped ringingly round the face. Opponents of spiritualism agreed with supporters in putting the qualities of the female body at the centre of the issue: denunciations tended to have a misogynist edge to them, and to be alarmed at the deceitful, uncontrolled physicality of spiritualist practices. (Mediums were celebrated but semi-respectable people, constantly guarding their reputations; but it could be argued that there was a certain structural kinship between the behaviour of mediums and what Lady Jane, universally admired, did in the service of her absent husband. Her impeccably ladylike presence stood for her husband's continuing absence; it acted first as emblem for him, then as his *memento mori*. Eschewing a 'strong body' herself, she reminded her audiences perpetually of the male bodies stranded in the Arctic. The far experience of exploration found a shape in her: the nation's medium for Franklin.)

In the same way, Lady Franklin's correspondents and counsellors of 1850 effectively made gateways, or channels, to revelation of their female bodies and identities. In tune with the perception of femininity as vague or fluid or unfixed, compared to masculinity, they emphasised that their utterances were ungoverned and unsought; it was the way they seemed to arrive without intention that gave them their fraction of authority. Speech like this recruited male prejudices in its favour. It conformed to expectations. As the test of the illiterate clairvoyante in Manchester suggests, men might find psychic predictions by women compelling because of their own assumptions about female ignorance. The mind of an unlettered woman must be a *tabula rasa*, a mental snowfield; she could have no opinion about Franklin's whereabouts, and therefore the steady movement of her finger on the map indicated the working of an inexplicable power. Whether slyly professional or innocently excited, the other visionaries too claimed sources for their visions in states of mind that were over the verge of conscious control: in trances, in reveries between sleep and waking, in the vague hinterlands of consciousness where images rose up and combined unbidden. Clouds rolled down and blocked the view when Lady Jane asked Ellen Dawson a question she could not answer (what direction the *Erebus* and *Terror* were moving in). It was one way of speaking on geographical, manly subjects – and being heard. And through the misty windows of these female bodies, the harder stronger bodies of the mariners could be glimpsed amidst the snows. When the news was good, the sailors tended to be arranged in stereotypical groupings; worshipping or receiving paternal authority, as the moral image of exploration suggested they would be. 'Sir J. was readg prayers to the crew, who knelt in a circle, with their faces upwards, lookg to him and appearing sorrowful,' according to E of Bolton. But bad tidings tended to strew the sailors direly about the ice, turning their hardness against them, producing a catastrophically physical tableau. The Manchester woman had Sir John himself alive, but the crews divided into parties and widely separated, with some dead 'in different postures under the snow'. She had seen one of the ships 'under water, with very thick timbers', a sunken skeleton rigidly disarranged. Though E of Bolton was generally reassuring, she said that, of the officers, 'one was dead (shelled)'. *Shelled* does not seem to have been a customary slang-word for *dead.* An *old shell* or, later, *shell-back*, meant an old sailor, weathered and toughened before the mast; *shell* could also name a tight military jacket for servicemen. Here, the associations with the sea and with a taut covering for the body seem to be supporting a precise and unpleasant visual image. She used the word as if the officer were a crab or a lobster, a crustacean ripped out of his protective armour, hardness meeting its nemesis. Something is perhaps at work here, a brutally unflinching sense of men reaching the end that men would, given their nature.

One case of supernatural advice stood out. Lady Franklin first heard of 'Weesy' Coppin of Londonderry when a letter reached her from a Captain Coppin of the Board of Trade.

About 12 months ago I lost a beloved Child and in about six weeks after her death she appeared to her Brothers and Sisters – I must remark here that I have four Children at present living, the Eldest Boy John 14 years old, the second is a girl named Anne of 10 years, the third a girl called Dora of 6 years and the 4th is a Boy called William of 2 years – the deceased was a girl a little under 4 years and between the 3rd and 4th child. The deceased Child Louisa appeared distinctly to the 3 Elder Children, and is constantly showing them scenes which I cannot now describe only so far as your interest is concerned the deceased speaks to her sister Anne by some chance the question was put is Sir J. Franklin Alive when to the surprise of Anne, the room they were in appeared to be filled with Ice some Channels and a Ship in one narrow creek or harbour between two Mountains of Snow and Ice in a Sort of delapidated State with Another in the distance and in a distinct Channel of water two Ships, the first had men on the deck and the second question put is Sir J. Franklin alive, if so make some signal, in a few Moments she describes a round-faced Man ascends the Mast and waves his hat the next question put Have they any Provisions, when the same person who ascended the mast takes a plate of flour and makes it into cakes, holds it to a fire described as made by throwing something like fat or oil on it. A [illegible] is also shown a Reindeer is seen on the ice and a man breaks a hole in the ice and takes up a fish. The question being asked what part of the Arctic ocean is S. J. Franklin in, the first scene completely disappears and on the wall are placed in large letters BS then P.RI – NF. These being the first letters shown and constantly lead me to believe that S John is in Prince Regent's Inlet off Barrow's Strait, likely in the Victory in Felix Harbour or not far from it at this moment. I am writing this the letters are placed on the wall the letters also E and T are after shown and SJF shall give you all the letters in rotation on the back of this sheet as they are described by the Child and perhaps you may understand them, from other circumstances which we have found [illegible] out as predicted by this Child.

Lady Jane took to Mr Coppin, who was prepared to put up a fair amount of money for her next Arctic search, and pressed her to check the truth of his dead daughter's suggestion. What his letter does not make clear, despite the vivid circumstantial detail and the intricate description of the cryptogram on the wall, is that he himself never saw any of the visions. 'Weesy' only appeared to the other children, who told their mother, who told Mr Coppin. We only have, as records of the affair, Coppin's transcribed letters to Lady Jane, and a much later book by an eccentric Liverpool vicar. Coppin presented the apparition through the filter of his own training as a surveyor, his own eager wish to be involved in the Franklin search. The Reverend J. Henry Skewes' *Sir John Franklin: A 'Revelation'* (1889) claims Weesy Coppin's message as a divine intervention. He improves the episode of the spectral writing so that it fits the celebrated biblical occasion when the hand of God spelled *Mene mene tekel upharsin* in Babylon, and he massages the content, to read 'in large round hand letters, about three inches in length . . . "Erebus and Terror. Sir John Franklin, Lancaster Sound, Prince Regent Inlet, Point Victory, Victoria Channel."' Which was the very place at which McClintock eventually found the traces of the expedition. On hearing the news, Skewes' Lady Franklin is supposed to have cried 'It is all true! It is all true!' Then, 'Light, as from an invisible world, now permeated her whole being. She was, as by seraphic force, raised to a plateau far above all the heights of human measurement.'

But there can just be retrieved, from behind these two screens, a somewhat different story, which suggests *The Turn of the Screw* more than the fifth chapter of the Book of Daniel. Apart from the two-year-old boy, the Coppin household was entirely female: since the death of Weesy, Captain Coppin had absented himself almost continuously on his tours of duty around Ulster. In the atmosphere of bereavement which clung to the villa, Mrs Coppin and her resident sister had heard, and not discouraged, the children's first tentative declarations that little Louisa was still about. With Mrs Coppin's nervous approval, Weesy's ghost developed into a spiritual barometer for the neighbour-hood, supposedly detecting the moment in the middle of the night when Mr Mackay next door expired. Such uncanny coincidences were the stuff of traditional folklore, and had nothing to do with the Arctic, but soon, with their mother and aunt's attention engaged, the children had progressed to relaying topical questions to Weesy. Mr Coppin had not yet heard of the manifestations. There ensued a series of comic attempts by Mrs Coppin to tell him during his flying fifteen-minute visits to the house to pick up clothes and travelling necessities. She finally arrested him with the information that invisible balls of blue fire were floating back and forth in the dimness at the corners of the ceiling. This was sufficiently electromagnetic an item to win the Captain's consideration, and the Arctic revelation, which followed shortly, held him for good. He took over, of course, redrafting his sister-in-law's unprofessional rendering of Weesy's magic chart; but though it then belonged to him to tell the world, the haunting, which had conferred domestic power on the children, and given the women an eerily pious occupation for their days, did have the immediate effect of making Captain Coppin's home interesting enough for him to stay in it. It is hard to avoid the conclusion that the entrance of the Arctic into the nursery might have had that aim, though without conscious acknowledgement. He had to listen, if he wanted the description of the round-faced man climbing the mast, and the sailor boring the fish-hole in the ice. He had to defer to the children's ability to see, and the women's ability to interpret, because he had missed the moment when (according to the unreliable Skewes) the snowy wastes materialising upstairs 'as if an actual Arctic reality, made [Anne] shiver with cold, and, as a consequence . . . clutch the dress of her aunt'. Once again it was taken for implicit evidence of the vision's authenticity that girls and women would not know what Arctic expeditions looked like, however many artists' impressions were printed in the illustrated papers. This time, however, with so eccentric a motive for the vision, it was a fine refinement that the absent body of a dead girl now pointed out the absent men: absence redoubled, or perhaps even tripled, if we figure in the absent Coppin himself, lost in the tundra of business beyond the front door. Weesy's vision retrieved, at least, one missing man.

There was a further association between the poles and the female body. The polar regions did not entirely elude the rage for personification which saw men plaster female identities to their ships and their railway engines, their nations and their arts. The naming of so many things as female inscribed the contemporary understandings of gender on every available surface. As a habit of mind, personification let Victorian men figure their relationships with objects, ideas, and places as repetitions (or enlargements) of their familiar relationships with women. It made a grammar from men's views of women as wives and daughters, sisters and lovers, that could be used to describe bays and headlands, schemes of urban improvement and shiny piston rings. But it dealt, of course, in imagined female types, rather than in individual observations: beneath the subtle and inflected uses it was put to, it was a crude grammar of the stereotypes that had the widest circulation, the greatest cultural potency.

Personifications of the poles were comparatively rare because the best-known characteristics of the ice worked as something of a deterrent. That cold, those scouring winds, that overt sterility: none matched the picture of motherhood in the grammar, or accorded with nymphdom. No goddess Arctica or Antarctica ever held up the horn of plenty in a mural. With a scientific effort of the imagination it *was* possible to make the marine fertility of the poles the basis for a personification: in the evolutionary romance *The Water Babies* Charles Kingsley seated 'Mother Carey' on an iceberg at the North

Pole, and had the numberless species of plankton flow out from her. At first Tom the chimney sweep can only see a peaked ice-form at the centre of the quiet polar sanctuary he has reached, where the good whales spout at peace, and microscopic life throngs, pink and opal and brown and yellow in the water. From nearer to, however,

it took the form of the grandest old lady he had ever seen – a white marble lady, sitting on a white marble throne. And from the foot of the throne there swum away, out and out into the sea, millions of new-born creatures, of more shapes and colours than man ever dreamed. And they were Mother Carey's children, whom she makes out of the sea-water all day long.

He expects 'to find her snipping, piecing, fitting, stitching . . . and so forth, as men do when they go to work to make anything'.

But, instead of that, she sat quite still with her chin upon her hand, looking down into the sea with two great grand blue eyes, as blue as the sea itself. Her hair was as white as the snow – for she was very very old – in fact, as old as anything which you are likely to come across, except the difference between right and wrong.

Instead of making the creatures, 'I sit here', she says, 'and make them make themselves.' She is in fact a new vision of Dame Kind, of female Nature – wittily adjusted to illustrate Darwinian biology, which Kingsley tweaks in turn to preserve the kindliness of Christianity. With her sisters Mrs Doasyouwouldbedoneby and Mrs Bedoneby-asyoudid, benign arbiters of the moral world, she presides over astonishing metamorphoses and gradual improvements in the world of living things; like Tom's own progress from blackened industrial chrysalis, to larval water-baby, to upstanding moral man.

But Kingsley's polar Mother Carey was exceptional, a piece of imagining that puts a name and a wise face to the providence Thomas Bewick had thought must have a purpose for the Arctic. And her body – which is really the process by which creatures generate themselves – scarcely resembles the declamatory female forms of the grammar. She dissolves into Nature itself. Only the marble of Kingsley's description agrees with the way that, for the most part, those personifications of the Arctic that there were set about giving it female flesh. With the obvious sorts of physical generosity excluded, these explored varieties of female chill, from cool chastity to deathly seductiveness. They gave their Arctics freezing bodies, whether for good or for ill; bodies from the mildly perverse pages of the personifying grammar, which dealt with imaginary women of power, icily splendid.

When Hans Christian Andersen's stories were first translated into English in 1846, they were immediately successful, reprinting in ever larger collections as he continued to write, until his death in the 1870s fixed the canon. Many adapted traditional Danish originals (Mrs Peachey's standard English edition was called *Danish Fairy Legends and Tales*, identifying Andersen as one of the wave of collectors who were cataloguing European folklore, nation by nation), but 'The Snow Queen', one of the most perfect, was entirely his own. It made an ideal winter's tale, for telling when the temporary snow of Denmark or England whitened the known landscape outdoors into a strange and incalculable terrain. In it he had invented a myth: new, but like the oldest myths organised around the most compellingly simple oppositions, between warmth and cold, emotion and reason, the wild and the tame. The Snow Queen herself is the presiding spirit of the cold, the queen of the bees that snowflakes resemble as they whirl in a winter wind. Little Kay succumbs to her because, with the fragment of glass from a goblin mirror in his eye, he cares more for numbers than the human heart. He sees the worm in a rose instead of its beauty. Only the inorganic, mathematical 'flowers' of the snow appeal to him. ' "See, how curious!" said Kay; "these are far more interesting than real flowers; there is not a single blemish in them; they would be quite perfect, if only they did not melt." ' Hitching his little sledge to her great one, the Snow Queen carries him away where snow never melts, to Lapland where, a reindeer tells Kay's friend Gerda, 'the Snow Queen has her summer tent; her strong castle is very far off, near the North Pole, on the island called Spitzbergen'. Even her summer house is the abode of perfect ice. 'The walls of the palace were formed of the driven snow, its doors and windows of the cutting winds . . . Vast, empty, and cold were the Snow Queen's chambers, and the Northern Lights flashed now high, now low, in regular gradations. In the midst of the empty, interminable snow-saloon lay a frozen lake . . .' Here

Kay labours at a monstrous ice-jigsaw, promised that if he makes the word *Eternity* the Snow Queen will give him the world and a pair of silver skates. Before he can seal his captivity with success at the puzzle, Gerda rescues him, and a warm tear washes the glass from his eye; but his seduction is of more present interest. What has the Snow Queen on her side, in the battle between her frosted adult femininity, and Gerda's warm innocent variety? Exactly the knowing rejection of childhood, and feeling, and change. She is a beautiful nightmare, not untender to her captive, and though she is an enemy to life – doves drop dead from their nest at her breath, while the guards of her palace are malign parodies in snow of snakes and bears and porcupines – right at her side the cold mounts to a height at which it no longer hurts, as in the fabled space at the centre of a storm. No-one likes to freeze, she says, inviting Kay in under her white furs. In place of cold she offers immunity, by surrender to a numbed null state, the sensation Keats called 'the feel of not to feel it'.

'Are you still cold?' asked she, and then she kissed his brow. Oh! her kiss was colder than ice, it went to his heart, although that was half frozen already; he thought he should die, – it was, however, only for a moment, – directly afterwards he was quite well, and no longer felt the intense cold around.

At her second kiss, Kay loses all memory of home. He begs for more, but ' "Now you must have no more kisses!" said she, "else I should kiss thee to death." '

Kay looked at her, she was so beautiful; a more intelligent, a more lovely countenance, he could not imagine; she no longer appeared to him ice, cold ice . . . in his eyes she was perfect, he felt no fear, he told her how well he could reckon in his head, even fractions; that he knew the number of square miles of every country, and the number of inhabitants contained in different towns. She smiled, and then it occurred to him that, after all, he did not yet know so very much . . .

The Snow Queen's manners are those of an amused *grande dame*, but she embodies the unbodying Arctic; a poised paradox. Were she a Snow King she might have the sombre grandeur of a cold god, a sort of blue-skinned Arctic titan on an ice throne; she could not, however, then represent, at least to small male Kay, the seductive attraction of frozen feeling, with that endless promise of more to learn, once fleshy distraction has ceased. And it is indeed in Kay, though Gerda is far more the heroine of the story than he is the hero, that the point of the Snow Queen's femaleness is registered. The two contending for him mirror each other. The Snow Queen is the inverse of Gerda; her sterility, her intellect, her icy composure, all take their force from being reversals of conventional female qualities. It is mythically apt that her roles as anti-mother and anti-wife should be vested in the lineaments of beauty, all emptied to white: white furs, white hair, white skin.

Dangerous kisses and the prospect of eternity also appear in George MacDonald's children's novel of 1871, *At the Back of the North Wind*. But 'North Wind' here, like Mother Carey in *The Water Babies*, is a figure of fantasy invented by an author with religious intentions, to mediate a Christian message; she serves, in effect, as an Arctic angel of death, and MacDonald means her to humanise his themes of hope and resurrection. MacDonald's child-hero Diamond, the ailing son of a carter, does not know the nature of the friend who steals in through the keyhole on a day of blast and bluster, and carries him away northward to the country 'at her back'. Diamond's innocence allows him to trust Death as she should be trusted, chattering amiably to her and receiving her caresses while they travel through the emerald and sapphire ice-floes. At the end of his journey he must pass on through her: she sits glacial and still at 90° north, allegorically Arctic, a 'doorstep' to heaven. Again the cold penetrates the boy-child, as the Snow Queen's kisses sank into Kay, but – so far as MacDonald is consciously concerned – to utterly different effect.

'You must walk on as if I were an open door, and go right through me.'
   'But that will hurt you.'
   'Not in the least. It will hurt you, though.'
   'I don't mind that, if you tell me to do it.'
   'Do it,' said North Wind.
   Diamond walked towards her instantly. When he reached her knees, he put out his hand to lay it on her, but nothing was there save an intense cold. He walked on. Then all grew white about him; and the cold stung him like fire.

He walked on still, groping through the whiteness. It thickened about him. At last, it got into his heart, and he lost all sense. I would say that he fainted – only whereas in common faints all grows black about you, he felt swallowed up in whiteness. It was when he reached North Wind's heart that he fainted and fell. But as he fell, he rolled over the threshold, and it was thus that Diamond got to the back of the north wind.

This was supposed to be a benign, if frightening, dissolution. North Wind's heart, as cold as death, loves Diamond fiercely nonetheless: the destination of his passage through her justifies its pain, which is, after all, for his own good. Her ice is purgatorial ice, with the same function as – the more common religious metaphor – purgatorial fire. But the degree of ascetic rapture in the passage remains disturbing. The fainting, the *swooning* loss of self Diamond undergoes resembles the anti-sensual sensuality of the Snow Queen's kiss; only MacDonald endorses it, suggesting an appetite set free, somehow, by the gendering of his story. His pleasure in North Wind cannot be named masochistic: that kind of label abolishes all delicate grades of intention. But where Andersen's tight and mythic design controls the implications of his Snow Queen, MacDonald's use of a female Arctic, looser and allegorical, spills extra meanings. North Wind has a distinctly erotic physical presence. Despite her mournful stance on her 'doorstep', she is most often seen in the story in violent motion, billowing and gusting and changing size, quite unlike the crystalline stillness of the Snow Queen. She has wreathed, sky-wide black hair; her enormous eyes are implacable pools of ultramarine; her strong white naked arms reach down from the sky to drown ships. Diamond's ease in her stormy company has the exposed feeling – in every sense the word 'exposure' has – of those dreams in which one finds oneself walking the chilly outdoors in one's pyjamas, or even less. For purposes of innocence, it seemed good to MacDonald for Diamond to spend the greater part of the novel in his nightshirt. Nightshirted he rides on her shoulder; nightshirted she stows him away among the nested flags of a German polar expedition; nightshirted he walks on the glassy surface of the bergs. Altogether this feminisation of the Arctic draws upon a profoundly ambiguous attitude to flesh, and on a view of women that is both fearful and excited. MacDonald sees the female body as gloriously punitive, ferociously divine. And, somehow, as being far bigger than the bare, forked bodies of men.

Immobile at last, her flesh not easily distinguishable from the ice, North Wind sits on her doorstep 'leaning forward with her hands in her lap, and her hair hanging down to the ground',

like one of the great figures at the door of an Egyptian temple, motionless, with drooping arms and head . . . Her face was as white as the snow, her eyes were blue as the air in the ice-cave, and her hair hung down straight, like icicles. She had on a greenish robe, like the colour in the hollows of a glacier seen from far off.

MacDonald may have been eccentric, but how common this posture is among the personifications! Mother Carey too sits like patience on a monument, and in a *Punch* cartoon of 1875 on the Nares North Pole expedition the convention can be seen at its most instant and unconsidered. *Punch*'s female North Pole is serenely virtuous and fixedly passive. The caption, WAITING TO BE WON, identifies her as a prize: no nymph of course, but a virgin of the snows signifying the chaste renown that the conquest of the pole will render to a determined suitor-explorer. Two polar bears snort at her feet. The berg she sits on, she also merges with: a sort of draped molar of ice sticking up into an arched dark space like an apse. Her veiling is icy. One extended hand adheres to the berg; the other holds a decorative spear. On her head she wears a spiked tiara of the same make as the crown on the Statue of Liberty. Her face is sub-sub-sub-Ingres, or, better, like the blank oval visage of an object in the artworks section of the Great Exhibition, displayed perhaps to illustrate the advantages of carving in soap, or the possibilities of a new method of electrolytic casting: for in her the metamorphosis into statue is complete, and the female Arctic finds a comfortably frozen form.

Meanwhile the enthusiasm of real women for the censored, moral version of exploration was attracting, as well as paternal approval, a small trickle of male contempt. Could women imagine the true conditions, the true harshness of exploration? It was one of those misogynist circles: middle-class women excluded, or 'protected', from adventurous physical experience then had their social limitations cited to them as evidence of their limited understandings. The language that had seemed to offer them common access to heroic experience might appear absurd to men. By the time of the 'heroic era' of Antarctic expeditions, the moral discourse of exploration had shifted its ground, becoming less sacrificial, more ingenuous and boyish, in tune with the Edwardian shift of the culture: but the episode of the group of schoolgirls who applied to join Shackleton shows the same incredulous response by men when women took the public image of exploration at its face value.

We are three strong healthy girls, and also gay and bright, and willing to undergo any hardships, that you yourselves undergo. If our feminine garb is inconvenient, we should just love to don masculine attire. We have been reading all books and articles that have been written on dangerous expeditions by brave men to the Polar regions, and we do not see why men should have all the glory, and women none, especially when there are women just as brave and capable as there are men.

It is immediately clear why Shackleton did not take this application seriously; it is equally clear that the three applicants had written in what they thought were just the right terms. The 'garb' and the 'attire' come straight out of the vein of neo-chivalric praise for courage – newspaper Walter Scott-ery – while the talk of glory and hardships reproduces the official tone of popularised polar literature. Quite as much as the slip into female diction at 'we should just love', the letter's thorough dependence on 'books and articles' declared it to Shackleton as being foolish: a message from another world of (from his point of view) second-hand experiences, apprehended through heroic words. The language that was supposed to win the girls admission in fact only ensured their request would be taken as harmless, rather than seeming improper. And that barely: Shackleton's gruff reply to the effect that there were 'no vacancies for the opposite sex on the Expedition' suggests that he had briefly imagined the situation of three teenaged girls among some tens of sailors and explorers.

Much turned here on women's grasp of geographical knowledge, on their skill with maps: to men, charts of places they might go or dream of going to, to most women variably opaque windows on places to which the imagination might pass, if the black squiggles of bearings and co-ordinates would yield sense. Husbands' and brothers' journeys lent urgency to the scrutiny of maps. But even the stature of female waiting, the acknowledged sphere of women's strength, might come into comical question, if it seemed to the male eye that women's awareness of where their absent menfolk went was faulty. In 1849, for example, the novelist James Fenimore Cooper published *The Lost Sealers*, a sensational potboiler which developed the American public's sense that whaling and the Wilkes Exploring Expedition had given them a stake in the poles. Roswell Gardiner, a Yankee skipper of great tenacity, has sailed for a group of secret islands in the Antarctic. For most of the book he battles with the ice, but occasionally the action returns home. 'I wish I knew all about this voyage of Roswell's,' says his sweetheart Mary, in 'one of the gentlest voices that ever fell on human ear'. Her uncle, a silly greedy old man who has bankrolled the voyage, cannot help much. 'It's desperate *cold* ice, the sealers all tell me, that of the antarctic seas . . . It's extr'or'nary, Mary, that the weather should grow cold as a body journeys south; but so it is, by all accounts. I never could understand it, and it isn't so in Ameriky, I'm sartain.' In desperation they turn to written authority, and Cooper pokes a little fun at their inability to comprehend it, the uncle because of native stupidity, the girl because 'Providence' has withheld the capacity to do so.

'It is all told in my Geography here,' answered Mary, mechanically taking down the book, for her thoughts were far away in those icy seas that her uncle had been so graphically describing. 'I dare say we can find it all explained in the elementary parts of this book . . . It says, sir, that the changes in the seasons are owing to "the inclination of the earth's axis to the plane of its orbit." I do not exactly understand what that means, uncle.'

'No, – it's not as clear as it might be. – The declination –'

'*In*clination, sir, is what it printed here.'

'Ay, inclination. I do not see why any one should have much inclination for winter, but so it must be, I suppose. The 'arth's orbit has an inclination towards changes, you say.'

'The changes in the seasons, sir, are owing to "the inclination of the earth's axis to the plane of its orbit." It does not say that the orbit has an inclination in any particular way.'

. . . One of the plainest problems in natural philosophy was Hebrew to them both . . .

Revealingly the error lies in trying to read the cold, the technical terms of geography as if they belonged to the world of human motives. Cooper presumably believed that the stock situation – Mary waiting patiently – was a strong enough fictional standard to survive his demonstration that his heroine was good for nothing except being sweetly pretty; but the humour removes all respect from her attempts to imagine Roswell 'far away in those icy seas'. It was not, anyway, an aspect of his story that particularly held him. He preferred to dwell on the conflict between men in the Antarctic, and on the perilous wonders they negotiate; knowing, as Mary cannot, that the hard-edged ice has no 'inclinations', and they must enforce their own upon it.

When, on the other hand, Elizabeth Gaskell was researching the Arctic whaling trade for her infinitely more distinguished novel *Sylvia's Lovers* (1863), she undertook a consciously female translation of the data she found in histories of Whitby, and the two magisterial volumes of Scoresby's *An Account of the Arctic Regions*. Arctic facts, Arctic economics, and printed Arctic narratives become oral resources. They become the fireside tall stories which men tell to women about their hair-raising adventures; they become the nearby sources of information that are available to women who wonder and imagine, as they wait for men to return from afar. Perhaps it was the novel's saturation by loss and longing which made Edward Lear choose it, half-tactfully, as a gift for Sophy Cracroft aboard the SS *Poonah* a year afterwards, a fellow passenger saluting Lady Franklin and her companion as acknowledged experts in the situation *Sylvia's Lovers* describes. Gaskell herself had had some social contact with the Arctic, meeting Scoresby, and holidaying in Morecambe Bay not far, as she put it in a letter, from 'Lady North Pole Richardson'. This was the wife of Franklin's comrade from his earliest expedition, Sir John Richardson. Interpolating his distinction into her name made a witty social label, and shows Gaskell's colloquial awareness of something more, the way that polar identity – and the subject of the poles – were funnelled to a woman via a man. The ice in Gaskell's name for Lady Richardson referred to Sir John, not to the map. In *Sylvia's Lovers* the bold 'specksioneer' (chief harpooner) Charley Kinraid comes to the Robson family's farm above Whitby, and he and Sylvia's father, Daniel Robson, vye with each other at telling polar yarns, while Sylvia listens entranced. Daniel remembers the feel on his body of the Arctic waters the time a whale's tail swatted him into the sea, a story taken out of Scoresby's section on the hazards of the fishery and converted into Whitby dialect. 'First, I smarted all ower me, as if my skin were suddenly stript off me: and next, ivery bone i' my body had getten t' toothache, and there were a great roar i' my ears, an' a great dizziness i' my eyes . . .' 'Talk o' cold!' he ends, 'it's little yo' women known o' cold!' Kinraid counters with a vision of hell's mouth opening in the Antarctic. 'We all saw wi' our own eyes, inside that fearsome wall o' ice – seventy miles long, as we could swear to – inside that gray, cold ice, came leaping flames, all red and yellow wi' heat o' some unearthly kind out o' the very waters o' the sea . . . yet never so much as a shred on 't was melted.' Sylvia is 'greedy and breathless' for more. It seems this is the Othello method at work for winning women's hearts, for Kinraid certainly wants Sylvia. 'Women is so fond o' bloodshed,' says her other suitor Philip Hepburn sourly. But he is wrong, or at least stiffly oblivious to Sylvia's particular nature, as he is throughout the novel, to her hurt and his own. 'All night long', writes Gaskell, in a coda to the storytelling scene that exactly situates Sylvia's response to these reported marvels, 'Sylvia dreamed of burning volcanoes springing out of icy southern seas. But, as in the specksioneer's tale the flames were peopled with demons, there was no human interest for her in the wondrous scene in which she was no actor, only a spectator. With daylight came wakening and little homely every-day wonders.' Beside the latter, the tales seem thin and lurid. What lends the immediacy needed for the Arctic to arouse Sylvia's interest is her growing attachment to Kinraid. As 'The Keel Row', the women's song that echoes through the book says, *Weel may the keel row, that my laddie's in.* For her the Arctic is then an extension of him, and where before she had gazed at ships on the horizon with 'no thought as to where they were bound to', she now joins the other women of Whitby whose men are sailors in 'the consciousness that there were men on board, each going forth into the great deep, [which] added unspeakably to the interest felt in watching them'. This is the form of women's participation, a kind of spectating intense enough to be an action in its own right; and it is Sylvia's life on shore that provides the action of the novel, rather than being a comical addendum to the sea.

Soon after the telling of the stories, there is a passage in *Sylvia's Lovers* which parallels Mary's confusion in *The Lost Sealers*. Philip has elected to educate Sylvia. In one sense the knowledge he brings of a wider world offers her an enlargement of horizons she truly needs; but his lessons are also an attempt at gaining a mental ascendancy over her. Gaskell's irony attaches to them as much as her scepticism attaches to Kinraid's heroics. Once again geography occupies the centre of attention:

Philip hailed her interest in geography as another sign of improvement. He had brought back his book of maps to the farm; and there he sat on many an evening teaching his cousin, who had strange fancies respecting the places about which she wished to learn, and was coolly indifferent to the very existence of other towns, and countries, and seas far more famous in story. She was occasionally wilful, and at times very contemptuous as to the superior knowledge of her instructor; but, in spite of it all, Philip went regularly on the appointed evenings to Haytersbank – through keen black east wind, or driving snow, or slushing thaw; for he liked dearly to sit a little behind her, with his arm on the back of her chair, she stooping over the outspread map, with her eyes, – could he have seen them, – a good deal fixed on one spot on the map, not Northumberland, where Kinraid was spending the winter, but those wild northern seas about which he had told them such wonders.

Here the self-deception, the lack of grasp on essentials, belongs to Philip, whose chosen posture of authority prevents him seeing aright. Although Sylvia will commit a major geographical error about Kinraid's whereabouts, it will not be a question of her geographical ignorance making her waiting foolish; it will instead be Philip's fault, he having betrayed Kinraid to the press-gang, that she thinks him dead in the North Sea when the Navy has carried him southward, and will be married with a child when he returns to claim her. *Sylvia's*

Lovers is a book of losses, of certain losses and uncertain spiritual recompense. It is only in part because it deals with commercial whaling, and is set seventy years into the past in a social milieu not given to high-minded moralism, that Gaskell omits, except in occasional glances, all reference to the moral interpretation of the Arctic. As the female lead, Sylvia has no sense that religious ideals grant her an understanding of the 'one spot on the map'. (Religion barely figures in her conscious thoughts.) So far as the novel reflects the contemporary preoccupation with exploration, Gaskell's concern is with the filtering of Arctic ice through the persons of individual men into the experience of women. Only in comparison to the patronage of a Fenimore Cooper can the novel be counted as a vindication. But far more than (say) a popular poem like Jean Ingelow's 'When the Sea Gives up her Dead', prompted by the Franklin affair, which deploys as a consolation the noble reason for the beloved's absence, *Sylvia's Lovers* inhabits the experience of waiting without the suggestion that the ice elsewhere has primacy; the experience of having the Arctic concentrated into a person; of imagining, for that person's sake, vistas remote from one's continuing life; of hoping for signs and portents, and watching the sea.

SEVEN

Relics in the Snow

In Poe's story 'A Descent into the Maelstrom' (1845), the terrified narrator sits perched upon a Norwegian precipice, surveying an 'inky', ship-eating expanse of ocean, toothed with islands. 'A panorama more deplorably desolate no human imagination can conceive.' Using a phrase sometimes applied to the poles, the narrator says he feels that he is looking at 'the ramparts of the world', its outer extremity. His guide enumerates the names of the islands: Vurrgh, Iflesen, Flimen, Sandeflesen, and more. 'These are the true names of the places – but why it has been thought necessary to name them at all, is more than either you or I can understand.'

The nineteenth century saw the Arctic pocked and chequered with new names, scribbled over with them. Why was it 'thought necessary' to pin on these labels that usually implied use, familiarity, habitation? What was involved? The cruise of Lady Franklin's yacht *Fox* in the summer of 1852 brought specimens of naming quite different in tone from the Nordic exotics Poe had carefully researched, half snarl, half sussuration. On 9 December that year, Alfred Tennyson added a postscript to a letter to his brother Frederick. 'Captain Inglefield has called an Arctic promontory Cape Tennyson after me which makes me as proud as Lucifer. So don't let your major-domo look down upon me!' Tennyson's pleasure is obvious. So, following hard on pleasure's heels, is his sense of absurdity. It was such a very intangible type of commemoration – one's surname applied to an inhospitable lump in a distant sea, a sea so distant that one would never set eyes on one's namesake cape. Following the success of 'In Memoriam', Tennyson was starting to grow used to forms of praise that, strictly speaking, had nothing to do with writing or reading. Celebrity was convertible coin. Tennyson's would bring him a peerage, in the end. These rewards naturally entailed obligation, and gestures of mutual recognition between different branches of Victorian endeavour. The poetry won the cape. Vice versa, on the strength of Cape Tennyson, Inglefield was able to meet the poet at the Geographical Society the following April, and rather later to present him with a copy of his *A Summer Search for Sir John Franklin*, inscribed 'To the Poet Laureate from his humble admirer the Author'. But being added to the Arctic map was a special kind of compliment. In the years before the twentieth century proved that established names were politically pliable, that Chemnitz *could* be Karl-Marx-Stadt, and St Petersburg turn into Leningrad, one could not expect to mark the face of Europe in the same way. English, French, and German landscapes, long tilled and long settled, were already full to the brim with names, mapped with customary identities for every field and hill. Across North America and Australasia, it was true, new names were being laid down that would be weathered into ordinariness by the new populations that lived among them, and spoke them habitually, so that (for example) the range of mountains in Canada named after British Prime Ministers would lose their artificial air. No such expectation of settlement attached to Inglefield's capes. There the names were supposed to persist without being used by the only humans who inhabited the northern ice; there, there was the sense of a landscape entirely available to be named by fiat, entirely open to acts of commemoration. This was so, however, because that landscape was thoroughly detached from use and population in the minds of many of its namers. It was open because humanly meaningless. Consequently the information that part of this vacuum bore your name was news you could do nothing *with*. Nothing followed from it. Real butlers would not be impressed; nor would it be sensible to style yourself Mr Alfred Tennyson, A.C. (Arctic Cape).

The Arctic and Antarctic now have their complement of names; sometimes, indeed, several competing names for the same feature. For a modern equivalent of Tennyson's situation we would need to turn to the scientist who finds a formal-looking envelope on her doormat one morning, and opening it reads that a comet has been called after her. Theoretically, her surname is now orbiting the sun in a tricky ellipse. She will not be visiting her chunk of high-velocity debris, any more than Tennyson could go to see his cape. In one respect she is better off than Tennyson. Once found, 'her' comet will stay found, because modern astronomical observations are a great deal more reliable than the observations of Victorian explorers in wooden ships. A note in Tennyson's collected *Letters* at the page dealing with 9 December 1852 adds: 'The Arctic promontory has not been identified.' It *ought* to be located on the south-eastern tip of Ellesmere Island, opposite Cobourg Island, at about 76° 15' N, 80° W; but Inglefield's chart is not entirely trustworthy. He did not land to verify Cape Tennyson's position, and on the day he named it, sailing past, 'Indifferent observations only could be obtained, for the drifting ice so encumbered the sea, it was almost impossible to be sure of the horizon, and here and there it was obstructed by vast icebergs, 150 feet in height.' Inglefield may have given the poet's name, not to a solid headland, but a chunk of perishable ice, moored temporarily across his field of vision. This seems an aptly indeterminate fate for a compliment so airily thin, predicated on emptiness.

The parallel with the modern scientist, however, is imperfect. It does not quite exhaust Tennyson's feeling at the news, which contained, I think, a further element of gratification, specific to his time. We already know that he was sympathetic to exploration, by temperament as well as through family ties; and Inglefield's compliment associated him with an enterprise he admired, a type of defiant voyaging much closer than any physical thing he would ever do himself to the 'yearning' desire in his 'Ulysses' (1842) to 'seek a newer world'. Tennyson had imagined Ulysses as an old man refusing his happy ending on Ithaca in favour of one last journey, 'to sail beyond the sunset, and the baths/Of all the western stars, until I die'. He 'cannot rest from travel', moves for the sake of movement itself. And also because

> I am a part of all that I have met;
> Yet all experience is an arch wherethrough
> Gleams that untravelled world, whose margin fades
> For ever and for ever as I move.

This Ulysses was the embodiment of restlessness, a restlessness that would often be taken as wholly heroic, indomitable in its refusals.

Certainly that was how Apsley Cherry-Garrard saw it when he persuaded his companions in 1913 that the last line should be carved on Scott's memorial cross in Antarctica, as a kind of credo: 'To strive, to seek, to find, and not to yield'. Tennyson himself was less certain (which only makes the use of the poem as a memorial that much richer, in feeling and irony). He had found the germ of the story in Dante, where Ulysses is being punished in hell for his last voyage's presumption. The monologue he wrote allowed for criticisms of Ulysses to register as well as admiration. The hero's rapt image of the arch for example, through which gleams the promise of journeying, never consummated, never exhausted, could be read to mean that Ulysses condemns himself to teeter perpetually at thresholds, expecting from voyages what he fails to discover within himself. ('Great pains, small gains for those who ask the world to solve them', as Captain Ahab says in *Moby-Dick*: 'it cannot solve itself'.) But read either way Ulysses' unyielding stance was a charged one for Tennyson. And the urge for departure was one of the foci on which his poetic attention was concentrated. Nor was the 'untravelled world' of the real snow far away in literary terms. The contexts, the publications in which his poetry appeared were often the same as those that featured the better-written polar reports. That opening issue of the *Cornhill Magazine*, for example, from which he read aloud the proof of Franklin's fate to his wife, Emily, contained alongside articles on China and chloroform and an episode of *Framley Parsonage*, the first printing of his own poem 'Tithonus'. Fifty pages separated 'Me only cruel immortality/consumes' from 'he found in the bottom of the boat two human skeletons . . .' It moved Tennyson, as it moved his contemporaries, that in extreme circumstances human beings should continue to assert their human powers. As a name, Cape Tennyson was both flattering and absurd. The act of naming it, however, was also absurdly brave: a statement of sorts about the power of language and intention.

Naming practices varied from expedition to expedition and from commander to commander. By custom it was both the commander's duty and his prerogative to name the new features that were charted, although informal names often circulated as well on shipboard to identify hat-shaped or kettle-shaped peaks, and the final nomenclature would be settled as much by accident as by official ratification. It helped if the names sounded well in the mouths of later expeditions. Inglefield himself was much given to christening things after famous people, or recent Victorian achievements, with slightly comic effects. He was a consummate practitioner of the polar placename as a social grace-note. Besides Cape Tennyson, he produced Cape Albert, Cape Faraday, Louis Napoleon Island ('in honour of the French President, from whom I had received some very flattering attentions') and Mittie Island ('after the daughter of one my friends'). On the east side of Smith Sound, 'some extraordinary table-topped cliffs attracted our notice, and so perfectly even and marked into galleries did they appear, that my mind associating them with the glassy sides of the Great Exhibition, I named them the Crystal Palace Cliffs'. Franklin, likewise, paid back patronage in placenames so furiously that a manuscript satire written by the Hudson Bay fur-traders just after his first Canadian journey took care to skewer the habit in a joke. The piece is full of professional contempt for amateur heroics. It caricatured Franklin's tendency to make a geographical meal of the landscape the traders worked in day by day without plaudits: 'In sailing along the Union Coast . . . we also discovered many shoals and islands unnoticed by former Navigators, in particular an extensive sand-bank which at low water forms an Island . . . This Island I have named Brown-Bottom-Island in honour of my Friend and relative Lord Brownbottom.'

But generally speaking polar names could be divided among a set of rough categories. There were the tributes to the great, the learned, and the powerful, whether these were notable scientists, notable poets, or the Lord Brownbottoms of the world. (It was also not uncommon for an institution to be commemorated. It did not sound strange to a contemporary ear for a mountain or glacier to honour, for example, the Royal Geographical Society *en masse*.) There were the names given, usually to rather smaller features, in honour of men actually on board ship, who had distinguished themselves in the affection or the estimation of their shipmates. There were private, family compliments, like Inglefield's Mittie Island, or Franklin's gift to Eleanor of a group of islets called Porden. There were names recalling specific incidents that had befallen expeditions, more often grim than happy ones: hence the coves named Starvation or Desperation, and on Scott's last expedition the neatly euphemistic Inexpressible Island. There were the purely descriptive names, which tried to fix in brief form the look or colour of a feature. Then there were the pattern-names, which ran exhaustively through the alphabet or the spectrum: these saved thought, and unified a whole cluster of features into something like a physical mnemonic. Instead of Richard Of York Gave Battle In Vain for the colours of the rainbow, you had a batch of polar places ordered by ABC. (Scott's three meteorological observation points in 1910–13 were Archibald, Bertram, and Clarence.) There were home names, reused with the addition of 'North' or 'South' or 'New' when a chance similarity with a familiar landscape disclosed itself; following more precariously the model of New England, Nova Scotia, and New South Wales, and producing North Devon in the Arctic and the South Shetlands in the Antarctic. Finally there were the occasional poeticisms, which drew on the sensibility or the reading of explorers. But there were comparatively few of this last kind; and even those polar placenames that seem aptly atmospheric often turn out to have arisen on different, prosaic principles. Erebus, for instance, makes a sombrely hellish name for the enormous live volcano that glowers over Ross Island in the Antarctic, all corrugated horizontals, shaped like a squashed Mt Fuji. But it only witnesses to the fact that Ross arrived beneath it in the 1840s in HMS *Erebus*. The classical habits of the Navy made the mountain Erebus, at second hand, not a separate act of classical imagination. The passage of time moreover, like a newspaper subeditor eliminating anything from copy that is too surprising or too idiosyncratic to fit house style, has tended to smooth away distinctiveness. The wasp-waisted landmass in northern Canada that the Victorians knew as Boothia Felix, by romantic analogy with the Arabia Felix of Roman geographers (but also in thanks for the deep pockets of Felix Booth, Sheriff of London), now appears on maps as the plain Boothia Peninsula. Photographed heroically by Ponting, suggestive of sublimity and endeavour, the Great Ice Barrier of the Scott era in the Antarctic has become the Ross Ice Shelf:

sensible, scientific, a pattern-name that conforms with the Weddell and Filchner shelves elsewhere around the continent.

In a sense, though, it was the function of polar placenames that conveyed the important feeling, rather than their style, which could seldom be called inspiring. (One of the rare pieces of writing on polar naming as such, a whimsical essay of 1942 by Frank Debenham, set out to explain why the names were, and had to be, so 'lacking in originality'.) The consensus eventually grew up that the best names were the descriptive type, which might actually help a stranger to recognise questionable features, and relate map to surroundings. But recognition is a term packed with cultural expectation. It is instructive to compare the explorers' Arctic namings with the Inuit nomenclature for the same landscapes, which usually interested the Victorians not at all; though in retrospect it is the indigenous names for the inhabited parts of the northern ice which seem substantive, and the European ones a ghostly overlay. The family of Inuit languages is agglomerative and accumulative. They build famously long compound words from a pool of prefixes, suffixes, particles, and modifiers. The grain of truth behind the legend that Eskimos have umpteen separate words for snow is the genuine existence of umpteen separate compound terms for it – which each translate quite unmysteriously, however, as 'wet snow falling very fast from the east' or 'light dry snow unlikely to last long'. These languages allow very precise, informal orientation to the surroundings, based on common knowledge of ice and horizons, and on the shared experience of hunters' journeys from A to B. Without the benefit of engrained familiarity with the landscape, Inuit namings would have come across to Europeans in faulty nineteenth-century translation as sets of vague instructions; to turn west at the shore, keep going for half a day, and look out for the big rock. Imported English and European names, by contrast, oriented ships in relation to latitude and longitude, in relation to previously known coasts and bays. When a mapped feature was recognised, it established a position, and on more than the purely practical level. Recognition situated a ship in relation to a previous history of endeavour and commemoration, to which the present venture might add. Two different senses were involved of knowing where you are. The European baptisms of the

Arctic used names as signs of known-ness, declarations of presence and discovery. The Inuit nomenclature assumed the familiarity of the home ice.

The European names were more fragile. Despite the weight of technology behind them, despite the expeditions' role in tying the North into a world of Christianity, capital and factory-made fishhooks, the European names were bestowed by men who knew they were only sojourners in this landscape. They lacked the sense, given by modern ecology, that they might damage it. The balance of probabilities seemed entirely the other way around. It would more likely damage them, and their capacity even to mark it seemed doubtful. So names, those utterly intangible markers, were at once powerful, because linked to the confidence of the world that had sent the expeditions, and frail beacons of meaning. There was no unacknowledged irony in calling some impassive rock after a dignitary; the irony was built-in, self-evident, almost the point of the exercise. The names exerted consciously slight grasps on the wilderness. They posed knowingly feeble challenges to the wilderness – which the act of naming, of course, assumed to be nameless, thereby helping to cement an influential view of the wild as a place to be defied. Each silly or prosaic name acted as a small gamble against the vanity of human wishes. (For human, of course, read European.) In one sense, a very Victorian style of glamorous self-pity was involved. But because the names were things *left behind*, so was a wider Victorian interest in discarded objects, in scraps and debris orphaned by time. The corollary to the acquisitive confidence of the 1850s and 1860s was an imaginative awareness of rubbish. Never had so much heterogeneous stuff been owned; never had so much been used up, worn out, and thrown away, to indicate the melancholy end of ownership. A fading stamp of human intention and human familiarity clung to a bundle of abandoned clothing, or to the broken junk that circulated through the very poorest shops in London. This was the period in which Henry Mayhew investigated the 'deposit' building up in the capital's sewer system. As well as human excrement and horse- and pig-manure, it included 'tin kettles and pans (pansherds); broken stoneware, as jars, pitchers, flower-pots, &c.; bricks; pieces of wood; rotten mortar and

. . . even rags' – altogether a sort of layered archaeological trove, the ruins of a city when it was still standing, which a special subdivision of the urban poor sifted full-time for items of value. This was also the period when Dickens' illustrator Phiz was providing, for the master's work, endless small indoor scenes in which the edges of rooms are lost in shadow. Somehow the dark of those walls and corners always suggests engrained dirt and rotten lath. Just beyond and around the figures, a chaos of decrepitude and broken objects lurks. Disgust was not the sensation that Phiz or Mayhew intended to convey; more a recognition, through things, of a pathetic transience. Broken objects spoke of when they were whole, rags communicated the fate of fine dresses. And if names left behind to dare the Arctic would not exactly shrivel or crack, the position of the wishes they represented amidst the waste was still eloquent. Anything deposited in the Arctic was lost in space, threatened with being broken by the indifferent expanse around it. From this point of view, Cape Tennyson too was a poor thing.

But names, perhaps because of their official status, and the chance at least they had of permanence on the map, were not the most affecting form of relic. For a reflective chill, for example, nothing in Captain Inglefield's sportsman's sketch of his 'summer cruise' matches his shipboard scientist's note on the destiny of rubbish dropped into the waters between Greenland and Baffin Island. There was an organic sediment down on the dark sea-floor, wrote Dr Sutherland. It could not be examined directly, but it surely contained besides the 'brownish slime' of diatoms, the remains of seals and 'other mammalia' including unfortunate humans 'blown away from the land upon the ice'. Finally, 'In the event of Davis Strait leaving its bed dry by a subsidence of the sea, or by elevation of the land, we should have to add to our list of natural materials, manufactured articles, such as ships' anchors and cables, broken pottery, and other unimportant, although enduring relics of civilisation.' Such a tiny, such an unimportant impact on the physical environment! Sutherland surely knew the effect he was creating, surely took a dry pleasure in relegating human corpses to the category of 'other mammalia', and civilisation's manufactured products to a negligible seam of debris. One of the rhetorical satisfactions of science was this ability to look at things on a new scale. Human lives were measured in tens of years, and for the individual man 'blown away from the land' his mischance was an all-encompassing catastrophe; but science's cold eye could consider the aeons required to raise a seabed, and see such individual tragedies as a minor organic process. Yet the dead unfortunates were more forcefully recalled for being sent to rot among the seals, and the broken things that civilisation had made would always declare a certain difference from the purely natural junk. A shade of sentiment would necessarily adhere to the fact that they *endured*; were 'unimportant but enduring'. Just as, a little later, much of the power Darwinian biology would have in the culture came from people's agonised inability to accept the picture of themselves as dispensable pawns in the game of selection, thus, here, the scientific account demanded resistance. Tennyson recoiled in 'In Memoriam' from a Nature 'so careless of the single life'; worse, so careless of whole species that the world was packed with their jumbled fossils. The horrible implication was that the single life, so absorbingly particular and important to its subject, meant nothing, and death erased even the illusion of significance. Tennyson asked if Man, with 'such splendid purpose in his eyes',

> Who loved, who suffered countless ills,
>   Who battled for the True, the Just,
>   [could] Be blown about the desert dust,
> Or sealed within the iron hills?

– an entropic nightmare that had deep roots in the Romantic tradition; for Wordsworth had imagined the dead 'rolled round in Earth's diurnal course,/With rocks, and stones, and trees', and now science threatened to confirm the vision. But the gulf lay too provocatively wide between what science said and what individual experience insisted upon. The vision could not be accepted easily, when each mind felt the importance of the thought passing through it that very instant, and each body passed on continual messages of presence and activity, as a hand stirred a teacup or batted away a wasp. I, I, *I* am here, making a link, buying a postage stamp, signifying. Reduction to objecthood was unthinkable. When likewise the picture was presented of an Arctic desert in which bodies were blown about, and away, and

Nature constantly promised a fatal reduction, it could not be granted that a description like Sutherland's was sufficient. The bodies must mean; even the objects, if they were constructed objects, had to be invested with something beyond indifference. Indeed, Sutherland was being knowingly provocative in omitting this dimension of human sense. Once again, I think, the irony was bargained-for, built-in, something that everybody knew. Sutherland did not write 'relics' in any spirit of dismissal. 'Relics' was the standard word to describe the leavings of polar travel, when these were found once more. It covered both things and corpses; a nice nod by a secularising age to a kind of mystery it could not afford to do without.

All expeditions dumped signs of their passage. The lavish equipment with which the grand expeditions set out made each a travelling storehouse of contemporary arts and technologies, a Crystal Palace afloat, crammed with stuff ranging from steam organs to electroplated cruets. It also made for diverse garbage, especially if things went wrong. Empty tins, broken oars, perished cloth, spoiled food, and domestic impedimenta were all abandoned in the snows. Where they were not crushed by ice, or dropped into the sea, the climate preserved many of them. Thoreau, ending *Walden* (1854) with a fantasia on exploration, did not forget them either: 'explore your own higher latitudes', he urged his readers, 'with shiploads of preserved meats to support you, if they be necessary; and pile the empty cans sky-high for a sign'.

Once frozen, it was not easy to distinguish at first sight between new rubbish and old rubbish. It was all laid down alike like the work of the ages, giving an odd sense of time abolished. Given the thousands on thousands of square miles the things were scattered in, it took considerable luck or detective work to turn them up; but, surprisingly often, they were found. Always touching when later explorers came across them, because the faint hint they gave of willpower and purpose contrasted so with the surroundings, the cast-offs of exploration took on a special significance in the case of the Franklin search. Then there was an additional pressure for found objects to have meaning. They became, explicitly, clues. Inglefield's sole new find (he was in fact looking in the wrong direction) was a manufactured knife uncovered in the Inuit settlement at Whale Sound. It had probably come north from a Danish trading-post, but the inscription on the blade ('B. Wilson, cast steel') was scrutinised and recorded. At that date, the discovery of a machined implement in northern Greenland deserved attention. The knife stood out; it did not match.

At the conclusion of the search, the *Cornhill* article carefully noted the diverse strew of things found by Lieutenant Hobson.

Quantities of clothing, cooking and working implements were scattered about near Point Victory, and a sextant, on which was engraved the name of Frederick Hornby, was found among the debris. Collecting a few of the most interesting of these relics to take with him upon his return, Hobson then pushed on to the southward, and when near Cape Crozier he discovered the boat above mentioned, by a small stanchion showing just above the snow. Clearing away the snow, he found in the bottom of the boat two human skeletons, one of which was under a heap of clothing. There were also watches, chronometers, silver spoons, money, &c., besides a number of Bibles, prayer and other religious books; and although one of the Bibles was underlined in almost every verse, yet not a single writing was found to throw further light upon the history of the retreating parties. There were two guns, one barrel of each being loaded and cocked, as if these poor fellows had been anxiously longing for a passing bear or fox to save them from starving; for nothing edible was found, save some chocolate and tea, neither of which could support life in such a climate.

These objects both told and withheld a story. They testified in some part to the last needs of the dead travellers, for food and for spiritual comfort, but they could never quite explain what the two dead men had intended – where they thought they were headed, how they had been separated from the others in the 'retreat', whether the silver spoons were loot or talismans, or, as Lady Franklin believed, keepsakes of her husband, whose monogram was engraved on them. The objects delivered the fact of death, but not the history behind it. They could only speak tantalisingly of a departed human presence, and wring hearts with the obvious truth that the rescuers had come much too late. The finds that Hobson collected were brought home to Britain, and given the different preservation of glass cases, to perpetuate their partial eloquence.

Of course the relics with the greatest power to move were human bodies themselves. Objects only bore an associative smear of intention, while bodies, now turned to dumb shells, had once been the actual vessels of will and decision. We tend to think that when the three Franklin graves were located by the anthropologist Owen Beattie in 1984, and the modern world found itself able to gaze into the faces of Franklin's long-dead crew, a unique avenue had opened into the past. The ice had preserved John Torrington, John Hartnell, and William Braine as yellowed revenants from 1846. Their lips had drawn back from their teeth, and their eyes, oysters of water-ice when the coffins were first opened, proved to have sunk back beneath the lids; still the three men's hair and features and clothes were just as they'd been on their last day of life, and it seemed possible to look across time. But this was not quite the modern sensation it appeared to be, as Beattie's photographs were reprinted around the world, provoking essays by novelists and disconcerted fascination everywhere. The Victorians, here the objects of our own backward gaze, knew the sensation too. In fact, as the book jointly published by Beattie and his associate John Geiger explained, Hartnell's grave on Beechey Island had already been opened by none other than Captain Inglefield, following up, at the end of his 'summer search', on the work of Sir Edward Belcher. Inglefield discovered nothing of practical help in the search, and the episode of the exhumation was not detailed in his book. But Sir Roderick Murchison did remark, as he awarded Inglefield the RGS's Arctic medal in 1853, that 'the coffin . . . was found in as perfect order as if recently deposited in the churchyard of an English village. Every button and ornament had been neatly arranged . . .' A private letter from Inglefield to Rear-Admiral Beaufort, retrieved by Beattie and Geiger from the archives of the Ministry of Defence, brings us much closer to the moment at which Inglefield, with Sutherland beside him, lifted the lid.

My doctor assisted me, and I have had my hand on the arm and face of poor Hartnell. He was decently clad in a cotton shirt, and though the dark night precluded our seeing, still our touch detected that a wasting illness was the cause of dissolution. It was a curious and solemn scene on the silent snow-covered sides of the famed Beechey Island, where the two of us stood at midnight. The pale moon looking down upon us as we silently worked with pickaxe and shovel at the hard-frozen tomb, each blow sending a spur of red sparks from the grave where rested the messmate of our lost countrymen.

Inglefield touched what we see. If he veered away from physical description of the corpse towards awed word-painting, preferring to dwell on the red sparks and the pale moonlight, it indicates rather a contemporary reticence than a failure to confront Hartnell's arrested gaze. It was 'curious and solemn' for him too, though Hartnell had only been in the permafrost for six years.

But then the preserving ice does something curious to history. It does not distinguish between the recent dead and the remote dead; all are glazed over alike, and in a place, furthermore, where the signs of *period* by which we make familiar judgements of historical time are almost completely absent. Imagine a group of explorers, black dots against the snow, and history almost reduces to the style of their garments. (It is this apparent shearing-away of social background and historic context which helps make it easy to feel intimacy with the characters of polar narratives: no matter that the vast majority of those who know, say, Captain Scott's final words would have been cut dead by him had they encountered him strolling up Buckingham Palace Road. The intimate gaze at the dead overlooks the dead man's world of caste certainties and social niceties.) When Beattie first looked at John Torrington in 1984, 'Despite all the intervening years, the young man's life did not seem far away; in many ways it was as if Torrington had just died.' What disturbs so much in the faces of the Franklin dead is a combination of remoteness and proximity in time; for Inglefield as well, the exhumed body mixed immediacy and distance, though because in his case it made him the immediate witness to a tragedy he might as well have been a hundred years too late to prevent instead of six.

And for that matter the Victorians did not only gaze on the recent polar dead. They also looked back across centuries, to a time as remote from them (or remoter) as theirs is from us. It was, furthermore, a time to which they particularly wanted to lay an intimate claim: the sixteenth- and seventeenth-century era of the great navigators. In the modelling of an appropriate past for their energetic present, they had seized on this period, reading a foundation for the contemporary romance of empire in the exotic travels of the merchant-venturers, constituting a mythology from the Renaissance blend of action and poetry; and calling the thing that emerged a national tradition. There were special attractions in the mercurial sensibility of the Elizabethans. Instead of proving that the past was a foreign country, it suggested to them that the phlegmatic Englishness of the present day inherited, despite appearances, the buccaneering virtues; it still had, somehow, the quicksilver touch. Macaulay's histories paid tribute to these glories. Carlyle relished imagining the Elizabethan sea furrowed by argosies, and the whiff of cinnamon and gunpowder that carried over from it into the trading, imperial present. By the end of the century Francis Drake and Walter Raleigh had honoured places in the storyfied versions of national history presented to children. This was a time that the Victorians thought they knew, and thought they recognised themselves in. And in accordance with the Elizabethan navigators' sympathetic boast that 'There is no land uninhabitable, nor sea innavigable', this past contained its quota of polar adventures. Sir Hugh Willoughby of the Muscovy Company had frozen to death in the 1550s with all his crew, on the way back from Archangelsk, while a few decades later Frobisher and Davis began the search for the North-West Passage through the Canadian Arctic. In the next century, English captains had raced the Dutch for possession of the Spitzbergen whaling grounds (and lost, but that was a detail). The feeling that these voyages formed the pertinent past behind current polar journeys was very widely shared. Parts 2, 3, and 4 of Chandos Hoskyns Abrahall's epic poem *Arctic Enterprise* (1856) surveyed polar journeying from the Vikings onwards, with particular emphasis on the sixteenth and seventeenth centuries, recruiting the entire history to prove by the beginning of Part 5 'The superior claims of Britain as an adventurer in the Arctic seas'. Charles Kingsley's theological intentions made him a heterodox interpreter of the Arctic in *The Water Babies*, as we have seen – where others saw territory to be conquered, he imagined the ice as 'a great white gate' locked by divine command to conceal Mother Carey's quiet pool. There are similarities between Kingsley's nineteenth-century use of the Arctic and C. S. Lewis' use of the solar system in his 'science-fiction' novels of the 1950s: both men, infusing their adventurous materials with allegory, reject discovery as an adequate goal. It was wrong for the mere sake of movement to stray too far from the place in creation that was ordained for you. But Kingsley was also the author of *Westward Ho!*, the single most influential evocation of Elizabethan swashbuckling in Victorian fiction, and the same past crowds around young Tom's otherwise eccentric swim to the North Pole. The seabirds who guide him are the ghosts of the great skippers, condemned to work out their sins by circling the ice. Then, much afraid, Tom sees, grinding amidst the pack, 'the wrecks of many a gallant ship; some with masts and yards all standing, some with the seamen frozen fast on board. Alas, alas, for them! They were all true English hearts; and they came to their end like good knights-errant, in searching for the white gate that never was opened yet.' But he dares the great dive northward anyway, and finds he 'was not a bit frightened. Why should he be? He was a brave English lad, whose business is to go out and see all the world.'

More than a routine overlap of ideas, a familiar conjunction of periods, was involved here. The Hakluyt Society, set up in 1846 to reprint the venturers' narratives for bibliophiles, had a deliberately activist aspect to it. Satisfying the desires of armchair travellers as well as pleasing the collectors of fine books, it aimed to make the achievements of the past available in the culture; a conscious part of it, even. When Tennyson needed historical background for his poem about the sea-fight of the *Revenge* (a gory, disastrous episode during the singeing of the King of Spain's beard), the Society's Secretary travelled down to the Isle of Wight in person to fill him in. The Society's conception of the national past had pronounced ideological overtones, and its membership were busy to a remarkable degree about the present business of empire and exploration. Subscribers to the Hakluyt editions tended often to be public-spirited as well as historically minded, with a distinct Romantic understanding of the national destiny. The Secretary who visited Tennyson was none other than the young Clements Markham, later to become Scott's patron, his finger already in many pies. The founders of the Society included Lord Dufferin, eventually Viceroy of India, and a classic exemplar of the idea that Britain found itself most truly in the brush with the far-off and the exotic.

It seems somehow inevitable that when Dufferin, as a gilded young Anglo-Irish peer, took a literary voyage in 1856 in his private yacht *Foam*, he should have chosen to sail north on an amateur Arctic cruise; even more so, that on a beach in Spitzbergen he discovered a body. Traces of early exploration had been uncovered round Hudson Bay, and up the coast of Greenland. Spitzbergen was dotted with relics of whaling, from ships' timbers to broken shelters and sad little crosses. The *frisson* of an encounter with the past was on the menu of Arctic travel, and available now to the non-professional, if he were as determined as Dufferin. Dufferin's *Letters from High Latitudes* displayed a charming devotion to his mother; contained a comically dour servant and a manly Icelandic guide; reported Dufferin's witty speech in Latin at a Reykjavik reception and exploited the picturesque qualities of the sagas; gallantly saluted the charms of Scandinavian women; were written in the best ornamented style of an unoriginal but very accomplished public schoolboy. Altogether the book (reprinted several times) made it engagingly plain that the author thought of himself only as a deferential guest at the banquet of letters. Tennyson naturally received a copy.

In the middle of the white night of 6 August 1856, the *Foam* 'came to anchor in the silent haven of English Bay, Spitzbergen' with its cargo of graceful reflections and well-turned quotations. The view had a mortal look about it, to Dufferin:

I think, perhaps, its most striking feature was the stillness – and deadness – and impassibility of this new world: ice, and rock, and water surrounded us; not a sound of any kind interrupted the silence; the sea did not break upon the shore; no bird or any living thing was visible; the midnight sun – by this time muffled in a transparent mist – shed an awful, mysterious lustre on glacier and mountain; no atom of vegetation gave token of the earth's vitality: a universal numbness and dumbness seemed to pervade the solitude. I suppose that in no other part of the world is this appearance of deadness so strikingly exhibited. On the stillest summer day in England, there is always perceptible an under-tone of life thrilling through the atmosphere; and though no breeze should stir a single leaf, yet – in default of motion – there is always a sense of growth; but here not so much as a blade of grass was to be seen on the sides of the bald excoriated hills.

The holiday was proceeding according to plan. Thoughts of deadness led swiftly to thoughts of the dead, sacrificed in the conquest of these silent seas. Dufferin, who recounts the story of Hugh Willoughby just before the landfall, was not lucky enough to sight a fleshed corpse. He can only recount what

I have been told by an eye-witness, that in Magdalena Bay there are to be seen, even to this day, the bodies of men who died upwards of 250 years ago, in such complete preservation that, when you pour hot water on the icy coating which encases them, you can actually see the unchanged features of the dead, through the transparent incrustation.

But the next best thing happened. A cry from the ship's surgeon brings Dufferin 'helter-skelter' to see a lesser marvel first-hand. 'Half embedded in the black moss at his feet, there lay a grey deal coffin falling almost to pieces with age; the lid was gone – blown off probably by the wind – and within were stretched the bleaching bones of a human skeleton.' Although the remains of an inscription unfortunately proclaimed that the skeleton was Dutch rather than English, and had only been *in situ* since 1758, a century astray of the target, the bones sufficed as a general Arctic *memento mori*.

A bleak resting-place for that hundred years' slumber, I thought, as I gazed on the dead mariner's remains! . . . It was no brother mortal that lay at our feet – softly folded in the embrace of 'Mother Earth' – but a poor scarecrow, gibbeted for ages on this bare rock, like a dead Prometheus; the vulture, frost, gnawing for ever on his bleaching relics, and yet eternally preserving them!

Dufferin's discovery of the bones of 'poor Jacob Moor' effectively furnishes the climax of his book: its most Arctic moment. Afterwards there only remained to be narrated Dufferin's rueful return, via Norway and reflections on the career of Harald Hardrada, to the 'foul, greasy, gas-discoloured mud' of London. He illustrated *Letters from High Latitudes* himself, and one dark, Gothic little picture shows the coffin on its beach, the inky sea washing below it, the equally Stygian sky gloomy above it. The exposed skeleton grins up. With its boxy ribs, and square skull pierced with rough holes like a Halloween pumpkin, it deliberately has the look of a woodcut from a previous century. It alludes to the emblematic death's head who would tell the readers of seventeenth-century pious works, *I eate you all*, or *Remember thou must die*. Dufferin fixes another motto to this Victorian exercise in ghoulish atmosphere. 'Et ego in Arctis': I too have been, not in the Arcadia which usually caps the quotation, but in the Arctic. He was pleased enough with the phrase to put the whole episode of the corpse under the same title in the running contents list for the chapter. 'No REINDEER TO BE SEEN – ET EGO IN ARCTIS – WINTER IN SPITZBERGEN' and so on. The dead man had been stripped too far by the weather, his coffin had been too much wrecked, for Dufferin to entertain the comfortable thoughts about village churchyards that the trim graves on Beechey Island had inspired in Sir Roderick Murchison; and perhaps his temperament better suited Gothic than pastoral anyway. The Arctic was not Arcadia, and Jacob Moor was too far gone to seem a 'brother mortal'. Here the discovered body presented no little island of order and decency amid the wilderness. It displayed the consequences of the Arctic for the human frame. But Dufferin, enjoying himself tremendously, finds these 'gibbeted' remains (if anything) more heroic. They have suffered a *Promethean* agony at the hands of the frost; have paid over their awful fate, like the Titan who offended Olympus by giving fire to man, as the price of knowledge. Jacob Moor is a forebear worth having. If the cold has not preserved his face, it has preserved, in the spectacle of his bones, the message Dufferin wanted to receive about the value, even unto death, of voyaging. And though the marks of mortal brotherhood have been obliterated, enough essential humanity (humanity perhaps rendered down to an essence) survives for Dufferin to sense a continuity between the corpses and himself. Fellow feeling returns through the clever ironies of the caption, for the declaration *Et ego in Arctis* of course applies as much to Dufferin himself. The spectacle included him. It offered him the place he expected as an observer of the past. He too declares that he has stood in the far North. He has looked

168

appreciatively upon the ghastly visage of past endeavour; confirming, with the eye of a connoisseur, the power of its relics.

Usually celebrations of the Arctic dead were less physically explicit, less aristocratic, less deliberately macabre. When Erasmus Brodie, unfortunate author of another epic about the Arctic search, remarked that 'them only I embalm in rhyme/Who, cold and far off, sleep in hyperborean clime', the effect was a mistake: the same mistake as shown in his choice of *Euthanasia* for an upbeat title. He meant, not that the cold had put down the Franklin party, like dogs given a lethal injection by a vet, but that they had met a good death, literally a *euthanatos*: virtuous, serene, stoical. Views like Brodie's were reinforced by the way that the physical aspects of an Arctic death were commonly imagined at home. It seemed a clean, an undisgusting way to go. The body's contents were not spilled out, war's mess of blood and entrails was avoided; the cold, it appeared, respected the integrity of the human frame, while life ebbed away. Neither the discovery of whole bodies (reticently reported), nor even of excoriated skeletons, disrupted the picture. A skeleton, having lost all its flesh, offered little information about the state of the flesh at the time of death. Though the symptoms of scurvy and frostbite were well reported, and the public were accustomed to hearing that some living polar hero's sufferings marked his body, these suggested no distinct visual image to most people – no exact close-up of sores, or morbid tissue whose cell-walls had been ruptured from within by ice-crystals. Already, folk wisdom had it that freezing was a gentle, drowsy way to die, a kind exit from the cold. The idea was so widespread that Dr Elisha Kane thought it worthwhile to record for once the actual feeling behind 'that lethargic sleepiness mentioned in the story books'.

I will tell you what this feels like, for I have been twice 'caught out.' Sleepiness is not the sensation. Have you ever received the shocks of a magneto-electric machine, and had the peculiar benumbing sensation of 'can't let go,' extending up to your elbow-joints? Deprive this of its paroxysmal character; subdue, but diffuse it over every part of your system, and you have the so-called pleasurable feelings of incipient freezing.

Still, in the minds of most people without direct experience, it seemed apt that a snowy end would come as softly as snow itself fell. If there was terror about it, it only lay in the terrible, irresistible fact of death itself, which shifted attention from the physical to the spiritual dimension of dying in the snow. As sensation ceased (so people imagined) the body dropped away from the victim's last passages of consciousness, almost as if in premonition of the future state for which the soul was now bound; the victim became all thought, all dream, perhaps in the best cases all prayer. It would be a mistake to think of this as a necessarily complacent line of thought. For the most part, certainly, it inspired comfortable reveries about the appropriate death of heroes, in which the incidentals like the whiteness of the snow were recruited to give hints of heaven. Blanketed here below by the snow, the dead would wear celestial robes more radiant still; buried on the shores of the frozen Arctic Ocean, they would don their crowns by the side of the 'glassy sea' of the Book of Revelation. Mention of the '*white* North', in Tennyson's epitaph for Franklin, helpfully led on towards the assurance that the Captain voyaged now 'toward no earthly pole'. In the verse Prologue Dickens wrote for the 1857–8 productions of *The Frozen Deep* he capitalised on the same associations. He proposed that the audiences take a mental journey

> To that white region where the Lost lie low,
> Wrapp'd in their mantles of eternal snow;
> Unvisited by change, nothing to mock
> Those statues sculptured in the icy rock . . .

Again the physical stillness and immutability of the Arctic are blended into metaphysical composure and changelessness; with the extra thought that in this beautiful calm the preserved bodies of the dead become their own best monuments.

At worst such pious imagining could turn the polar regions into heaven's antechamber, culling souls with a feather-touch. But the removal of physical suffering from the picture could make it seem that the idea of the snowy death confronted you in the purest possible form with the essential coldness of dying – of quitting the whole world of warmth and movement, sustained only by the difficult hopes of religion. Finding the comfort in such a death might be the hardest test of faith. Emily Dickinson, living habitually expectant of death and resurrection, experiencing the Four Last Things of religion as pressing sensual realities within the four walls of her New England frame-house, felt her way into the idea of the cold death several times. She was alert to the imaginative potential of the poles: Lady Franklin even makes a personal appearance in a poem of about 1864, as the 'lone British Lady', a model of faithfulness. In 1862 she incorporated death by freezing – 'A Quartz contentment' – into her lyric 'After great pain, a formal feeling comes', using it as an idiosyncratic metaphor for the null aftermath that would follow the bouts of anguish in her spiritual life.

> This is the Hour of Lead –
> Remembered, if outlived,
> As freezing persons, recollect the Snow –
> First – Chill – then Stupor – then the letting go

The absence of physical pain hardly counts, here, as a consolation. It is a *datum*, a given foundation on which to build a complex structure of acceptance. A poem completed the previous year, the famous vision of the 'meek' dead sleeping 'Safe in their Alabaster Chambers', had troubled her for an apt conclusion. She wanted to convey the chill stasis of being dead, an equivocal 'safety' lying at the end of change. She had tried a verse that summoned the cold literally:

> Springs – shake the Seals –
> But the silence – stiffens –
> Frosts unhook – in the Northern Zones –
> Icicles – crawl from Polar Caverns –
> Midnight in Marble – Refutes – the Suns –

But it was her final version, in which the spheres go on revolving but all human movement lapses away; in which there comes a silent wintry universal downfall; in which 'Diadems – drop – and Doges – surrender –/Soundless as dots – on a Disc of Snow –' that made the single reader, her sister Sue, say, 'I always go to the fire, and get warm after thinking of it, but I never *can* again . . .'

Death could come in many ways in the Arctic. It could be exacted as the price for a simple mistake over clothing or food that would have been harmless enough elsewhere. It was this sense of disproportionate penalties attaching to everyday actions that made people think of the Arctic climate as *unforgiving*, waiting to pounce, it seemed, on anybody less than meticulous. Death could come suddenly and unpredictably, as when Bellot dropped abruptly out of sight through an ice-crack. A shrug of the ice, moving at the call of forces which quite dwarfed the activities of explorers, and a man was gone. Equally, though, a polar death was often the outcome of a long, failing struggle, a prolonged exertion that spent all a party's reserves of willpower and fortitude in vain. It came after a traveller had roused himself over and over to march again, to plan again, to consider expedients. From the narratives of polar survivors, the public had already grown used to stories shaped by hope deferred. Franklin's record of his first expedition was a case in point. As Franklin and his companions had done on their dreadful boot-eating march back from the Arctic in 1821, so the readers of his *Narrative of a Journey to the Shores of the Polar Sea* also pinned their hopes on the hut at Fort Enterprise. It provided the promised goal of the explorers' overland return, and even it seems utterly out of reach at first. The porters mutiny, the party divides, starvation walks among them. When Franklin reaches Fort Enterprise, after much suffering, after an apparently final effort, it proves empty of stores and fuel. The promised relief recedes indefinitely. The fair, the proportionate close to the story turns out to be, so to speak, a false wall; the real end to the narrative is much farther off. Once more the travellers must conjure a day's life from a meal of leather and charred bones; and then another day's; and another, and another, until they have so little strength left that ordinary tasks take hours. Very slowly they saw a log, or turn themselves over on the hard floor, or argue with 'a kind of unreasonable pettishness' amongst themselves, apologising every few minutes. 'Dear me, if we are spared to return to England, I wonder if we shall recover our understandings,' remarks one. Only then, after the expected limit of suffering has been repeatedly breached, and action has slowed into a nightmarish, all-absorbing succession of trivia, does relief arrive. It might have been, it nearly was, death that instead ended the struggle. This became one of the classic forms of the polar narrative: the unexpected redoubling of the plight itself an expectation in the reader's mind. And it was perhaps this kind of long-drawn-out polar death that most commended itself to the contemporary imagination, and to contemporary reverence. (All the signs suggested that it was indeed how Franklin's last expedition had died.)

Despite the gradual breakdown it implied of mental strength as well as physical resistance, despite the unmistakable truth that an expedition which had died had therefore failed, it was this species of mortal defeat at the Arctic's hand which most gave authority to the relics of the dead. To die having resisted to one's utmost was better than departing in an accidental split second. Such a death spoke most of courage. Such a death was most filled with dogged meaning, and with the curious quality of triumph some Victorians associated with the remains of the dead, wherever they lay. 'Heaven forbid' (wrote Dickens, in the first of his two *Household Words* essays)

that we, sheltered and fed, and considering this question at our own warm hearth, should audaciously set limits to any extremity of desperate distress! It is in reverence for the brave and enterprising, in admiration for the great spirits who can endure even unto the end, in love for their names, and in tenderness for their memory, that we think of the specks, once ardent men, 'scattered about in different directions' on the waste of ice and snow, and plead for their lightest ashes.

Such a death most required, too, the vigilance of the living in maintaining the reputation the dead left behind. A death justified by the remarkable conduct it elicited needed to be sustained in the minds of posterity. Returning to the same imagined vista of scattered bodies which had moved him before, Dickens took up cudgels again at the end of his second essay, against indifference to the polar dead.

Utilitarianism will protest, 'they are dead; why care about this?' Our reply shall be, 'Because they ARE dead, therefore we care about this . . . Because they lie scattered on those wastes of snow, and are as defenceless against the remembrance of coming generations, as against the elements into which they are now resolving, and the winter winds that alone can waft them home, now, impalpable air; therefore, cherish them gently, even in the breasts of children. Therefore, teach no one to shudder without reason, at the history of their end. Therefore, confide with their own firmness, in their fortitude, their lofty sense of duty, their courage, and their religion.

Though the result was a corpse lying in the snow, a vacated property, palpably undone by an environment too vicious to survive, some Victorians were prepared to take the death as a victory because it had elucidated qualities in the dead man which made the snow irrelevant. Instead of displaying the triumph of an indifferent wilderness over humanity's best efforts, it could seem to show the exact opposite.

If this strikes us as an unlikely thing to believe, it should be remembered that there are different degrees and sorts of belief. This was a satisfying reflection given house-room because it spoke irresistibly to wider anxieties about human resistance and human self-sufficiency. No connected, certainly no practical, thinking about the Arctic was involved; in fact, while this response to the spectacle of the polar dead revelled in the details and the atmosphere of exploration, it shied away from a full and prosaic understanding of the subject. Its power lay in being vaguely sensed. And in place of the Arctic as a geographical region, there could be substituted an Arctic which was an arena for the imagination.

Dickens did just this in the verses he supplied as an overture to *The Frozen Deep*, when his family and friends mounted Wilkie Collins' Franklin-inspired melodrama at home in Tavistock House. (In its way his Prologue is as public a document as Tennyson's engraved epitaph on Franklin in Westminster Abbey, for after the extraordinary success of the amateur production it was spoken from the enormous stage of the Manchester Free Trade Hall, and declaimed to Queen Victoria at a command performance.) It opens with an allusion to *Robinson Crusoe*, that sustained tribute to the sovereign power of the individual mind. While 'soft music' played, and the lifted curtain revealed only 'mists and darkness', Dickens' friend John Forster recited:

> One savage footprint on the lonely shore,
> Where one man listen'd to the surge's roar;

Not all the winds that stir the mighty sea
Can ever ruffle in the memory.
If such its interest and thrall, O then
Pause on the footprints of heroic men,
Making a garden of the desert wide
Where PARRY conquer'd and FRANKLIN died.

These lines depend on shaky syntax to make a shaky meaning cohere. The deeds of explorers, says Dickens, endure because they are imprinted, like Man Friday's footprint, beyond the reach of wind and tide. Where? On the surface of the mind; in some region formed, like memory or great fiction, according to the priorities of 'interest' and imagination, against which mere weather is powerless. The great oddity of asserting that exploring achievements are as real as fiction passes unnoticed, for here fiction – or the world of imagination fiction represents – counts as more real than any actual beach or snowfield. It takes better impressions, and retains them longer. In the calculations of this sort of immortality, Parry conquering and Franklin dying register as equally grand impressions. The difference between the two things hardly amounts to a contrast. Dickens, so lavishly privileging the imagination over the material world, needs the audience's belief as well. The syntactical clumsiness of 'O then/Pause on the footprints' creates a nice ambiguity. Do the footprints of the heroic men make 'a garden of the desert wide', or does the audience's own willingness to 'pause'? Dickens loved the conventional artifices of theatre, and among them of course the tradition of the address to the audience which prays their help in dissolving workaday reality. But here the audience are being asked, implicitly, to do something more than to clap their hands if they believe in explorers (so to speak). Endorse the precedence Dickens gives to imagination over brute matter, and you grant the traces left by the explorers a kind of transforming authority. Their footprints can change the nature of the wilderness, at least where it truly matters, in imagination.

Dickens was not just indulging in a literally florid metaphor, though for decades to come explorers were conventionally praised in similar terms, credited with illuminating, making bloom, and generally putting in its humble place the terrain they struggled through. (Dr Wilson 'beautifully lit up the wastes' of Antarctica, said his *Times* obituary.) Nor was he only venturing a sublime inversion, super-imposing a touch of the English cottage garden onto the frozen plain. Dickens took almost comical pains to get *The Frozen Deep* right where the small things of polar exploration were concerned. He ordered authentic props and costumes, boasting in a letter:

I believe that anything so complete has never been seen. We had an act at the North Pole, where the slightest and greatest thing the eye beheld were equally taken from the books of the Polar voyagers. Out of thirty people, there were certainly not two who might not have gone straight to the North Pole itself, completely furnished for winter!

He practised with the 'Snowboys' who were to drop, from above, the paper snow he had had manufactured whenever the door at the rear of the stage was opened to show the howling Arctic. (In fact, a slice of the back garden of his townhouse, specially enclosed in a wooden shed, and whitened.) And the garden referred to in the Prologue was a direct allusion to a particular discovery on Beechey Island that had wrung the heart of the nation. The searchers had found a little plot, scratched hopefully in the soil, intended for a garden. Some mosses and small anemones still survived. This forlorn effort to cultivate the wild had a special pathos. Of all the ways of defying the Arctic, gardening seemed the gentlest and perhaps the most resonantly English, besides which, as Dr Kane remarked, 'A garden implies a purpose either to remain or to return: he who makes it is looking to the future.' But Dickens used it in a different fashion altogether, turning the touching gesture of defiance into a symbol of victory, an apt vindication of all the intangible qualities that could be opposed to the null surroundings, and which, in the truer Arctic of imagination, successfully seeded it with virtue. Bodies, strangely, have a role in this immaterial or anti-material vision. The homage to 'the Lost' in their snowy mantles follows immediately after: the 'footprints' surely include the whole trail of Arctic evidence, from the littlest relics to the revered corpses themselves. The gardening metaphor does not quite reckon with them – Dickens tossed off the Prologue verses with the pell-mell facility he brought to loose, occasional writing. The bodies are not envisaged as seed-pods, for example: in fact Dickens' sense of their authority depends on them not popping open, but remaining closed, for ever the same, making the desert bloom with their integrity. This was primarily a moral wholeness, as befitted his fantasy of an immaterial Arctic, though the physical preservation of 'the Lost' came in by way of poetic reinforcement.

Yet the shift into fancy we see in Dickens' Prologue – and the wish-fulfilment – are not decisively detached from the prosaic history of exploration. They consume that history imaginatively in a way that develops the moral assumptions already implicit in it. Lady Franklin was already working to have her husband's achievements judged on moral grounds. When Dickens took sides in the cannibalism controversy, he was both protecting Sir John's reputation and defending his own imaginative investment in an idea: the idea that men in the white North could preserve themselves, entire and irreducible, no matter how enfeebling their experience. If disaster could weaken explorers' bodies *and* minds, pressing to the limit the power of circumstances over character, yet still left unaltered some essential core of self which forbade corruption, it suggested a broader hope that an individual far from the Arctic could cling to.

Some grounds for the home attractiveness of this interpretation of Arctic adventure can be seen in the story of Dickens' passionate involvement with *The Frozen Deep*. He was going through a very bad patch. His writing and editing commitments had begun to exceed even his formidable energy, and, amidst the strain of continual obligations, he could find no relief in his private life, for his marriage itself was at deadlock. 'I find that the skeleton in my domestic closet is becoming a pretty big one,' he confided in a letter of April 1856. He felt completely encased; and, within the tight carapace of circumstances, increasingly unsure of his purposes and intentions. The best he could muster was an image of himself journeying fatalistically, trudging onward beneath his burdens. From the same letter:

However strange it is to be never at rest, and never satisfied, and ever trying after something that is never reached, and to be always laden with plot and plan and care and worry, how clear it is that it must be, and that one is driven by an irresistible might until the journey is worked out! It is much better to go on and fret, than to stop and fret. As to repose – for some men there's no such thing in this life.

He could not yet allow himself to envisage escape, unless it came through doing something that gave meaning to endurance. Dickens needed an outlet, a chance to inhabit his stoicism differently, a safe but bolder way of understanding his journey. It looks as if acting in *The Frozen Deep* gave him this chance. He threw himself into the business of rehearsals; he positively enjoyed the disarray caused in the household by the production, writing away at *Little Dorrit* with a rare sense of refreshment while all around him carpenters hammered, gluepots teetered on stepladders, and buckets of distemper boiled on braziers. Most of all, he relished being someone other on the minia-ture stage the carpenters erected. Amateur theatricals at Christmas time in Tavistock House were an annual tradition; but this year was exceptional, for the scale of the enterprise, for the public acclaim it aroused, for the intense release it afforded the chief actor. He remembered it as a blessed moment of free self-expression. 'The domestic unhappiness remains so strong upon me', he told Wilkie Collins in March 1858 – by which time matters had grown, if anything, worse – 'that I can't write, and (waking) can't rest, one minute. I have never known a moment's peace or content since the last night of the Frozen Deep.'

In part his performance so transfigured him because it let him come at his craft of writing from a new angle, without the labour of forcing the plot along, and the association that had become engrained in him between the solitary effort of composition and his loneliness. One of the invited critics, John Oxenford of *The Times*, observed that Dickens' minutely detailed physical creation of his character was somehow un-actorlike: a novelist's performance, with a novelistic density far in excess of the basic needs of the part. 'Writing' his character moment by moment in stance and gesture, Dickens himself recorded, added an element of public catharsis to the familiar pleasures of good technique.

1 'The Ice Islands'. Cook's crew successfully mining iceberg fragments for fresh water on his Second Voyage; engraving of a drawing by William Hodges in *A Voyage Towards the South Pole*, 1777.

2 'Landing the Treasures, or Results of the Polar Expedition!!!'
by George Cruikshank, 1819.

3 Drawing by George Back of Franklin's party on his overland expedition
to the Arctic coast foraging for 'tripe de roche', an edible moss.

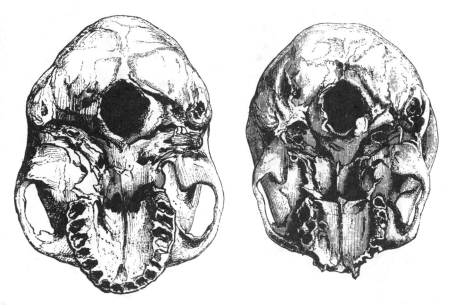

4 Skulls of 'an Eskimo' (left) and of 'one of Napoleon's Guards killed at
Waterloo', from Robert Gordon Latham's *Natural History of the Varieties
of Man*, 1850.

5 Dickens (left) as polar explorer. Nathaniel Powell, a wine–merchant who
lived next door to Dickens at Tavistock House, sketched his host and the
other actors as they performed *The Frozen Deep* in 1857.

6 'The North-West Passage' by John Everett Millais, 1874.

OPPOSITE
7 Alictu and Kanguagiu, Inuit drawn by John Ross *c.* 1835.
8 The elusive Cape Tennyson, shown with misleading certainty on
Inglefield's 1853 map of Baffin Bay in *A Summer Search for Sir John
Franklin*. Note also Mittie Island, and other compliments in the form of
placenames.

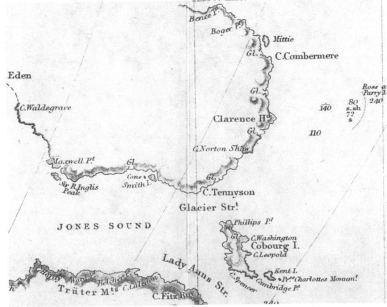

WAITING TO BE WON.

(ARCTIC EXPEDITION SAILED MAY 29, 1875.)

9 'Waiting to be Won', *Punch*, 5 June 1875. Verses overleaf continued the
pin-up treatment of 'the White Ladye of the Pole' (*sic*):
But still the white Witch-Maiden, that sits above the Pole,
In the snow-bound silver silence whose cold quells aught but soul,
Draws manly hearts with strange desire to lift her icy veil:
The bravest still have sought her, and will seek, whoever fail.

10 'I Decided to Go as Aurora', *South Polar Times*, vol. 3, 1911. The Australian geologist Griffith Taylor, writing as 'Jessamine', contributed a 'Ladies Letter' to the Scott expedition's winter newspaper, illustrated by Edward Wilson with cartoons of many of the expedition's personalities in drag. (Birdie Bowers appeared in maiden-aunt rig, with bustle and parrot-headed umbrella.) Jessamine's prediction for the next season's sledging wear was 'the new material *Gaberdine* – in greens and greys . . .' Here she is describing a simple frock for the midwinter celebrations, consisting of 'ribbons in shades of magenta, purple, and aniline blue'.

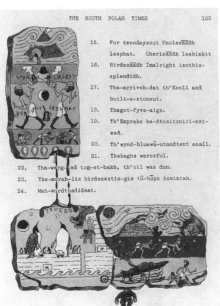

11 'Antarctic Archives' in the *South Polar Times*: a mock-ancient record of the Winter Journey to Cape Crozier, with pictures by Wilson showing the party playing at being Egyptians rather than Inuit, while their makeshift igloo blows away

Player's Cigarettes.

CAPTAIN SCOTT.

Player's Cigarettes.

CAPTAIN OATES.

Player's Cigarettes.

LIEUT. BOWERS.

Player's Cigarettes.

COMMANDER EVANS.

Player's Cigarettes.

Dr WILSON.

Player's Cigarettes.

AN ADÉLIE PENGUIN & HIS MATE.

Player's Cigarettes.

A SLEDGE TEAM.

12 Player's 'Polar Exploration' Cigarette Cards, 2nd series, *c.* 1915–16

I derive a strange feeling out of it, like writing a book in company; a satisfaction of a most singular kind, which has no exact parallel in my life; a something that I suppose to belong to a labourer in art alone, and which has to me a conviction of its being actual truth without its pain that I never could adequately state if I were to try never so hard.

Dickens managed to convince the audiences, too, that they were witnessing a uniquely truthful, uniquely faithful portrait. But the 'naturalness' that the critics described is hard to account for now from the reported style of Dickens' acting. The slow burns, the elaborate facial tics that were supposed to convey contained violence, the buttonholing delivery – none of these distinguish themselves especially from the acting conventions of the time. All seem as contrived as the play's bouts of eerie music ('Those Evening Bells' and 'Farewell to Lochabar'). It appears more likely that the audiences were responding to the intensity of Dickens' own conviction. Revived ten years later by a professional company, without Dickens' 'frenzy' (his word), the play flopped and no-one could remember the reasons for the former excitement.

What truth was he imparting? Where the actual writing of the play was concerned, Dickens had also taken a hand, less by using his pen than by marshalling Wilkie Collins' text to support the performance he had in mind for himself. When Collins, under Dickens' wing as a young staff writer on *Household Words*, presented his draft version for Dickens' approval, the play revolved around the fate of 'Frank Aldersley', a British lion of a romantic lead who found himself stranded in the Arctic on a lost expedition, another of whose officers, the venomous 'Richard Wardour', was unbeknownst to Frank the spurned suitor of his sweetheart Clara, sworn to kill Frank at the first opportunity. The march-till-you-drop plots of the polar narratives, while dramatic, were not easy to mount on stage. Collins had solved the problem by grafting on a romantic melodrama of conventional type, with a well-tried source of dramatic tension, and a set of relationships that unfolded reliably from the main premise. (Facing a related difficulty, the poet Jean Ingelow handled her spoony, gushing Franklin poem by superimposing a similar romantic situation onto the resistant material. Her narrator lamented that when

Thou didst set thy foot on the ship, and sail
    To the icefields and the snow;
Thou wert sad, for thy love did nought avail,
    And the end I could not know . . .

Love made icebergs tractable.) On seeing this first script Dickens at once chose for himself the role of Wardour, the villain of the piece as the piece then stood. Barring a few simple refinements to the staging, the revisions he arranged with Collins ('some cuts', 'mostly verbal', suggested to a junior writer 'exceedingly quick to take my notions') were all designed to refocus the play on Wardour. The prophetic powers of the Scottish nanny were burlesqued, so that providence was relieved of the task of bringing Aldersley safely home. That was now made dependent on a change of heart in Wardour; who inherited, indeed, Aldersley's original leonine character, and now carried the limp former hero back from the ice in his jaws, depositing him at Clara's feet. 'I see the lamb i' the grasp o' the lion,' shrieked the nurse. Still harsh, still saturnine, Wardour ceased to be thuggish. The revised Wardour opened his mind to a fellow explorer, gaining an inner life, while judicious amendments upped the danger to the whole expedition, bonding the threat posed by Wardour with the natural violence of the elements. Dickens' character became the only source of dramatic tension in *The Frozen Deep*. In its amended form the play still found little use for the Arctic landscape revealed from time to time through the door at the rear of the stage, where a Union Jack provided a splotch of colour, 'blowing out straight and bold in the icy breeze,' (enthused one critic) 'as much to say, "Where am I not? And where I am aloft, who despairs? who has not heart and hope and resolution?"' At the beginning of the 'Arctic' Act Two, the script set the scene with a cheerfully absurd exchange which suggests no-one took the exotic location very seriously. A seaman reports that 'it's pinching cold'; 'And that's no news in the Arctic Regions,' replies an officer, 'with the thermometer below zero indoors.'

Curiously, however, it was Dickens' changes which stopped *The Frozen Deep* from being *entirely* a melodrama with an unusual backdrop, principally to be admired for its topicality and resourceful carpentering. Instead of showing a good man, Aldersley, beset by the twin perils of (a) the Arctic and (b) a dangerous rogue, it now portrayed the struggle of Wardour against his internal iciness, a theme signalled as the true moral of the play by Dickens in his Prologue. He asked

> that the secrets of the vast Profound
> Within us, an exploring hand may sound,
> Testing the region of the ice-bound soul,
> Seeking a passage at its northern pole,
> Soft'ning the horrors of its wintry sleep,
> Melting the surface of that 'Frozen Deep'.

This was the old, old metaphor, of no great particularity. Yet the displacement of the play's emphasis onto an individual's 'wintry sleep' already suggested a relegating attitude to the physical dangers of ice and darkness; and one final innovation where Wardour was concerned gave the absolute primacy to immaterial qualities that Dickens desired. Wardour is immune to the cold. The others have weakened, but Wardour has not: a sign, not of health, but of an overriding sickness where it matters most. 'Look at me!' he declares, in one of the passages of self-explanation Dickens had had inserted,

Look how I have lived and thriven, with the heart-ache gnawing at me at home, with the winds of the Icy North whistling round me here! I am the strongest man among you. Why? I have fought through hardships that have laid the best-seasoned men of all our party on their backs. Why? What have I done that my life should throb as bravely through every vein of my body at this minute, and in this deadly place, as ever it did in the wholesome breezes of Home? What am I preserved for? I tell you again, for the coming of one day – for the meeting with one man.

Wardour, as Dickens acted him, is a figure of supreme physical independence of environment. Here was the occasion for Dickens' electrifying identification with his role. Here, his chance to work through in a distanced and highly melodramatic way, subtle-silly, silly-subtle, his own passionate wish to be remade from within, forged anew within the constraints of circumstances as icy and deadening (he felt) as the Arctic. And here as well, in the question of environment and selfhood, the assurances he chiefly cherished in his Arctic reading came in, into play and into *the* play. It has been pointed out that Wardour's characterisation differs markedly from Dickens' portrayals of the lost sailors in his *Household Words* articles; but it is the difference between a photograph and its negative, where black and white replace each other within the same outlines. For Dickens, the value of *The Frozen Deep* was as a reticent, yet expressive psychodrama. He wanted to get at the meat of the matter, I think, by turning on its head the premise that good men might survive morally: instead assuming physical survival as the starting-point for the moral conflict, and throwing into high relief the anomalous case of a man 'preserved' in the wrong sense. Wardour has succumbed to the Arctic ('I like it,' he growls) in every way except the physical. Having finessed young Aldersley away from the main returning party, he intends to dispose of him in the icy solitudes. But he carries Frank safely homeward instead, his moral renaissance resulting, with inevitable symmetry, in his physical collapse and pathos-filled death on stage at the play's finale. His paradoxical inviolability has been reordered. Now properly immune to the cold as good men are – morally, that is – his flesh suffers the less important consequences of the snow, a right relationship restored. Dickens wore a wild grey wig for the last scene, because Wardour is (of course) so changed the others do not recognise him. Propped on one haggard elbow, he describes the moment of his conversion, and the true limits of the Arctic's power as he has discovered them to be. The pressure of the place (a refining wind) actually helped to dislodge his wicked intention, but it cannot touch the virtuous intention that replaced murder in his heart: 'I heard the night-wind come up in the silence from the great Deep. It bore past me the groaning of the ice-bergs at sea, floating, floating past! – and the wicked voice floated away with it – away, away, away for ever! Love him, love him, Clara, for helping *me*! No wind could float that away!' With all their mighty cold, and powerful *drift* – a morally suggestive sort of movement – the poles are helpless in the face of virtue.

But then the audience, if it were alert and in the mood to make connections between this preposterous entertainment and the general sentiments that exploration inspired, would have known long before that Wardour's crime will miscarry. At the climax of the second act, as he ushers Aldersley out into the wilds, Wardour utters a threat that invokes the full erasing power of the Arctic, that raises the ultimate and annihilating fear the Arctic aroused. He says: 'Come over the Snow and the Ice! Come over the road that no human footsteps have ever trodden, and where no human trace is ever left!' Which Dickens, at least, will have understood as a self-confuting polar heresy, an empty bogey of a fear. For the traces *were* left, and the traces *were* found, and they made all the human difference in the world, if you did not class men under 'other mammalia'.

EIGHT

Imagining Eskimos

Following out the traces, deciphering and sustaining their meaning, depended on shared possession of the relevant history. For the older relics, that meant the mythicised history of a buccaneering English past, which was (piecemeal) coming to underlie English identity in the industrial present. For the traces of recent expeditions, what was required was a knowledge of a current and immediate tradition, along with the conviction that exploration had obvious value, as the expression of restless English virtues. This shared world of necessary understandings formed one pillar of the perception of exploration as something national, *owned* nationally despite the absence of borders in the polar regions. 'Cherish them gently, even in the breasts of children,' Dickens had written, over-the-top but undeniably tapping a vein. The horrors of exploration became acceptable, educational horrors. Franklin suffered in texts for children alongside Lord Nelson losing his arm and eye. Polar stories took their place among the other tales of glory presented to the young in order that they might know what they were inheriting, and that Englishness might be reproduced and re-created in their minds. Englishness bequeathed you a kit of narratives, assumptions, and values. It allowed you to read shared codes.

John Everett Millais' son was shooting springbok in the Karoo Desert of South Africa at the end of the century, when he suddenly came upon a print of his father's epic painting *The North-West Passage*, hit of the 1874 Royal Academy spring show. He describes the encounter:

a tropical thunderstorm compelled me to gallop off to the nearest shelter – the hut of a Hottentot shepherd, some miles away – and there before me hung a gaudy German oleograph of this picture nailed to the mud walls – the only adornment of the place. Anywhere else I should have been disposed to laugh at it as a ludicrous travesty of the original; but here it seemed like the face of an old friend bidding me welcome in the wilderness.

The North-West Passage, eventually donated to the nation and now hung in the Tate Gallery, celebrated the British polar tradition just as Sir George Nares was preparing the departure of the century's last north-bound British effort. It was an excellent psychological moment: the new expedition, it seemed, was just about to refresh the achievements of the past. (In fact, Nares' lumbering man-hauled sledges failed ignominiously to reach the pole, and scurvy broke out, the wrong tradition revived.) But at the time, with crowds jostling in the RA for a sight of Millais' work, Nares complimented the painter on having influenced the spirit of the nation. For a consciously national piece, it was interestingly indirect. It had a mild quality of a puzzle about it. Instead of showing ships sublimely ice-bound, or sailors actively thrusting through the snow, it was a domestic interior. On a stool centre-right a young woman sitting in the pale pool of her long dress reads aloud from a large book to a grizzled old man, left, wearing a heavy outdoor jacket and enthroned erect on an upright chair. She looks down dutifully at the pages: his sharp, pensive gaze comes straight out of the picture to intercept the eye of the onlooker. A second examination reveals that the room is stuffed with naval, and more particularly polar, mementoes. The old man's hand lies at the foot of a widely unfolded map of the Arctic archipelago; a telescope rests on a side-table; one print on the wall shows a full-rig blue-and-white Navy officer from the earlier 1800s while the other, part-shrouded by an enormous flag, reintroduces the expected sledging-scene in the form of a miniature water-colour. Even the safe sea of a south coast resort, seen through the window at the extreme left with little boats drawn up on its beach, recalls that other boreal sea too far off for the telescope to see it. Like Millais' equally famous *Boyhood of Raleigh*, which left its audience to fill in the maritime glory waiting for the doubleted child playing on Plymouth Hoe, *The North-West Passage* relies on those who saw it being able to supply the appropriate narrative. They could, of course. A daughter was clearly reading a printed polar narrative to her father, equally clearly an old sailor, who had brought traces of the poles home with him to his retirement. Most of all, the pensiveness and fierceness of his features now assembled themselves as signs of his cold experiences; the transports of painful memory accounted for his lifted gaze, by meeting which – like entering into a contract – the viewer entered too into the story of polar endeavour, possessed as vestiges and recollections in an English sitting-room. Millais' son can gloss the picture expansively in the memoir of his father from which the Karoo anecdote comes.

He is at home now – this ancient mariner, stranded on the sands of life, like the hulk of an old ship that has done its duty – but as he listens to these deeds of daring, the old fire burns within him, and in every lineament of face and figure we see how deeply he is moved.

The North-West Passage keeps faith with the English past, and Millais junior, seeing it, keeps faith with his father *and* with that. He does not only think of the picture as an old friend because what he now meets as a cheap print out in the wilds of the Karoo, he first knew as an enormous original canvas in his childhood home. He belongs to the nation whose traditions it encodes; he owns the common history which makes it easy to decode. Asked what *he* thought of it, the Hottentot shepherd on the other hand pointed to the Union Jack in the top right of his oleograph, and said: 'I like that cotton goods. It would make good clothes.'

Hottentots were at the bottom of the racial heap in nineteenth-century South Africa, a sad suppressed aboriginal people, far lower in the scheme of things than the aggressive tribes – the Zulus, the Xhosas – white men had contended against for the land. The herder's comment could not possibly disrupt the sense that the artist's son read from the picture. It was too tangential, too off-beam, voiced from too far out on the margins; the audience the painting had been designed for were too confident in the story it told. In fact the younger Millais took it as wholly, charmingly comic. He put it into his memoir among the other anecdotes, biographical sidelights and snippets calculated to entertain those who saw a flag as a flag rather than a potential shirt.

For the same reason – good copy – he filled in the identities of the models used for *The North-West Passage*. As the old sailor, Millais had the testy, eccentric, semi-charlatan Captain Trelawney sit for him. A pushy friend of the Romantic poets, a witness of that distant day on the Italian beach when Shelley's body was burned on a pyre dressed with oil and wine, Trelawney now owned a part-share in a Turkish bath. He demanded payment in kind for his modelling services. Every time he came for a sitting, Mrs Millais was obliged to take a steam treatment at his bathhouse. She sweated six times in the cause of *The North-West Passage*.

But the very irrelevance of the Hottentot's comment draws attention to how exclusive, and excluding, the preoccupations of the painting are. The picture is impervious because complete without his response to it; it does not need someone like him to understand it. Yet it also performs its evocation of the English exploring spirit without needing to make any reference whatsoever to those tens of thousands of other 'natives', as remote as any Hottentot from the national community primed to interpret it, who have a rather closer connection with the Arctic: the indigenous inhabitants of the ice. It seems that *The North-West Passage* is complete without Inuit either. No harpoon or fur or vanishingly tiny tacked-up drawing of a kayak represents them, though they appear in almost every account of almost every journey. What makes Millais' omission particularly telling is that in this he appears to go against the grain of Victorian fascination with the polar peoples. They were far from being generally ignored. Indeed the 'Eskimos' (as they were called invariably, from a rude Canadian Indian term meaning *raw flesh eaters*, until they gained enough clout in the later twentieth century to insist on their own name for themselves) were already the single most studied 'primitive people' in the world. Studied, photographed, repeatedly described and marvelled over: the recipients of concentrated attention by a Europe and an America fascinated by their position amidst the ice, strung out along a circumpolar skein of settlements from Greenland to Alaska. In relation to their numbers, they held a conspicuously privileged position in the European imagination. While the Dayaks of Borneo (say) occupied the attention of a few early anthropologists, and of the traders and officials who dealt with the East Indies, the habits and customs of Eskimos, or at least a garbled version of them, formed part of common knowledge. Eskimos rub noses, Eskimos swap wives, Eskimos build ice-block houses. Since Ross' encounter, meeting these genial locals furnished an inevitable incident in the British polar tradition. But their absence here, where an artist has consciously selected for the emotive essence of exploration, brings out a certain doubleness in that tradition; it alerts one to a tacit, but firm, distinction between the aspect of exploration which involves visiting the Arctic, and the aspect concerned with travel in the Arctic – the struggle to reach x. Unlike the mixed logs and journals, Millais' painting presents the iconography of the second aspect alone. And on examination, in fact, most of the nineteenth-century polar narratives allow little more role to the Arctic's natives than the painting does, when it comes to the explorers' success or failure at traversing the landscape. The Eskimos belonged in descriptions of the region, in accounts of its natural history, studies of its folklore, word-paintings of its scenery. They did not belong in the stories of discovery and achievement.

Up to a point, this reflected a genuine difference of purposes between explorers and Inuit in the landscape. The kind of enterprise represented by an expedition had no possible basis in Inuit society, and equally the idea of 'an expedition' had no place in Inuit culture. Hunting ranges and living patterns varied across the arc of settlement, but usually groups of Inuit families migrated short distances in an annual cycle, back and forth between winter and summer food sources, concentrating their energies first on the means of supporting life, then on living the life their efforts made possible. Getting and spending calories, in short: getting them from whales, reindeer, fish, birds, and seals, spending them on love, art, blood-feuds, gossip, and religion. An Inuit hunter might go on an odyssey beyond familiar territory, returning (or not) to be celebrated for his feat, and incidentally perhaps to astonish an outsider with his skill at drawing accurate freehand maps of his route. A shaman might undergo a solitary ordeal in the snow, ragged and hungry, in order to glimpse the secret faces of holy animals. Neither journey resembled the organised

European pursuit of geographical goals in the Arctic, any more than the hunter or the shaman's decision to wander much resembled the calculations of loss and gain that preceded a Victorian sailor's decision to sign on for an Arctic voyage. When a wooden ship arrived in the ice containing tens or hundreds of European men, with specialised occupations, arranged in a naval hierarchy, and accompanied by a long-term stock of food, something was purposed that made little sense to the Inuit, who never travelled to reach invisible point x. The Inuit name for the North Pole translates as 'the Great Nail': it was coined in the nineteenth century after hearing Europeans talk about the northern axis of the earth, on the assumption that the goal which prompted such efforts must be a physical object, evidently of some bulk and value. And iron was particularly valuable in the North, once its advantages over bone hooks and knives had been demonstrated. In effect, they attempted to envisage the Europeans' activity in Inuit terms. When realisation dawned (as happened way out on the sea-ice to the four north Greenland hunters employed by Robert Peary on his successful polar journey of 1909) amazement or derision followed. So, although individual Inuit frequently participated in expeditions, they did not initiate them, and would not have chosen to. It could reasonably be pointed out that the explorers were trying something new to the Inuit, for good or for ill; something which truly exceeded Inuit practice in the demands it placed on organisation, transport, and determination.

But the European perception of polar travel as an activity *wholly* separate – in mood and technique, aims and expertise – from the Inuit experience of inhabiting the Arctic, also indicates that the spectacle of the Inuit, living their domestic lives in a place Europeans were considered heroic for reaching, aroused a degree of tension. It is not hard to see how the Inuit presence would complicate the visions of exploring bravery predicated on the idea of an empty Arctic. If they did not 'explore', their daily routines amidst the snow nonetheless overlapped with what explorers did to survive. After all, they too negotiated, in an unsettling matter-of-fact way, the struggle with the environment that so fascinated the polar audience; and moreover they succeeded in the struggle. (As a people, if not as individuals. Inuit also died of injuries on the ice, of diseases, of starvation. Before the regular role played in Inuit existence by dearth and famine was understood, Europeans who encountered Inuit communities on the edge of starvation could adopt a straightforward attitude of pity. These were wretched people, in a wretched place: the environmental paupers of the world. The travellers could then figure themselves as the only stalwart and capable denizens of the ice, or even as the godsent relievers of the Inuit. Parry distributed spare ship's supplies to one hungry village. 'Poor child of chance! hath Winter shrunk thy store?', glowed Chandos Hoskyns Abrahall. 'Fear not, – there is a Briton at thy door!')

They too left human traces in the Arctic; they too constituted specks of human warmth and intelligence in the wastes, which demanded some response from the well of feeling which fed English tears for Franklin. It was possible to map out similarities as well as differences, especially when the tools of early anthropology became available. The Victorian science of mankind assigned the much-studied Inuit a place alongside their white visitors in the common story of human development, even if there remained small role for them in the tableaux of exploration. Yet it was on the footing of perceived similarity that the possibility arose of unwelcome contrasts between Inuit and European adaption to the Arctic. With a reflex protectiveness towards their own culture's self-definitions, rather than any conscious decision, most observers managed their reports of the Inuit to avoid such contrasts. It needed doing. For while the Hottentot's reaction to *The North-West Passage* only prompted laughter, would an Inuit's have been as funny? Suppose an inhabitant of Thule or Angmassalik had studied the background of the painting, and said: why are those men pulling a sledge themselves? Where are their dogs? Or: what peculiar snowshoes. Or: those clothes don't look warm.

This was, of its nature, an unacknowledged threat. The nineteenth century saw no explicit avowals of a truth which has become evident in retrospect. Until the invention of petrol motors efficient at low temperatures, Inuit methods worked best for polar survival, even though these had to be adapted to explorers' different ends. Explorers prepared to learn from the Inuit succeeded. Those who ignored the fur clothes, the lightweight elastic sledges and the dog-handling techniques failed when they attempted long journeys, or even died, Franklin providing the extreme case. But there was no Victorian polemic corresponding to the essay published, with hindsight, by the Canadian explorer Vilhjalmur Stefansson in 1939. 'The Lost Franklin Expedition' begins stingingly:

One of the most baffling problems of Canadian exploration is how Sir John Franklin and his party of more than a hundred contrived to die to the last man, apparently from hunger and malnutrition, in a district where several hundred Eskimos had been living for generations, bringing up their children, and taking care of their aged.

Contrived to die – Stefansson was in no doubt that a total catastrophe like Franklin's required a wilful refusal to benefit from Inuit example. 'The main cause', he concludes, '. . . was cultural.' He accuses the English of a stubborn unwillingness to shape their behaviour to their surroundings. They dressed inappropriately. They treated hunting as a sport, not a necessity, till it was too late. They ate preserved food, supplemented by the Admiralty issue of anti-scorbutic lemon juice, useless after one year frozen, instead of fresh meat rich in vitamins. They insisted on regarding early signs of scurvy, like lassitude and apathy, as morale problems. Stefansson's lip can be heard curling as he notes that, instead of paying attention to proper cooking methods, they tried to fight dietary deficiency 'with merry song and with entertainment'. He shakes his head over the bumbling English, so wasteful of their lives; he regrets the deaths, but has no sympathy whatsoever for the romantic rigidity that helped to cause them.

This mournful briskness clears the ground wonderfully. As an enthusiastic advocate of the idea (he coined the phrase) of 'the friendly Arctic', which only kills the ignorant traveller who cannot detect the food all round him, Stefansson saw the complete, practical folly of *resisting* the environment in the Victorian mode. His concerns were practical, but he opens up the intimate connections between disaster and disdain, an immensely suggestive diagnosis. At the same time the very lack of sympathy which lets him cut through the alibis for

Franklin's failure inadvertently draws attention to the strength of the cultural obstacles he himself finds it easy to push aside. His own view of the Inuit was culturally conditioned, in a way as invisible to him as the views of the 1840s were invisible to their possessors. Throughout the essay his allegiances show, to a later and different set of racial protocols, and to another variety of polar hero-worship. Born in 1879, author in 1913 of *My Life with the Eskimo* after four years sojourn in Alaska and the Canadian Arctic, Stefansson shared the preoccupations of late nineteenth-century anthropology, including the biologically inspired belief (which we shall come to) in the superior adaptability of white men. His great respect for the Inuit did not prevent him from thinking that their environment contained and limited them. Whites on the other hand – sensible ones, at least – could fit themselves to any climate. The Franklin crews ought, Stefansson's essay argued, to have been *more* successful in the ice than their Inuit neighbours, absorbing all that the locals had to offer while keeping the advantage of their firearms and their trained, youthful masculinity. By 1939 he believed he saw proof that the lesson had been learned in the achievements of the new generation of British explorers, like Gino Watkins. Watkins' Greenland expeditions used dog-sleds on the ground, planes in the air. Civilised innovation and organisation were combined with Inuit experience, which the new school had received indirectly through study of the methods of Amundsen and Nansen, breaking conclusively with the Franklin tradition and its last upholder, Scott. (A strong element of Scandinavian pride featured in Stefansson's detachment from the sentiment surrounding Navy pride and Navy catastrophes: the English mystique of 'The North-West Passage'.) And if now, why not then?

The blood of Englishmen was the same a hundred years ago as it is to-day. There is no reason other than mental why these healthy young men of 1845 could not have had as much fun every month of the year as is now the rule when graduates and undergraduates from Cambridge and Oxford go off on their exploring expeditions to Greenland, Spitsbergen, the Antarctic . . .

The Franklin tragedy, one can tell, frustrates him. It need not have happened. The reasons why it did seem correspondingly trivial – a matter of wrong-headedness. He fingers 'culture' as the culprit, but reduces the meaning of that word in the act of using it, until beneath the pressure of his indignation it only signifies 'the social and mental outlook of the period. A point of view brought scurvy; the scurvy brought death, both as a disease and as a cause of starvation.' For the outlook which divided necessary tasks according to social hierarchy, Stefansson would see substituted a proper flexibility. For the outlook which ignored the Inuit settlement in the middle distance except as a source of interest and conversation, he would substitute a readiness to learn. Stefansson's syllogism is both neat and probable. But it fails signally to reckon with the culture he accuses on the solid and inclusive terms on which the dead sailors experienced it. You can change an outlook. You ought to, urgently, if the stakes are life and death. Those stakes Stefansson sees vividly. Only in the form of empty, impractical words did he recognise the other matters at stake – which the 'social and mental outlook' sustained, which made of it in fact far more than a point of view. 'There is no doubt' (he wrote bitterly) 'that the disciplined officers and sailors of the Franklin expedition met their fate with a high average of resignation and courage.' His use of 'resignation' here represents a later period's sarcastic and half-comprehending nod to the values of its predecessor. To Stefansson the word recalls all he finds most infuriating, most passively pious about Victorian attitudes; attitudes he measures by their destructive practical effects.

It is instructive to compare Stefansson's strictures of 1939 with a passage from the *Narrative of an Expedition in HMS 'Terror'* (1836), not only written from out of the thick of the past culture almost exactly a century earlier, but, it happens, actually penned by one of Franklin's close associates and a chief upholder of his polar practices. George Back reflects upon the scene revealed by one of those constitutional winter walks officers took in lieu of the hunting trips Stefansson would prescribe:

Then from the sterile summit of the hill to gaze, far as the eye could stretch, upon a dreary plain of rocky ice, relieved only by the frost-smoke issuing here and there from a few holes or lanes of open water, and suddenly to turn to the small dark speck which denoted the ship, the abode, alas how frail! of living men imprisoned amidst this 'abomination of desolation.' What a multitude of reflections rushed into the mind! – the might of nature – the physical feebleness of man – and yet again the triumph of spirit over matter – man, trusting in his own unquenchable energy and the protection of an omnipresent Providence, braving nature in the strongholds of her empire, and if not successful in the encounter, yet standing up unvanquished and undismayed!

One can imagine Stefansson's reaction to this bravura confirmation of his complaints. What chances Back loses! Why has he not set men with guns and harpoons to watch those 'holes or lanes' of open water? Why has he reduced himself to trusting in the 'triumph of spirit over matter'? Why does he insist – a self-fulfilling prophecy – on the sterility, the desolation of the landscape? But Back's paragraph can equally be read as a concise statement of all that he gains by his attitudes, or all that he continues to be able to feel. There is no reason to doubt that the reflections Back describes did 'rush' to his mind, with the involuntary speed that word suggests. That is how the potent assumptions of a culture present themselves: as an almost inevitable train of thoughts, if not as simple responses to stimulus: the most available, most natural-seeming ways of situating yourself: comforting and flattering too obscurely to register amid the quick succession of them: providing a real and rooted solace.

We can, however, glimpse the positive force of those same attitudes – and the extent to which contemporaries would reflexively defend them – on the occasion in the 1850s when Inuit and white chances of Arctic survival were most nearly contrasted in Stefansson's style. Stefansson did have great respect for one mid-Victorian explorer, 'John Rae, a man exact and truthful, and in his methods of travel a generation ahead of his time'. This admiration was not surprising: the chief areas of Dr Rae's expertise that distinguished him from his fellows were indeed his beliefs about travel, and about polar diet, the two subjects on which Inuit methods offered the most lessons. Rae, a responsible and virtually autonomous civil employee of the Hudson Bay Company, made repeated overland journeys without the publicity or the enormous support structures of the naval efforts. He commanded small parties of Canadian Indians, Inuit and half-breeds, drawing on their skills in a matter-of-fact way which anticipated Amundsen's or Nansen's approach. They could all hunt, and his dog-sledges carried few provisions. He formed no great polar friendships: his journeys were not crucibles of emotion. He viewed the natives of the North through eyes both colonial and commercial, without sentimentality or detached benevolence. But he was willing to learn, and where he gave his respect was not determined by philanthropic categories. Given the chance in 1846–7 of observing Inuit icecraft in detail, he put himself to school. Later he would always press, unsuccessfully, for British expeditions to use the light, elastic, low-friction Inuit sledge design rather than the lumbering Navy model. He praised the slitted Inuit snow-goggles, the retrievable segmented harpoons used for the seal hunt, the architecture of the Inuit hunter's overnight snow shelter, warmer than a tent and almost as quick to erect. More importantly, to the Ethnological Society in 1865 he described these inventions as products of 'scientific skill', a remarkably unhedged term to choose, because unlike the commoner tributes to Eskimo 'ingenuity' it implied that the Inuit hunter with his resources of bone and sinew was engaged in exactly the same technological activity as an English engineer. He even speculated presciently about the causes of scurvy in the light of Inuit freedom from the disease on their all-meat diet. An Admiralty committee in the 1870s heard him deduce the existence of vitamin C nearly forty years before its chemical discovery. 'I consider scurvy a blood disease caused by the lack of something that it gets from vegetables and that when you have no vegetables or no bread there is something that the system wants which is in very small quantities in animal food and therefore you have to eat a very great deal more than you want to get at the quantity from meat.' If anyone had listened, here was a suggestion of a rationale for the carnivorous binges Inuit would go on immediately after a whale kill, which were usually put down to gluttony or improvidence.

Rae's recorded opinions give the impression of a man who had somehow sidestepped a whole tranche of contemporary feeling, perhaps as a matter of temperament, perhaps because he had worked too long together in Canada for received opinion in Britain to influence his work. On polar questions theory weighed much less heavy with him than practice, though in other things he conformed with his times – he was a recognisable type of Scottish imperial patriot, and later in life an ardent volunteer in the equivalent of the Territorial Army. He was therefore not best equipped to weave his way diplomatically among the impractical, the cultural, the *imaginative* aspects of the cannibalism controversy when he shocked the nation with his report of the kettles of English flesh. He knew it. He was aware (he could hardly fail to be) of the powerful sentiments attending on the affair, and that, since he did not precisely share them, he possessed no quick and sensitive grasp on public reaction. He was also crucially bad with words, the medium in which exploration was created for the public as much as in real, polar actions. His attempt to defend the character of his Inuit informants, once Dickens had published 'The Lost Arctic Voyagers', brought him up against, as he put it with a certain simplicity,

a writer of very great ability and practice. To oppose this I have nothing but a small amount of practical knowledge of the question at issue, with a few facts to support my views and opinions, but I can only throw them together in a very imperfect and un-connected form as I have little experience in writing and, like many men, who have led a wandering and stirring life have a great dislike to it.

It is true that some amateur guile is at work in this statement, an accurate if clumsy notion on Rae's part as to the strengths he ought to be playing from rhetorically. Look at me, the passage tries to say, I have *knowledge*, I have *facts* (what does Mr Dickens have?) and my *life* has been stirring even if my prose falters. Rae did sense that the persona he adopted would be important for the reception of his report. Its dependence on the uncorroborated testimony of the Inuit – 'meagre and unexpected' tidings, he called it in his initial letter to the Admiralty – required that it have a frontman, a mediator to smooth its passage through the world of official gazettes and unofficial opinion. Unfortunately the pitch he chose was one that has rarely prospered when more exciting rhetoric is available, an image of the explorer that has been regularly outbid by more seductive versions. Ranked on

Dickens' side in the argument there were arrayed all the eloquent emotions aroused by the figure of Franklin, expressive victim, focus of public pathos. Consider for a moment Rae's implicit challenge to Franklin's competence, and his situation can be seen as an anticipation of Amundsen's, after Scott's brilliant final testaments reached the press. (Rae and Franklin, Amundsen and Scott; somehow the same pair of contrasted types seem to recur over and over, the laconic competent explorer versus the catastrophe-prone legend who none-theless holds the lien on public sympathy, because he thinks of himself as the public thinks of him. Their pairing is permanent in polar history, like Don Quixote and Sancho Panza, only Sancho's concern for survival and a full belly arouses precious little sympathy here, in a field of endeavour so slanted, apparently, towards the quixotic.) There was no great appetite among readers for Rae's incommunicative efficiency. When he did not speak of impossible horrors, he talked about things much less arresting than the customary run of polar adventure. The particular circumstances in which the Inuit resorted to cannibalism, for example, and the degree of linguistic difference between separate Inuit groups.

Consequently the report lacked the sort of effective sponsorship which could make it count, and response to the claims in it flowed round and past the figure of Rae. Although, as we have seen earlier, the controversy damaged his standing behind the scenes, alienating Lady Franklin's goodwill and spoiling his chances of a knighthood, the Admiralty eventually authorised payment of the Franklin reward money, including £210 to Rae's Inuit interpreter Ouligbuck (who Rae said spoke English 'perhaps more correctly than one half of the lower classes in England and Scotland'). And in print he was generally treated with politeness. Damned with faint praise, in fact. Either he was relieved of blame for the unpleasantness of his news at the price of a distinctly unflattering implication that he had let himself be imposed upon by grimy, deceitful savages; or he was simply commended for his diligence in bringing any information to light, however suspect. 'It is not material to the question that Dr Rae believes in the alleged cannibalism', wrote Dickens, going on to call him 'manly' and 'conscientious'. 'With these remarks we can release Dr Rae from this inquiry, proud of him as an Englishman, and happy in his safe return home to well-earned rest.' With Rae himself thus bypassed in the argument, the accusations of man-eating instead could not help but be perceived, by Dickens and others, as a direct challenge, from outside civilisation, to a civilised achievement. Attention was directed for once at the Inuit as possessors of a viewpoint on white exploration. Attention – or as Rae described it indignantly thirty years afterwards, 'a quantity of scurrilous abuse of the people of whom the writers knew nothing'. The Inuit ceased, temporarily, to be England's favourite natives.

The Inuit were execrated precisely because, at this rare moment, it was impossible to avoid perceiving a conflict between different perspectives on the Franklin tragedy. And the abuse was intended to lift the threat to the cherished, familiar perspective by reasserting the gulf between Inuit and explorers so firmly that comparison would again become impossible. Dickens used a ragbag of traditional ideas about savages to discredit 'the gross handful of uncivilised people' who were appearing in the unusual character of witnesses.

The word of a savage is not to be taken for [cannibalism]; firstly, because he is a liar; secondly, because he is a boaster; thirdly, because he often talks figuratively; fourthly, because he is given to a superstitious notion that when he tells you he has his enemy in his stomach, you will logically give him credit for having his enemy's valour in his heart.

Along with this straightforward attack went the suggestion that Rae's interpreter would have told him whatever he thought Rae wanted to hear. But Dickens also meant his passing phrases of description to wipe away all common ground. Explorers talk, in 'The Lost Arctic Voyagers': natives 'chatter' or emit a 'vague babble'. Explorers eat disgusting things, and it is a sign of their tenacity: Inuit are defined by their repulsive diet, they have 'a domesticity of blood and blubber'. So far as he could, Dickens presented the Inuit story of white men eating one another as a malevolent projection onto the explorers of habits natural to the Inuit. We have already seen how his essay supports Lady Franklin's domestic battle for a moral assessment of her husband, as against a geographical or a technical one. The same key passage needs to be read again in the light of the cannibal accusation's source;

Dickens' language of disgust at the Inuit also marks it. He had written that in cases like this 'the foremost question is – not the nature of the extremity; but the nature of the men. We submit that the memory of the lost Arctic voyagers is placed, by reason and experience, high above the taint of this so-easily allowed connection.' Why 'taint'? Even when selected as an easy, idiomatic metaphor for contaminated honour – 'smear' does the same work – the word preserves its original vivid association with meat. Corrupted meat, meat gone bad, is 'tainted': condemned meat, in its ultimately repellent form, is exactly what the flesh of explorers cannot be allowed to have turned into. But the story that Franklin's men did go from true grit to true gristle comes from mouths that themselves eat blood and blubber, meat never cooked, and therefore never translated from raw flesh into safe food. A sort of horror at the thought of rawness runs through 'The Lost Arctic Voyagers'. (At one point Dickens argues that the sailors could not have eaten corpses, because they would have had no fire to cook them on.) It links the authentic tales of maritime cannibalism Dickens tells with the Inuit diet; and here, I think, it displaces the polluting 'taint' from the explorers onto their accusers. 'Reason and experience' lift Franklin's men 'high above', leaving the Inuit imaginatively fixed in a world of ungoverned eating, taboo appetites. To defend the 'nature of the men' Dickens disinfects and disconnects them from similarity with the Inuit; restoring, with rattled ill temper quite unlike the ordinary run of the century's attitudes towards the polar natives, the categories for once disordered by Rae's news.

Dickens used no ammunition that was not part of the common stock of information about the Inuit. Indeed, references to their disgusting eating habits are a constant in descriptions of them, the difference being that, where the picture is more settled, disgust becomes an easier part, almost a more comfortable part, of a natural history of Inuit life. Authors report the reaction of their noses on first entering an igloo. They pattern it, then, into their assessments, weighting it more or less against other factors revealed to their curiosity. Not only is physical disgust often offset by appreciations of Inuit physical prowess in other areas, or subordinated to religious judgement. Inuit domestic squalor could seem so pronounced as to be a sort of natural marvel, wondrously repellent, and therefore gratifying to confirm by the evidence of one's own senses. It was a rare explorer who did not know, at least in outline, what to expect. Nineteenth-century encyclopedia entries under ESKIMOS give a useful register of these expectations: they mediate between the explorers' first-hand accounts and wholly digested 'facts' about Inuit of the proverbial kind. They compose the pictures of the Inuit into smoothed, ready information; they frame them as common knowledge according to the learning of the moment. And, intended to be authoritative in a minor and uncontentious way, once circulating they cycle on through the culture influencing later judgements. The seventh edition of the *Encylopaedia Britannica*, for example, gave this composite report on igloo manners in 1842, the author neatly dovetailing the accounts he cites.

In their domestic economy, however, they are uniformly filthy, and disgusting in the extreme. 'The Greenlanders,' says Egede, 'in their manners and their common way of life, are very slovenly, nasty, and filthy; they seldom wash themselves, will eat out of plates and bowls after their dogs without cleansing them, and, what is most nauseous to behold, eat lice and such like vermin which they find upon themselves or others. They will scrape the sweat off their faces with a knife, and lick it up.' Captain Lyon's description of the interior of an Esquimaux tent is to the same effect. He found accumulated 'an immense heap of flesh, blubber, bones, birds, eggs, &c., which lie at the mercy of the heels of all who enter; the juices forming an intolerably filthy mud on the shingle floor. From this profusion of delicacies thus jumbled together, it may be unnecessary to add that the food of the family is selected as wanted.' Details similar to the above are given by others who have visited these countries, but they are too disgusting to be quoted here.

Decency might restrain some gastronomic details from being printed, as it did the details of Inuit sexual frankness. (The first collection of Inuit folk-stories appeared in English in 1875. An ethnological landmark, Henrik Rink's *Tales and Traditions of the Eskimo, with a Sketch of Their Habits, Religion, Language and Other Peculiarities* gave a circumspect translation of Inuit wordings like the boast of 'The Woman Who Wanted To Be A Man' to her male rivals. According to Rink, she says, 'I'm a better man than any of you!' A modern translation of the same sentence produces: 'My clitoris is bigger than all your penises put together!') Yet the refusal to go further nicely settled the impression already created. On top, as it were, of Captain Lyon's description of the trampled floor-salad – its nauseating effect curiously heightened by the way the Inuit *select* chosen *delicacies* from the mush, in the fastidious language of the civilised table – the passage above assures readers that even grosser things are true. It flinches late enough for curiosity to be satisfied; it flinches too soon for the dietary rules the Inuit themselves find important to be investigated. (In fact, with a few consciously bold exceptions, right across the Inuit domains sea foods and land foods were kept separate as zealously as meat and milk are in a kosher kitchen. Lyon's horrible heap would have been ritually clean, even if not hygienic.) Attention here was concentrated on their blithe indifference to familiar rules. Lice-eating, egg-squashing, dog-spittle-licking, unspecifically lubricious; the Inuit compelled fascination in part for the very extravagance with which they were different.

Mental acquaintance with the 'Eskimos' as human curiosities began early in England. With the Danish recolonisation in the seventeenth and early eighteenth centuries, Greenland entered the orbit of European society, as a distant object of knowledge and comment. The easy paradox of its name fixed it in the memory; its ice was known, along with its population of evangelists, Danish administrators, and lascivious Eskimos. Almost a century before Ross' encounter Polly and Macheath had sung to each other in *The Beggar's Opera*, back and forth, of their sweetly global dalliance, which could revel in Greenland's ice as well as tropical palms: anywhere together, 'over the hills and far away'. On a black December night in 1762, James Boswell was sitting awake over the journal of his life in London, updating its winning record of his vanities and dissipations, when 'I inadvertently snuffed out my candle . . . Downstairs did I softly and silently step to the kitchen. But, alas, there was as little fire there as on the icy mountains of Greenland.' Later, he 'carried on a short conversation by signs with some Esquimaux who were then in London, particularly with one of them who was a priest'. But Dr Johnson refused to believe he had made himself understood, he noted with chagrin. Still, 'No man was more incredulous as to particular facts, which were at all extraordinary . . .' Extraordinary too, and very affecting to the eighteenth-century mind, was the Greenlanders' fondness for their inhospitable home, which seemed to show how universally home pulled on mankind's heartstrings. The fourth edition of the *Encyclopaedia Britannica*, in 1810 still a repository of sensibility in the eighteenth-century style, glossed an old story of Inuit home-sickness as an indignant little narrative of sentiment. King Christian IV of Denmark had had Greenlanders kidnapped in the late sixteenth century for his inspection. 'Nothing', wrote the *Britannica* contributor,

> can be more inhuman and repugnant to the dictates of common justice than this practice of tearing away poor creatures from their country, their families, and connections . . . When first captivated, they rent the air with their cries and lamentations: they even leaped into the sea; and, when taken on board, for some time refused all sustenance. Their eyes were continually turned towards their dear country, and their faces always bathed in tears. Even the countenance of his Danish Majesty, and the caress of the court and people, could not alleviate their grief . . . at length, seeing no prospect of being able to revisit their native country, they sunk into a kind of melancholy disorder, and expired.

Late eighteenth-century men wept buckets proudly at the thought of distress. This easy, tearful sympathy for the victims of another power's imperialism would change as men changed – and as Britain developed Arctic interests. Stories of transplantation with the same dismal outcome would be reported in quite different terms, and tones: still complimentary towards the Inuit transplantees, but impermeably convinced that they must have benefited by the experiment, as in the case of Kallihirua or 'Erasmus York', taken to England to be educated. Touring the Great Exhibition he was mistaken for a Chinese. Quite soon, he died. 'During his illness he was as patient and gentle as ever,' wrote the English lady who witnessed his final decline in Newfoundland, 'and thankful for all that was done to relieve him.' Victorian benevolence towards the Inuit would often take the form of confidence – in Clements Markham's words – that they were 'capable, after instruction, of the highest virtues of civilised men'. Only observing from a distance as yet, eighteenth-century English opinion was more likely to approve Inuit life as it already seemed to be. The scarcity of information left more room for speculation, for a more boisterous projection of philosophic notions onto the Inuit. Their society's total lack of civil and military hierarchy would seem undeveloped later; it appealed immensely to an age which cherished the idea of primitive happiness, of a wig-less and law-less counterlife which Europeans had lost, but which continued elsewhere among the savages. Some of the customs of these particular savages were bizarre, if correctly reported, and their character naturally enough appeared to reflect the chill of their home. Greenland provided a provokingly unexpected site for Rousseau-esque contentment, the 'Eskimos' themselves made un-usually tubby, lice-ridden vessels of virtue. All the better. Few civilised observers actually wanted to throw off their wigs, or touch the blubber; only to believe that the Inuit preserved the original brightness of social intercourse, before artifice had done its tarnishing work. 'In their dispositions', said the article of 1810, 'the Greenlanders are cold, phlegmatic, indolent, and slow of apprehension: but very quiet, orderly, and good-natured. They live peaceably; and have every thing in common, without strife, envying, or animosity.' Opposition to the sentimental image of savage simplicity came from those like Dr Johnson who saw civilised manners as *enabling* virtue, the freedom from them in savage societies as a barbarous lack. Johnson, perhaps scorning Boswell's Eskimo conversation for this reason, certainly squashed his biographer on every other occasion when Boswell talked modishly of the subject (30 September 1769):

I attempted to argue for the superior happiness of the savage life, upon the usual fanciful topicks. JOHNSON. 'Sir, there can be nothing more false. The savages have no bodily advantages beyond those of civilised men. They have not better health; and as to care or mental uneasiness, they are not above it, but below it, like bears . . .'

Opposition also came from the missionary writers themselves, whose authoritative descriptions served as the source of most knowledge about Greenland – the facts of the *Britannica* article, for example, were largely drawn from David Crantz's *History of Greenland*, available in English translation. They objected to the alarming implication that the Inuit, already peaceful and good, did not need Christianity to make them so. Crantz and Egede's books, as well as being investigations of Inuit custom and practices, were sustained attacks on the sufficiency of those customs without the quickening spark of faith. The Inuit, they reminded readers, lived without the divine light; unregenerate, their apparent virtues were hollow. If you believed that savage life preserved an original human happiness, you could pick and choose among historical analogies; the *Encyclopaedia Britannica* made their sharing of property sound rather like the early Church, where the apostles famously owned 'every thing in common'. Charged in the extreme from the missionary point of view, the evangelists could only admit this comparison on strictly limited terms. The happy congruence of one aspect of Inuit life with the New Testament would only be welcomed as a promising sign of their ripeness for conversion. Otherwise, it needed to be stressed, the Inuit existed in original darkness, the state of humanity before the preaching of the word. Reginald Heber, soon to be Bishop of Calcutta, may well have read Crantz and had his diagnosis of the Inuit in mind when he wrote his famous missionary hymn in 1811. English congregations began to sing –

> From Greenland's icy mountains
> To Java's coral strand . . .

Heber's hymn spanned as broad a geography as John Gay's prison duet for Macheath and Polly, to entirely different ends, for it stipulated a world where

> . . . every prospect pleases
> And only man is vile.

That included the seeming graces of peoples like the Inuit as surely as it did their obviously vile cuisine. Only the inanimate landscapes of the world escaped condemnation.

But both these eighteenth-century views of the northern natives worked to chronologies which were about to change, along with the sense of what was meant by an origin, or an original state. At the back of the evangelical opinion lay Christianity's sacred history of the globe; behind the enlightened sentimental opinion, an idea of past time inherited from classical mythology, from the readings of Virgil and Hesiod common to the education of almost every gentleman. The world, agreed both mythic patterns of the past, was recent, yet decrepit, stumbling downward to a close. Creation had been best at its beginning. Indeed, there had been Eden at the start; either the literal and actual Hebrew Eden of the Bible, or its counterpart in Greek and Roman myth, the Golden Age, when seasons were unknown and the kindly fruiting earth fed humankind without labour. Then decay. For Christians, the sudden catastrophe of the Fall, or in the pagan scheme (maintained in Christian Europe for its poetic sense, its explanatory beauty) a slower decline, through a tarnished Silver Age to the present hard Age of Iron. The two histories differed, though, on whether the first glory of the world had definitely departed, for all humans, everywhere. In the Christian scheme it had, and the Garden was closed for good, leaving only God's promise of redemption – while a lingering glow of the Golden Age might be thought to shine out still, here and there. Thus if missionaries agreed with mythologists in placing native peoples somehow nearer the beginning of time, the *earliness* of native lives meant quite different things to each party. The earliest time to which an evangelical eye could assign (for example) the Inuit mode of existence was the moment of complete loss and wreckage after the Fall, with God's first plan for humanity ruined through human sin, and news of the second chance He offered not yet arrived. Without the definitive rupture of the Fall to contend with, dividing early time into *before* and *after* beyond hope of appeal, the whole first part of the downward gradient of time seemed tinted at least with gold, and the savage state as gleaming too, for its earliness. Still, there was agreement again that the contrast between savage and civilised offered a moral lesson to the beholder, a moral comparison of epochs, whichever way the moral tended.

In the first half of the nineteenth century a new chronology replaced both of these. (They ceased to function, at any rate, as serious, widely shared frames of reference. They did survive in pockets and bubbles of the culture. The gold–silver–iron plan of time remained useful as classical furniture for poetry, whose readers were expected to suspend their disbelief. Bible history remained real, literal history for those believers who entirely refused nineteenth-century discoveries in biology and geology. In their insulated congregations, the old clock ticked on.) A little while before rocks proved that the planet was neither a recent object nor tottering on its last legs, archaeology proved the same thing, more modestly, for the shorter record of human history. It was a Danish archaeologist, working in the 1830s on burial sites in Jutland, who proposed a new sequence which ordered the artefacts he was finding in the earth. Iron objects lay nearest the surface (at least in an ideally undisturbed deposit, for this was a general principle rather than an invariable prediction) and therefore nearest in time. Deeper and farther off bronze would be found. Beneath again, and remotest of all, stone implements came to light. These gave names to a trio of ages, modelled satisfyingly after the classical succession, but utterly different in implication. Modern Europeans still lived in the Age of Iron, their steel-forging and metal-bashing a wonderfully elaborate development of the first iron knives and pots; but the Iron Age had become the highest of the three ages, the apex of achievement so far. Stone, Bronze, Iron: now the gradient of history ran upward, from simple to complex, from crude to subtle. Human history, measured by human *making*, had become progressive. And its tempo seemed to be quickening. As far as archaeologists could date matters from the scattered evidence available, each age had lasted less long than the one before. The Stone Age had been slow and sluggish, the era of bronze – when written records began – paced slightly more briskly. Then the Iron Age seemed to push on through discovery after discovery, through time inscribed more and more thickly with recorded events. Indeed the archaeologists could see material advance visibly speeding up around them, the shapes of their own phase of the Iron Age beginning to rush by, to flicker, they changed so fast. History played *accelerando*. First there had been progress in ponderous breves, then a patient rhythm of crotchets, like a hammer beating on an anvil; and so onward to the hectic semi-quavers of the present.

Like Bible history or the mythological three ages, the new sequence was intended to be universal. It was supposed to tabulate all human progress. But because it named the materials tools were made from, instead of dealing in divine dispensations applicable everywhere, or metaphors for a world sliding from precious to base, it was universal in a different way. It indicated an apparently universal process; it did not produce a unified picture of humankind, or tell a unitary story. For archaeologists, and soon for ethnographers and anthropologists, it made masses of disparate instances or specimens intelligible, by showing which preceded which. It helped one decipher whether a given artefact or custom faced forward or backward on the line of a particular history – whether one was looking at progression or retrogression. In effect, it pencilled in the direction of time's arrow. In the first place it divided history into stages of development, and only secondarily into specific periods of past time. So far as the Stone, Bronze, and Iron Ages had dates, they were the dates at which a given population had happened to pass through the corresponding stages of tool-use. Dates, or amounts of time elapsed from a notional beginning to history – which was receding anyway, into the remoter past – now mattered less. The distinction between past and present blurred, lost its fundamental importance, if you were primarily interested in telling whether a human accomplishment (exogamy, ploughshares, manufacture of efficient poisons) aided or retarded the great progression in human affairs. It was no accident that the scholarly disciplines of archaeology and of anthropology and ethnology developed in such close alliance, even though archaeology dealt with the past and its sisters with the present. The same Victorian savants were often active in both. The techniques involved overlapped; but more than that, the object of inquiry was the same, whether you dug for your evidence or sought it out among the living. Archaeology provided a sort of anthropology of past times, and anthropology a kind of archaeology of the present moment. Since the rate of human advance was obviously neither constant nor smooth around the globe, or even within a single society, it seemed that every stage of human development was there to be observed, on the earth or under it; all the living and all the dead struggled with their separate phases of the ascent, with their historical clocks set differently according to the stages they had reached.

But this diversity was never interpreted to mean that all calendars had equal value. In fact authoritative dates were established for the ages: the dates at which *European* society had happened to pass through them. Against these the progress of other societies was judged as slow, slower, slowest. Against the present state of the civilised countries, the state of other cultures was judged as backward to the exact degree to which they failed to resemble Europe. As the anthropologist Edward Tylor put it, in his magnum opus *Primitive Culture: Researches into the Development of Mythology, Philosophy, Religion, Language, Art, and Custom* (1871):

The educated world of Europe and America practically settles a standard by simply placing its own nations at one end of the social series and savage tribes at the other, arranging the rest of mankind between these limits according as they correspond more closely to savage or cultured life. The principal criteria of classification are the absence or presence, high or low development, of the industrial arts, especially metal-working, manufacture of implements and vessels, agriculture, architecture, &c., the extent of scientific knowledge, the definiteness of moral principles, the condition of religious belief and ceremony, the degree of social and political organization, and so forth.

Not only technical achievements, the 'industrial arts', then, were calibrated by the European standard. With a self-approval coinciding remarkably with the most ranging curiosity, the 'educated world of Europe and America' erected their own moral habits and social arrangements as the peak of progress so far, and construed different moralities and social structures as more and less rudimentary forms of the same things. (Sometimes it proved hard to show how other customs were leading up to the European norms. Monogamous marriage gave special trouble: you couldn't readily trace the tendency that ought to exist for marriage everywhere to become the familiar Victorian institution – the pressure towards wedded bliss, railway-villa style.)

All this radically changed the way in which a people like the Inuit were perceived as 'early'. The word *primitive* gained its modern sense over the course of the nineteenth century, in line with the revision of what it meant for something to hark back to early times. It had expressed an uncorrupted simplicity, a first rightness, as in the phrase 'the Primitive Church', or the consequent choice of an eighteenth-century sect to call themselves 'Primitive Methodists'. Without ever quite losing its complimentary meaning, it also began to convey roughness, underdevelopment, a first crudity. By the mid-century, a woman's wardrobe could be described as primitive if she had only one bonnet. When applied to cultures, as Tylor used it in the title of his book, it carried the specific message that the culture in question was composed of rudiments, scarcely shaped components, however complex their patterning into that culture's stories and mythologies. The new understanding did make many aspects of Inuit thought intelligible to Westerners for the first time. It was an instrument of great explanatory power, though not the key to fit all locks which it thought it was. Furnished with a theory of primitive religion, observers rightly stopped trying to see the Inuit as pagans on the Roman or Greek model. The fruitless search ended for a pantheon of 'Eskimo' gods and goddesses. John Francis Smith's digest of current scholarship in the 1842 *Encyclopaedia Britannica* still credited the Inuit with a female deity and a subordinate polar bear god. He wrenched around an Inuit description of the soul's journey after death so that it sounded like an Elysian afterlife, adding, 'With such fond anticipations of coming bliss do these poor savages contrive to cheer a life of extreme privation, in a state little elevated above that of the animals on which they subsist.'

Soon, in place of this, there came an appreciation that another kind of belief preceded the formal worship of defined gods, and that the Inuit indeed inhabited that spirit-saturated shamanic landscape, where animals counted for much more than food. Observers began to guess at descriptions better than 'magician' or 'conjurer' for the Inuit *angekuks*, or men of spiritual power. Later *Britannica*s identified the Inuit as animists. At the same time, however, the new scheme of understanding could impose new distortions on the picture of Inuit life. The conviction that social advance everywhere pointed towards the European standard made some customs essential to Inuit survival – their rules governing ownership, for instance – look like wilful obstacles on the path of progress. Wealth never accumulated in Inuit society. If they went on like this, they would never discover the limited-liability corporation. The ethnologist Robert Brown, introducing the English edition of Rink's Inuit folktales in 1875, noted that 'the idea of improving and securing the comforts of life by the aid of property is only very scantily developed in them'. 'Long habit', thundered the ninth edition of the *Britannica* (1875–89), 'and the necessities of their life have also compelled those having food to share with those having none, – a custom which, with others, has conduced to the stagnant condition of Eskimo society and to their utter improvidence.' Rather than drawing moral comparisons, observers now drew developmental ones, contrasting accomplished with rudimentary, elaborate with embryonic, stagnant with flowing societies. This was now the basis on which the Victorians measured the unlikeness, and likeness, of the Inuit to themselves.

Yet the earliness of the Inuit remained an exciting thing. If it were now established that the whole difficult history of advance, from the opening of the struggle to the last word in Great Exhibitions and scientific manufacture, separated European civilisation from Inuit savagery; still, there the Inuit were at the opening of things, arrested near the point at which human society began. For them it was all yet to come. Beginnings have a peculiar glamour, especially if you consider you know what follows, the involutions and mis-steps and thick incredible complications. Studying the Inuit was like re-reading the very first pages of a long, long novel – whose plot the Victorians thought they knew, because they thought that they themselves lived its latest pages – and being reminded that once, remarkably, the cast of characters you almost knew too well had been strangers, glimpsed casually for the first time. Everything that they may become, that they *will* become, waits to be revealed. In the Inuit Victorians glimpsed the primitive, the lumpishly original forms of human making and doing. Their fascination was of a piece with the contemporary interest in defunct mythologies; where, said Carlyle, you found an 'incipient' truth.

It was granted, of course, that the Arctic landscape helped form the special qualities of Inuit culture. Indeed the thinking going on in Germany and elsewhere about the growth of nations (a classification of humanity which scarcely figured in the developmental scheme) stressed the way soil and climate, sky and earth, moulded the identity of human groups, just as the character of a wine reflected the chalky or acid *terroir* that produced it. The Arctic ice furnished the Inuit equivalent to the formative clay of Prussia, or the treasured crumbly black earth of Russia. They reflected the stuff of their home. What Emily Dickinson ascribed in a poem to the hemlock plant, growing 'Upon a Marge of Snow', could have been said about them:

> The Hemlock's nature thrives – on cold –
> The Gnash of Northern winds
> Is sweetest nutriment – to him –
> His best Norwegian Wines –

Robert Brown wrote of the 'scarcity of objects', the 'scanty materials' feeding the Inuit sensibility in Rink's collection of stories. The stories presented, he said, 'a true picture of what is likely to have formed the principal objects of the people's imagination, of what is considered great and delightful on one side, and hateful and dreadful on the other . . .' The influence of the place on the people gave their tales the land's austerity. It made reading them 'uniform and rather fatiguing to us', like the uniform and fatiguing effect on European eyes of staring at unvaried Arctic vistas. Land and people could be seen as one: could even merge into each other. When Brown constructed a deliberately popular portrait of the Inuit in the first volume of his *The Races of Mankind* (1872), he had them emerge dramatically from the 'dreary' scenery, hardly distinct from it at first, like human outcroppings, despite their 'egg-shaped and good-humoured faces'. 'As we pace the snow-covered deck, alternately gazing on the snow-covered, glacier-intersected land, and the snow-laden, frozen sails and shrouds, we are startled by a clear sound through the still Arctic air. We listen; surely it cannot be the sound of man; surely no man lives in this hope-forsaken place.' Icily, squalidly, and cheerfully however, men do, as he proceeds to explain, and later he tells the story of the dying Eskimo on his way home to Greenland who cried continually 'Do you see the ice? do you see the ice?'

But place in this almost alchemical sense, as a crucible which transmutes human identity, mattered less in developmental thinking. Geography principally determined the materials available for tool making, which in turn set a position on the scale of development. One could fix areas chronologically. Like the red deserts of central Australia and the dripping rainforests of New Guinea, so Greenland, with its agriculture-preventing ice-cap, its treeless coastal margins and its total lack of metal, was 'in the Stone Age'. Or more accurately, since the Inuit used materials outside the scope of the original classification, in the Bone Age, the Ivory and Skin and Sinew Age. It is hard to convey how literally the later Victorians took this idea. They did not mean it as an engaging metaphor, vulnerable to experience, liable to lapse when in real conversation with an Inuit. Directly and straightforwardly, they perceived themselves to have travelled in time when they travelled across the space of the North Atlantic to Greenland. It was as if the globe were effectively divided into chronological reserves; as if tracts of past time persisted here and there which could be visited. A ship cruising off the north Greenland coast sailed through the earliest segment of history. Your steam-boilers forged in Manchester or Pittsburgh powered a time-machine. If you looked from the deck at an Inuit settlement on shore, at Inuit men sitting outside their dwellings in the sun, you were watching the Stone Age happening that moment. If they laughed, they were exhibiting the human propensity for humour which their very laughter demonstrated was already present at the dawn of things. If, bone needles in their mouths for threading with seal gut, they repaired the trim of a kayak, you were seeing *homo faber*, man the maker, at work on his first handicrafts. If they kicked an over-curious dog away, that displayed the domestication of draught animals (*and* a cruelty to dumb beasts no civilised society would tolerate). If one stabbed another, and no policeman took the culprit away, no court punished the action, you knew you witnessed the state of society before the notion of justice was born. There was lost time before you – found.

The Inuit had their own versions of history, and their own feelings of location within it. The people of Tikigaq ('Point Hope') in Alaska, the ritual metropolis of the westernmost Inuit, divided time in two. From their standpoint, living in an earth maze of subterranean *iglus* beneath a hummocked forest of bone stakes and tripods, the first era of creation was also in some sense continuing, but as a primordial pattern of existence against which to place the quotidian, imperfect living moment. Memory of people's names and characters endured for five generations, during which *uqaluktuaq* or ancestor stories were told. Then those ancestors dropped into oblivion, or, much more rarely, joined the cast of the other sort of stories, the permanent myths corresponding to the permanent foundation of time in which Raven Man was still rising up for the first time from the cosmic grandmother's blubber-lamp sediment.

For outside observers, though, these local chronologies proved the arrested, prehistoric nature of Inuit life. They could be assessed for mythological patterning, gleaned for buried clues to events which interested ethnologists, such as migration; they paled in the face of the potent sense the observers gained of immediate personal contact with 'the dark backward and abysm of time'. (A quote from *The Tempest*, especially popular in the century of geological and biological revolution.) Those explorers who solidified the developmental explanation of the Inuit into a perception had Science's authority behind them. An ethnographic manual compiled by the Royal Geographical Society for the use of the Nares expedition in 1875 advised the sailors that 'here, in the far north, there are tribes still living . . . in a stone age'. Matthew Henson, controversial right-hand-man on Peary's Arctic expeditions, could speak fluent Inuit. He wrote in *A Negro Explorer at the North Pole* (1912), 'I was to live with a people who, the scientists stated, represented the earliest form of human life, living in what is known as the Stone Age . . .' Vilhjalmur Stefansson himself left one of the best accounts of the sensation of time travel, mixing categorical scientific pronouncements with the excited freedom of fancy enabled by such scientific confidence. The passage is worth quoting at length. Stefansson had studied prehistory, and now the moment had come when reconstructions on the pages of books would give place to living actuality:

Our first day among the Dolphin and Union Straits Eskimo was the day of all my life to which I had looked forward with the most vivid anticipations, and to which I now look back with equally vivid memories, for it introduced me, a student of mankind and of primitive men especially, to a people of a bygone age. Mark Twain's Connecticut Yankee went to sleep in the nineteenth century and woke up in King Arthur's time among knights who rode in clinking mail to the rescue of fair ladies; we, without going to sleep at all, had walked out of the twentieth century into the country of the intellectual and cultural contemporaries of a far earlier age than King Arthur's. These were not such men as Caesar found in Gaul or Britain; they were more nearly like the still earlier hunting tribes of Britain and of Gaul living contemporaneous to but oblivious of the building of the first pyramid in Egypt. Their existence on the same continent with our populous cities was an anachronism of ten thousand years in intelligence and material development. They gathered their food with the weapons of the men of the Stone Age, they thought their simple, primitive thoughts and lived their insecure and tense lives – lives that were to me the mirrors of the lives of our far ancestors whose bones and crude handiwork we now and then discover in river gravels or in prehistoric caves. Such archaeological remains . . . tell a fascinating story to him whose scientific imagination can piece it together and fill in the wide gaps; but far better than such dreaming was my present opportunity. I had nothing to imagine; I had merely to look and listen; for here were not remains of the Stone Age but the Stone Age itself, men and women, very human, entirely friendly, who welcomed us to their homes and bade us stay.

Stefansson insists that he did not have to sleep, like Twain's Yankee, to cross the gulf of time, that the meeting was better than dreaming; but theories can be as potent as dreams, and the effect of seeing this one – this ordering dream of nineteenth-century learning – apparently confirmed to his waking eyes, lent the whole scene something of the quality of an enchanted sleep, of a kind of Rip Van Winkle slumber in reverse, from which the dreamer rises to find that the calendar has run backwards. Dazed with wonder, Stefansson stepped forward to accept the Inuit's invitation to supper.

It is evident how involving the encounter was, and not only because Stefansson happened to be fulfilling a personal ambition. Dreams tell you about more than the individual dreamer: Stefansson's emotional investment in the scene went beyond a student's delight that the reading of his twenties has become the experience of his thirties. Development theory brought the Inuit close to home for contemporaries – close to the quick of civilised self-definitions once more – in the discovery of a resemblance between these present savages and 'our far ancestors'. 'Mirrors', Stefansson calls Inuit lives, and of course they reflect European faces. In any case, the idea of extant zones of past time applied the world over, and certainly at home too, if less straightforwardly. The British Isles in general (say) might be at the highest stage of development, yet chequering the landscape of home, and visible more in manners and fragmentary customs than in entire modes of life, earlier stages persisted. Development was uneven. Pockets of surviving feudalism, or of degraded pagan lore, might escape the general pressure of progress; and therefore confront the observer with the ancestral past as the Inuit did. Anthropology, with its double appetite for past and present evidence, treated a garbled ploughman's song, left over to puzzle the nineteenth century, like the freshest news of some primitive system of belief in current practice far away. The study of one led to the study of the other. Tylor devoted a long section of *Primitive Culture* to survivals close at hand. As he put it, 'Survival in Culture . . . even now sets up in our midst primaeval monuments of barbaric thought and life. Its investigation tells strongly in favour of the view that the European may find among the Greenlanders or Maoris many a trait for reconstructing the picture of his own primitive ancestors.' Spotting survivals was a popular semi-scholarly pastime. Anachronisms fascinated a culture conscious of its extreme novelty, of the pace of change that could be felt within each individual Victorian life. When capitalist economics made it seem, in Marx's words, that 'all that is solid melts into air', throwbacks and survivals, those stubborn local things which remained solid, attracted a gritty pathos to themselves, and held out the possibility of an understanding of roots and beginnings. They spoke of an identity which was not wholly at the mercy of the dissolving present. Boatmen on the river Trent, Carlyle told his lecture audience in 1840, still call a certain vicious eddy of the water an *Eager*, after the Viking god of tempests Aegir. 'Curious; that word surviving like the peak of a submerged world! The *oldest* Nottinghamshire bargemen had believed in the God Aegir. Indeed, our English blood too in good part is Danish, Norse . . .'

The systematic approach to anachronisms in development theory offered a more elaborate foundation for imagining. Towards the end of the century, the idea began to appear in novels. To see the most gnarled and settled aspects of the English landscape through the lens of the theory might be a peculiar sensation; familiar contours turned strange when it was suggested they had an affinity with the shapes of savage life. It was not expected that maypoles and well-dressings, or the nosegay the hero presented to the heroine, should be viewed in a spirit of detached archaeology. But besides the gain in freshness of vision, the advantage to the writer in her or his perennial attempt to describe things anew, the idea brought vigorous new understanding to the difficult, irregular relations between change and continuity, of old and new, near and far, of the familiar and the exotic. Thomas Hardy's *Return of the Native*, written between 1876 and 1878, tells of the return of Clym Yeobright to the territory of his birth in southern Wessex. But the novel aligns Clym's journey home with the tricky returns to Tierra del Fuego or Greenland of the other sort of 'native', the primitive tribesmen plucked away in many celebrated cases to be educated in the civilised world and dressed in formal Victorian clothes, then transported back to their starting-points. Victorian opinion was deeply curious over the fate of these men, eager to learn whether they could re-adapt to their old life, and what (if any) use they found for the infusion of 'higher' knowledge they had received. Perhaps the frock-coat would only be abandoned in the snow. Back from Paris, 'the centre and vortex of the fashionable world', Clym Yeobright resembles 'Erasmus York', whisked away from the Arctic by Admiral Ommaney, because for all his native soil is located in deepest England, Egdon Heath is an 'obscure, obsolete, superseded country', precisely a pocket of the savage past. 'Civilisation was its enemy', Hardy wrote in the grand invocatory first chapter of the book. On its brown impervious scrubland Egdon preserves an almost nomadic manner of human life. It keeps the past inviolate, for good as well as for ill, since 'to rest on a stump of thorn' there brings a consolation like Carlyle's claim of Viking blood, 'ballast to the mind adrift on change, and harassed by the irrepressible New'. Hardy even found something Arctic about Egdon, an ancient constancy which appeals like 'a gaunt waste of Thule' to the modern spirit glutted on fashionable beauty.

The notion of survival could be potent in fiction even where an author felt no tolerant interest whatsoever in primitive life. Unconcerned with growth from roots – in fact, deliberately deracinated, uprooted, like its author – *Heart of Darkness* (1902) did not discover the past literally alive in England. The Thames Valley as Conrad's narrator Marlow imagines the Romans seeing it, with threatening forests lining the shores and 'here and there a military camp lost in the wilderness', has vanished; or rather persists along the valley of the Congo, enforcing a grim dark-adapted version of development theory. Conrad's use of it was crude in the extreme from the anthropological point of view. The savages of the Congo *are* what the painted Britons *were*; Europeans now act towards them as the Romans did towards the Britons, risking corruption and contamination in the endless struggle to civilise. Yet naming the two situations as the same almost abolishes the difference in time. The Romans felt their fear and loathing for the savage Thames only a blink of time ago in the scheme of an indifferent eternity, compared to which human lives last as long as lightning flashes; 'yesterday', says Marlow. The two rivers fuse, and while Marlow evokes the primaeval Thames in language of colonial immediacy – calling the hinterland of Middlesex 'the bush', conjuring a homesick Roman officer who thinks like a modern subaltern – the past effectively awakes, and savage Britain coalesces again around Marlow's audience, the woods reaching out to entrap, the zone of lost time asserting its 'cold, fog, tempests, disease, exile and death'. You cannot be consoled in the face of change by the survival of the past, in *Heart of Darkness*: rather the opposite. Conrad too, however, offers a reassurance of sorts, also derived, though in a very different way, from the persisting patterns revealed amidst apparent flux by the notion of development. Since the struggle between civilisation and savagery, 'light' and 'darkness' repeats itself grimly through history, Conrad can point to the role of civiliser as a permanent identity. The peoples who occupy the role change, but the identity itself remains. Conrad implicitly invites the reader to take for his forebears, not his literal ancestors, but whoever in the past did unto those woad-wearing forefathers what he now does unto Africans. Again, interestingly, there is a hint of *ultima Thule* in Conrad's estranged description of the familiar landscape. We are to imagine the Roman officer at 'the very end of the world'. ' "And this also," said Marlow suddenly, "has been one of the dark places of the earth." '

The final jigsaw piece in the scientific recognition of a direct resemblance between the Inuit and the remote British past fell into place during the 1860s. It concerned climate, and the deep history of familiar landscapes. Glaciology had found out the Arctic past of Europe and North America. Controversial and largely spurned when the Swiss scientist Louis Agassiz first proposed it in Britain in 1840, geologists had since come to agree that enormously expanded ice sheets must have scored and polished land-forms as far south as New England and the middle of France. By now the idea of one or more recent glacial eras was spreading excitingly across the disciplines, reorganising the botanical past and the zoological past to take account of ice. At the greatest expansion of the polar caps in about 13,000 BC there had been ice hundreds of feet thick across Hampshire and New Hampshire, eliminating species of plants and animals, grinding the bones of the earth. Then the ice had retreated spasmodically over the centuries, quitting continental Europe, clearing southern England, lastly withdrawing from Scotland and Scandinavia, and carrying gradually northward behind the receding white wall bands of Arctic and sub-Arctic weather, until by about 4000 BC the ice occupied only its present place in the world. In Scotland in particular, where bare rock made the signs of glacier action nakedly legible, geologists eagerly examined U-shaped valleys and smoothed boulders. And they looked from the places the ice had left to the places where it remained, with a new sense of the way Arctic and temperate geographies mapped onto one another, and perhaps illuminated each other. The ubiquitous Scot Robert Brown reminded the sailors of the Nares expedition, in his section of their RGS Arctic primer, that it was 'only by the study of a country like Greenland' that explanations might be forthcoming for 'the puzzling deposits of late geological age in Britain'.

But most arresting of all were the implications of an ice-bound Europe for the study of human development, now that students of humanity reckoned the age of homo sapiens in tens of thousands of years. The chronology of the glaciologists' Ice Age overlapped the chronology of the anthropologists' Stone Age. The last time, at least, that the ice had engulfed Europe, the human animal had been among the species adapting to life on the glacier verges. The first European experiments in chipping flint had taken place while powder snow blew down from Arctic skies to blue the hands of the toolmaker. That savage ancestor of the Victorian savants had worn furs while rummaging for suitable stone; had set deadfall traps for Arctic hares on the snowy slopes of the Weald or the Massif Central, or hunted larger prey with spears across the European permafrost. The hunter had taken the kill home to an unwashed band of men and women whose weapons, whose customs, whose laws, whose stories, whose lives were perhaps as close to those of modern-day Inuit as an Alpine plant is to an Arctic one. A veritable polar setting had now been added to the parallel between the Inuit, in their continuing Stone Age, and the embryonic stage of the existence Victorians knew. The parallel was irresistible, and the recent discovery of the painted caves at Lascaux had given bold, pictorial backing to it. You could imagine the Arctic at home; dig out its cold presence in the deep layers of local scenery and local identity; reconstruct it, even, in the clangour of London, as Edward Tylor did in a deliberately striking passage of *Primitive Culture*:

There the antiquary, excavating but a few yards deep, may descend from the debris representing our modern life, to relics of the art and science of the Middle Ages, to signs of Norman, Saxon, Romano-British times, to traces of the higher Stone Age. And on his way from Temple Bar to the Great Northern Station he passes near the spot ('opposite to black Mary's, near Grayes inn lane') where a drift implement of black flint was found with the skeleton of an elephant by Mr Conyers, about a century and a half ago, the relics side by side of the London mammoth and the London savage. In the gravel-beds of Europe . . . where relics of the Palaeolithic Age are found, what principally testifies to man's condition is the extreme rudeness of his stone implements, and the absence of even edge-grinding. The natural inference that this indicates a low savage state is confirmed in the caves of Central France. There a race of men, who have left indeed really artistic portraits of themselves and the reindeer and mammoths they lived among, seem, as may be judged from the remains of their weapons, implements, &c.,

to have led a life somewhat of the Esquimaux type, but lower by the want of domesticated animals.

Behold the London Eskimo, buried between Temple Bar and the Great Northern Station. His black flint tool lies beneath the soot-black and Windsor-soup brown colouring of the modern capital. This was not Tylor's only rhetorical recourse to London when he wanted to call up the pre-eminent type of urban modernity, its gas-lit matrix. Elsewhere, comparing savage and civilised 'moral standards', he cautions the reader that 'in sober fact, a Londoner who should attempt to lead the atrocious life which the real savage may lead with impunity and even respect, would be a criminal only allowed to follow his savage models during his short intervals out of gaol'. That conclusive and *necessary* a distance separated London's deepest deposit from the life on its surface. At other times, of course, Tylor's contemporaries were not sure that the topmost layer of London could be counted as civilised through and through. Fear of those who did not share in the unprecedented wealth of London could lead to the poor being characterised as 'savages', as if the East End were a tribal encampment pitched uncomfortably close to the civilised city. And social investigation, as well as social anxiety, could bring in the language of savagery to describe the present-day city. The preface to *London Labour and the London Poor* (1851), Henry Mayhew's great survey of costermongers and night-soil collectors, prostitutes and scavengers, had experimented with the thought that the fluid life of the streets might somehow recapitulate the existence of nomads wandering the steppes. This would not be an instance of cultural survival, but of regression. It was not really possible to confine primitive London to the strata of the London earth: London, in the common phrase, already had 'lower depths' of misery and depravity, without you having to dig for them. Tylor's attention elsewhere to unequal development acknowledged this. Here though he was concerned with the roots of modern life, not its present unevenness. (Modern civilised life always tended to homogenise in the Victorian imagination when savages were under consideration, to become one unified confident thing that the student or the traveller had at his back for support.) He kept his syntax conditional: *should* a Londoner behave like a primitive, he *would* go to prison. Yet so long as the feral Londoner in question belongs to the distant past, he allows his return. In the sober whimsical way of a scientist discharging his duty to entertain while he enlightens, Tylor countenances something like an imaginative eruption of the London Ice Age to the surface. His artful play with placenames makes it hard to avoid the thought of the Eskimo walking *on* Gray's Inn Road, out of place since out of time, but indubitably at home. (More at home than the strolling Inuit visitors Boswell met on the street.) If the effect seems vaguely familiar, perhaps that's because it recalls the spattered, and even more primaeval 'megalosaurus' Dickens sent waddling through the mud and fog of the London streets in the famous opening set-piece of *Bleak House*. Tylor's passage also awakes the old sublime satisfaction in superimposing the bleak on the placid, in suddenly subjecting the August garden to snow; he alerts his reader to the Ice Age overlaying – or rather underlaying – the prosaic map of the metropolis.

Nor was this an isolated fancy. Well beyond anthropological circles it was taken for a truism that the way to understand the remote past was to study the present life of primitive peoples; and the Inuit, far from being the recherché enthusiasm of a few specialists, were the primitive people most studied to this end, the main focus, for a while, of Europeans' roundabout curiosity about themselves. 'The principal aim of this abridgement', wrote Brown in his 1875 preface to Rink's *Tales and Traditions of the Eskimo* in English

has been to make these accounts more available to readers engaged in archaeological studies, or investigations of the earliest history of mankind by comparison of the traditional tales, languages and religious opinions of the more primitive nations, in which respect the Eskimo, and specially the Greenlanders, have been studied more minutely, perhaps, than any other similar people.

Given the opportunity posed by the RGS manual of the same year, of directing the attention the Nares expedition would pay to the Inuit, the different contributors banged home the point again and again. Clements Markham reminded the sailors that

The discoveries of geologists have recently brought to light the existence of a race of people who lived soon after the remote glacial epoch of Europe, and who were unacquainted with the use of metals . . . A close and careful study of [the Inuit race], therefore, and more especially of any part of it which may be discovered in hitherto unexplored regions, assumes great importance, and becomes a subject of universal interest.

A. W. Franks, Keeper of Ethnography at the British Museum, gave the same reason when he asked for Inuit artefacts:

It is most desirable to make as complete a collection as possible of everything illustrating the Arctic tribes; for the intercourse with Europeans must in time modify or extinguish many of their peculiar implements, weapons, or dress, and it is believed that the Arctic races would furnish valuable illustrations of the condition of the ancient inhabitants of the South of France, &c., during the cave period . . .

And in an appendix the eight invited experts pressed eager, insistent questions, reaching towards still more minute knowledge of Europe's favourite, most pertinent savages. What was the state of the decorative arts among the Inuit? What was their attitude to war? Did they personify the sun and moon? Had they legends of a golden age? Or memories of living elsewhere?

Despite the 'universal interest' felt in a people who preserved alive the early history of all mankind, the perception of kinship with them could not be straightforward. For all their deepset importance, and their charm as objects of contemplation, they remained too remote for intimacy. Though concerns of lively popular interest composed the journey of imagination required to link Inuit and Europeans, the track of evidence and consequence to be followed was long; and other Victorian preoccupations interposed, scuffing and criss-crossing the trail. The broad success of development theory only made for a broad agreement *that* development took place. Within that consensus, many schools of thought contended over *how* it happened. What mechanism, or mechanisms, brought a people up from stage to stage? Perhaps the unvarying laws of physics led different peoples to the same discoveries quite separately, so that the significant inventions which transformed cultures were arrived at independently around the world as a matter of course. Some practical problems had only one solution which worked. You could point to the common design of all efficient arrows, no matter who fletched them. And domes used the same counterbalancing stresses to hold a roof up whether Brunelleschi built them over a Renaissance church, or an Inuit hunter popped in the key-block of an ice igloo. That would make nature the tutor of material advance. Or perhaps the fundamental likeness of human beings meant that their minds were stocked alike with the same possibilities, the same capacities for awe. The Maya of Central America and the ancient Egyptians had both built pyramids, hitting on the same imposing, giant shape. On the other hand it might be that the lightning of innovation struck much more rarely, maybe only in one people at one place at one time. In that case progress would have diffused from a few sources. Advance would depend most on how far a people migrated during its history, and whether they came into contact with other peoples of 'higher' or 'lower' accomplishments. Responsible scholars tended to treat these as interlocking factors, more or less influential in the particular situation of a particular people, however committed they were to 'independent invention' or 'diffusion' as the foremost tool of explanation. The recorded history of Europe alone offered too many examples of each of the possible mechanisms doing the work of change, for any to be discarded. Progress, it was acknowledged, was the composite effect of many causes. The other mechanisms remained factors to be considered when diffusionism became the orthodox opinion towards the end of the century. (Then, German philologists led an attempt to trace the whole of Indo-European culture back to a single starting-point somewhere in central Asia. Their goal, the modern counterpart to the fountain of eternal youth, was a sort of fount of Johns: a primaeval home out of which had flowed all the nations which called their sons John, Jean, Hans, Ivan, Ian, Ján, Yani, Johann, Jonah, Hanif, or Arjuna.)

But behind the battle of the theories lay a fundamental argument over the capacity of different peoples to advance themselves, an argument over the connection between knowledge and biology. Each of the different positions you could hold on the means by which humanity advanced was shadowed by a view of humanity itself –

physical, embodied humanity, whose thoughts and actions were somehow produced out of flesh which varied from place to place, in bulk and colour and features. Here we come to the question of race; which indeed had never been absent in anthropology from the beginning, and assumed even more importance when the seductive metaphors of Darwinism entered the subject. To some, Darwinian thinking suggested irresistibly that the different divisions of mankind should be thought of as semi-distinct species, engaged in evolutionary competition with each other. There was a related debate over whether the thinking ape homo sapiens had evolved once (monogeny) or several times over in several places (polygeny), in which case the 'white' and 'black' and 'yellow' kinds of people were actually separate branches on the biological tree. But the developmental account of human culture directed attention to race anyway, without assigning it a definite function. The scale of advance which Tylor described, running up from the lowest cultures to the highest ones, supplied an incidental racial hierarchy. 'Few would dispute that the following races are arranged rightly in order of culture: – Australian, Tahitian, Aztec, Chinese, Italian.' Of course it did not necessarily follow that 'stone age' natives occupied the lowest point on the scale *because* of their race. Tylor for one argued that it was 'both possible and desirable to eliminate considerations of hereditary varieties or races of man, and to treat mankind as homogeneous in nature, though placed in different grades of civilization.' To him it hardly mattered 'how far tribes who use the same implement, follow the same custom, or believe the same myth, may differ in their bodily configuration and the colour of their skin and hair.' Increasingly, though, drunk on the torrent of evolutionary data showing the link between animal behaviour and the 'bodily configuration' of species, later Victorians were ready to wonder if noses flatter than their own might determine 'lower' forms of society. Perhaps the physiology of a race like the Inuit restricted them to inventing primitive tools and singing monotonous songs; perhaps race was destiny. In modern terms, anthropology simply grew more and more racist as the turn of the century approached.

In its investigations into custom and craft, anthropology had always been accompanied by its little medical brother, physical anthropology.

Physical anthropologists recorded the finger-length and skin tones of savage peoples in the same way that the scholars of the main discipline collected their pots and necklaces. But the physical study of primitive humans also abutted onto zoology. The procedures for weighing, dissecting, and analysing were the same, whether a human body was the object of scrutiny or the ligaments and ribcage of a bird. The skull, as the seat of the brain, was particularly important. Quite naturally, the head bones of the fascinating Inuit were measured: as far back as 1850, Robert Gordon Latham's *Natural History of the Varieties of Man* illustrated the contrast between 'dolycephalic' and 'bracycephalic' types with two engravings, on the left the 'Skull of an Eskimo', on the right the 'Skull of one of Napoleon's Guards killed at Waterloo'. At first glance Latham's two heads look like nothing human at all. To bring out the difference in the skulls' dimensions front-to-back, Latham gave a view from beneath, staring up into the empty socket of the spine. Till you make sense of this very alienated perspective, you seem to be gazing at the monstrous relics of a pair of Cyclops, whose single eyes sit centrally on an obscure, wrinkled plane of bone. Only then, with a somersault of vision, do you see as intended that the jug-handle loops at the bottom of each picture are cheek-bones, far larger and more curved in the Inuit's skull; that the bulges above are the backs of the two crania, compactly rounded in the case of the Grande Armée veteran, while his neighbour's makes a pointier, extended arc. (You notice too that the Arctic hunter had much better teeth.) Later the classification of human skulls was refined. The Inuit moved from the dolycephalic or long-headed category to the class of mesocephalic, middle-headed, peoples. Among the experts invited to pose questions in the 1875 RGS manual, a skull-calibrating doctor duly appeared, calling for exact information, and from the ninth edition of the *Encyclopaedia Britannica* until the eleventh, from the late 1870s until 1911, the general reader found figures giving the height/breadth ratio of Inuit heads in the ESKIMO entry. 'Their skulls are of the mesocephalic type, the height being greater than the breadth; according to Davis, 75 is the index of the latter and 77 of the former.' Thereafter new editions quietly dropped this piece of data, which shifts in scientific perception made clear was mumbo-jumbo, irrelevant at best.

Indeed, what might follow, scientifically, from the skull ratios was never evident. You could relate the form of a bird's wing to the pattern of its life. The equivalent functional link, between the back of an Inuit's head and his or her marriage customs, eluded observation; since, as Victorians of course recognised, human behaviour possessed a complexity far exceeding that of other animals. The only tools available were clumsily macroscopic – rulers held up alongside savage heads, inside leg lengths tabulated in notebooks. Nineteenth-century biology lacked methods commensurate with the complications of the human animal. (And when the techniques did become available, when the genetics of populations could be mapped, the whole racial supposition became untenable anyway. The part of the genetic code which produces ethnic characteristics takes up a negligible amount of space. Two individuals of the same ethnic group differ much more from each other genetically *as* individuals than they resemble each other because they share a skin colour. The only behaviours which seem to be physically determined, hard-wired into us as human animals, are those shared across the species as whole. Language acquisition, for instance.) It is as if a century fascinated by quantity and amount, simply measured whatever could be measured about a people like the Inuit. This kind of physical anthropology was not innocently pointless, though. If it could not lead to scientific conclusions, it could certainly secure social and psychological results. It helped produce the vague but deep-seated feeling in European explorers that a gulf almost like the difference between a cow and a horse separated them from the Inuit. It encouraged a willingness to treat the people of the Arctic as specimens. In the most notorious case, a small party of Inuit brought back to the United States by Peary in 1897 sickened and died, victim to bacteria which didn't exist in their antiseptic homeland. The flesh was rendered off their bodies, and their skeletons, articulated with wire, were displayed in the Museum of Natural History, as further samples of Arctic fauna among the walrus tusks and the stuffed seals.

There was, so to speak, an incentive to feel the difference between whites and Inuit this way. It simplified matters. It defended explorers' conceit of themselves, especially where the contentious skills of the

Inuit at making do in the polar landscape were concerned. It answered more directly to a white traveller's sense of personal superiority, than the careful reasoning could which was generated by a non-racial explanation of white men's higher level of development. And there were problems with applying those cerebral explanations. When Tylor, for example, came to consider the exceptional areas of expertise in which savages sometimes surpassed a modern civilised type, he had this assurance to offer:

It is true that these exceptions seldom swamp the general rule; and the Englishman, admitting that he does not climb trees like the wild Australian, nor track game like the savage of the Brazilian forest, nor compete with the ancient Etruscan and the modern Chinese in delicacy of goldsmith's work and ivory carving, nor reach the classic Greek level of oratory and sculpture, may yet claim for himself a general condition above any of these races.

Tylor treated all these accomplishments, impressive or beautiful though they might be, as essentially obsolete; important for past and present people who depended on them, but no longer useful at the point on the road of development where 'the Englishman' stood. He couldn't shin up a eucalyptus, catch an armadillo, beat gold to airy thinness, or declaim in the market-place. He didn't have to, when instead he could buy butcher's bacon, hire-purchase an electro-plated epergne for the sideboard, and play his part in public life by reading the parliamentary columns of *The Times*. The trouble was that a 'general condition' of superiority did not help in the explorer's situation, when the Englishman found *himself* in the jungle or out on the ice, far from the developed material framework of his society; when in the stone age zone of the Arctic the Englishman discovered it was presently necessary to be able to manage the knotted thongs of a dog harness, and he couldn't do it, while an Inuit could. At home the Englishman did not need to possess as individual skills all the technologies that made his life advanced. Indeed specialisation, the complex distribution of different tasks to different men in factories and offices, was central to higher societies as Tylor envisaged them, freeing the individual Victorian to ride on a train without having to be capable of building his own steam locomotive. Things were different in the Arctic. There individual Englishmen confronted individual Inuit who did each aim to possess the total of knowledge required to survive, and thrive. Following Tylor's kind of argument, the individual white might try to preserve his general superiority by imagining that he bore his whole culture in little inside him, that he had the schema for the whole coded into his fractional self, so that, like a Japanese paper flower expanding in a cup of water, he could blossom out the entire panoply of Crystal Palaces and Brummagem-ware teapots and wage relations if necessary. (Long before, in a potent text for the imperial imagination, Daniel Defoe had imagined just this: alone, but replete with know-how, Robinson Crusoe had unfurled a complete familiar order of things on his island.) But this was a precarious rigmarole to go through for the sake of securing a comfortable sense of status under polar circumstances. Much more probably, and much less consciously, explorers resorted to believing that their civilisation inhered in their whiteness, an individual quality after all, as concrete and immediate as the shade of their skin. Elaborate explanations always tended to collapse back into simple convictions about European and Inuit bodies. If Inuit, short and plump and ovoid, were animals adapted to endure the Arctic, what were white men, tall and beefy and muscular? Animals independent of any particular environment, perhaps; whom you would not say, in the same manner, typified the fauna of the rainy British Isles. (The *Inuit* impression of white men's physique played little part in these deliberations. Inuit onlookers were routinely astonished at the weights their visitors could lift in a single heave: but whites also struck them as prodigal with energy, short on stamina, easily exhausted.)

Analogies with animal behaviour eased the cognitive strain caused by the slender, retrievable Inuit harpoon, and its efficient like. The perfect V made in the air by flying duck stirred no alarm in the beholder, nor did the impeccable hexagons built by bees worry European architects. Suppose that the Inuit production of elegant survival kit also shaded over into instinctual behaviour, and you usefully detached your attitude to the people from your attitude to their tools. The tools could command admiration without the admiration escaping control. This sleight-of-mind gave a refined, biological sheen to a mental knack found all around the imperialised globe, wherever there were objects or buildings to admire. Things and the makers of things could be placed in separate mental compartments of the European mind, as if there were only a tenuous or accidental connection between them, despite the one having constructed the other. Sometimes it seems as though the nineteenth century positively devoted itself to avoiding recognition of other cultures' accomplishments. The managed vision which could view a gorgeous mosque in the Middle East as a triumph of religious art, and still see the Friday worshippers there as aimless Asiatics, is familiar from Edward Said's *Orientalism*. A modest northern counterpart could be written called *Borealism*, and it would have much to say about animal imagery.

The hint that the Inuit survived their snows instinctively could be seen at work back in the 1850s, in *Peter the Whaler*, a phenomenally popular boys' adventure story with a strong evangelical bent. Little Lionel Tennyson got a copy for his eighth birthday in 1862, along with a pocket-knife; the Popular Library made it one of their first hundred classics in 1908; it was still being given as a Sunday school prize in the 1930s. Pell-mell 'Adventures in the Arctic Regions' are half the point of the book. The other half was the moral reform of the hero, at the opening a ne'er-do-well who smokes and poaches. ' "Peter," said my father with a stern look . . . "this conduct, if you persist in it, will bring ruin on you, and grief and shame on my head and to your mother's heart." ' After a breakneck succession of shipwrecks and thrilling catastrophes, Peter finds himself marooned in Greenland for the winter. The Inuit figure here as serene, lovable Good Samaritans, prompt to render the assistance which makes the daunting task of survival possible. 'The natives live; and we must try to find out how they do it,' says one of Peter's implausibly pious sailor companions. English dignity must be preserved, though. The same man puts the same point in the course of the same conversation, in a different and distinctly rivalrous manner: 'I do not see why we should not manage to live, as well as the ignorant natives who inhabit this country.' Soon, concerned at the thin walls and skimpy insulation of the hut the Englishmen have erected for themselves, the nearby band of Inuit mount a bravura display of igloo-building. Up go the domed walls on a circle of beaten snow, piece by piece, 'While we stood looking on with amazement at the rapidity and neatness with which the work was executed.' The author's description conveys directions quite precise enough for English boys reading the book to try building their own, should the English winter oblige with sufficient snow. They probably could not achieve the expert shaping of the Inuit original – 'Indeed, the house thus rapidly formed was perfect in every respect.' But relieving any tension caused by walls like 'the most shining alabaster' and interior light 'tinted with the most delicate hues of blue and green' comes a tell-tale simile. The Inuit architect of all this splendour exits his finished work 'as a mole does out of his mole-hill'. And a curious sense of racial punctilio prevents the English lads in the story from occupying this igloo, built expressly for them. They do not quite like the thought of living so close by the Inuit; more important, they cannot take survival as a direct gift. Instead, 'Andrew suggested, that though we might not use the hut they had built, we might take a lesson from them, and cover in our house with snow of the same thickness as their walls . . .' Peter and his friends resolutely pass the winter in a driftwood shack, coated like an igloo on the outside, English within. They are 'tolerably comfortable, though we had to own that . . . the Esquimaux were better able to make themselves so'.

Yet the earnest heroes of this polar yarn do learn from the Inuit, do consent to 'take a lesson'; and perversely it was the recourse to a racial guarantee of dignity which helped allow some real explorers in the real Arctic to absorb native instruction. These men felt able to learn, at least in part, because they now felt themselves secure. Their ignorance before they put themselves to school with the Inuit need not be troubling, need not set loose too many doubts and uncertainties. The arts of the ice were simply adaptations to circumstance Europeans had not had to acquire; now, with a brisk, ubiquitous flexibility, wise explorers could confidently add the local knowledge of the Inuit to their own repertoire. In the last years of the century a belated transfusion began of Inuit technologies into exploring practice. What had been a rare willingness to learn in Rae became a hungry appetite for the useful details of sledge-runners and clothing among the most innovative explorers, who tended to be Scandinavian or American.

The social or scholarly or commercial encounter with the Inuit became, often, an explicitly instructive occasion. Nansen spent a month during the winter of 1888–9 near Godthaab in Greenland, enjoying Inuit company, forcing down 'such delicacies as . . . frozen crowberries mixed with rancid blubber' and methodically bettering his skills. That winter his whole party, bar one, mastered the kayak. Nansen's disciple Amundsen seized the opportunity of contact with the Netsilik tribe while overwintering in King William Land, part way through his successful traverse of the North-West Passage in 1899–1900. About 150 miles away from the spot where Franklin expired in his English cloud of unknowing, Amundsen got himself and his crew trained, with incredible rapidity, in igloo-building, anorak design, dog-handling, and icecraft. 'In 3 hours we had erected 2 magnificent igloos. We lack practice, which we will get later.' A 1932 biography of Nansen, then two years dead, praised him in connection with the Inuit for his 'ability to enter into the life of whatever people he might meet'; more surprisingly, Roland Huntford's *Scott and Amundsen* applauded Amundsen in 1979 along the same lines, for a 'perception and humility' extraordinary among 'civilised men'. It did, of course, require personal imaginative sympathy on Nansen's part to learn as he did: his biographer was not wrong to link his willingness to eat the Inuit diet, and re-orient himself in the world by a different compass of food, with his later humanitarian work for the League of Nations. Likewise Amundsen had to find a remarkable individual tact in his dealings with the Netsilik. Other 'civilised men' might very probably have learned nothing: he demonstrated the same respectful brilliance in prompting assistance from the Arctic natives that he used to win the best work from his crews that they were capable of. But beyond their individual resources, both men gained by their feeling that their relations with the Inuit were on a secure footing of difference. Nansen saw in his hosts a 'humble contentment with life as it is', an *adapted* fitness to the Arctic; Amundsen believed that his teachers' techniques were an *evolved* response to the cold. Both men's intelligent appreciation of the Inuit depended obscurely on the contemporary understanding of race. Perhaps the racial substructure of their views seems to disappear in retrospect because it did not translate into racial hostility as we now recognise it. Indeed, once freed from anxious comparison, these founders of the modern tradition of exploration were able to record in unembarrassed detail how much they owed to the Inuit.

There remained the risk that too close an association with Inuit ways of doing things might rub off on the over-flexible traveller – the fate Peter's fictional party avoided by keeping themselves physically separate from the Inuit settlement. The perception of races as fixed, settled categories co-existed with the sense that there could be movement between levels of civilisation. The exceptional experience of Matthew Henson at the turn of the century demonstrates the multiple possibilities for racial alarm which resulted. It was well known that Inuit could be uplifted, improved, and made over into something better. Henson recalled the adoption of a favoured Eskimo child on Peary's successful North Pole expedition of 1909: 'After this boy was washed and scrubbed by me, his long hair cut short, and his greasy, dirty clothes of skins and furs burned, a new suit made of odds and ends collected from different wardrobes on the ship made him a presentable Young American. I was proud of him, and he of me.' But by the same token, an explorer could slip downward from the civilised standard, become degraded, literally de-graded. A degree of threatening fluidity existed in the situation. The same expedition discovered a white man left behind in north Greenland by Peary's rival Dr Frederick Cook. This polar castaway was squalid and demoralised, the very image of the danger involved in reverting to the primitive. And Henson himself, his rare gift of fluent Inuit speech making him the chief conduit for the Inuit expertise that Peary (a spikily obstreperous Navy type, whose moustache stretched slightly wider than his head) could not obtain, contended constantly against suggestions of regression in his own case. As a black American in the white Arctic, his presence was already racially provocative. It constituted a disruption of European and American images of exploration, hastily restored after Henson's participation in the final dash to the pole by journalists' descriptions of him as Peary's 'valet' or 'manservant'. More even than his white colleagues, Henson had cause to insist that he hadn't lapsed from civilisation among the Inuit. No doubt his experience of life in

Maryland and Virginia under the Jim Crow laws contributed to his sympathy for the non-white Inuit. 'Many and many a time, for periods covering more than twelve months, I have been to all intents and purposes an Esquimo, with Esquimos for companions . . . enjoying their pleasures, and frequently sharing their griefs. I have come to love these people.' The esteem was returned, and no doubt too it was a relief after months spent in wholly white company, steadily ignoring provocation (one man called him nigger, and said he'd shoot him: 'a good friend of mine', Henson recorded blandly), to cease being honest, unassuming Matthew for a time, and become the joking, adroit Mahri-Pahluk, approvingly remembered in Greenland to the present day. But Henson had to insist there was nothing *natural* about his affinity with the Inuit, that he had only made the same qualified journey into *and out of* the Inuit world as his white colleagues. 'I was to revert to that stage of life by leaps and bounds, and to emerge from it by the same sudden means.' He conceded humble terms for his participation in the polar conquest – writing his *Negro Explorer* he claimed just to have 'accompanied' Peary, a politely passive term – but the racial ground he was willing to locate himself on was the rising ground staked out for black Americans by Booker T. Washington, who introduced Henson's book. It could have nothing to do with the Inuit's presumed physical adaptation to the North. Negotiating issues of racial identity his white counterparts never had to deal with, Henson had all the greater reason to use the same animal imagery to sweeten his dependence on the Inuit. He was supporting his own contested status as an explorer. The Greenland Inuit, he wrote, were like the Greenland huskies: they had 'all the characteristics of the dogs, including the dogs' fidelity'.

But for some, incorporation of Inuit ways into exploration, even when cushioned to preserve explorers' self-respect, was something to be resisted. Though exploration was still differentiated from the Inuit's modest aim of living in the Arctic, and explorers continued to occupy the centre of attention, the kind of books that Frederick Cook, Peary, Nansen, and Amundsen wrote betrayed the subtle alteration in the tone of polar expeditions which resulted. The Inuit's domestic, intimate familiarity with the polar landscape was making incursions into the explorers' unfamiliarity with it; pressing home the possibility of other, prosaic responses to it, even if they were the dogged responses of doggy people. A realism about means and methods was emerging which gave less and less scope to immaterial resources, to spiritual resources in the conquest of the snows. As exploration became more conditioned by Inuit precept and example, it seemed less self-evident that explorers' success demonstrated virtues held in high esteem at home. Above all the sacrificial validity of exploration seemed to be slipping away, in favour of displays of competence. English Arctic exploration had been in abeyance since the failure of Nares in 1875. It was partly in a spirit of resistance towards the Inuit example that when polar activity in England revived, still in the hands of those faithful to the naval tradition, it was directed towards the truly empty, definitively personless Antarctic, where no natives complicated the performance of exploration, and penguins, the most human-seeming thing alive in the Great White South, only clustered comically around explorers' knees. It is suggestive, too, that the men who most insisted on traditional means, when the English went south, were those least willing to countenance descriptions of the Inuit which allowed for imitation. Clements Markham wrote a description of the seasonal life of the 'Arctic Highlanders' for the RGS manual of 1875. It is a charming portrait: affectionate, rigidly benign, almost pastoral in its tranquillity, quite closed to the thought that the tools of the natives might be of anything other than scholarly interest.

During the long night they are engaged in mending sledge-harness and preparing harpoon-lines and bird-nets; and the women chew the boot-soles and bird-skins, and make clothes with ivory needles and thread of split seal sinew. Summer brings a bright and happy time of sunshine and plenty. The children drive along the babies in miniature sledges, the boys play at hockey with rib-bones and leathern balls, or catch the rotches with nets attached to long narwhal horns, and the hunters are busy in their attacks upon larger game. All emerge from the dismal *iglus*, and exchange their darkness and filth for the well-ventilated seal-skin tents; and thus they move from place to place along the coast.

These were people one might come across, people to study if there were time. If an example were to be held up, it would be the example of the English, for the benefit of the Inuit. When Markham conjugated a sample verb, in his attached grammar of the Inuit language, he picked a verb illustrating a topic on which explorers were always giving guidance, and Inuit, alas, resisting it. He chose the verb 'to wash'. His conjugation inks out an expected relationship. There are plain usages, in past and present and future tenses: *He washes, he has washed, he will wash.* There is a rather resigned future form: *He will wash sometime hence.* There are a stern conditional, and a polite request: *If he washes, please to wash.* There is something close to pleading: *Let me wash.* And there is the imperative: *Wash!*

NINE

Comfortable Barbarians

By the time the nineteenth century ended, a few polar references and images had trickled into public circulation in the commemorative form of pub names, or names for streets, or household souvenirs. These were the small change of fame and patriotic sentiment: decoration on a mug or a biscuit tin, faraway places or national heroes borrowed to christen a row of terraced houses, and naturalised into the brick geography stretching between a mill-building and a railway siding. At the height of the Franklin search, the Staffordshire pottery industry had extended its line of loving couples in china by issuing Sir John and Lady Jane. The figurines of the pair updated the traditional shepherd-and-shepherdess group for the mantelpiece without much changing it. Later – as British polar exploration revived at the turn of the century after a twenty-five-year gap – there were cigarette cards devoted to polar heroes. On slips of pasteboard Scott and Shackleton, Edward Wilson and Captain Oates would be tucked down the back of packets of Woodbines, *circa* 1915, pictured in the rich smeary tones of early colour lithography, their lips a surprising vivacious red. The London A–Z street directory lists an Arctic Street in Kentish Town, and a North Pole Road near Wormwood Scrubs prison: both late nineteenth-century creations, neither very long, neither very important. Pub names turn over quickly, registering today's topical heroes, or a new landlord's sense of what's notable in the world, but some survive each shake of the sieve of generations. You can still drink in 'The Lady Jane Franklin' in London. These names sometimes commemorated real experience. Opening a pub was a traditional option for naval ratings retiring from the sea with a gratuity in hand, so a steady run of ex-petty officers enlivened the geography of port cities with drinking-houses called after things they had done, places they had been, the poles included. A touch of celebrity sold beer. People might step a little out of their way to have a pint pulled by a landlord who'd seen the far North or South. Petty Officer Edgar Evans planned to run a pub when he returned in triumph with Scott, and he would almost certainly have called it 'The South Pole'. Tom Crean, distinguished lower-deck veteran of Scott's last expedition and of Shackleton's boat journey a year afterwards, did in fact go home to Ireland, and die in 1938 the proprietor of the South Pole Inn, Annascaul.

But polar terms made a rather poor showing in slang. (Even 'Great Scott!' refers to Sir Walter, not Robert Falcon. 'Great Scott, the ontological argument is sound!' cried Bertrand Russell in 1894, when the explorer was still an obscure torpedo lieutenant.) Perhaps the Arctic and Antarctic were simply too far away. A slang marks out the group who use it: it sets an identity test. It also keeps the most frequently summoned thingummyjigs and whatsits of a life close by the speaker, in the topmost linguistic compartment, within easy mouth's reach. Unless you count the technical jargon built up by ships' crews with business in cold seas, what slang needed to refer habitually to icebergs and walruses? Yet the nineteenth-century expansion of the world that was known of and reckoned with did bring in a couple of trophies. 'Ask where's the North?' Pope had written. 'At York, 'tis on the Tweed;/In Scotland, at the Orcades; and there/At Greenland, Zembla, or the Lord knows where . . .' *North* in eighteenth-century slang meant clever; it drew on stereotypes of canny Yorkshiremen and cunning Scots. *Too far north* meant too clever by half. By the second half of the 1800s, at the very least, almost everybody knew where a north was in terms larger than the compass of the British Isles, leaping straight from York to the ice; that north was a place where the Navy went. The new slang sense of *north* from the 1860s on, meaning strong, where drinks were concerned, came from the Navy. Grog that was *due north* was absolutely neat, no water in it at all. *Too far north* – desperately, incapably drunk – now carried the sense of being hopelessly lost up there in the *ultima Thule* of booze. Elaborated into a jovial saloon-bar or shipboard witticism, it even brought together the degrees proof of spirits with the degrees of north latitude. *Another point north, Steward*: mix that a bit stronger, won't you?

Eric Partridge's enormous historical *Dictionary of Slang* records one more Arctic item, the arrival of *North Pole* as rhyming slang for *arsehole* around 1870, interestingly close in time to the preparations for the Nares expedition, last British effort before the hiatus – so if not in response to the rising profile of the Arctic in newspapers, at least within its topical shadow. It would be nice to think that *North Pole/ arsehole* represents a scabrous view of the round frozen Arctic sea as anus mundi, the puckered rectum of the world: the North-West Passage, so beloved by the Admiralty, so fussed over and revered in solemn print, as the back passage to China. Much more likely, of course, it implies no attitude whatsoever towards things polar. If indeed it isn't just pure linguistic opportunism, generated by the chime of the sounds and the neat way a *pole* turns a *hole* inside out like the finger of a rubber glove, it probably stems from a general reaction towards a whole class of subjects that happened to include the poles. From the point of view of working-class life and experience, the North Pole, along with the wonders of the natural world and the joys of moral purity, would have belonged in the category of things that authority grew excited about. It lay in the province of schoolteachers, curates, and public speakers – it was demonstrably a bee that buzzed loudest in the bonnets of a section of the middle and upper classes. Given that polar exploits had been judged suitable for use in education, it would not be surprising if mention of the North Pole were associated in people's minds with a set of lecturing, reproving, order-keeping tones of voice.

The White Cross League for Male Purity, for example, put out a collection of 'Papers for Men' called *The Blanco Book*; by 1909 they had distributed 24,000 copies 'with care and discretion' to soldiers and sailors and men in the street. *The Blanco Book* attacked the sexual double standard. Before it grappled with the question of why 'some men are so beastly', or proceeded to the medical testimony by a doctor who had 'no object in view in writing on so disagreeable a subject as lust . . . except your good', it encouraged 'those who think meanly of human nature' to consider the story of Greeley's American Arctic expedition. There, readers who doubted their capacity to resist fornication could 'see for themselves the infinite possibilities of self-sacrifice and self-control that lie hidden in common natures . . .'

Deflating this kind of thing must have been irresistible sometimes, it ground its axe so obviously. It tried so transparently to ingratiate itself: 'what a good fellow the private soldier is at his *best*', a lieutenant-colonel reflected elsewhere in *The Blanco Book*. 'What a smart, clean, cheery, hard-working chap he can be.' The gaudy red-white-and-blue enthusiasms of the press – more and more expertly whipped up, as the century ended, by the newspaper baron Harmsworth, sponsor of several polar ventures – equally invited you to see through them; but the laughter was directed at the way in which they were offered. Laughing did not mean you could not be moved at the same time, or that you did not feel patriotic pride. Assent to the images of national heroism and greatness was virtually universal in working-class Britain until the experiences of the Boer War, and then, conclusively, the Great War, demonstrated their hollowness. The badges of British identity, some of which the story of British exploration furnished, were familiar and important; only it might be with a sense of derisive familiarity that the response came to any version of them couched in terms designed to win you over, or improve you. 'I never read the proclamations of generals before battle', George Orwell would write forty years later, or 'national anthems, Temperance tracts, papal encyclicals and sermons against gambling and contraception, without seeming to hear in the background a chorus of raspberries from all the millions of common men to whom these high sentiments make no appeal.' Yet it was Orwell's point that 'the high sentiments win in the end'. *North Pole/arsehole* maybe blew one of Orwell's raspberries. Perhaps it was comparable to a sudden hoot – who said that? *who* said that? – out of the back row at an Empire Day celebration in an elementary school. Dr Edward Wilson in fact taught a Bible class of slum children at the Caius College Mission in Battersea, before his first departure to the Antarctic on the *Discovery* expedition of 1901. They drummed their iron boot-soles on the floor, they fought over forbidden toffees, they kept up a shouted conversation with other children clustering round the window outside. Wilson would try to pacify the horde by reading aloud dollops of Kipling. 'All the while I am telling them how nice it is to be like Christ and how soon they will get to the "jungle book" if they'll only be a little quieter . . .' These snotty, resistant objects of benevolence probably said *North Pole* for *arsehole* , though not within Wilson's earshot.

Nonetheless the crudity of the phrase seems appropriate to the blustering era between the last decade of the old century and the outbreak of war in 1914: not because a crude dismissal of polar feats typified it, but for the opposite reason. Belief *in* them now grew appreciably cruder, among those who did believe. Polar enthusiasm took on a strenuous certainty, for this was the time when the cloudy solution of Victorian culture was clearing, to precipitate out the coarser deposit that formed Edwardian civilisation.

Victorians had set a high value on doubt. They had had to, if they were willing to digest the implications of Darwinism; eventually, scepticism had come to seem an essential mark of a mature mind. A style of seriousness had prevailed which operated in a thick brew of suspended questions – was there a God? did human existence have a purpose beyond the imperative to reproduce? – and could pride itself on doing so, despite the discomfort, and at times the emotional pain, of the resulting collisions between wishes and evidence. Much of the richness of Victorian thought and feeling had come from this sometimes bold, sometimes melancholy admission of the world's difficulty; its diversity; its huge shadowy past and unguaranteed future. But the willingness to live amid unresolved issues would often strike the Victorians' successors as a fondness for vaporous, seemingly endless hedging. They were irritated by what they tended to regard as a habit of having things both ways. Victorians themselves had constantly accused each other of hypocrisy. It had been a Victorian truism that theirs was an age of artificial virtue, systematic lying, fake proprieties. But when Edwardians made the accusation it often applied to the Victorian tolerance for uncertainty. The Victorians had been subtly, painfully unsure about gender; about capital and labour; about faith and science; about authority; about empire and ethics; about race and identity. The world of their successors buzzed with insistent solutions to each of these problems. One current scholar of the era sees the chief characteristic of the Edwardian temperament – the fundamental point on which even the fiercest opponents might tacitly agree – as the desire to reconcile and re-unify the fissured understanding that had been inherited from the Victorians.

While it had been an exciting, if tremulous, business for Darwin's contemporaries to pull on loose threads, and watch antique convictions unravel, the feeling was different for those born into the cultural landscape which resulted. To them, the generation who would be influential at the beginning of the new century, the ethical blankness of the evolutionary perspective, its silence on matters of human definition and value, seemed a crippling lack, rather than a prompt or an opening. Havelock Ellis, Edwardian critic and sexual reformer, born in 1859 into a vicarage family, lost his faith in a model Victorian way after reading Darwin as a teenager in the 1870s, but materialist science, he wrote in *The Nineteenth Century* (1900), 'never taught the art of living', 'could never furnish any guide to life'. It was 'a blank and empty desert': it only revealed 'an alien universe of whirling machinery'. James Ward, future psychologist, found that his break with religion as a young man in 1872 brought him hard up against a vision of himself as a bundle of reflexes over which he had no choice and no control. 'I have no dread of God, no fear of the Devil, no fear of man, but my head swims as I write it – *I fear myself.*' To fill the silence, to fertilise that desert, the Edwardians looked to kinds of belief which could co-exist with the inescapable truths of science, but repattern them. They drank down new sureties like a tonic.

Beside the dun shadings of the old scepticism, the restrained motley opinions and the subdued liberal diversity, how bright the ideas were that the Edwardians cherished! Primary coloured, in fact, loud verging on lurid, bold and attractive, wittingly extreme or just extremely silly. Fairies existed, said Sir Arthur Conan Doyle. Jesus Christ was 'a first-rate biologist', proposed Bernard Shaw. Scouting prevented decadence. Syphilis could be conquered by increased vitality. The social investigator Charles Booth, to Edwardian London what Mayhew had been to the Victorian city, suggested that the poorest eighth of the capital's population should be removed to 'State slavery' in labour colonies. Or, a group of young Liberals wondered, perhaps they could be sterilised. The history of the world was the history of sea-power. Friendship dissolved class barriers. Body and spirit worked as one on a cycling holiday.

It seemed a safe world to be extravagant in. The difficulty for us, gazing backwards in the hope of catching the Edwardians in the act of being themselves, is that it is hard to believe in their perception of their safety, without rendering it picturesque, or monstrous, or merely self-deluded. Some of the component pieces of this past time are completely unfamiliar, so much so that we now receive the image of them without any of the amalgam of probabilities and meanings which kept them, then, likely and proportionate and everyday; on the other hand some pieces – like the Edwardian inventions of the telephone, the aeroplane, the car, and the radio – speak their later twentieth-century sense to us so easily we're misled: we imagine (say) the phone in every house constantly abolishing distance rather than the 'operaphone' service Proust subscribed to. He listened to his expensive instrument in his bedroom for three hours: a factotum in evening dress stood in the opera house all the while pointing a mouthpiece towards the stage. This was another world, chequered here and there by the embryonic development of our own. For one thing, it stood at that phase in the cycle of technological and social change when the consequences of the new set of objects and practices that have just appeared are still obscure. That things *were* changing was evident, and exciting. Against 11,000 licensed hansom cabs, London possessed only two motorised taxis in 1904. By 1910, a declining fleet of fewer than 5000 hansoms competed against 6300 taxis. The motorbus and the tram ejected the horsebus from the streets at the same time and at the same pace. A man returning from any of the polar expeditions of the period found London suddenly smelling distinguishably less of horse manure. Observers could see that the petrol engine was full of possibilities. It aroused a mass of predictions both shrewd and foolish; but Edwardian curiosity was not ballasted down yet by any sense of what London, and the rest of the country, might be like when the car became normal. That the roads themselves might widen to accommodate the new traffic was scarcely imagined. In the same way Edwardian science fiction was unabashedly, eagerly speculative, cheerfully assigning roles and characters to future decades, or even (in Wells' *The Time Machine*) future millennia. Yet its confident way with the future reflected a sense that the ways of the present were eminently solid, quite as much as it indicated dissatisfaction.

In fact the economic prosperity of Edwardian Britain, like many of its favourite answers to troubling questions, was shakier than it looked. Edwardian analysts noted that German and American industry were already winning the commercial initiative, innovating more and re-investing more than the complacent companies at home. Still, British industry's books bulged with orders from the captive markets of the empire; the volume of British trade outweighed all competitors; since the last Victorian slump in the 1870s wages had risen steadily to 1900 while food prices fell, and even when wages once more stagnated over the first decade of the century and prices rose, profits continued buoyant. The national balance of payments glowed with health. Edwardian commentators observed that for the first time young working-class women were avoiding domestic service where they could. Mrs C. S. Peel, 1902: 'The young working-girl of today prefers to become a Board School mistress, a post-office clerk, a typewriter, a shop girl, or a worker in a factory' (a typewriter was a person who operated a typing machine). Still, of the four million women employed in Britain, one and a half million worked as servants. Across the whole range of middle-class households the sight of the maid about her work at the endless task of domestic maintenance, blacking grates, boiling clothes, saving the labour of her employers, gave a daily demonstration of the social hierarchy. The equation involved was very simple, and so ordinary it faded from the notice of most who benefited by it: the servitude of some made time for the freedom of others. Unusually sensitive to the drudgery being performed around him, Edward Wilson imagined being called to account on the Day of Judgement, 'brought face to face with them and asked what we have done with our lives, and the time they gave us'. The rest of the pyramid-shaped structure of subordination lay further from the view of the comfortably-off. But with the industrial revolution a century or more established and the industrial class structure several generations old, with thirty years of male working-class voting behind it and few upheavals recorded, British society seemed to have settled into something like a permanent form. It was stratified and engrainedly deprived (Rowntree's survey of the city of York showed that large numbers of respectable working-class families could only stay on the right side of his newly labelled 'poverty line' by spending nothing at all on alcohol, insurance, doctor's bills, newspapers, tram fares, or union dues). Yet it seemed placid, at least as the middle classes experienced it, until the explosion of strikes in the last years before the outbreak of war. The same set of facts which spelled misery also spelled order. And Britain had been placid so long that many people took placidity for the natural state of things: counted on it continuing, at some deep level of their minds: assumed its permanence, whatever they themselves did, so that they could securely imagine Wells' Martian war-machines rampaging across Surrey, or advocate root-and-branch surgery on the nation, and just the same remain utterly sure that they would descend the stairs next morning to tea and the newspaper. Things would trundle on along their familiar course.

Between the habits, tastes, and expectations of the different social strata gaps opened so wide that much potential class hostility was lost in them. It was in the relationship with one's immediate social superiors and inferiors that resentments or snobberies congregated. A working-class area of a city had its local landlords or fat shopkeepers to be hated; the upper reaches proper of the class structure lay outside the scope of the everyday calculations of status. They climbed away into vague and shadowy grandeur – the social sublime – and a respectful awe for the gold and red of national splendour, and the peacockry of high society, marked attitudes towards dukes, MPs, and generals, especially among the unskilled. 'It was their belief', recorded Robert Roberts ruefully in *The Classic Slum*, his study of the Edwardian Salford of his childhood, '. . . that the middle and upper classes with their better intelligence and education had a natural right to think and act on behalf of the rest.' Exasperated socialists, still making relatively little headway, noted like Harry Quelch of the Social Democratic Federation that British workers were 'the most reverential to the master class' of any of the European proletariats. Deference oiled British manners. The respectful formalities that would certainly govern an encounter between people of very different social strata if they met as officer and batman, or hat-buying customer and milliner, mostly carried over to rule, as well, the looser and more unpredictable meetings of city life. The apparent pliability of the poor (often in fact a defensive reserve) meant that very seldom was their betters' understanding of what was happening challenged or disturbed, that very little prevented the middle and upper classes imagining that they did indeed 'think and act on behalf of the rest'. A patriotic speech given in a slum district would echo back unobstructed to the ears of the speaker. Even when, acting on hierarchy, the privileged occasionally meddled in a thing universally acknowledged to be the rightful possession of working-class Britain, they were allowed their intervention, and sometimes admired for it. Football, for example, had become a professional working-class sport since the 1880s, drawing millions every Saturday. Nearly 111,000 fans went to the 1901 FA Cup Final. The public schools had abandoned soccer, once the rise to glory of full-time clubs like Aston Villa doomed amateur efforts. But there was an exception. For a little while longer, the single best team in the country was a gentlemen's side named the Corinthians, made up of army men, Oxford and Cambridge blues, and other enthusiasts. The Corinthians often contributed players to the England team for international matches, but at home they only took part in 'friendly' games. They played, inevitably enough, with negligent grace, wearing their prowess lightly: all saunter. In 1902 Bury won the FA Cup by a record-breaking 6–0 against Derby County; a huge triumph, focus for much pride in industrial Lancashire, which set Bury at the very top of the professional ladder. Immediately afterwards Bury played the Corinthians for the Charity Shield – and lost 10–3, their record margin of victory neatly bettered, to the amateurs in the dazzling white cricket shirts and deep blue shorts of unique design. A historian of football calls the Corinthians 'much-loved'; and perhaps they were.

For the same reasons it was curiously easy to be private in public places, if you were eminent or rich, if you gave off the right aura of power. There was no exact equivalent in British politics for Kaiser Wilhelm I's twenty-year habit of meeting Bismarck on a park bench in

Berlin in the afternoons, when Emperor and Chancellor could chat in Prussian uniform about affairs of state, confident they would never be molested or annoyed. That had too feudal a flavour for England. Already, in England, the press would pursue politicians without mercy if a story was breaking: Arthur Balfour had to slip out of the country in disguise in 1902, to receive his appointment as prime minister from the King at a French resort. But journalists did not encroach on the ordinary business of government, nor dog the steps of notable men in their private affairs. Balfour's predecessor Lord Salisbury travelled back from Downing Street alone every evening to Hatfield by train, admittedly in a private compartment of a corridor-less carriage. Nobody ever bothered him, except once and famously a lunatic, whom Salisbury politely carried home with him, convinced that this amiable person must be an acquaintance whose name he'd forgotten: the point of the story being that only a madman would have so intruded. And Balfour himself liked to tell the story of the time Gladstone had come to stay with him at his place in the Highlands one summer during the 1880s (for the rising young Conservative Balfour had been on excellent terms with the Liberal leader, then in office – yet a third prime minister). Alone, host and guest had walked to the station across the moors, but found themselves late for Gladstone's return express south and had to run for it through pools and streams. Balfour sprinted ahead to hold the train, the Grand Old Man panted along behind. They made it, and as the express drew out 'I saw with intense thankfulness a pair of wet socks hanging out of the carriage window to dry. I had at least not inflicted on my distinguished guest the added horrors of a head cold.' Balfour described the scene as a spectacle of comic incongruity, but again what underlay the joke was a complete, imperturbable assurance of dignity. Within the array of rigid manners and punctilious courtesies there existed a little cupped space reserved for the ludicrous and the informal. Indeed the rigid manners allowed for the informality, protected it from misconstruction. Even bare-toed, Gladstone was Gladstone. All was well.

The satisfying sense that each thing and person occupied its proper place extended literally world-wide. If you were, in particular, a devotee of empire (and more than ever before, more than ever after, those who gave their imaginations over to it could feel they had the sanction of the times); or a cog in the imperial bureaucracy (which for this short reach of time seemed to offer a career central to the life of the nation, and attracted young men of high seriousness); or a child in a prosperous nursery (and Edwardians gave the view from the nursery unprecedented status), you looked out on a panorama of order coterminous with the globe itself. Farther and farther out from the ritual of teatime in Kensington or Camden Town, with two kinds of cake laid for eating and the trams clanging by beneath the window, there stretched away ranged circles of dominions and possessions, colonies and protectorates. London might not look like Vienna or Berlin, military-grand, all razored avenues of trees standing to attention, leading up to barracks and ministries; but lately and belatedly one central cell in the brick body of the city had been metamorphosed into marble. Now conscious imperial splendour edged St James' Park: from the ornamental bridge the fantastic mock-oriental spires and domes of the India Office glimmered white in the rain. Beyond the city lay the home counties, whose soil had recently been declared immemorial, the idea of patchworked survivals simplified to the idea of ancient continuity, the little mill still clacking, in the proem to *Puck of Pook's Hill* (1906), that 'has ground her corn and paid her tax/Ever since Domesday Book'. Then the North, where the machines were made and the folk-song collectors went. Then Scotland, and loyal blarneying Ireland. Then the broad ocean – the enchantment really beginning – creased by the wake of battleships and the liners of the P&O, BSA and White Star companies, all listed on page 2 of *The Times* every day. Beyond again, the almost endless other lands, huge and tiny, of every conceivable climate, progressively wilder and stranger, in cavalcade.

This was the age of geography-by-rote. Knowledge of the world meant Chief Ports, Largest Rivers, and Principal Products. The child or the adult gazing outward knew the height of the Himalayas, that Australia exported wool, beef, and opals. But the order of things conveyed by such information did not seem static, or fixed in place. What was suggested was a world in ordered motion, humming and buzzing, everywhere energetic. The closer you looked, the more there was to see, as if an optical trick were being played. It was a very old one. 'O Lord, how manifold are thy works!', the psalmist had written, surveying creation piece by piece, and making each piece seem to come alive when mentioned, by land or by sea. 'There go the ships: there is that leviathan, whom thou hast made to play therein.' The ships are set going in the act of describing them, the whale sports in the waters that very moment. So now, seen through the windows provided by a pictorial encyclopedia or a stamp album, innumerable distant people kindled into activity, each at a task or an occupation typical of them. At that moment, Zulu women were pounding sorghum in a *kraal*; Egyptian fellahin were tilling lentil fields beside the Nile; an Australian aborigine outstared a lizard, boomerang in hand; the Mounties chased crooks across a British Wild West; and all over India trains whistled, Sikhs drilled, ghats smoked, clerks scribbled, jute flowered, and caste-marks were painted on fresh. Everything was happening at once. The sun was coming up and the sun was going down. A hurricane was battering a merchant steamer outbound from Newcastle, New South Wales, with a cargo of coals. A snowmelt drip in remote mountains was fattening the waters of the Brahmaputra. In a district entering its fourteenth month of drought a white man was squatting, testing the baked earth with his fingers. Here and there a patter of rifle-shots announced the swift outbreak and resolution of a small war, but that was to be expected. 'Everyone can help', would insist Alfred Milner (whose dry fervour as High Commissioner in South Africa helped provoke a disturbingly large war there). Everyone British, *he* meant; everyone born, in a slum or a manor house, to the national destiny of empire, who could feel themselves bodily included in Lord Curzon's statement that the empire 'is part of us. It is bone of our bone and flesh of our flesh.'

In another sense everyone, really *everyone* within the ten million imperial square miles, was already helping, it seemed, playing their appointed part. The aggregate of their actions, great and small, innumerable yet patterned, constituted the empire daily. They made it solid and factual. For the child's abridged vision of empire, these many acts scaffolding the sum of things could be presented as invariably happy. But it did not need to be so. Adults could see that the harmonious fabric might well be shot through with ironies, that private bitterness and shame could equally serve the whole. The laureates of empire – Kipling and Conrad – acknowledged the thankless tasks and the crushed individual hopes, feeling a dash of self-pity and a touch of pride. Moriarty, in one of the *Plain Tales From the Hills*, 'did his work well in the four years he was utterly alone; but he picked up the vice of secret and solitary drinking, and came up out of the wilderness more old and worn and haggard than the dead-alive life had any right to make him'. Imperial experience came in all colours. A favourite fiction of the imperially minded – there were many versions – dealt with the arrival in one colony or another of a soft and despicable theorist from home, usually a supporter of native rights or some other airy fad. (Birdie Bowers, toiling dutifully in the Royal Indian Marine over the years before the sailing of the *Terra Nova* to Antarctica, fulminated just this way against 'cheap-labour specimens' who stirred up the coolies.) As the story was told, with its ideal come-uppance, the troublemaking type would lecture and pontificate as if Hampstead held him, not Durban or Delhi. He'd be ludicrously simple amidst obvious complexities. Then the surroundings would strike him with all the force of the real, and strike him dumb too. The immense sufficient *fact* of the empire was all the argument required. For there it was, after all, prosaic yet overwhelming, apparently permanent: complete, capacious, and various, or at least enough of each of these three things as was necessary to satisfy a child gazing forth, or an adult eager to believe.

In the quarter of the earth's land surface which the mapmakers coloured red, the unknown had not lost its power to shock, and different customs had not been rid of their disorienting effect. These things had, so to speak, been regularised. They had been put on a comfortable footing and made part of the expected panoply of empire. As such they were no longer quite seen as foreign. In fact, consciousness of empire had altered the way the British thought of 'abroad'. Abroad only began now, in its full sense, beyond the boundaries which the appropriating eye of imperial imagination could not cross. France, so near across the Straits of Dover, was abroad; Russia and Germany emphatically were; the United States was abroad too, despite the best efforts of propagandists to claim Americans as 'Anglo-Saxon' brethren. Jamaica on the other hand might be over the seas and a long way off, but was not abroad. Neither was the Sudan, nor Singapore, nor 'British India'. No matter if a place might be a scrubby plain roamed only by a testicle-collecting tribe of cattle-drovers who bleached their hair with cow urine; no matter if the place happened to be a city largely populated by Chinese families. However strange, however remote, it did not qualify as wholly foreign so long as it was held within the compartmented structure of British rule, and a visitor immersed in its strangeness or an observer contemplating it nevertheless knew that the strings of all this strange life were ultimately gathered in a British hand. What made Boulogne, by contrast, decisively foreign was the lack of this final degree of reference to England and home. Though the people there dressed far more as the British did, and had so many aspects of industrial European experience in common, their existences referred to a different centre, to a separate, self-sufficiently French identity.

Like the idea of a steamship acting as a time-machine, this geographical assurance is hard to credit now. It is important that we should believe it if we can, because it is implicit in Edwardian attitudes towards the very farthest places on earth, the cold zones stretching into guesswork at the very edge of the imperial map, yet still susceptible to the claims of possession. With claims to possession went claims of familiarity. The British sense of proprietorship over Antarctica partly rested on the curious conviction that the continent was *not foreign*. Amundsen offended against British views of sportsmanship; he also trespassed against the sense that the Antarctic, a howling wilderness, somehow did not count as abroad, but as a wild annex of England. Both in 1901 and 1910, Scott sailed to Antarctica down a corridor of Britishness. He went to the end of the earth, without ever quitting the scenes that St James' Park gave onto: he only passed into the remotest one. His ships called at Cape Town to refuel and collect supplies, then at Melbourne where Australian scientists boarded, then at Lyttleton in New Zealand for final arrangements and last goodbyes. Nowhere along the route London–Cape Town–Melbourne–Lyttleton–Ross Island did the expeditions touch any port where English was not the master tongue, where the coins were not the same size and shape and denominated in sterling, where the officers were not fed mutton and sherry at dinners given by local notables and the men could not go to the pub. To be sure, Table Mountain above Cape Town was not the Downs, and Lyttleton Bay was not the Thames estuary. The crew had welcomed King Neptune aboard as they crossed the Equator; there'd been Maoris to see, and South Africa's host of different peoples, black and 'coloured' and Chinese and Indian and even Hottentot. But weighing by imperial measures Scott had travelled into much more truly alien country on his brief preparatory trip to consult Nansen in Norway. And once settled under Mt Erebus at 78° S, nothing at all – except the news of Amundsen's arrival at the Bay of Whales in 1911 – impeded the reign of British certainties, obstructed the sense that even at this distance the expedition existed within the envelope of a familiar order. There were not even any inhabitants, only seals and penguins; and they, like the trackless expanse of the Barrier and the terrifying question mark of the polar Plateau, fell under the heading of 'nature'. The ships *Discovery* and *Terra Nova* had pushed through the pack-ice into natural space rather than foreign space. The continent had of course to be kept that way. Finding it so, making it so, and keeping it so were all fused together. During the agitation in the 1890s for Britain to resume exploration in the Antarctic, there had been a patriotic consensus among the luminaries of the learned societies. They disagreed bitterly about what form of British return should be made to the territories discovered by Ross in the 1840s, but the essential agreement that there should be one stretched from the eager scientists, for whom the national motive supplemented their urgent interest in polar geomagnetism, to not-terribly-bright men like the Marquis of Lothian. The chief agitator Clements Markham had already wishfully divided up the south polar landmass on paper like a hot cross bun, into four 'quadrants' with irreproachably English names. The Marquis of Lothian put the matter with naive clarity to a meeting designed to win funds from the Australian colonies. Small Belgian and German expeditions were preparing to nibble threateningly at the edges of Antarctica. The Marquis thought that 'the work of Antarctic research should be done by Englishmen'. 'I should not like', he said, 'to see foreign names upon that hemisphere where all civilised points are inhabited by our countrymen, and belong to this country.'

It seems appropriate that it should also have been in Antarctica that the Edwardian world lasted longest. After the period ended a tiny bubble of pre-war feeling and expectation persisted there in the form of Shackleton's marooned *Endurance* expedition. Probably Shackleton's men were the last Europeans on the planet still inhabiting the lost paradigm in 1916, year of the Somme: 'I suppose our experience was unique,' he wrote. The war had already just begun when they sailed in August 1914 to try the first crossing of the Antarctic continent, but the England they left was in the very first phase of high excitement. All they had seen was the Edwardian nation mobilising, not a single casualty list published, not a single telegram of condolence sent. The war had no colours yet except the patriotic ones. They heard their last instalment of news in Buenos Aires in October, where the received wisdom still held that the battles would end crisp and quick within six months. After that they passed beyond communication, 'not without regret' at their exclusion from the great adventure, as if the European catastrophe already unrolling behind them were a spreading stain they had accidentally outrun. Shackleton's plan failed. Before *Endurance* even reached the Weddell Sea coast of Antarctica it was immobilised by the ice, gripped, and eventually crushed. Two years and a desperate boat journey later, Shackleton, Worsley, and Crean stumbled into Stromness whaling station on South Georgia, back within the war's range. They were revenants from the previous age, polar Rip Van Winkles. The time-freezing effect of the poles which seemed to keep the Eskimos in the stone age had kept their clock stuck at 1914. In Shackleton's extended description of their awakening – to news of 'nations in arms, of deathless courage and unimagined slaughter . . . of vast red battlefields in grimmest contrast to the frigid whiteness we had left behind us' – the war still sounds slightly muffled, still stirring, though in the 'grimmest' of keys now. But his book *South* (1919) best conveys the bursting of the bubble in an exchange of dialogue as sudden and blunt as the inrush of the new world that it brought about. As soon as the three scarecrow-like travellers had established who they were to Mr Sorlle, the manager, and what they were doing wandering through his whaling station frightening children, 'Tell me, when was the war over?' Shackleton asked. 'The war is not over,' he answered. 'Millions are being killed. Europe is mad. The world is mad.'

(Perhaps Shackleton's enforced ignorance of half the Great War never rubbed off completely. One effect of the 'stunning return' was to sharpen his unease that they had left at all in such times. He had offered up the expedition complete for war service. PROCEED, the Admiralty wired back. He felt he must insist that the expedition had not run away. His mind on courage, and the possible shame of absence, he maintained an understanding of the war slightly out of sync with the general disillusionment at home, one which allowed a place for individual valour despite the machine guns. *South* takes care to point out how many of the lives heroically saved on Elephant Island during the expedition were then heroically lost 'in the wider field of battle'. And as that phrase suggests in itself, so far as he could he equated the war with the 'strenuous campaign' of the expedition. Reprising the red/white imagery, he dedicated the whole book 'To My Comrades Who Fell in the White Warfare of the South and on the Red Fields of France and Flanders': when it was far commoner among polar veterans of the 'heroic age' who also served in the war, and who paired the experiences, to see in their exploring at most a distinct and 'clean' counterpart to the ruck that followed, the Great War's better equivalent.)

Because Europe's madness shredded so many Edwardian certainties, the time before the war often gets judged innocent. The happy anticipation of the war in chivalric clichés, the recruiting booth doing great business in the foyer of the theatre where Guy du Maurier's *An Englishman's Home* played, the half million who enlisted at Saturday football matches before the war's first December: all famous signs of a naive leap over the brink, by people who understood none of the terrible possibilities of their world. The war's coming presents an irresistibly potent image of fracture, visited again and again in imagination over later decades by observers who come to see the moment when innocence and experience divided, and the nature of the twentieth century became apparent. But it is an innocence that needs very careful definition. It did not feel like an innocent age at the time. The Edwardians were innocent of the future, of course. H. G. Wells (in *Anticipations*, 1901) could look forward to a stern New Republic in which life would be 'a privilege and a responsibility, not a sort of night refuge for base spirits out of the void; and the alternative in right conduct between living fully, beautifully, and efficiently will be to die'. He could predict the gassing of the 'feeble, ugly, and inefficient' without the prospect carrying any freight of horrible, specific images. The future cast no backward shadow on the Edwardians. They were not forewarned. Wells might foresee gas-chambers (in fact he soon retracted) but he never expected cattle-trucks, extermination quotas, the industrialisation of death; he was imagining some utopian form of euthanasia, angelic guardians leading away those too feckless or wretched to enjoy the garden cities and eugenic marriages of his future state, away down trim sunlit paths to a peaceful death on a couch designed by William Morris. Arts-and-crafts annihilation. Yet annihilation was still not an innocent proposal, and Wells, proposing it, did not feel innocent any more than the advocates did of any other of the countless illiberal schemes put forward by the Edwardians for the cure of this or that social evil. So the idea violated every religious rule about the sanctity of life, and every legal principle about the rights of the individual. But the snotty urchins treated by Wilson at the university mission in Battersea were snottier, iller, and more stunted than any previous generation of the poor (in part because British diet had reached its all-time, nutritionless nadir: a fact which eventually had polar implications). What had Victorian piety or Victorian enthusiasm for constitutional liberties achieved lately in such places? When had either favourite panacea of the past ever made inroads into the problem of poverty? A sharp mind would now see these restraints as illusions, whether he or she solution-mongered on the left, or garnished projects on the radical right with Milner and Joseph Chamberlain and Kipling. (The concerns of the two overlapped to a surprising degree. A Fabian like Karl Pearson, author of *National Life from the Standpoint of Science*, could satisfy both socialists and imperialists with his demand for 'a decently-bred and properly-fed herd' of Britons.) Wouldn't it restrict 'the liberty of boys' if the novelist Galsworthy's scheme of 1911 were put in practice, and every poor male between fourteen and seventeen were carried off for compulsory outdoor training? 'What liberty have they in the present muddle? What liberty have boys of the more fortunate classes? Why should boys have liberty?' Beneath the flippancy Galsworthy, like Wells, felt bold, tough-minded, conciously shocking, and even *realistic*.

It was not just that the Edwardians tended to project futures where every restraint would still hold true except the one they planned to abolish, and the decencies they took for granted would continue to operate, insulating and domesticating their wildest notions. They were also sure that they viewed the present with clear eyes. They were already persuaded that they understood the uncomfortable truths; how much more likely the world was to be harsh rather than kind, how the balance of nature favoured the strong and condemned the weak. When it came, the Great War brought about so great an expansion in the scale by which horror and violence were measured that the scale the Edwardians had counted these things on seemed minuscule in comparison. But the sense of restricted scale existed only in retrospect. At the time, the Edwardians inhabited a full-sized world, the one and only real world, where a perfectly good working definition of modern warfare existed. Total war was defined by events in South Africa. British casualties in the dragging struggle to pin down the Boers were the highest of any war to date; British tactics were unprecedently nasty, and had included the use of dum-dum bullets and invention of 'concentration camps' to pen up Afrikaner women and children. A writer could show a tough familiarity with suffering by alluding to South Africa. A statesman could point to the experience to show the hard logic, the inevitable callousness of power politics. Edward Wilson (who thought imperialism was 'the vilest of sins') reacted to a hard-boiled newspaper report of 'our' 'bombardment of Kronje in the Modder' with a revulsion just as intense as the revulsion that people of conscience would feel in later decades reading about atrocities committed by their own side. The technological scope of the violence would expand year by year: gas attacks in World War I, carpet-bombing in World War II, napalming in Vietnam, the pinpoint aerial charring of the Iraqi column on the Basra road. But the helpless reaction had already formed fully in 1901, and would remain the same: 'It made me cry like a baby and I threw away the paper in perfect disgust.'

Wilson conceded that the 'cruelty' shown in the bombardment of Kronje was also 'as things are, necessary'. That was his point of common ground with the large number of Edwardians who read what he did but were not ashamed, who could view cruel actions with equanimity because they were cruel-but-necessary. Unlike their Victorian predecessors, they thought, they faced up to the need for such cruelties as made the world work or would make it work better. For some time British culture had leant towards admiring strength. Self-congratulation played a part here: finding itself on top of the world, as it seemed, Edwardian Britain liked to remind itself of hierarchies and pecking orders. So did the simplified 'Darwinism' (really no such thing) that drew parallels between the struggle of species for survival and the struggle of human nations and individuals against one another. Maybe Nietzsche even had some influence, for his ideas about the 'will to power' and the superman were just beginning to be popularised in Britain by a few converts. But Edwardian enthusiasm for toughness, tough tactics, and toughened moral fibres was very widely diffused. They were less willing than mid-Victorians to recognise the delicate and ambiguous kinds of mental endurance, but they admired strength of character. They enjoyed shows of force, in the form of military parades, ranked fleets of battleships, and exhibitions of scientific boxing. They were keen on programmes of exercise that would build up bodies and lead to physical 'fitness', itself a term only carried over since the 1870s from biology. The word had gained its modern, muscular meaning while still suggesting readiness for the evolutionary scrum. In a time of alarm about the poor physical condition of most British men, those who did match the brawny and deep-chested Edwardian ideal stood out; and they could be frankly appreciated. Scott frequently remarked that this or that member of his expeditions 'stripped well', and in common with many others aboard the *Terra Nova* he seemed almost mesmerised by Birdie Bowers' chest size, he mentioned it so often (forty inches).

Literature too had changed. Oscar Wilde's sudden disgrace in 1895 had deleted 'decadence' (meaning a witty suspension of judgement as well as sexual unorthodoxy) as an acceptable school of letters, leaving the field temporarily dominated by a muscular and masculine writing. The taste for the fatalistic social novels of Hardy and Gissing was also fading. Contemporaries in fact assigned a date for the beginning of the trend. George Eliot had died in 1880. Since then, the roomy and fluid Victorian novel, with its frequently female authors, its domestic and local sense of what constituted serious subject-matter, and its acknowledged openness to the forms of women's experience, had been gradually replaced as the model for fiction by the briefer thing that one critic calls 'the male romance'. Stevenson, Kipling, and Conrad – the famous names among a legion of lesser workers in similar veins – wrote seriously crafted, seriously considered stories about subjects that would have seemed the stuff of genre fiction for boys thirty years earlier. Fiction now explored jungles, engineering exploits, war, piracy, ships at sea, what it might be like to be a wolf or a husky. Such writing often took its central dilemmas, its drama, from the half-formed, half-controlled strength of young men. And often it expressed an attraction for these big boys' freedom from restraint while they found their place in the hard adult world: the same cathartic attraction perhaps that Dickens had played out on stage in a false explorer's beard, now made over into a mainstay of the literary mood. You can distinguish a phalanx of these heroes. Jim Hawkins, a streamlined prototype, laughing as he shins up the mast out of reach of Israel Hands in *Treasure Island* (1883); Jim of Conrad's *Lord Jim* (1900), the subtlest of the crew, his cowardice and bravery the occasion for Conrad's meditative searching of both; Stalky of *Stalky & Co.* (1899), foraging the Devon countryside like hostile territory, too exaggeratedly unscrupulous, too much a junior Spartan for the critics to stomach. By setting these figures so high in cultural estimation, Edwardian writers were doing rather more than acting out the perennial pleasure adults feel in the grace and ardour of the young. They also expressed a confidence that youthful wildness fitted perfectly comfortably into the adult order. Pompous elders abounded in fiction for the young to see through; but there were also always appreciative guides and patrons – Conrad's narrator Marlow suddenly crying out to his cronies as he tells Jim's history, 'Wasn't he true to himself, wasn't he?' This connoisseur's approval (layered with conscious irony in Conrad's case) rested on the sense that the world (not being breakable) could stand a little rough handling from those whose wild strength after all served just the same ends as the sober and responsible acts of the greyheads. Mowgli grew up in one story Kipling wrote into a forest ranger, the servant of the Raj. Alarm over delinquency lay well in the future. In the meantime the public was imaginatively on the side of cadets who abducted complacent MPs, subalterns spoiling for a fight, and the kind of students whose behaviour prompted the rhyme about 'the upper class/who like the sound of breaking glass'. High spirits was almost a justification in itself.

If much fiction blurred the line between stories for boys and stories for men, that was the point; and indeed the writing about (and for) younger children at which the Edwardians also excelled did not see its subjects as innocent either. Partly, the Edwardians paid more realistic attention to children than their predecessors had. The little angels of Victorian children's books were fortunately dead, except in the least ambitious kind of evangelical pulp. Child readers could now see brother-and-sister squabbles faithfully reflected by E. Nesbit's Bastables and Railway Children. But the times also favoured an alarmingly *eager* vision of children as conscienceless imps, changeling creatures who existed outside the adult moral scheme altogether. It was not so much that you could call Peter Pan, or one of Saki's imperturbable little manipulators, bad, or even morally equivocal in any adult sense; they were non-moral, or in Peter Pan's special case, pre-moral and determined to stay that way. Peter, J. M. Barrie reminds readers several times, is quite without pity. He has grace instead. Edwardian children really did enjoy the playful horror of Belloc's *Cautionary Tales* and Harry Graham's *Ruthless Rhymes for Heartless Homes*:

> Billy in his nice new sash
> Fell in the fire and burnt to ash.

And now, although the room grows chilly
I haven't the heart to poke poor Billy.

Saki imagined children who really might burn a detested uncle at the stake, at any moment, seeing no reason why not.

From here some Edwardians went on to relish the sensation of ruthlessness. These admired not just strength, but what strength could inflict; they did not only accept the need for cruelty, but also thrilled at it. Yet their fundamental sense of safety held all the while. It manifested itself in an expectation that the violence would stay within manageable bounds, within a proper arena almost, around which you could spectate. It would never crash out into the stalls, as Siegfried Sassoon imagined a tank doing in a poem to punish those who spectated on through the Great War. Joseph Chamberlain, the orchid-wearing Colonial Secretary from 1895 to 1903, played to this gallery, and perhaps sat there himself, for all his power to move real armies. 'I think', he wrote to Lord Salisbury after the Kaiser had telegraphed support to the Boer president Paul Kruger, 'what is called an "Act of Vigor" is required to sooth the wounded vanity of the nation. It does not much matter which of our numerous foes we defy, but we ought to defy someone.' Chamberlain made such a successful power-broker because, as in this astonishing remark, he shared the reflexes he was manipulating. He lost power when his own mood ceased to coincide with the national one, and he grievously misread the level of support for his 'Imperial Preference' tariff scheme. For now, 'wounded vanity' was right. The long experience of being on top had led a large part of the British public into that spoilt, petulant state (more familiar in the late twentieth century among Americans) where any check to the national pride was interpreted as a monstrous affront. The humiliations of the first phase of the South African war drove civilian feeling at home to new heights of theoretical fierceness. In *The Psychology of Jingoism* (1901), not quite the serious study it sounds but an impassioned tract, J. A. Hobson disgustedly assembled a catalogue of brutish behaviour, from the wealthy war-fan who presented a Maxim gun for service and promised the troops a bonus for each dead Afrikaner but a deduction for each prisoner taken, to the Lord

Lieutenant of a county receiving 'prolonged cheers' for suggesting 'three inches of bayonet' should be rammed down Kruger's throat. Kipling saluted 'Good killing at Paardeburg, the first satisfactory killing of the war'. The Anglican Archbishop of Armagh praised the fertilising effects of 'war's red rain'. 'Mild and aged clergymen; gently bred, refined English ladies; quiet, sober, unimaginative business men, long to point a rifle at the Boers, and to dabble their fingers in the carnage.' Hobson blamed malignant right-wing newspapers and immature voters, who had indeed nodded the government back into office at Chamberlain's neatly timed 'khaki election' of 1900. But reactionaries held no monopoly on salivation, on being eager to see harm happen. A few years later, with the Liberals in office, the radical journalist H. W. Nevinson detected an equally unpleasant excitement among wealthy West End sympathisers of women's suffrage. Like him, they went to WSPU rallies to deplore the treatment of feminist hunger-strikers in prison. Yet they also attended, as he thought, making the theatrical parallel explicit, to feel 'the thrill of vicarious danger, implying no risk whatsoever to themselves . . . If the Liberal government had burnt one of the leaders alive on stage, they would have shrieked with indignant delight, and gone home to tea.'

These were, of course, the very grossest manifestations of the Edwardian taste for sensational extremes. But the readiness to subscribe to absolute solutions of one sort and another ran deep, even among dissenters. With his fellow social reformer Octavia Hill (who founded the National Trust) Nevinson pioneered military drill for poor boys at the city 'settlements', which attracted his idealism as they had Dr Edward Wilson's. He might not have wanted the boys to become little jingoes, but he did see an instinctive rightness in the disciplined movements of drill – something to set against the chaos and irresolution of slum life. And Wilson, Scott's confidant and spiritual counsellor on both his Antarctic expeditions, though so free of some of the symptoms of Edwardian machismo, conformed to the times deeper down.

He was gentle with others, at the cost of being fanatically hard on himself. He wore his quiet, pacific faith like a too-tight shoe that squashes the bones of a foot. It came from many sources. His polar colleagues found him a little otherworldly, rather than simply pious, because he could not be pigeon-holed; he was not a book Christian, nor one who followed a denomination's rules; his faith impressed them as entirely authentic and somehow self-made. He believed, in fact, that no Christian precept could be truly taken to heart until you had proved its truth on yourself by living it out. St Francis was his spiritual ideal: 'I admire the man more than anyone else I ever heard of, and that's a thing no one can do without trying to follow him.' But the tradition he had found for himself, of spiritual exercises and spiritual self-fashioning, became in Wilson something as strenuous, and in its way as reckless, as the life of a Kipling hero. He set himself a fierce regime of humility and devotion. At Cambridge, his biography delicately records, 'He took out-of-the way means to acquaint himself with the experience of pain . . .' Later he found that everyday duty provided a perfectly adequate hair-shirt, if you allowed yourself no respite from it at all. He came from a comfortably-off country family, but as a medical student in London between 1895 and 1898, he made himself live on eight shillings a week, eating potatoes and watercress. Early each morning, before the other residents at the Caius Mission were awake, he worked at a home-made commentary on every chapter and every verse of the New Testament. (Where Jesus says, in St John's Gospel, that the spirit must be born and live, like the flesh, Wilson interpreted the saying to mean that soul grows at the expense of the body.) Then, shabby but scrupulously neat and clean, he walked across London to St George's Hospital; worked there until about 5 o'clock; walked back to Battersea, ate, taught, and doctored slum children for two hours; perhaps chaired a meeting or a debate. He would read in bed until late in the small hours, leaving perhaps four or five hours at most for sleep before the cycle began again. At the height of the discipline he imposed on himself, he noted in his diary every moment he thought he had wasted in 'idle chatter' or 'pottering', terms which covered everything that was not deliberate attention to God, or medicine, or useful knowledge. 'I never feel', he wrote to his mother, 'that I have suffered for any of my sins half enough, so that I should feel in no way surprised or disappointed by any bodily ailment that happened to me, such as losing a hand or getting Consumption . . .'

Sure enough, he did develop TB. Three weeks of dogged hospital work while ignoring a high fever, on top of a year or two of his usual habits, let the bacillus romp through his system. He was forced to spend a year and a half ill or convalescent, in Switzerland and Norway. After that, though he still believed that bodily strength was given to be used up rather than hoarded, he moderated his experiments. He was no longer solitary. Always, in theory, he had recognised that the needs of other people had an equally absolute claim on his conscience. What separated self-denial from self-absorption was that, as God required, you put yourself at the service of whoever needed you. And now both his marriage to Oriana Souper (happily ascetic on both sides), and the interknit communal life of Scott's expeditions (where each depended on all, and Wilson could salve conflicts) shifted the focus of his spiritual ambitions, brought other kinds of striving forward. The peacemaking touch, the sweet temper, and the limitless patience his polar friends admired were also deliberate creations. They were the equivalent in his human dealings of the potato and watercress diet, and he had had to struggle sternly to stick to them. He would indicate disapproval by withdrawing – a damning chill would settle on his face at 'indecent' humour – but he had conquered a naturally caustic tongue. As a child he'd been known in his family for fits of rage when he would lay about him verbally, and Wilson the Cambridge student had sometimes talked daggers; these had gone, though at close quarters aboard *Discovery*, he wrote to Oriana, 'God knows it is about as much as I can stand at times, and there is absolutely no escape.' Expeditions required restraint. They could not work socially without it. Wilson's remorseless interpretation of the divine command to love thy neighbour made him, in this sense, a consummately gifted explorer. And he faithfully discharged the corresponding obligation he now saw, to look after himself so far as it lay in his power. He treated his body on expedition as an item of equipment his companions would need, and would need to find in good repair. The cold, absolutely dry air of the South indeed healed his lungs, so Antarctica was positively good for his health. Still, there can seem something frightening about his composure in his last, intensely moving letters, written while he lay dying on the Barrier in 1912. It is as if, once he has satisfied himself that he has done all he can to survive, for the sake of Oriana and his companions, once he has legitimately failed to live despite his best efforts, the old reckless disregard is waiting serenely to catch him. He had fulfilled the conditions for a good death he had set down back in 1900. All that was wrong with suicide, he had written then, was the terrible presumption involved in taking a decision that ought to be God's. 'It is no sin to long to die, the sin is in our failure to submit our wills to God to keep us here as long as He wishes.' Now he could say, 'We have struggled to the end and we have nothing to regret.' 'All is well.' He is sorry 'to be the cause of sorrow' to Oriana, sorry at leaving her and 'all the things I had hoped to do with you', but he is not exactly sorry to die. Hearing the clear tones of welcome in Wilson's voice, and knowing from the record of his earlier history that they were not entirely generated by the starved and hopeless state of the polar party, some recent writers have wanted to name Wilson's condition equally plainly, without pious applause. The good doctor gives them the creeps, understandably: they diagnose a death wish. (Roland Huntford scouts out evidence of morbidity everywhere. He even finds it 'morbid' that Wilson took along 'In Memoriam' for his nightly reading on the *Discovery* sledge journey, making Tennyson's great poem of faith and doubt sound like a primer of gratuitous gloom. You wonder what bright, perky book Huntford thinks *would* have been appropriate.)

But this seems too simple a resolution of the case, too unequivocally black a reading by far of a life spent being delighted *at* life. Dying, Wilson quitted a world whose beasts and birds and flora he had studied with the Romantic sense that the life of each gleamed with something beyond itself. More than anyone else on Scott's enterprises, he was the direct inheritor of the Keatsian and Tennysonian passion for the earth as a 'round of green', edged by gold light, and endlessly, sensuously variegated. The rifle, the scalpel, and the formaldehyde a working biologist used to come closer to the transcendent beauties of creation did not bother him. He had the taxidermist's unsentimental way with an animal specimen: he and his skinners were known on the *Discovery* as 'the blood and guts brigade'. But to draw nature right, and to understand its living processes, was to praise it, to be involved in the great network of it, just as it had been a mode of praise for the poets to find the exact word for the movement of leaves in a breeze. The 'large leaves of the sycamore', like dry flat hands, *fluctuate*, Tennyson decided in 'In Memoriam'. Wilson wanted it to be possible to tell from his drawings what the characteristic movement of a creature would be, sinuous or jaunty, grave or nervous; and he was proudest when he thought he had conveyed in an animal's pictured stance the particular motion it alone possessed in the swimming, flying, scuttling, intricately interjoined order of creation. He did not recoil from the parts of nature which were not pretty. He felt no distaste at the interesting worms that live in a seal's rectum, nor at the squirted bright-pink excretions of baby penguins. He seems only to have excepted himself from appreciation.

I think this sharp distinction between self and world is the clue to him. In him the Edwardian taste for pushing things to their limit turned exclusively inwards. He would never willingly contemplate harming someone else, and the parade-ground fantasies of the period seemed dangerous and wicked to him. But you might say he drilled his own soul. Rather than assuming that the order of the world was unbreakable, and therefore safe for adventure, he had the martyr's sense of the world's fragility, and the likelihood of hurting other people if he did not apply the greatest delicacy and caution. Only himself did he see as the imperialists saw Africa, or the reformers saw the social system, or the warmongers saw Germany. Only when he looked at himself was his imagination presented with a recalcitrant lump against which strong measures were called for. If he succeeded in breaking *that*, he had the assurance of a greater safety for a reward. Once, shortly before Scott first accepted him for the *Discovery*, Wilson managed to draw his idea of St Francis, 'with an expression that somehow satisfies me'. It is a very bad picture. Human subjects did not usually attract Wilson's attention, and his lack of artistic training showed far more when he attempted them. The saint is gazing out with rapt, impersonal tenderness from a skull barely covered by skin. Brows and cheekbones join into a complete ring round each hollow eye. Wilson's biography cites the picture's minute pencil-strokes, too fine to be distinguished except with a magnifying glass, as evidence of

Wilson's 'extraordinarily keen eyesight'. But it also looks like the work of somebody who believes that goodness – the saint's, his own – must be the result of a terrifying, heedless concentration.

Since their lives did end so soon before the world they took for granted did, it is always tempting to wonder what would have become of the five men dead in the snow if, instead, they had survived, reached base at Cape Evans, and had to cross over like Shackleton into the juddering, unsafe times that followed. It is surprisingly hard, though, to summon a satisfactory mental picture of Wilson in the Jazz Age, or Oates as a superannuated major at Dunkirk. There are the histories of the real survivors to draw on: Frank Debenham pursuing his sensible scientific career, and becoming director of the Scott Polar Research Institute in Cambridge; Cherry-Garrard sad and isolated; Teddy Evans bouncing through the decades undaunted, ending up as an improbable Labour peer in 1945. But they in turn are surprisingly little help, and not just because, in the case of the extinguished Polar Party, there would have been the incalculable private effects of their failure to take into account. There was a natural gradualness to the real polar afterlives. The survivors altered with the altering present day, even when they loathed it. The effect of tracing their continuous adjustment to new prospects is quite different from the effect of suddenly projecting the dead men, in imagination, forward across time. It's like the difference between observing a child's growth, and scanning two photographs of the same child ten years apart, apparently metamorphosed between clicks of the shutter. To imagine the Polar Party out of the time that formed them involves a blatant transposition of their age onto another. It makes them unlike themselves as you know them. David Thomson's book *Scott's Men*, for example, offered a brilliant, speculative glimpse of an older Scott, a public man out of his depth in a new world: 'not a leading politician perhaps, but a token hero who might have been used by other men. One can see Scott on the angry political platforms of the 1930s, speaking tensely and passionately, unaware of uglier forces beneath whatever hope for regeneration he might be urging.' Yes, this seems possible. The far Right of the '30s courted heroes, liked the anti-flesh rigour of the ice; the public-school Left of the '30s lapped up the image of explorers as capable titans. Nostalgia for the mutual loyalty and common feeling of Edwardian exploits could indeed lead men of Scott's background into bewildered support for groups who promised that those things lived again in totalitarian dreams of perfect unity. And it is true that the Edwardian relish for ruthlessness, and capacity for unreasoning belief, did plant some of the seeds that eventually germinated into the totalitarianisms. Many later horrors were Edwardian fantasies acted out literally, after the Great War had demonstrated that anything, anything at all, was possible. But Thomson's thought-trick reminds you by the impossible speed of the transformation, how distinct the Edwardian heroic mood was from its successors. The seeds of the future were only seeds then, the fantasies only fantasies. Nor was the thinking or the feeling of Edwardians in any sense organised to become the thinking or feeling of the postwar century. Over and over, if you follow back a notion, rancid or respectable, to its Edwardian genesis, you find it closely constellated with other ideas which later developments have moved to far distant areas of the cultural firmament. Edwardian culture was a mass of strange bedfellows, weird elective affinities. The cause of free school milk was entwined with the cause of empire. Psychic research fascinated poets and prime ministers. Housing reform interested militarists. Arguments over women's rights interlaced with arguments about eugenics. (One suffrage poster showed a tall, queenly young woman in academic dress beside a sly flat-craniumed male straight out of a textbook on the criminal physique. Why should she be deprived of the vote? the poster asked. Why, when this squat specimen had it whose tubes should evidently be tied forthwith in the interests of public health?) The classifications we're accustomed to using for ideas don't work on the Edwardian cultural scene. So much that was characteristic about it lay in just these links between ideas, in attempted reconciliations and wished-for pairings. In retrospect they look frail and temporary – unstable marriages between sense and nonsense, often – but at the time they meant that the culture had a peculiar self-sufficiency. It does not work, for this reason, to interpret the era as our recognition of some things in it, our unfamiliarity with others, most invites us to do.

The presence of two expeditions side by side in empty Antarctica in 1911 yet apparently at opposite poles of modernity and antiquity from the technical point of view makes the invitation almost irresistible. When the *Terra Nova*, happening on the *Fram* in the Bay of Whales, actually moors next to her, and those aboard Scott's chosen ship wonder at the *Fram*'s petrol tanks, and the individual cabins aboard her for every man from captain to cook, it neatly resolves the sense of times colliding to reflect that while Scott seems to inhabit a 1911 only forty years on from the 1870s, Amundsen's 1911 seems only forty years in advance of the 1950s. But that was not a possible thought then, and it does no justice to the curious truth that Scott – friend of Barrie, husband of a New Woman, eager reader of new literature and new science – was on his own terms an advanced thinker. We cannot simply refer one set of elements in the period to the Victorians, others to the emergent twentieth century, and see it as a struggle between the fading old and the burgeoning new. Stove-pipe hats did not fight it out with trilbies till the trilbies won. More than most times, this was a time separately absorbed in itself, estranged from its future.

And also from its past. If it is surprising to find what a supposedly modern movement like feminism began by meaning, and being open to, it is equally odd, often, to see in what peculiar forms pieces of Victorian doctrine and sensibility ended up among the Edwardians. They transmuted much of what they inherited. Because no cataclysm divided them from their predecessors, as a major war did from their successors, this was not always visible to them. On the contrary: they frequently thought they were expressing their trust in ancient continuities. Once again the Edwardian readiness to believe made the difference – and the particular quality of their belief, literal and categorical, inclined to hyperbole. When applied to the past it produced exaggerated visions. Those who rejected their inheritance built up the sexual, financial, religious, and philosophical habits of the preceding century into a bogey called 'Victorianism', which crouched on your chest and choked your emotions; Samuel Butler's oracular anti-Victorian novel *The Way of All Flesh* (1903) had the Pontifex family withered and blighted by their joyless submission to the monster. But the conservatism of the groups in Edwardian England like the Church, and the larger part of Scott's Navy, who looked back with approval, was not much less polemical, or selective. These institutions appeared precedent-ridden, pinioned in sticky webs of tradition: and that is how Scott's naval background is now described by authors making contrasts with the innovative, mercantile Norwegian attitude to the sea. Many traditions that gave the effect of antiquity, though, were brand spanking new. Edward VII's coronation service in Westminster Abbey, for example, with its hieratic gestures and complex passes through the air around the monarch, was devised by Anglican ritualists freer than any of their predecessors had been to use the delightful apparatus of bells and ornamented robes and holy oil. Ceremonies had been a prime cause of argument throughout the ambiguous history of the Church of England; now the liturgists managed to suggest instead a serene unbroken chain of succession in Church and State between Edward the Confessor and 1901, and they noted complacently that they had done a much better job at being ancient than those who contrived the last coronation in 1837. Victoria's had been a slapdash affair – tawdry in comparison. Other traditions did have a previous history, short or long, but had been inflated from precedent until they became something new and musclebound; a cartoon of past practice, taken horribly seriously. Sometimes the tacit transformation of the past happened because the Edwardians took straight and earnest what had been figurative and even flippant. Anthropologists might have recognised this turn of events. The 'stiffening of metaphor' was, Tylor had written in 1871, one of the 'intricate and devious operations' that promoted the formation of myths. He had been thinking of primitive cultures (the study of modern and urban mythologies lay in the academic future), but the way its public memory worked made civilised Edwardian England itself remarkably prone to 'the mythic fallacy'. A large number of Edwardians preferred the past to be a repository of certainties, a body of heroic story like a body of mythical lore, discreetly in the modern manly taste. The origin of that certainty in the appropriation of past metaphor vanished. Another ceremony was a case in point. Disraeli, expert at lush language, liked to whip up the fact of Britain's Eastern empire into a froth of romantic images for

Queen Victoria's pleasure. And after the Indian Mutiny was suppressed, and she became Empress of India, he arranged with the Viceroy Lord Lytton for her to have a sumptuous accession day in India. At the 'durbar' elephants processed and troops marched past in many colours; a parade of Indian rulers from all over the subcontinent swore oaths of fealty to her. The occasion of course expressed a real subordination, of the Indian princes to British rule; but its function as a picturesque metaphor was acknowledged. It could be recognised, and *was* recognised by a critical press, as a de luxe oriental fantasy typical of both Lytton and Disraeli. Then the metaphor stiffened. The durbars held for Edward VII in 1903, and George V in 1911, were grand and zealous and wholly solemn. Lord Curzon, the imperial ideologue who was Viceroy in 1903, treated the ceremony as a sanctified instrument of British power, a literal enactment of a relationship, in effect turning a dish of imperial zabaglione into a load-bearing pillar of governance.

Where some of the qualities relevant to polar exploration were concerned, the emphasis of a thought had sometimes been unconsciously shifted, or a belief hollowed out and refilled with a different feeling. The idealists of Scott's expeditions would have agreed with Franklin's fans, with Dickens, that such a thing as a moral triumph over the snows was possible. Indeed that the conquest of the physical world represented by a journey into the cold was intrinsic to the spirit and purpose of exploration. They used many of the same words. They gave the dangerous prominence to immaterial factors, as against speedy movement and successful planning. That *was* the British tradition at the poles, after all. At the last, faith was more important than competence for the naval officers of the 1840s and 1850s. At the end of *The Worst Journey in the World*, the questions arising from the débâcle of 1910–13 that Apsley Cherry-Garrard believed 'ought to be studied' all revolved, similarly, around 'nerve' and will and imagination, resources still preferred in the cold over well-nourished bodies. 'Why do some things terrify you at some times and not at others?' But the polar enthusiasts of the mid-nineteenth century believed in a moral dimension to exploration independent of its physical outcome. They did not dispute that cold froze you or that lack of food starved you. Dickens, saluting the lost sailors of the Franklin expedition, did not bother to argue with the technical critics, the 'utilitarians', over the material cause-and-effect of the sailors' deaths. He was talking about bodies dying and souls living – though the soul had become something defined more by fancy and desire than religion. He only insisted that the Franklin expedition told a second, spiritual story which took priority over the material one; it recounted to those with ears to hear a victory in the explorers' hearts and minds, which registered where it mattered most, in the hearts and minds of their compatriots, or even in an ideal Arctic truer than the gross Arctic shown on maps. It was moral force, naturally, that kept an explorer like Franklin going while the faintest hope still flickered. Yet the defining characteristic of exploration's spiritual achievement, as understood in 1850, lay in the 'beautiful resignation' Vilhjalmur Stefansson spat fire at. When legs and arms could do no more, the dying discoverer rose above the physical problem of survival, sealing his final victory over the whole inert waste of snow and ice by letting go. The Edwardians did not much relish resignation. Nor were they happy (as we have seen) with a science – a vision of the material world and its forces – so deterministic and mechanically minded that to applaud human intentions you had to rise above the material domain altogether. By the time that Scott first sailed south the background of thinking out of which thought on the special case of exploration emerged had changed subtly. Edwardian scientists looked at the flaws in Newtonian physics. They looked at the natural world, and thought that it did not much resemble the geometric test-bed postulated by Newton's laws. They looked at human behaviour and refused to believe that it could be calculated from any statement of external forces and stimuli, however complete. Quantum mechanics was about to resolve one set of these dissatisfactions by substituting a new paradigm in physics. Others of their complaints against geometry anticipate the perceptions (of, for example, leaf forms and weather systems) that have led very recently indeed to chaos and complexity theory; but that was not the direction in which Edwardian scientists were looking. Instead, some decided that where living creatures were concerned a special force must be active, and they channelled their dissatisfaction into theorising about it. This force, Life with a capital L, took on properties that had formerly been the province of the soul. It was the 'highest' attribute of a person, it was noble, it deserved reverence. Like the soul, it had no physical characteristics of its own, no smell or colour or weight. But unlike the soul it was an integral part of the human organism, and it could exert material influence. Eminent men had begun to suggest that being alive might alter the working of physical laws. 'Life', wrote Sir Oliver Lodge, 'introduces something incalculable and purposeful amid the laws of physics.' The psychologist James Ward argued that life actually created energy. The result was that it no longer seemed certain that there was a physical limit on what bodies could be made to do, if 'Life' urged them on. People might, for example, evolve voluntarily, passing on acquired skills to their offspring by sheer vitality. Or they might march further through polar snow than the calories contained in a ship's biscuit strictly allowed. The implications had diffused into literature, contributing an apparently scientific rationale to the period's manly bounce. 'If the world does not please you,' wrote H. G. Wells in *The History of Mr Polly*, published the year the *Terra Nova* departed,

you can change it. Determine to alter it at any price, and you can change it altogether . . . There are no circumstances in the world that determined action cannot alter, unless, perhaps, they are the walls of a prison cell, and even those will dissolve and change, I am told, into the infirmary compartment, at any rate, for the man who can fast with resolution.

When British explorers believed in the primacy of spiritual resources, they now tended to have in mind qualities tinged with a magical power to obtain results. Scott and Bowers both liked to say that difficulties were made to be overcome; remarks indicating more than individual temperament, because they encoded the wider refusal to believe in the insurmountable. Cherry-Garrard's list of questions sounds medical as well as spiritual, because he thought of the immaterial 'nerves' as a kind of second source from which the body could draw strength, an alternative to pemmican. 'What is the ratio between nervous and physical energy?' he asked. 'The man with the nerves goes farthest,' he stated. Wilson came closest to perceiving the matter in the old way.

For the rest, those who spent the long winter night at Cape Evans in 1911 at the officers-and-scientists table, in 'an atmosphere of pleasant and quite interesting conversations' about recent discoveries, about horses and biology and theatre and Japan and The Woman Question, 'which sometimes degenerated into heated and noisy argument' while the blizzards clamoured outdoors and the gas light hissed, had at their backs – like a butler poisoning the wine – an age gently decanting, into the old spiritual bottles, a belief in the unlimited powers of effort which was still more dangerous.

But the chief fact behind the peculiarities of British polar exploration as the Edwardians practised it was that there had been none for twenty-five years. The inglorious results of the Nares expedition (itself a carbon-copy revival of earlier naval ventures) discouraged the Admiralty from trying the experiment again, and from Nares' return in 1876 until the *Discovery* voyage of 1901, no British expedition on the grand scale had been mounted, either to Arctic or Antarctic. British ships of course continued to visit the northern and southern waters that had already been charted, but those places now fell within the orbit of the familiar, and the prospect of these businesslike whaling or trading voyages could not arouse the original complex of expectations associated with discovery, whatever their practical hazards. Increasingly, there were also streamlined private and semi-private expeditions in small ships, whose success in their deliberately modest aims should have delivered an essential message about appropriate techniques: but the informal life aboard them did not stir onlookers as the display of sub-zero social niceties had. For twenty-five years, the tradition of the large hierarchical expedition magniloquently devoted to Science could be found only in memory, national and individual, where it accreted all those other significances tied to nostalgia in the minds of the nostalgic. The paper existence of exploration had always been as formative as the actual experience of it. Throughout the gap between Nares and Scott it existed in Britain only on paper. It passed into the possession of memory; it passed into the possession of boys' stories. There writers used it to induce icy thrills and excite heroic urges, slipping a young protagonist or two into the well-known situations of a polar voyage.

G. A. Henty, author of the prototypical series which featured a boy *Under Wellington's Command* or *With Cochrane the Dauntless* – each book a boy's-eye-view of a splendid crux in national history – did not take up the polar locale; but his emulators did. *Peter the Whaler* kept reprinting. Jules Verne contributed two thrillers, *The English at the North Pole* and its sequel *The Field of Ice*, which paid 'Anglo-Saxons' his usual bizarre compliment of portraying them as monsters of reason, scarcely flesh and blood at all. Captain Hatteras in *The English at the North Pole* walks and talks as if his legs were springs, belly a furnace, brain clockwork, eyes cameras, and stiff upper lip a steel plate adjoining the cigar-smoking machine of his English mouth. 'Have no fear. For each degree north you make from this day you shall receive £1000 sterling. We have only reached the 72nd yet, and there are 90. My name will guarantee my good faith. I am Captain Hatteras!' More typically, *le fameux flegme anglais* appeared in its home-grown version, in the form of light-heartedness and plucky battles against over-whelming (environmental) odds. A sentimental song about home might be sung. There was certain to be a good polar death at some point, performed by a character neither too major nor too minor. The patriotic 1890s saw the adventure genre higher than ever in critical and educational esteem. Even after the departure of the *Discovery* there was time for Dr Gordon Stables to publish *In the Great White Land: A Tale of the Antarctic Ocean* (1903), gaining in topicality from Scott, yet still just able, before Scott's return reintroduced first-hand knowledge, to work a vein of pure fancy, where Walt and Charlie and Captain Mayne-Brace (*sic*) of the good ship *Walrus* sat down together in high latitudes to a plum-duff 'studded with real raisins, like the stars of an Arctic night in number. Those raisins were well within hail of each other, and not simply dotted and dibbled in here and there as with the point of a marling-spike.'

Exploration's sojourn among perfect suet puddings and perfect British behaviour left it, when it returned to the realm of the real, with a water-marking of unreality; and it was guided jealously back into existence by a man determined that it should produce exactly these boyish pleasures.

Sir Clements Markham – President of the Royal Geographical

Society, President of the Hakluyt Society, glutton for facts, transplan-
ter of the quinine-producing cinchona tree from Peru to India, queen
bee of polar committees, expert in so many adjacent disciplines that a
moiety of the tributaries feeding the passion for the poles flowed
through him – had been nine, laid up with mumps at boarding school,
when a reading of 'Parry's Polar Voyages' won him over lifelong. His
later enthusiasm never quite lost its connection to the original impress
made on a boy's mind. He liked boys. He liked them in several senses,
as a matter of fact. He had been a pretty fourteen-year-old himself,
slight and delicate with fine hair and coloured cheeks, looking rather
like the young Thomas de Quincey, or one of the appealing waifs
shown holding up a biscuit or a cup of hot chocolate in an
advertisement; and he was always quirkily responsive to male looks.
But if he acted on the homosexuality he kept buried beneath a
respectable marriage and an array of academic honours, he did so far
away from home. Certainly far away from the midshipmen of good
family, the bright-eyed merchant marine cadets, whom he began to
make his companions in his middle age. In them he valued the
stereotypical qualities boys were supposed to have, the unbounded
high spirits, the insatiable appetite for cake, the ardour for adventure,
the singlemindedness an adult might envy before sexuality clouded
the picture. His attraction came in, if it came in, as an additional
savour of boyish company, unacknowledged as much else was
unacknowledged in his clenched life. He joined the board of governors
of the merchant-service training ships *Worcester* and *Conway*. 'His
house', wrote his cousin and biographer Admiral Albert Markham,
'became the resort of the Worcester boys.' Somehow, amidst his
dovetailing commitments, he made endless time for treats and outings.

There was nothing Markham would not do that could conduce in any way to
their pleasure, their happiness, or their instruction. He would spend whole
afternoons . . . taking them to the Tower of London, the Zoological Gardens,
Westminster Abbey, the Aquarium, or any Exhibitions that might be open;
then home to tea or dinner, winding up the day with a theatre.

Later his cousin's command of the Navy's Training Squadron,
equivalent to the *Worcester*, led to an open invitation and for some

years Clements spent months in succession cruising the West Indies, the Baltic, and the Mediterranean on the Squadron's sail-rigged flagship *Active*, scarcely touching shore. He carried on his ceaseless studies aboard: his cousin remembers him during an Atlantic gale that rolled the ship through 42°, 'engaged in drawing up a careful pedigree of the Kings of Aragon!' It was through the Training Squadron that he first, famously, encountered Robert Falcon Scott, then a midshipman aboard another of the four training ships, the *Rover*. At nineteen Scott was a little long in the tooth, but still personable. Several writers have remarked how like a boy's adventure the scene of the talent-spotting is, as Markham constructs it in his unreliable history *Lands of Silence*. Scott takes part in a race between ships' cutters. The signal gun booms. The seamen in each make sail, urged on by a young officer. The boats are away! They round the first buoy – the second – out flash the oars – the competing boats pull for dear life back towards the finishing mark. Who's ahead? Who has won? It's Scott, Scott of the *Rover*! Whose destiny beckons as he steps up to receive his prize under the approving eye of the distinguished geographer. Like a boy's story Markham's account suggests that merit always gets its uncomplicated reward. Like a storybook too, it promises that success at something you really can do, something within the bounds of boyhood such as sailing a small boat, fits you magically for a starry role in the great enterprises of adulthood. Winning a race may catapult you directly to Captain Mayne-Brace's table; even *make* you Captain Mayne-Brace. But at the time Markham had an inconvenient preference for another youth, edited out afterwards. And he was surrounded by boys, 'an especial favourite' of the gunroom, 'a sort of oracle on all matters'. It pleased him to sit in the corner of the forecabin, revising proofs or perhaps preparing a special lecture for the boys, while they had their lessons. When no other adults were present, he thought of himself as an honorary boy, included in games, spurring the company on. He grew frolicsome:

Then, chaos reigned supreme, and would continue until summarily put a stop to by the Commodore, or other high official. Although it would not be fair to assume that their guest was the instigator of these somewhat irregular disturbances, yet it was generally conceded that there was never any cause to complain of their unseemly conduct when they were entirely by themselves!

On another occasion he drove across the island of Barbados with a carriage-load of midshipmen who were throwing fireworks and trying to lasso the coachman's hat. This delight in mild riot deserves comment. It implied, of course, no secret vein of delinquency in the very ordered mind of the savant. Instead it shared in the turn-of-the-century certainty that the escapades of the young were perfectly congruent with tradition, order, and discipline. The unvarying routine of the naval day would always restore calm among the boys, and their innocent rowdiness be absorbed back into the good of the service. Markham would undoubtedly have seen himself as one of the supple-minded adults, the guides and accomplices of the young, who (like the appreciative housemaster in *Stalky & Co.*) could see the rough goodness in boys, and thus act as go-between in their dealings with authority. His underlying assurance about the young fills the apparently puzzling passage in his *Personal Narrative* of the *Discovery* expedition where he explains why his absolutely tradition-bound project nevertheless requires a stripling for a leader:

The fatal mistake, in selecting Commanders for former polar expeditions, has been to seek for experience instead of youth. Both cannot be united, and youth is absolutely essential. Elderly men are not accessible to new ideas, and have not the energy and capacity to meet emergencies. How can novel forms of effort be expected from stiff old organisms hampered by experience! Where a youthful intellect has only to grasp the new idea, the old intellect has first to comprehend the new thought, and secondly to conquer the tendency in his mind to formulate the idea in question in his old accustomed way. His powers, far from being stronger than those of young men, are considerably weaker. The inexperience and haste in decision of young leaders are disadvantages which sometimes accompany their youthful energy, but they alone have the qualities which ensure success. Old men should supply information and the results of experience, and should stay at home, making way for the younger and therefore more efficient leaders. New ideas, new situations meet with cordial welcome when young men are at the helm.

Taken literally – though the emphasis on total inexperience is odd – this would be a manifesto for flexibility and improvisation. Neither is a quality readily associated with Clements Markham, who believed (his cousin's loyal gloss) that the man-hauling system of the 1850s 'has been handed down for all time as the pattern to be followed in Polar exploration'. The evidence shows that he had no patience in practice with the unmanageable virtues that he was applauding here in theory. Since debunking scrutiny began, then, the passage has usually been read as part 'sentimental', part Machiavellian; which it is. From the practical point of view there existed an overwhelming advantage to selecting a leader quite without polar training. Someone not set in their own ways could much more easily be set in Markham's. As mentor to a youthful leader whose mind was as blank on questions of technique as the Antarctic map was empty of features, Markham could act as the monopoly supplier of 'information'. He made himself the chokepoint, the bottleneck, through which British polar lore passed on its way to Scott. His position ensured that the smallest decorative details of the *Discovery*'s equipage could be as he wished. He was glad to report that 'at my suggestion the officers of the Antarctic Expedition continued the tradition' of flying swallow-tailed heraldic banners from their sledges. 'Tradition', that authoritative word, guise for so many contemporary inventions, in fact stood for a complete exercise in fancy by Markham alone. The 'tradition' had begun in 1875 – again, 'at my suggestion'. *La tradition, c'est moi.* He designed the flags himself. They were three feet, two and a half inches long.

But Markham's endorsement of new thoughts, new ideas, new situations, new forms of effort, primarily took its cue from his particular cult of boyish freedom, with its built-in guarantees. Crucial because it served as Markham's rationale for choosing the polar virgin Scott, the passage in the *Personal Narrative* was above all a connoisseur's judgement. The stiff old organism with the power to decide complacently bends his knee to youth, in order to look up and admire, perfectly sure of what he will see. Markham only expects all these potentially disconcerting novelties – all these spasms of initiative – to be manifested as they are manifested in a midshipmen's rumpus. Really the young are keen as mustard to do what they're told. Youth is enclosed, directed, justified by age's appreciation. In this Markham was tellingly aligned with the whole Edwardian strand of eagerness for boys to be properly uppish, his cooing over the naval young a straitened special case of a wider phenomenon. Right through the period adoring attention to breakneck exploits by subalterns co-existed with perfect faith in the wisdom of generals.*

Can Sir Clements Markham be claimed as an Edwardian? A time is never unified; the different generations who share it travel side by side without their perceptions necessarily merging, like the different bands of grit that a glacier carries separately downwards. Besides the broad band of the generation whose time this is for activity and maturity, there are always children, for whom the most important events of the day form only the ingredients for a remembered childhood atmo-sphere, and the old, continuing in great part the lives they had up to whatever point it was at which they ceased to feel the times were theirs, and instead pursued their familiar certainties in private. Those people we call Edwardians were generally those born between about 1865 and 1890, who reached the decade before the Great War ready to take its dimensions as the natural shape of the world. Scott, the oldest man aboard the *Terra Nova*, was born in 1868; Wilson in 1872; the most junior members of the wardroom, lodged in a cabin inevitably christened 'the Nursery', at dates running through to the late 1880s. Clements Markham on the other hand was a silvery supercilious seventy-year-old in 1900: he had been born in the reign of William IV,

---

*The Great War killed this pattern of feeling, though afterwards there were forlorn attempts made by eminent Edwardians to accommodate even the Western Front in it. You can see its threadbare remains, disturbed by grief and genuine humility, in 'Courage', an address given to the students of St Andrew's by J. M. Barrie in May 1922. He read aloud Scott's final letter to him, 'which I think will hearten you'. Scott's courage meets his listeners' case, as they face adulthood, because like a body preserved in a glacier, or the honoured dead of the war, 'Scott and his comrades emerge out of the white immensities always young'. The old have failed the young, he says boldly, led them down a 'brimstone path'. The young are right to be angry. Many of his audience have returned from the trenches. But he urges them to believe that the 'aim' of their anger 'is the opposite of antagonism, it is partnership'; he tells them, with a frantic desire to reconcile, how wild and happy he was in London at twenty, 'not knowing a soul, with no means of subsistence'; he tells them how their ardour is needed, appreciated, loved by their elders. And he gracefully compliments General Haig, who sits in the audience, the doom of youth personified.

the son of one of the royal chaplains at Windsor. He cried when told that King William had died, because the name of the monarch would have to change in the household prayers, and already he hated change. (Also because the King had sent little Clements bonbons via his father.) At his golden wedding anniversary in 1906, according to his biographer, he contemplated 'with a sorrowful regret the happy time he spent when there were "no bikes, no bridge-parties, no beards, or golf and motors"'. This fogey's roll-call seems to place him quite securely among the ancients travelling on in distant parallel to the concerns of the age. But you were also an Edwardian, no matter how old you were, if the tastes of the time allowed things in you to flourish that you had never been able to act on before: if something in the time answered some need in you, however belatedly. Clements Markham may have abhorred the dress, manners, recreations, and modes of transport of the early twentieth century but he needed its florid appetite for bravery, its bravura self-deceptions.

To a degree extraordinary in someone involved in the management of expeditions, who had actually served in the Arctic himself during the Franklin search, he was a *fan* of polar exploration. Even as he produced it – made it happen – he consumed it, like a star-struck impresario who knows exactly what is happening backstage but falls for the magic of the performance every time. He preferred exploration's public face, the smooth perfection it could only have when reflected second-hand in newspapers or official accounts. It was in the paper re-creations of the poles that he found the tones and incidents he wanted to dwell on. He had carried his own boyhood enthusiasm back from the real Arctic significantly intact. His voyage with Sir Erasmus Ommaney in 1850–1, just before he resigned his midshipman's commission, not only lived up to expectations. As he chose to remember it, it reproduced exactly the bland good-fellowship he had read about. 'There never were more united messmates,' he wrote; 'hot arguments in abundance, anecdotes and good stories innumerable, and never told twice, but never an unpleasant or ill-natured word, never a sentence to cause regret or annoyance.' And this was not a statement intended for publication, but his private judgement on the direct experience of two years' cramped life at close quarters, written for his own eyes and hoarded up for his own pleasure. It proved to be an invariable judgement. He would always insist that any ship, any polar venture he had to do with, was perfectly happy, superbly equipped, supremely well prepared; the kind of thing a patriotic journalist might say in hazy retrospect formed Markham's first-hand impressions. 'A nobler set of fellows never sailed together', he wrote after travelling out to Greenland as a guest on the first leg of Nares' voyage. On the *Discovery* in 1901, 'The warrant officers are one and all good men, and the men as fine a crowd as one would wish to see.' Assessing Scott's 'most striking characteristic' in a *Times* obituary after the *Terra Nova* expedition had come to grief, he returned to the same mental picture of explorers completely united, completely harmonious: Scott, he said, 'won the love of all who served under him'.

Markham's recorded statements about the purposes of polar exploration are startling enough. At the top of his list of achievements by the Nares expedition stood '1. The creation of a young generation of experienced Arctic officers.' The 'main object' of the *Discovery* expedition, he wrote, 'would be the encouragement of maritime enterprise, and to afford opportunities for young naval officers to acquire valuable experiences and to perform deeds of derring doe'. Exploration existed so that young men could be excitingly brave. But in a peculiar way you can almost learn more about Markham's frank appetite for vicarious adventure from his handling of the argument-from-geography; the justification by science, which his cousin stoutly insisted in the biography 'was, of course, the primary consideration', and which Markham held 'derring doe' 'would lead to'. Map-making, the most purely factual aspect of geography, wore the crown. He could see benefits in the study of polar magnetism, oceanography, meteorology, biology, and geology: 'but these', he noted slyly in his *Personal Narrative*, 'are springes to catch woodcocks'. To his mind they mattered mostly because he could use them to win support from oceanographers, biologists, and so on. 'The real objects' were otherwise. The plotting of coasts and triangulation of mountains, on the other hand, were close to his heart. He used *them* to secure the altogether vital distinction between himself and a mere gawper. 'He was always most emphatic in his views', wrote Albert Markham, .

regarding what he was accustomed to stigmatise as 'sentimental and popular exploration,' such as a rush to the North Pole or the search for a North-West Passage; for such 'discoveries', he maintained, would be of no substantial or commercial value or utility. What he desired, and so strenuously advocated, was the correct mapping of every portion of the world, known or unknown, in the interests of geography generally.

The geographical justification for exploration as Markham deployed it kept something out, an unflattering image of the sentimental exploration buff, whose tears over polar tragedies could not be allowed to resemble Markham's own responsiveness. It also kept something in: locked his sentiment into the concrete details of exploration, which would forever evoke his deep feeling on the subject while leaving him defended, and feeling terribly practical. He treasured details, of every kind and on every subject, from the exact positions of the furniture in his childhood home to the 'cicatrix' (scar) on the left big toe of one of Nares' crewmen. He took notes obsessively. 'Nothing was omitted, nothing was too trivial.' Even his loyal biographer could not help remarking that 'in many cases the trivialities were entered at greater length and were more conspicuous, than those of a more important and perhaps more scientific character'. In the kind of human information which could not be set down in the form of tables, lists, and charts he was not interested: that was, precisely, what his collection of facts substituted for, or in effect embodied. Facts stimulated his emotions without him having to look at the emotions' source. Markham, it is clear, had a truly thorough case of the hobbyist's syndrome. Like beer bottle-cap collectors who buy the house next door for their exhibits, he located his passion in a mesh of *stuff*. Thomas de Quincey had observed in 1833 in his autobiography how many 'of our deepest thoughts and feelings pass to us through perplexed combinations of concrete objects . . . in compound experiences incapable of being disentangled'. You could turn that truth the other way around, make the process voluntary and habitual. Clements Markham did not wish the perplexed combination of facts conveying 'derring doe' to him to be disentangled at all. He had taken infinite pains to entangle them in the first place.

We have his handwritten dossier on the *Discovery* expedition, one in the long series of meticulous files he had kept on every project he considered belonged to him. (After his death his cousin discovered detailed notes among his papers on all one hundred or so of the foretopmen he had been put in charge of aboard HMS *Collingwood* in March 1847.) The dossier forms the centre-piece of his *Personal Narrative*, deposited at the Scott Polar Research Institute and only published in 1986. Some of the information it contains was necessary for an expedition organiser to have, like the contact addresses for each man's designated next-of-kin. But much was baroque detail for its own sake; and all of it, useful or not, is laid out like treasure trove. Markham's dossier is a little book devised for private reading, a labour of love or of some other emotion. Character assessments of the expedition personnel are studiously avoided, except in the most generalised and predictable terms, although every so often Markham will make an idiosyncratic comment on appearance. Of T. V. Hodgson, biologist, aged thirty-six: 'He is young to have a bald head sometimes needing a skull cap, but otherwise apparently strong and healthy.' More often he confines himself to listing places of birth, birthdays, parentage, pet names, special expedition responsibilities, the name of the comic song an individual sang at the pre-departure entertainment, and the number of teeth they had dealt with at the mass dental examination at Guys' Hospital in July 1901, when '178 were stopped, and 92 pulled out. Bill £62.4.5'. There are views of the *Discovery*'s deck and stowage arrangements pasted in. Officers' photographs are accompanied by hand-painted coats-of-arms, or the 'devices' Markham has kindly invented for those gentlemen unlucky enough to lack a shield. Portraits of the three really notable persons involved are mounted on pages of their own, within a ruled frame of two or four ink lines, headed by coloured blazons: Scott; Markham; the secretary Cyril Longhurst, a languid-looking Oxbridge youth who was possibly Markham's lover, and whom he paid £1000 for his year's work – more than 1% of the entire budget, more than Scott himself received. On one page Markham sets out the pedigree of Charlie Royds, the first lieutenant, taking the family tree back to ancestors in 1675 on one side, and to the Domesday Book on the other. The genealogical tables on another page don't go back so far; it takes only four or five generations to prove that the officers Scott, Royds, Barne, and Mulock are all related to Sir Clements Markham. He must have devoted days to his toy, with pen and ruler and gluepot and paintbox. It could be the work of a neat-fingered boy of eleven. For decoration, he has stuck the *Discovery*'s special stamp to the bottom of his hand-lettered title page. The stamp shows a penguin on an iceberg against a rising sun, and it is carefully labelled 'The Postage Stamp Of The Antarctic Expedition'.

Within the small precinct of his *Discovery* album, a parade of stout hearts and elaborate memorabilia pushed every other aspect of the poles out of sight. But this could not be his whole experience of exploration. He *was*, after all, the organiser, contriver and guiding spirit of a large expensive national undertaking; and its unscrupulous guardian when, part-way through the preparations, a group of Royal Society delegates on the planning committee tried to turn it into an intolerably scientific affair, staffed for research rather than adventure. Nor did his preference for the blandly heroic in polar matters stem from insensibility. It was not that he was a thick-skinned man. He was, on the contrary, temperamental and easily offended; a touchy pedant who alternately secreted a sentimental syrup (when everything was to his liking) and a torrent of bile (when it was not). He vented the latter on his committee opponents, using his longstanding expertise at bureaucratic infighting to revenge himself for the shock they gave him. It was probably bad enough having his pet project, nurtured in private, passed round for comment. Seeing it opened to revision was unspeakable, and his description of the proceedings is full of spite. At the worst moment for him, Professor Poulton – 'a dull stupid man, with a genius for blundering' – committed the sin of reading aloud a poisonous private letter of the kind Markham was in the habit of sending to those who displeased him. The outraged author stalked out of the room, pursued by shouts in (as he put it) 'a rude tone of voice'. He left behind him a temporary majority of votes for a plan by which Scott would act as mere naval ferryman to a scientific team leader. However, 'the conspiracy was exposed and thwarted' by the simple means of getting the committee reconstituted, and Markham saw his original scheme safe once more, in what he called, like the climax of a pantomime, a 'Grand Transformation Scene', where the good emerged triumphant and the wicked were utterly routed. Thinking it over gleefully, Markham assigned roles to his enemies. Poulton was 'Clown'; Professor Buchanan, 'another wearisome bore', was 'Bird of Prey'; the hydrographer Tizard, just 'Villain'. *'But no more performances on this stage'*, crowed Markham. The name-calling was typical, as was the foundation of the nicknames in Buchanan's large nose, Tizard's 'forbidding countenance'. Markham had always found other people's faces intrinsically funny, especially if they had any 'peculiarities' or 'blemishes'. Despite his sunny tributes to the good-fellowship he had found in the Navy, on no single voyage he made as a midshipman did he fail to get the wardroom newspaper suppressed by inserting hurtful jokes in it, about the weak chins and goggling eyes of his shipmates.

The discord between Markham's cherished image of exploration and his practical behaviour in support of it is striking. The gap between the version of events he recorded in *Lands of Silence* and elsewhere, and the less attractive manoeuvrings in which he was actually involved, has led to a current, and in a sense incontrovertible, judgement of him as a liar. He certainly processed the truth. Even so trivial a thing as the sequence of his early meetings with Scott has been improved in his account. Scott, pointed out Roland Huntford in *Scott and Amundsen*, remembered the chance encounter in the Buckingham Palace Road in June 1899 as the moment when the good impression left by the boat race twelve years earlier was first renewed. Markham on the other hand chose to recall Scott's follow-up visit to his house as the first meeting, and therefore 'a remarkable coincidence. Scott was then Torpedo Lieutenant of the *Majestic*. I was just sitting down to write to my old friend Captain Egerton of the *Majestic* about him, when he was announced' – out of the blue, seemingly, wafted across the world by the breath of destiny. He must have known it was not so; and yet here, as where greater matters were concerned, he was surely aiming to take himself in as well as future readers; turning the events in which he had participated into the type of events he treasured. What we see, when Markham massages the record, gilds the humdrum circumstances under which he made the expedition happen until they shine as satisfactorily and as distantly as the Elizabethan exploits he edited for Hakluyt volumes, is the passage of fact from one to the other of two mental categories he managed to keep separate. Some acts of counterfeiting are too compulsive to count as lies, though they may be conscious and deliberate. With part of himself reserved for business and part for dreaming, Clements Markham had had to develop a double mind, and he found it perfectly possible to believe (on different levels of awareness) in incompatible things. 'I daresay you haven't had much practice', says the White Queen when Alice tells her 'one *ca'n't* believe' the impossible. Markham had practised the art from very early on. It had already been characteristic of him for seventy years. He coped with unhappiness, especially, by translating painful circumstances into ideal ones, then holding to the perfect image. One wonders how large a part the need to conceal his sexuality played in this process. But it also recalls the psychological release built into the sublime, where fear becomes admiration. If something is hurting you, you identify yourself with the large and powerful force doing the hurting, rather than your frail self. Markham, in the *Personal Narrative*, warmly recommended the no-nonsense Navy treatment for one or two of the *Discovery*'s junior staff. He thought that the geologist H. T. Ferrar, aged twenty-two, was

A capable young man but very young, very unfledged, and rather lazy. He has a good deal in him, but it will require some bringing out. I like to imagine him after a year's training in a gun room, and through some process of this sort he must be made into a man in this ship. He gets a good deal chaffed and sat on by the young lieutenants, which is already bearing fruit.

We know, in fact, that the young Markham had particularly hated being jovially suppressed and cut down to size by his superiors. Mostly he had contrived to be a favourite, thus avoiding being 'sat on' altogether; but he had not responded with anything resembling gratitude in the single instance where he had faced the rough side of the naval tongue. Instead, brittle creature, he had mounted a spectacular sulk: announcing that he would despise the offending officer for ever, walloping the Gunnery Lieutenant over the shoulder with a wooden sword, and – horror above horrors – refusing the

Captain's sacred invitation to breakfast. After much blandishment, he was brought only to the grudging admission, in his cousin's words, that 'in punishing him as he did, [the Captain of the *Collingwood*] only intended to carry out what he conceived to be his duty'. His determination to leave the Navy began with this incident: and every lavish compliment he paid to hierarchic discipline afterwards, every little love-letter to Navy bounce, strategically metamorphosed a memory of humiliation. He had not even much liked ragging and rumpusing when he was a real boy, and not an honorary one. When the *Collingwood* crossed the Equator in 1844, preparations started for the ritual rough-house, with a dunk in a water-filled sail for those who'd never crossed the Line before. Markham and his friends bribed the seaman playing Neptune to be let off.

'I decided that he should be one of the Antarctic heroes.' Markham wrote that astonishing sentence about Charlie Royds, and the whole division of his sensibility is present in it. Royds was a twenty-three-year-old lieutenant 'in the destroyer flotilla at the Nore' when he volunteered. He was naturally without polar experience of any kind. If Markham made him a hero, it would be an entirely arbitrary act of patronage on Markham's part, an entirely artificial nomination to a heroic status that Markham clearly considered was conferred from the moment he made the decision in Royds' favour. Of course, once Royds reached the southern continent, heroic behaviour would be up to him, for Markham's ability to influence and stipulate ended with the *Discovery*'s departure. He could only start the game with pieces of his choosing, and hope it played out right: but the implication is that Royds needed only to conform to a template of heroic activity in the Antarctic to justify the role he'd already been assigned. 'Please, dear Lord,' Tom Wolfe says that the astronauts of the Mercury programme were thinking as they waited for lift-off, 'don't let me fuck up.' Royds, from Markham's point of view, was being sent on a mission constructed with an equally negative criterion of success. All he had to do to stay a hero was not fail, not fuck up. His actual experiences and intentions took a definite second place behind the task of not disturbing a heroic image. Once again the processed and derived meaning of exploration – its paper identity – took precedence. And, 'I decided'. Markham took a pleasure he did not bother dissembling in his power of decision. (The sentence was written in his *Personal Narrative*, a raw text he never expected to see published as it stood. When he had cooked his account of the same events nicely for *Lands of Silence*, no such boast appeared.) He could make a hero just as he wished; make a hero as entirely apt for his reflective pleasure as square-jawed, wide-mouthed, high-bred Royds, with his intricate family tree. He was treating Royds as a living toy. Yet none of this acknowledged artifice interfered in the slightest with Markham's ability, at the same time, to feel the most genuine and worshipful admiration for Royds, which had ignited *in vacuo* at the exact moment he made his decision. When he wrote that Royds had become a hero to him, he meant it. Into the space designated by Markham's collection of trivial information about Royds, a space kept carefully vacant of obstacles by Markham's fundamental incuriosity, rushed the quickening sensations he had variously associated with mercurial Elizabethan buccaneers, with Parry, all the heroes he had cherished in the safety of his reading. Markham could build an idol, quite cynically, then worship it, quite sincerely. Perhaps in the world off the page he could only really adore heroes he made himself. When he encountered the contemporary equivalent of the unpredictable Elizabethan style, he recoiled. He was allergic, in particular, to any hint of vulgar showmanship; which was unfortunate, since the character of success-ful expedition leaders usually included a healthy dash of it. Surprisingly often, indeed, the non-polar activities of such men verged on the fraudulent, the same inventiveness that made them equal to the snow leading them, at home, into fly-by-night business schemes and dodgy deals. Markham, by contrast, looked for an impossible combination of bravado with docility. In this he rather resembled the true-believing elders of Cuba and the Soviet Union much later in the century, who continued hoping that their pacified, regimented, secret-policed young might yet somehow become the New Men and New Women of socialist theory. As it happened Royds did fine in the South, displaying a common touch and a gift for tactful management of men which had no connection with Markham's endorsement of him; though he did not grow into a specially notable figure in public eyes, a fact put down by Roland Huntford to Scott's jealous regard for the public's, and Markham's, attention. With Scott himself Markham succeeded beyond his dreams, a testament to the resonance between the wider hero-worship of the era and the unlikely mind of Clements Markham.

So Scott presented himself for service, susceptible (as his sister said) to 'the romance of ice and snow', ignorant till he educated himself of the technical aspects of exploration, but sensitive to the impalpable relationship between ice and England; so Markham's brain-child the *Discovery* sailed, 485 tons of purpose-built ship, freighted with a nostalgia which had got out of hand, a reverie trying to be real. Absorbed in the erection of idols, Markham had effectively restricted the equipment the *Discovery* might use in the Antarctic to those he remembered in boyhood. He did not determine how Edwardian exploration would proceed on the Great Ice Barrier; he did not cause Scott's eventual death. But his influence, his choice of personnel, made it that much more likely that the tentative experiments made with dogs in 1901–4 would fail, and that Scott would conclude – learning, he was sure, from experience – that man-hauling ennobled men, while dog-driving was cruel to dogs. Markham valued immensely a small, silver model of a man-hauled sledge, presented to him by the *Discovery* officers. He liked to gaze at it. It is traditional that the person behind a disaster should die in bed at a ripe old age; and Markham did just that. But he did so in a violent and stubbornly symbolic way, the bedclothes aflame, the shock too much for a man of eighty-five; because, in January 1916, he insisted on reading by candlelight, like a midshipman in a bunk. Over the charred sheets hung the electric bulb he had preferred not to switch on.

But before that come the expeditions of the *Discovery*, *Nimrod*, and – above all – of the *Terra Nova*; when, as Scott wrote, 'for one brief moment the eternal solitude [of the Antarctic] is broken by a hive of human insects; for one brief moment they settle, eat, sleep, trample, and gaze, then they must be gone, and all must be surrendered again to the desolation of the ages'.

TEN

I Have Always Taken My Place, Haven't I?

29 November 1910

Seagulls scream; the crowds on the shore scarcely do less. The *Terra Nova* is underway from its positively last civilised port of call – for though Lyttleton was the official point of departure for the Antarctic, it has been necessary to make an additional hop down the New Zealand coast, to add yet more coal to the stores cramming the hold, and bulging on the deck under lashings. So it is Port Chalmers that sees the end of the series of departures, the true cessation of speeches and bunting. Herbert Ponting, the expedition photographer, cranks his cinematograph on deck: his lens records the jouncy progress of two decorated tugboats keeping pace with the ship along the sheltered water of Otago Bay, and the waving and the shouting of the sightseers on them. Boaters and parasols, early afternoon sunlight, hankies bobbing in fists. A wag aboard billows about an expedition tablecloth, in exaggerated salute back, large to little. Quiet on the bridge in long dresses, the three senior expedition wives watch as the headland approaches where the open sea begins. There they must leave the ship; the moment is at last in sight that the exhausting round of farewells has sometimes made seem to float ahead of them, always imminent but never quite reached, like a door at the end of a long corridor in a dream. Till now each grand dinner has only given way to the travel arrangements for reaching the next one. They have been saying goodbye for months. Indeed Kathleen Scott has known this moment would come since she agreed to marry Scott two years before – it was written into that agreement, an acknowledged factor in her decision – and Oriana Wilson has understood for even longer that when Scott organised another expedition, her husband would be part of it. But now the moment comes quickly. Now Taiaroa Head is abreast of the flotilla: now, suddenly, the moment has arrived, is passing, is undemonstratively over, and Mrs Scott, Mrs Wilson, and Mrs Evans are handed over the rail onto one of the attendant tugs. The tugs peel away, and *Terra Nova* sails on, shrinking to nothing on the horizon. 'Ory was with us on board to the last,' Wilson will write in his diary that night, '. . . and there on the bridge I saw her disappear out of sight waving happily, a goodbye that will be with me till the day I see her again in this world or the next – I think it will be in this world and some time in 1912.'

On the tug, as it turns for the shore where the holiday mood is still going on, the appearance of happy support is not being maintained without effort. 'Mrs Wilson was plucky and good', writes Kathleen Scott assessingly in *her* journal. Hilda Evans on the other hand, much younger than the other two, 'looked ghastly white and said she wanted to have hysterics'. Landed, and disentangled from well-wishers, neither woman falls in with Mrs Scott's proposal when she tries 'to muster them for tea'. Immune to radiations of jollity, 'Mrs Wilson sat sphinx-like on the wharf.'

In fact the three do not get on at all. Mrs Evans' unconcealed dread makes things harder for both her companions; she finds them respectively bleak and intimidating. Mrs Wilson tries to avoid active dislike, but wishes that her hard work of renunciation were being disturbed by neither Mrs Evans' schoolgirl tears nor Mrs Scott's worldly vigour. Mrs Scott finds Mrs Wilson's armour-plated goodness only marginally more congenial than Mrs Evans' emotional demands, which form part of a running contest for social pre-eminence. With her wit, and her status as consort to the expedition's leader rather than to his mere lieutenant, Mrs Scott wins every encounter: but Mrs Evans is an irritant. That same morning has seen the latest in a succession of disputes that reflect the tensions between the husbands, as well as the women's very different incarnations of the role of polar wife. Scott has just reinstated his lower-deck protégé Petty Officer Evans, after Lieutenant Evans has sacked him from the expedition for public drunkenness. 'All went well, till on the wharf we met the Evanses, both in a tearful condition. Apparently she had been working him up to insurrection and a volley of childish complaints was let fly.

Such as that Con [Scott] had cut his wife's dance, and many others too puerile to recount, and that therefore he must retire. Their tantrums spoilt the day and prevented us from being happy. If ever Con has another expedition,' she concluded, 'the wives must be chosen more carefully than the men – better still, have none.'

An earlier one of these spats has been described gleefully by Captain Oates in a letter to his mother. 'Mrs Scott and Mrs Evans have had a magnificent battle, they tell me it was a draw after 15 rounds. Mrs Wilson flung herself into the fight after the 10th round and there was more blood and hair flying about the hotel than you would see in a Chicago [*sic*] slaughter house in a month.' Oates claims he is a misogynist. 'Who doesn't like women?/I, said Captain Oates/I prefer goats', they sing in the *Terra Nova* mess. He is certainly ill at ease in female company. A little while ago he has been forced into formal clothing for a photo on deck with Mrs Scott: she was caught hand on hip, in pleated artistic dress and birdbath hat, saying something forthright – while he stood mute on his mark, arms tight behind back, his gaze a curiously boyish ironic protest out of a face that will still seem handsome eighty years later, in a heavy-browed Al Pacino mould. The formal suit seems to be the substance of Oates' problem with women, as well as its symbol. He chiefly associates them with social constraint; they represent, for him, every obligation to be polite, to make small talk, to translate enjoyable bodily activity (riding, hunting, sailing) into acceptable words. When he was eleven, his sister Lilian hit him over the head with a cricket bat so hard he spent two days in bed with concussion, but outside the family he has found that females refuse to go in for this sort of commendable directness, and the world of women is a domain of protocol. 'The visitors and women are a great nuisance as we can't get really dirty.' Scott has often toured his wife, and the other wives, around the *Terra Nova*, offering them assurance in the spectacle of the ship. It is the same spectacle, the same assurance about the men who will be absent, that Parry mounted for Isabella. Work has stopped while the women inspect hatches and companion-ways where preternaturally polite sailors answer questions and open doors. So far as Oates is concerned, the impression of exploration that the women receive is a simple sham. Oates perhaps has heard Kathleen Scott announce that she, too, dislikes women and their works. If he has, though, he has undoubtedly set it down as another inexplicable female affectation. He does not know that she has rather enjoyed him as a male type (noting him, for example, slouching through 'a most brilliant and overdressed crowd' at Sydney racetrack in 'marvellous trousers, and an indescribable hat, quite unconscious'). Nor would he care, if he knew, about the idiosyncrasies of her own attitude to the worlds of men, of women, and of snow.

Scott sees his wife as the antithesis of protocol: a nature-girl, a person constructed in opposition to the ranked and predictable life of the Navy. When she had met Scott in 1907, she was indeed a free agent. She first saw his 'rather ugly' face, and his 'eyes of a quite unusually dark blue, almost purple', at 'a luncheon party of lions' given by Aubrey Beardsley's sister Mabel in London: in other words, on the cultured ground that a naval officer could win access to if he had done something extraordinary, and socially exciting. She was a sculptor and it was her territory, not his. 'He's not of our world at all,' she told one of her legion of bohemian admirers. She lived in a cheap flat in Cheyne Walk on her own. Moreover, unlike Eleanor Porden, whose acquaintance with an exploring husband began at the same point of social intersection, her independence was not vested in one place, one house, one hard-won sphere of autonomy. It did not depend on a piece of female space within which she was not answerable. Her parents dead early in her childhood, she had slipped with some ease from the supervision of her ten older brothers and sisters, and 'vagabonded' away to Paris on her tiny inherited income. There she had studied under Rodin; befriended Isadora Duncan; and formed romantic friendships with numerous ardent and devoted men who were however, as she intended, held safely at bay by her talismanic (or as she would put it in her memoirs, her 'masterful') virginity. Men who expected she would become their mistress or their wife, discovered that they had gained instead a comrade for dawn dips in the Seine, or chaste nights sharing a blanket under the stars. She did not mean to tease her admirers: it is doubtful that she was interested in imagining what the state of suspended devotion she required felt like from their side. For her part she enjoyed the display of male manners, male ambitions, and male confidences.

She thinks herself ideally situated if she finds herself the sole woman amongst a throng of interesting menfolk. And if she shows a sometimes astonishing lack of tact towards individual men, she feels enormous loyalty to men in general, men as a class. She is, she makes it clear, on their side (though not at it). In Paris she nodded with sympathy at Schopenhauer's 'contempt for, and rage against, women'. While Scott is away she will take her New Womanhood into the gender wars as an *opponent* of women's suffrage, on one memorable day spending the morning arranging her contribution to an exhibition of women's art ('although I hate being among women'), and the evening at an anti-suffrage rally in the Albert Hall. She will never really explain why she should want to second men's rage and contempt. Perhaps there was a hint of a sort in the two names she proposed for her coming child when she was pregnant last year. The child would be Peter, if a boy, after Barrie's icon of perpetual youth; or very strangely, if it should be a girl, Griselda, many women's least favourite name because of its association with 'Patient Griselda' of the tale, who let herself be abused without complaint. It was as if, perhaps, she could envisage only two possibilities, an exultant crowing masculinity versus a mute and passive female destiny. If those were the options, who would choose womanhood? Who would go down among the despised women for company and stimulus? In the event, of course, she gave birth to a Peter, and satisfied a long-held desire to produce, herself, a splendid man for the world. She had been consciously foraging the male genepool in pursuit of 'my son's father' for years. 'Corn-coloured hair and a crooked smile, maybe, but not the father for my son.' Of a willing law student: 'He's nothing much except tall and strong and very vital and moving, with the minimum of inhibitions.' It was in this biological light that she first considered Scott, and the polar achievements which might signal he possessed the eugenic right stuff: the hero as potential sperm-donor.

But she had equally often wished she could have a son without a husband. Since the unrespectable solution attracted her not at all, she had had to reckon up, like Eleanor Porden, the chances that she would be able to preserve the freedoms she found essential, once she threw over, in a marriage, the protections that had kept her autonomous till then; or 'self-sufficient', as she preferred to put it. In her case the chief protection had been a mobile thing, a persona of bold innocence, which she had always been aware might not work successfully in the more dangerous stretches of the male world, for it was a kind of bluff. The courtship of the sculptor and the explorer turned out predictably bumpy, on–off, on–off, but she did not need to dispatch any ultimatums during it, in part because Scott was a man of far larger imaginative sympathy than Franklin. So far as he could he entered into her difficulties with the marriage, promising her (for example) an escape-hatch any time she cared to back out. And he took her work seriously, as an exciting manifestation of the new world of London art and literature he had been admitted into. At the same time, qualities in him less immediately attractive than violet eyes reassured her. On the obvious credit side of the ledger, he was sensitive, quick to follow a thought, eager for intellectual companionship, willing to trust her sense of honour if she spent the time he was at sea vagabonding some more with his rivals ('Perfect man!'). But he was also moody, diffident, sometimes withdrawn to the point of apparent catatonia, and endlessly anxious about money. These tendencies in him, all in their way retreats back into the shell he had developed when a naval bachelor, ensured that she found him unfrightening. They allayed a fear that had always quietly shadowed her adventures. Alongside the 'lovely lads' and the proffered hearts, she remembers being suddenly, physically sick the first time she saw a naked man in a life class; she remembers how it felt that her Paris flat could be gazed into by an alarming Russian neighbour who hanged himself; she remembers that she relied on the 'veil' of foreign languages she 'only half-understood' to 'dim' the 'crudities' of some suitors, and 'transform a grossness from a blow into a caress'. Once she testified at the trial of an anarchist dynamiter she'd inadvertently befriended, and heard the court chuckle when the defence counsel argued it was no proof of guilt that the man had been caught with a bomb on him; after all, smiled the lawyer, 'Quoique moi-même j'ai tout ce qu'il faut sur moi pour violer une femme, ça ne dit pas que je l'ai fait!' [While I have everything I need on me to rape a woman, it doesn't mean I have!] What made these moments fearful was the reminder they contained that it lay in the power of men to ignore the rules of her innocence, and relegate her to the ranks of the victims, the done-unto, the Griseldas. Any woman would have felt threatened in the French courtroom, and she had been made to feel like any woman. However sharply she separated herself in her mind from the common run of femininity, she could be pushed back there.

She does not often express female solidarity. One of the few times she has was in an exchange of letters with Scott over a fashionable 'sex problem' play they had both seen. Scott thought 'this subject' was crowding off the stage all the more interesting things men were doing in the world: 'it's the women I believe who keep it in so foremost a place'. 'Of course it's the women who keep up the interest in the sex problem,' she snapped, '– it's their *life*, whether they will or no. They can't get rid of it, however intellectual or well-educated they are.' She hates male brutishness, which she thinks of as masculinity running out of control. She has channelled her fear into a particular horror of drunkards. For her a man loosened by alcohol concentrates all male dangers. Scott is quite unlike this, with his contrary fear that service life has given him a 'hard crust'; consequently he is free of the touch of nightmare. It was not that she had wanted a weak husband, whom she could control. She depends on self-control in men. It guarantees her pleasure in them. She needed a husband who lived within the restraining codes of masculinity.

They were married on 2 September 1908 in the chapel at Hampton Court, Kathleen whispering her admiration of the best man's looks to Scott. 'Can I marry *him*?' 'I shall be sending you some hideous presents in a day or two,' promised Max Beerbohm. From the beginning Scott was away a good deal, captaining HMS *Bulwark* of the Channel Fleet, which ensured Kathleen a straightforward measure of physical independence. They wrote letters; he dashed home at weekends and snatched sudden opportunities for leave, while she calculated likely times she might become pregnant; otherwise she worked in her studio as before, dined and lunched out on her own account as before. She could deal breezily with his occasional assumption that he had a say in her art. But still her solitude had a different feeling about it now. The tie to Scott inevitably impinged; the sense that his character now slightly overlapped with hers, like two circles in a Venn diagram, accompanied her, sometimes happily and sometimes not, even through her old rituals and routines of self-determination. Being married was a continuous state. 'I never thought I should become just exactly like all the other women', she wrote at one low point, 'and be dependent on one man's moods and comments, especially when they are so utterly illogical.' A few days afterwards: 'There is something terribly real about you. I never used to know anything about loneliness. Have you robbed me of my self-sufficiency?' She knows now, in New Zealand, that Scott's much more definitive absence on the *Terra Nova* will not restore her original sense of herself either, though her situation alone in London with Peter during the expedition will come ironically close to her first ideal of happiness. 'I used to say I wanted a baby but not a husband,' she will reflect in ten months' time, when gripped by another surge of despondency, 'and I've got it, but with a difference. One hasn't got one's husband in the body, but one has got him so firmly in the spirit that it spoils everything.'

Whether their marriage is genuinely rocky, or whether these are only the emotional urgencies of the early phase when two personalities hammer out an accommodation, Scott and Kathleen will never have the time to learn. Scott *has* learned that he made a mistake about her in one respect. At the beginning, he had supposed that he ought to become more like her; that this was, in fact, his chance to break his crust and gain some of the vagrant freedom he never tired of saluting in her. 'I see the beautiful things you strive for, I see your glowing independence of thought. I know you are impatient of the great mass which lives by rule, and ever eager to appeal to nature and individual right, – but oh dear me, how will it all sort with the disciplined, precedent-seeking education of a naval officer?' He practised bohemian attitudes: 'By nature I think I must be a freelance. I love the open air, the trees, the fields, the seas, the open spaces of life and thought.' But she distinguished sharply between the welcome awakening of emotion in him, and any suggestion that he might himself be a round peg in the square hole of the Navy. She was not looking for a convert. She found his attempts at resemblance implausible, and even, when they seemed to be feeding on his melancholic side, a little frightening. She told him so. 'I wonder how we shall do?' he wrote, on the eve of a battle exercise in the Channel that would be professionally important to him. 'I don't mind much. I do mind about you. What does it all mean?' 'How dare you say you don't mind?' she replied fiercely. 'You *do* mind. You must and shall mind.' By protecting Scott's career when he seems apathetic, she is protecting the tricky equality their marriage maintains between two different centres of hope and ambition. Neither of them can be allowed to collapse onto the other, or it would be the end of mutual independence. But it is also vitally important to her that Scott live up to his destiny. She is sure he has one, and like all the great actions of the gender she idolises, it lies in a sphere of masculine endeavour at once heroic and properly coded. Scott's imagination must remain contained within his naval persona; what she has come to perceive of his private self must remain congruent with the splendour and the purposefulness proper to men. Those are the terms of her admiration, and the terms of her participation when she meets braided admirals at parties, talks poetry with politicians, or admires (free herself, dressed by Liberty's) the glorious ceremonies men stage. At parties and luncheons in London, in fact, she promotes Scott's advancement to an Admiralty job as skilfully as Lady Jane Franklin might have done, only her style is bold rather than insinuating, remarkable rather than exemplary. It will always make her indignant when men let their best selves lapse, even for a moment. She cannot understand how they can let themselves down so: how a man can drink in public, knowing he risks discredit; why Asquith, a close friend later when he is coalition Prime Minister during the war, should send her a 'flippant' note. 'It angered me; it seemed to justify the criticism often made of him.' Her work embodies this vision of men. When it doesn't portray babies, her sculpture, for the rest of her life, will represent male dignitaries or allegorical figures looking as they should, the characters appropriate to their callings vivified by her admiring observation. Her bust of Asquith will look pensive and responsible; a statue of Lord Delamere will gaze amused yet noble at the Kenya he governed. After the war, commissions for memorials will come helter-skelter, including one from her son Peter's school, where to his considerable embarrassment she will erect, not a tragically brooding Tommy, but a pubescent bronze boy, nude, ardently aspiring over the legend 'Here am I, send me.' And there will be the hewn, monumental figures and busts of Scott for churches, for the Polar Research Institute in Cambridge, for the spot his death reserves for him in Waterloo Place by St James' Park, in the tract of the capital where the official images of the whole imperial world converge.

By the time that the preparations for the *Terra Nova* were completed, she active in the cause throughout, Scott's perception of her had shifted ground. Now he sees her as his inspiration, the custodian of his courage. He must explore well for her sake. 'You needn't worry about my attitude under adversity,' he writes, as if he too has her 'in the spirit', personifying all that he believes he has to prove. In the flesh, as one of the *Terra Nova*'s officers, he will have her brother Wilfred Bruce observing him all the way to Antarctica, which must heighten his sense that all his acts refer back to her. She does not mind the election to muse and taskmistress; but she did not choose it, and again Scott has perhaps slightly misread her. The Woman One Must Strive For is a cartoon out of the male mind, and only approximates Kathleen. It is true that she plays up to it. It is true that she has something of the presenter of white feathers about her, blithely demanding bravery in circumstances her gender prevents her from experiencing. But her vicarious involvement in his polar life is more generous than that, and her emotions more detached from the public failure or success of the expedition than Scott imagines. Their marriage would not be ruined (as he sometimes fears) if he returned having failed to reach the pole, or (now his fears have coalesced into a Norwegian) having failed to beat Amundsen. The self-invented code she lives by has an eccentric stoicism as a main tenet. Nothing will be allowed to hurt enough to take the joy out of her life. When Scott moped once about the future, she had replied, in italics, '*I shall be happy whatever things happen and that is true!*' She would contrive to be happy if he came home defeated; she would manage somehow to make it not matter; though whether he would be able to endure that particular demonstration of her self-sufficiency is another question.

At any rate he has gone. The *Terra Nova* is over the curve of the earth, with those aboard cracking 'some awfully flat jokes' as departure sinks in, and the long summer day is fading to twilight in Port Chalmers. Kathleen Scott, the fanfare she glories in dying away, but with it the onus on her to inhabit the rather dull role of model wife ('discretion'), begins packing her bags for Australia, and discharging some final tasks. A duty letter to Scott's mother: 'I had a very busy time the last few days marking their clothes. I sewed on 31 dozen tapes!' On another momentous day two years hence, she will be given the message of Scott's death as she returns by liner to New Zealand to greet him. A tropical sky, a transmission in Morse to the radio room, the Captain's hands shaking as he breaks the news: and immediately, in her diary, she will cast her feelings, and their marriage, into a matrix that has been available for such moments since Parry and Isabella started praying together. 'I am afraid my Con has gone altogether, except in the great stirring influence he must have left on everyone who had knowledge of him. I think he has made me twice the man I was. Certainly I couldn't have faced this with complete self-control but for his teaching. Ever since I knew him I have worked striven and strained that he might applaud ever so little . . .' Grief will demand a past that had an unequivocal point, and an end in view; grief will reconstruct their marriage, on the instant. But now at the end of a day in 1910 it is only the same negotiation of two solitudes that it has been since they began. The independence of the one who stays needs restoring against the independence of the one who has gone, and she responds to his absence by doing what she always does when she needs to know that she is still there. She embarks for Sydney. She spots among her travelling companions 'a young South African, intelligent and adventurous, who could be trusted, without a doubt, to fall in with whatever plan I suggested'. She carries him chastely away into the Blue Mountains, with a blanket.

Her farewell to Scott had been unemphatic. 'I decided not to say goodbye to my man, because I didn't want anyone to see him look sad.'

2 December 1910

'Then dawn came and with it everything began to go wrong again at once.' Wilson wakes in one of the few bunks still dry on the ship, and finds that the *Terra Nova* is no longer floating because it rides on top of the sea, but because its wooden hull and deck planks enclose a roller-coasting bubble of air, outside which water hammers on all sides for entry. Yesterday's 'fairly manageable' westerly gale has grown into the familiar monster of the South Fifties, a hurricane mangling sea and sky together, which the *Terra Nova*, overloaded, heavy in the water, is in no state to resist. They guess that the waves coming at them from the west are thirty-five feet high, but they can only guess as the ship pitches up a crest, wallows down into the dangerous troughs between, the engine labouring to keep the prow pointed safely. If the angles of floor and bulkheads shift less violently than they did, that is a sign of dwindling buoyancy. Solid green heaves of water cover the waist of the *Terra Nova* almost continuously, tearing at the mounds of coal and pyramided petrol cans there, which have begun to flex and slide about in an unpredictable rushing mass, like a random battering ram. Birdie Bowers has spent much of the night diving for petrol, trusting to his grip on a rope when the ship rolls and he slides sideways underwater towards the rails; the dogs tethered on deck wash about around him, snatching breaths. Even on the bridge Scott is often waist-deep in the sea. All this weight of water on deck wrenches the planking. It pulls open the seams between, in rhythm with the arriving waves. All through the night, Wilson has heard 'the thud of a sea on the decks overhead and a water cart full of water pour down upon the wardroom floor'. With the water, trickling downward into the hold to reduce their besieged bubble of air, come little greasy balls of coaldust from the ruined sacks. Around dawn these clog the pumps down below; and in rapid consequence, the water in the stokehold where the steam-boilers are fuelled, already sloshing knee-deep from wall to wall, rises suddenly to threaten the furnaces. The fires have to be put out. The engine stops. They are now in a logical impasse. They cannot get at the clogged mechanism of the main pump to clear it without opening a deck hatch: the pump is only reachable from above. They cannot open any hatch on deck without inviting the whole

Southern Ocean in. 'It would have meant less than ten minutes to float,' Bowers will explain in a letter to his mother. They try a small hand-pump, but the pressure is too low, and it will not raise the water from the hold up to the deck. Lieutenant Evans takes the Chief Engineer and the carpenter below and starts cutting through the steel wall isolating the blocked intakes, a twelve-hour job at least. Meanwhile at 7 a.m. all the ship's officers who are not working the ship at that moment, and all the scientific staff and gentlemen volunteers not absolutely incapacitated by seasickness, are called to the narrow well that rises the whole height of the ship, from engine-room to the lee doorway up top. Puking (some of them) every few minutes, they cluster on the iron ladders clamped in the well, the bottom-most men naked in the steaming bilgewater hissing off the engines, those higher up progressively more and more dressed. 'A couple of engine-room oil-lamps whose light just made the darkness visible' (Wilson) swing as the well – an inky tube – itself sways back and forth across the vertical, like the arm of a metronome. They are passing buckets of water up the well; and as they bale, as they vomit, they sing. 'I went to bale with a strenuous prayer in my heart', Bowers writes, 'and "Yip-I-Addy" on my lips . . .'

'Yip-I-Addy' is a patter song in waltz time. It began as a Broadway hit of 1908, but London music halls took it up quickly. Really you need a female voice and a cello for the full comic effect. The twenty-odd inaccurate tenors, basses, and baritones on the ladder do the deep tones and the girlish tones as best they can:

> Young Herman Von Bellow, a musical fellow,
> Played on a big cello each night;
> Sweet melodies rare, in a dance garden where
> Dancers danced round and round with delight.
> One night he saw dancing a maid so entrancing,
> His heart caught on fire inside,
> And music so mellow he sawed on his cello,
> She waltzed up to him and she cried:
> Yip-I-Addy-I-Ay, I-Ay!
> Yip-I-Addy-I-Ay!

Even in these straits, a measure persists of the larkiness with which the gentry aboard the *Terra Nova* go about routine shipboard tasks. 'How the custom of the ship arose I do not know,' says Cherry-Garrard, 'but in effect most things were done by volunteer labour.' It's a small world where 'unselfishness' determines your social standing. When the call goes out, eager young men compete to act as dogsbodies, to be the donkeys for donkey-work. Geologists reef sails; naval autocrats in the making help in the galley; Cherry-Garrard himself has had a try at stoking the furnaces. (It was 'a real test of staying power', he decided.) Some, older or more sceptical, chafe at the atmosphere that results; the greater part of them like it. Many have already tasted authority in their professions. Before he signed up as Scott's stores monitor, Bowers had commanded a 255–ton Royal Indian Marine gunboat, alone for days on the grey-green River Irrawaddy with a crew of Lascars. Oates was the lackadaisically efficient adjutant of his regiment in India (as well as Master of the Mhow Foxhounds). By joining the expedition they have voluntarily demoted themselves, but the tasks they do on board are so far beneath their class's roster of possible destinies that doing them does not feel like any conceivable backward step, it feels like a holiday. They have become gloriously junior again, responsible to each other yet free of the persona of responsibility. And they are allowed to pitch in and get dirty. Jobs that are ordinary for the sailors are fun for them. Work about the ship has become a sort of social comedy, with a comedy's lightning mobility of roles. You exit as a specialist in geomagnetism, you re-enter immediately as a bilge-scrubber. Perhaps too the tasks they stumble through under the expert gaze of the crew revive the earliest thwarted ambitions of middle-class boyhood. Oh, to make things go! Oh, to have a set of tools of your own! What Papa does is mysterious, but the lordly men who drive trains and mend clocks know something worth knowing. Oates has enjoyed himself so much like this that a practical joke practically had to be played on him. At Lyttleton, while he was perched on the foremast helping the ship's carpenter, his head shaved, his shirt filthy, his mouth full of nails, 'a parson came up belonging to the Missions to Seamen. He heard I was a soldier and came up to me. He said he had been a private soldier and had raised himself to a parson and it was sad that I who had been a

Captain of a Cavalry Regiment should have come down to be a carpenter's mate. I think somebody had been pulling his leg.'

But Oates is not among the band forming the bucket-chain, and trying not to think about what will happen if baling does not hold the water level down. (They have been baling for hours now, in two-hour shifts.) Since the storm began his station has been in the fo'c'sle, where he and another notably silent man, the second surgeon Atkinson, have been struggling to keep fifteen frightened ponies on their feet, and therefore alive. Each wave rushes through the makeshift stalls: 'on occasions', Lieutenant Evans notices when he and Scott visit from time to time, 'he seemed to be actually lifting the poor little ponies to their feet as the ship lurched heavily to leeward and a great sea would wash the legs of his charges from under them'. Oates lifts and coaxes and soothes and shoves and lifts and coaxes and soothes and shoves. One horse has already drowned. Probably a mounting anger helps propel him through his invariable cycle of actions. The ponies were a set of wind-sucking old crocks in the first place, a botched buy. They ought not (no horse ought) to be exposed to this battering. Yet Oates *is* responsible for them. Scott's travel plans in the Antarctic may depend on them, or on whatever demoralised quota of horseflesh Oates can contrive to bring through this; and Scott may blame him for the deficiency. It is striking him more and more that all this altruism makes for a rather vulnerable social contract. You give your best, and then you rely on the other man being equally just and self-sacrificing. What if he isn't? 'Scott has always been very civil to me . . . but the fact of the matter is', he will fume later, 'he is not straight, it is himself first the rest nowhere and when he has got all he can out of you it is shift for yourself.' Oates is probably the only man to say 'fuck' on Scott's Last Expedition. Soon another pony dies.

> Yip-I-Addy-I-Ay, I-Ay!
> Yip-I-Addy-I-Ay!
> I don't care what becomes of me,
> When you play that sweet melody.

Nobody else quite feels Wilson's relish for the situation ('I must say I enjoyed it all from beginning to end'). Oates says, 'I can't remember having a worse time.' But everyone, without exception, is responding with understatement. They grow universally clipped, imperturbable. 'I thought things were becoming interesting,' writes Wilson. 'Captain Scott was simply splendid, he might have been at Cowes,' Bowers notes admiringly. By maintaining this yachting demeanour, Bowers adds, Scott 'behaved up to our best traditions at a time when his outlook must have been the blackness of darkness'. Bowers himself likes to pop on his dressing-gown – 'a lovely warm thing' – whenever a pause in the action allows. The words *death* and *drowning*, present in everybody's minds, are banished from speech. Instead they use the code-words *interesting* and *exciting*, which will be convenient many times over later. It is a group style, and (though they find it inside themselves, ready for an emergency) it also has an immediate group imperative behind it. While every single account of the storm they write afterwards reveals a perfect comprehension of their peril, most of them imagine at the time that there are innocents close by who must be protected from the dreadful knowledge: 'None of our landsmen who were working so hard knew how serious things were,' says Bowers, and in turn each scientist in the well labours under the same illusion where his neighbours are concerned. So they converge, unknowing, on the same manner, reinforcing it in each other, offering each other a constant mutual display of sang-froid. Ignorance of the true state of affairs is not, after all, completely impossible in theory. Suppose you are a 'landsman', a non-sailor accustomed to earth beneath your feet. You go to sea, and to begin with every lurch of the ship seems potentially dangerous. You don't say so of course. Only the bearing of your companions aboard reassures you that all is well, that ships do naturally move like that. You accustom yourself to pitching, tossing, rolling, yawing, dripping water in your bed, sudden painful creaking sounds from the timbers in the middle of the night. You know your own starts of fright furnish no guide to this wet world: the point at which real trouble begins seems, if anything, still more obscure, till experience teaches you. Just conceivably then you might ride out a hurricane unaware, if the sailors stay calm, that this time matters have genuinely slid past the incalculable danger line. But 'calm' does not exactly describe the behaviour of those in command now. It is an intensification of calm until calm becomes something else; something else perfectly intelligible. If any scientist balancing on the ladder had not made the obvious deduction from the rising water, he would have been able to read it like a book in the short answers and uniform good cheer of those around him. In fact the last person aboard to have grasped the situation is probably Oates, not because his reasoning powers are defective, but because, isolated in the fo'c'sle, he has had to wait for the evidence of his senses rather than taking the quicker cues in faces and voices. 'About 4 in the morning the fo'castle got half-full of water and on looking out I found the whole forrard part of the ship deserted and one solitary dog washing about. I began then to think that things were getting a bit serious . . .' Oates needed no group around him to turn stoical. 'He . . . appeared quite unconscious of any personal suffering,' Lieutenant Evans notices when he looks in on the struggle in the fo'c'sle, 'although his hands and feet must have been absolutely numbed by the cold and wet.' With Oates, it is only a deepening of his habitual reserve.

As will become famously clear in the British trenches of the Great War, the understated style, the phlegmatic manner, when apt to a dreadful situation can be extremely expressive. Then it will register a sense of horror that would leak away in ordinary description, and vanish completely if you try to match horror with hyperbole. 'Move to trenches Hebuterne', Private R. W. Mitchell will write in his diary in June 1916. 'Strafing and a certain dampness.' Now, it is true, the voices to be heard on the *Terra Nova* register less bleakly, they aim at lighter tones; but still they achieve irony, not euphemism, to those who share the mortal knowledge producing the light tone. (Which is everybody.) They can catch the absurdity in sinking to the bottom of the Southern Ocean only a couple of days after setting out to astonish the world with polar feats. 'It looked as though [the storm] had come', writes Wilson, 'to save us a great deal of trouble and two years' work . . .' Bowers is tickled by the contrast between today's waterlogged chaos and Tuesday's big send-off. 'God had shown us the weakness of man's hand,' he writes cheerfully, 'and it was enough for the best of us – the people who had been made such a lot of lately – the whole scene was one of pathos really.' The baling party joke glancingly about their own impotence.

Nor does their manner exclude fleeting moments at which they register the unwanted grandeur of the forces beating on them. Burke would not recognise the conditions for the sublime being met here: there's no real place of safety here from which to find satisfaction in this swirling flood: yet still the absorption of the work in the well interposes a kind of frail shelter in the mind between them and the hurricane. They are thinking constantly of what they can do, the hurricane still lies just beyond the confines of the present instant. When Wilson calls the waves 'really terrific', he does not only mean they are terrifying. When the moment the logic-trap closes is described as 'thrilling', fear is not the only component of the word, bravado and denial of danger not the sole motives for employing a term from the vocabulary of appreciation. 'Thrilling' half-expresses, half-mocks a sensation that pierces with wonder even as they bale for their lives.

Frank Debenham, a young Australian geologist, staggers back below decks, his mind full of the vista above, 'an abomination of watery desolation, giant waves . . . racing towards me whipped by a shrieking wind'. Birdie Bowers, overtaking, slaps him on the back. 'Isn't that a wonderful sight – didn't I tell you that a sailor's life is the only one worth living?'

> Yip-I-Addy-I-Ay, I-Ay!
> My heart wants to holler 'hurray!'

Bowers is terrified. Bowers is also profoundly happy, as high as a kite on the continuous exertion the emergency demands. He has not slept except in snatches for something like sixty hours, which gives all his perceptions an exhilarated clarity. He craves work and he has got it in abundance; he craves a hero to worship and he has found one in Scott; he loves good company, and all around him a constellation of nicknamed friends, Uncle Bill and Titus and Deb and Cherry and Sunny Jim, are labouring away. They call him Birdie, latest in a long line of nose names. And if the ship doesn't sink he is on his way to the place he has most desired to see since he was seven, when he mixed Antarctica up with the picture-book igloos of his geography lesson, and wrote: 'Dear Eskimo, Please write and tell me about your land. I want to go there some day. Your friend Henry.' Jesus came to Henry one night when he was nineteen, on the deck of a merchant ship homeward bound from Australia. He had just learned that girls were put off by his turkey-cock appearance. Jesus

showed me why we are here, and what the purpose of life really is. It is to make a great decision – to choose between the material and the spiritual, and if we choose the spiritual we must work out our choice, and then it will run like a silver thread through the material. It is very difficult to express in words . . . but I can never forget that I did realize, in a flash, that nothing that happens to our bodies really matters.

Bowers has a very kind heart. 'There was nothing subtle about him,' Cherry-Garrard will remember; but he brings a kind of jocular delicacy to bear on the mysterious areas of life in which he does not expect to be included. If he senses your heart is troubled, he slams you heartily between the shoulder-blades, he ducks you in ice-cold water, he wishes you all the best. In all the world, he is only frightened of one thing, spiders. And only the thought of his mother gives him pain now. His father dead at sea before his first birthday, she raised him alone. (Perhaps in some ways he is a religious woman's idea of what a manly man ought to be.) She never wanted him to become a sailor; she certainly does not welcome him disappearing now to the ends of the earth. Again and again in letters he has tried to reconcile her wishes and his. It does not work. He cannot find a way to fit together the pleasures of decorating the house for Christmas, or playing athletic tennis while his mother looks on, with these present sensations. Instead it seems to him that he must simply be a person who pulls in two directions. 'Why did you give me this nature that loves and longs more than anything else to be at home, and yet when away at sea glories in the fact.' Glorying, he heads down for his next turn at the buckets. See him: a compact sphere of adrenalin bouncing along the companion-way.

> Sing of joy, sing of bliss,
> Home was never like this,
> Yip-I-Addy-I-Ay!

They have baled long enough. The borehole to the pump succeeds. The holds empty. The storm abates. The ship sails on.

31 December 1910–4 January 1911

Out of the rolling storm, into the rigid pack-ice; at a snail's pace through the tricksy lanes between the floes where the Adélie penguins squark 'a guttural Aha or Wahah' at the sight of humans, and grow 'most excited' when Bowers sings to them; released from the metamorphic ice, thick with resemblances and reflections, into the open Ross Sea beyond, as if they had passed ringed defences on their way to the core of the Antarctic. The New Year approaches like (says Teddy Evans) 'the opening of a new volume of an exciting book', and the *Terra Nova* moves sweetly in the bright night of Antarctic summer over shadowed and silvery waves. It is still a few hours short of midnight; surgeon Atkinson shakes Cherry-Garrard's shoulder. 'Have you seen the land? Wrap your blankets round you, and go and see.' Men of all watches are gazing off the starboard bow at 'the only white in a dark horizon': mountains 'like satin', high and so far away that they seem to float untethered above a band of dark. The clearing air transmits the peaks pin-sharp across 110 miles of sea, and over the next days, the last of the voyage, as they cruise to the Ross Sea's terminus at the Great Ice Barrier, then round the shore of Ross Island in search of winter quarters, the weather steadily takes on a fragile summer perfection. The sea calms, the wind goes gentle, clouds abolish themselves, the air dries completely. This is the air that cured Wilson's TB; it is a pleasure to breathe. It has a slight edge to it that you feel when you inhale, tingling when it meets the warm blood in your lungs, as if the vestige of a shiver were dissolved in each chestful, but the result is a heightened wakefulness, and a sense of your body working superlatively well. Scott calls it 'inexpressibly health-giving', Bowers says it is 'permeated with vitality'. Rather than sleeping, they sit on the deck in the nighttime sun. During the final approach to landfall, Cherry-Garrard writes, 'Many watched all night, as this new world unfolded itself, cape by cape and mountain by mountain.' The air conducts light extraordinarily. First they see a stark white Hollywood glow on the horizon dead ahead – the 'ice-blink' announcing the Barrier. Out of it rises the cone of Mt Erebus, then, as Wilson describes it, 'a brilliant white line' running away to the left as far as the eye can see, which thickens until it has 'developed' into the unmistakable wall of ice. Wilson ransacks his paint-box to name the colours that the light infuses into sea and ice, the colours that will withdraw too when the light does. Cobalt blue, 'inky' blue, sage green, emerald green, holly green. The sage green is the result of 'innumerable yellow and orange tinted diatoms floating in blue water', like the overloaded field of psychedelic flecks used for testing colour blindness. Suddenly a swarm of penguins ('brown from above with white edges') are in wild submarine motion in the clear depths siding the ship, 'leaping in and out like little dolphins', 'and the water was as though hundreds of rifle bullets were dropping in around us everywhere'. At the Barrier wall, pitted and luminous wherever wave action has scooped a cavern, they turn for Cape Crozier, where the long ice sheet runs aground on basalt rocks, but to land is impossible – too much surf, too much rotten ice in the surf – and they steer on towards the next likely landing sites in McMurdo Sound. Ponting wishes Scott would slow the ship as planned for cinematography, but this little frustration drowns in his tide of excitement. Like the expedition artist, the photographer is recording the sun-shot scenery for all he's worth. He has only a few frames of an experimental colour film, but he is scurrying to do all the justice he can to the light on monochrome plates, and at least in words. 'Ponting is enraptured', writes Scott, 'and uses expressions which in any one else and alluding to any other subject might be deemed extravagant.' Ponting actually has two styles of enraptured expression. Number One: 'The midnight sun was shining with such brilliance that I was able to make focal-plane photographic exposures with an aperture of F_{11}, using a Zeiss Protar lens of 16 inches focus, with a K_3 colour screen in conjunction with an orthochromatic plate.' Number Two: 'In these wondrous grottoes played hundreds of Peter Pan fairies – rainbow-hued flashes of light, mirrored by the dancing, lapping wavelets.' Both are professional. Scott allows that this is Ponting's rightful area of expertise, but he finds the photographer ever so slightly vulgar: he thinks constantly in terms of *effects*, both visual and verbal, both the 'remarkable pictures of priceless educational value' these scenes might become, and the picturesque patter that will go with them when he darkens a room and a magic-lantern-show of the Antarctic appears on a wall. Effects do come constantly. The ship is in motion, glittering icebergs are in motion, near shores and far peaks seem to move against each other with the parallax of the ship's passing. As McMurdo Sound – calm today – opens around them, cape slides out from cape, new reaches of still water open and close, forming and re-forming a kaleidoscope of views, a little light pack-ice here and there 'composing well into foregrounds'. It is not long after the *Terra Nova* finally moors that Ponting takes his famous photograph of the ship framed by an ice-cave's mouth shaped like the cross-section of an aeroplane wing.

These are rare days, and in fact these are rare perspectives. The Southern Continent will scarcely ever again show them this serene face, or offer such perfect visibility. Sometimes from their base at Cape Evans the mountains thirty miles westward across McMurdo Sound will return into focus, to remind them of their first pristine vision of the place. In the ordinary run of things the air will not be glass-clear, or permit this level, sustained, revealing light; it will be bright but not clear, clear but only moon-lit; at worst the endless permutations of cloud and darkness will lock down their vision to objects a mile away, a hundred yards away, five feet ahead of a groping arm. And only with the advantage of a far perspective is it possible to see Antarctica spread wide and whole, as it was before they closed with it. Bowers writes, 'The inhospitable mountains look from the distance inviting and grand beyond conception.' *The inhospitable mountains*: they sound like the Delectable Mountains in *Pilgrim's Progress*, always unreachably far, only requiring a human eye to read their invitation. They fill Bowers with the restless, acquisitive desire to do more with a landscape than look at it, to go among the peaks and put his foot on them. Closer to (like the tempting islands seen by St Brendan that turned brackish and foul when approached) the line of sight shortens, the angles go against you. Already the creased, intricate heights around Erebus and Terror have scrunched together, until, as they sail close under the bulk of Ross Island, only a single swart volcanic cliff can be seen, and one sufficiently forbidding first foothill above it. And the white shoulders of the mountains prove to be snow fissured in all directions, the edges of the island to be crevassed ice-falls. It is all dangerous. There is none of the land, none of the sea, that you can cross without laborious planning. You would not want to set your foot on anything you were not sure of.

Of the sixty-five men on the *Terra Nova*, eight have been here before, on the *Discovery* expedition or with Shackleton only two years ago, in the *Nimrod*. They had these vistas as memories and dreams while they worked at ice-less jobs in England; now memory rises up into overlap with all they see, and continues in phase with it. The polar landscape does its trick of freezing time. Wilson writes: 'All these things are strangely familiar and it seems but yesterday that I was clambering over them roped up with Cross and Whitfield . . .' They pass a message post hammered into a beach 'which we put up ten years ago and on it the two cylinders, the lower one of which I attached myself': all preserved, all immunised against change, as the remains of this present expedition will also be, down to the last half-eaten biscuit. Scott's heart lifts at the 'sight of the old well-remembered landmarks'. (During the weeks in the pack-ice he hardly spoke, Wilfred Bruce remarked.) 'It was good to see them again . . . It gives one a homely feeling to see such a familiar scene.' The newcomers find it all familiar in a different sense. It is prepared for, hoped for, expected; Antarctica comes to them as a confirmation as much as a revelation. They bring ready images, if not memories. 'As for the Barrier,' Cherry-Garrard explains, 'we seemed to have known it all our lives, it was so exactly like what we had imagined it to be, and seen in the pictures and photographs.' But they cannot feel the veterans' sense that they have a place in it. It's exciting, it's even – on these particular fair days – seductive. But its calm and its hugeness make for a beauty utterly detached from human uses and human needs. Teddy Evans is placed midway between veterans and tyros, for he has called here before, on the *Discovery*'s relief ship *Morning*, yet never lived with these views, never felt his way into this landscape. Usually so rapid-fire chatty, he has been feeling 'odd thrills'. 'To me those peaks always did and always will represent silent defiance,' he remembers afterwards; 'there were times when they made me shudder,' as if the shiver in the air amplified at the sight. Least of all can the newcomers find the panorama homely. Their prefabricated house of matchboard and rubberoid is packed in the hold, and in all the thousands upon thousands of square miles of the continent only the two indistinguishable dots of the previous expedition huts keep out the weather. It's homely's opposite, for which the German language has the perfect word. *Unheimlich*: uncanny. They stare and stare.

18 February–3 March 1911

White-out. Compared to the Great Ice Barrier, Ross Island is only a volcanic bobble. Across the sea-ice twenty miles south from Cape Evans, where the carpenters are still fitting out winter quarters, the Barrier seals the end of McMurdo Sound. Beyond, a huge plated wedge of ice larger than France fills the whole indentation in this side of the continent; a cracked white tabletop stretching poleward all the way to the foot of the Beardmore Glacier. Blown snow freezes into rippled ridges, or sets to a crust that hisses sharply when your foot goes through, or gathers into powdered, floundery drifts. Moving fast to seize the remainder of the summer sledging season Scott and ten others leading ponies or driving dog-teams have laid a curved line of supply dumps out here for next spring. 'Let's leg it,' he likes to say. Now, about 150 miles south of Cape Evans, Scott has decided that the ponies can go no further. They have built the bulk of their food and fuel into a neat heap called One Ton Depot, and turned for base, split into separate parties. They travel by night so that the ponies may rest during the warmer daytime hours. Northward in a thick whiteness, then, step Bowers, Oates, and Tryggve Gran – a young skier who is finding it quite hard being Norwegian in this company just now, but promised Oates a few days ago he would fight for England in a war, and won a handshake. Each guides an exhausted horse by the head. The horses are roped together in series; their breath whiffles beside the walking men.

'That march was extraordinary,' writes Bowers,

the snowy mist hid all distant objects and made all close ones look gigantic. Although we were walking on a flat, undulating plain, one could not get away from the impression that the ground was hilly – quite steep in places with deep hollows by the wayside. Suddenly a herd of apparent cattle would appear in the distance, then you would think: 'No, it's a team of dogs broken loose and rushing towards you.' In another moment one would be walking over the black dots of some old horse droppings which had been the cause of the hallucinations.

The foot-high snow ridges, *sastrugi*, float off the ground and become white downland lying across the route ahead. Stepping up onto what seemed the beginning of a long incline, their feet lift right over the whole hill. 'After going about ten miles we spotted a tiny black triangle in the dead white void ahead, it was over a mile away and was the lunch camp of the dogs.' The following night it is much clearer, and the optical effects reverse. The same unending plain lies before them, but now the horizon is further away than the senses suggest. The white sheet they look forward over comprises miles of snow, instead of yesterday's few yards, and mirages lift even remoter expanses into view, the shimmer producing a persistent illusion of open water. One of the cairns marking the route appears in the distance and then stays there: 'the only trouble about seeing things so far off is that they take such an awful time to reach'. Resolved not to make yesterday's mistake twice they overcompensate and identify another 'dark object' ahead as the dog-teams' encampment again. More steps, and 'it turned out to be an empty biscuit tin, such is the deceptive nature of the light'. February 22 brings a single night of ideal conditions, 'clear as a bell'; otherwise they march in growing obscurity night after night, in an atmosphere of imminent blizzard. Autumn is coming, 'the midnight sun was already cartwheeling the southern horizon . . . also the season had undoubtedly broken up'. They pass unexpected snow-cairns that prove to contain the corpses of two beasts belonging to the other pony party. Their own, emaciated from twenty-four-hour exposure to the Barrier, need constant nursing. Gran has dropped a small but crucial component of the primus stove, somewhere in the 'fuzzy nothingness' that engulfs them, on and off, all the way to the rendezvous at Safety Camp on the Barrier's edge. 'Cold food stared us in the face!' Still, 'we legged it into the void . . .'

313

The juggling confusions of the Barrier are new to Bowers; they disconcert him, but do not overbear his imagination; he even finds them amusing, till the 'novelty' wears off. He records them with a navigator's accuracy and an ingenuous curiosity that such things can be. Bowers has the quality Melville praised in whales and recommended for humans, 'the rare virtue of thick walls'. Seeing the Barrier phenomena through his eyes is like gazing through a thick, square block of glass. It is different for Scott, up ahead with a dog-team. Scott has been hammered thin by anxious calculations of weight and distance, by, too, the evident suffering of the horses as blizzard winds on the way out wasted their flesh under its thin hair coat. His eye is wide and scarcely defended against the loom and waver of objects in the mist. He notices acutely the forms of the snow, the hugeness of the Barrier, the sounds you hear from the tent when you are on the verge of sleep. In his diary he has been writing a series of 'Impressions' which show that, at however many removes, he has picked up hints from the new poetry of concise images beginning to shape the literary scene in London. If his notes do not quite match the prototypical Imagist comparison of faces in the Underground to 'petals on a wet black bough', they are nonetheless hyper-attentive. 'The wind-blown furrows', he writes. 'The small green tent and the great white road.' 'The gentle flutter of our canvas shelter.' 'The drift snow like finest flour penetrating every hole and corner – flickering up beneath one's head covering, pricking sharply as a sand blast.' Then, more ominously, the impressions gathering speed and turning into something like the hyphenated précis of contents at the head of a chapter of disasters in a Victorian travel book, 'The blizzard, Nature's protest – the crevasse, Nature's pitfall – that grim trap for the unwary – no hunter could conceal his snare so perfectly – the light rippled snow bridge gives no hint or sign of the hidden danger, its position unguessable till man or beast is floundering, clawing and struggling for foothold on the brink.'

This *is* a chapter of disasters, logistically speaking. The experience of the outward journey has proved that ponies cannot work in the blizzards which prevail at the beginning and end of the 'sledging season': therefore next year's departure for the pole must wait for a month after the date Scott had in mind. And perhaps, Scott thinks wretchedly, there may not be a departure. Since he overruled Oates' advice that they should write off the weakest ponies, and push One Ton further south, stashing pony-meat for dogfood as each horse failed, the ponies have been keeling over anyway on the road back. 'I have had more than enough of this cruelty to animals,' he had said. Now 'Blossom' and 'Blucher' are dead in the snow where they cannot do any good, and when Bowers' party catches up at Safety Camp 'Weary Willy' promptly expires too. Next year's essential transport is steadily disappearing. As if he had foreseen it, Scott has also had a sudden, scrabbling close shave with a crevasse. And, to ice his cake, a message has just arrived from the *Terra Nova*: Amundsen is ashore at the Bay of Whales with 110 dogs. Beside this item 'every incident of the day pales'. But this is not the end of the skein of catastrophes. There follows an astonishingly intricate final piece of ill-fortune. As they set off once more from Safety Camp in their different groupings for the last leg of the journey, across the frozen sea to Cape Evans, Bowers loses sight of Wilson, whose dog-team is supposed to be acting guide for the following ponies; in 'a black mist' he leads four ponies, Cherry-Garrard, and Seaman Crean onto ice that creaks underfoot and leaks black water along fracture lines, and though he thinks he has found safe ice for their camp that night, Bowers wakes in the small hours on a broken ice-floe drifting out to sea. Elaborate rescue operations and much bravery save the humans, but 'poor Guts' vanished when the sea opened, 'Punch' and 'Uncle Bill' have to have the *coup de grâce* administered. Oates, who had advised a humane revolver shot at One Ton, ends up driving a pickaxe through Punch's brain as the animal struggles in the water. 'I shall be sick if I have to kill another horse like I did the last,' he says. Bowers sees to Uncle Bill. Around them a dozen or more killer whales ram their heads up methodically through the masking ice: all teeth, all appetite. Six ponies gone of eight. 'Everything out of joint,' writes Scott.

Scott puts the expedition's incessant stumbling down to bad luck. He does not cease to find nervous fault with his companions, or to make minor distributions of blame; but he takes the stricken Bowers aside and comforts him with words about the impossibility of some

315

situations. In the face of the biggest blow of all, Amundsen's arrival, he takes a stance part dignified, part denying. 'The proper, as well as the wiser, course for us is to proceed exactly as though this had not happened.' The others are proud to see him so 'philosophical', when they have felt a momentary gust of rage at the news. Of course, it conveniently relieves Scott of personal responsibility if the last day's events have been fated accidents. This is what Oates sees, and what will still madden him six months afterwards: 'the loss of the ponies,' he will write, 'was Scott's fault entirely'. But Scott's state of mind is altogether less comfortably evasive than Oates allows. Wrought-up, wound-up, Scott may be salving his nerves when he talks about luck, but he has always believed that he was ill-starred, bound to stumble. He takes events personally in another way: they seem targeted at him. Out here, to a man who jumpily monitors every shift of cloud or change in snow texture beneath the sled runners, who feels events as a pressure mounting from the subtly invasive flick of flakes inside a balaclava to the eruptive attack of the killer whales, it can begin to seem that an obscure message is being delivered. Scott's ordinary feeling that an impersonal fate obstructs him germinates into something else, his sense of the mammoth indifference of the physical universe to his efforts shades further over with each successive mishap into a nudging conviction that there is a purpose at work. It's a perception common on the expedition. You can't not try to read the great document of Antarctica for meaning. In these surroundings the pattern-seeking habit of the human mind wakes a vague instinct of faith even in the most secular and scientific of Scott's men. As Debenham will put it years later: 'one cannot live for a while amidst the vast, lonely and yet magnificent scenery of the Antarctic . . . without feeling dwarfed by the scale of everything one sees and in the hands of a Providence or a Power. An intelligent man cannot really be satisfied with saying it is a matter of Chance, or if he does he really means that there is Something behind the Chance.'

Wilson and Bowers, now, are sure they know what lies behind. Bowers: 'My own opinion is that it just had to be, the circumstances leading to it were too devious for mere coincidence . . . everything fitted in to place us on the sea-ice during the only two hours of the whole year that we could possibly have been in such a position.' Wilson: 'The whole thing was just a beautiful piece of education on a very impressive scale.'

There is another candidate than providence. Scott is not a believer, but he is a romantic, conscious of Nature's ambiguous force; conscious as well of its blind selecting violence. 'I'm obsessed with the view of life as a struggle for existence,' he explained to Kathleen in 1909. In a world without God, the purpose you detect in your setbacks may be the fearsome otherness of the natural order, orchestrated for a moment to extinguish you. A Something never defined stirs behind Scott's conventional images of a hostile Nature; Something wakes in those deliberate pitfalls, traps, and snares. 'All visible objects, man, are but as pasteboard masks,' said Ahab to Ishmael. 'But in each event – in the living act, the undoubted deed – there, some unknown but still reasoning thing puts forth the mouldings of its features from behind the unreasoning mask.'

But you cannot harpoon Antarctica; and Scott – who is not crazy, only driven to distraction, heaped and tasked by schemes that fall apart, until he sees malignity out of the corner of his eye – knows you cannot even fight it. Sledging is like swimming. If you lose your temper with the sluggish medium you move in, you only thrash about and sink. You can only defy the snow by a held-in persistence, which keeps you going, impatient perhaps, but steadily butting forward at whatever speed the snow permits. Scott lacks the technical, the tactical, and the cultural qualities which ease progress. If he were Amundsen, schooled by the Inuit, ingenious and perfectionist, he could take the continent at a dog-powered glide. He has, though, the moral component: determination. It's his strength as an explorer, 'sheer good grain,' says Cherry-Garrard, 'which ran over and under and through his weaker self and clamped it together'. Whatever opposes him, whatever mistakes of his own return to thwart him under the name of 'bad luck', he will interpret as tests of behaviour. This means that in the end, in a curious way, he is less vulnerable to setbacks than Wilson, certainly than Bowers, both of whom subscribe to the Edwardian spiritual commonplace that you are never tested beyond your power to endure. Scott will never recognise his own contribution to the malignancy of his fate, but by the same token expects no favours from providence. He sees no limit to how wrong things can go. He's on his own. He just grips tighter.

When the party at last returns to Cape Evans, via a chafing wait at the old *Discovery* quarters while the sea freezes again, to contemplate the ten ponies remaining for the attempt on the pole, the rhythm of winter life soothes Scott. The white features that had seemed infiltrated with intent – imperceptibly fatted with presence, on the verge of writhing into hostile movement – still themselves. The mask is only a mask. Scott writes a diagnostic letter to Kathleen. He says, 'I am quite on my feet now, I feel both mentally and physically fit for the work.' He says that he has shaken off a malaise which had spread through his relations with the men he leads. 'The root of the trouble was that I had lost confidence in myself.' Next summer, as they slug their way up the Beardmore Glacier towards the pole, he will cry lightly 'How's the enemy, Titus?', when a stint of man-hauling looks about to end. Oates will look at his watch, report the hour. 'Oh, well, I think we'll go on a little bit more then . . .' Knackered, underfed, the others will curse under their breaths and follow.

4 June 1911
Rising bread dough. Sour-sweet yeast working in the lobed white mass, swelling it slowly in the night hours, carrying upward the steel disc placed neatly on top in the dead centre of the bowl. The disc touches the metal lid. Contact: a small red bulb goes on in the dark hut, the only light except for the oil-lamp beside the man on night watch. He picks his way among the sleepers at the other-ranks' end of the wooden building, finds Thomas Clissold, the cook. The bread machine Clissold invented used to ring an electric bell, but there were complaints. 'Clissold!' (A whisper.) 'Your bread!' Clissold, early twenties, Navy crewcut, little blond beard – who looks as if he'd be renting Kung Fu films from a video shop, if there were Kung Fu films, if there were video shops – rouses, and silently begins to knead his breakfast loaves at the galley table. The watchman settles back to his station by the acetylene plant in the porch. He must patrol for fire every couple of hours, and check the ponies in their icicle-encrusted

stable alongside. Otherwise this time is his, to write or think or be private. Teddy Evans has contributed a canister of China tea for the watchman's comfort. On stormy nights, when the blizzard blows down off Erebus, whichever officer or scientist has the watch may have to wrap up, go out through three successively colder doors, and feel along the side of the hut in the whirling drift for the ladder secured there. The intake pipe of 'Dines' Anemometer' on the roof tends to clog if too much loose snow flies in. If it's blizzing, too, the Anemometer becomes the most spectacularly noisy of Simpson's meteorological devices. The bottom end of the pipe broadcasts a continuous moaning howl, rising and falling like a banshee's wail, waking Ponting (who sleeps lightly) in his cubicle near by, or giving the photographer peculiar dreams of waterfalls and cataracts. The hut vibrates. The warm dark space, fifty feet by twenty-five, seems truly besieged then. But tonight is quiet, yesterday's wind a memory by midnight. Outside an enormous frosted hush; inside the ticking of all the chronometers from the far corner where Teddy Evans sleeps. At 5 a.m. or thereabouts a candle lights at the table next to Evans: Wilson is up, has prayed, and is painting. His brush jiggles against glass in his water-jar, moves to the box of colours in obedience to the pencil notes he made when he was sketching, hands out of mittens just long enough to snatch down a line of coast, a smudge of smoke, a mountain contour in the autumn afterglow. 'Put Hut Point in darkness – deep brown & purple snow against any western summit of deep orange.' 'Cambridge blue of the ice foot.' 'Greenish ice.' Clocks counting the minutes, preserving the exact deviation from Greenwich time necessary for navigation; Wilson working fast on wetted paper; Clissold baking; the watchman's last night rounds. Nothing else disturbs the dreamers' mutters from the remaining twenty-two sleepers, or the profound snores from Bowers, until, with no lightening of the sky, 7.30, designated as morning, arrives. The acetylene gas is switched on, flows to the shaded gas mantles around the long room; is ignited, with a soft fierce *woomf* of white light.

'Good *morning*, Farmer Hayseed,' cries Bowers to Oates, one bunk along from him in the genteel-squalid district of the hut known as The Tenements. 'How's the hay?' Oates grunts, stirs, swears with a delightful predictability, while around him the other Tenement dwellers collect themselves under the imperious eye of Oates' single ornament, a small print of Napoleon. Cherry-Garrard hooks his thick glasses round his ears. Across the way the rival encampment of Australian scientists dress behind their curtain, the only curtain in the Antarctic, they boast, which Oates declares makes their quarters look like an 'opium den' or 'a lady's boudoir'. Then Oates gathers up Anton – a Siberian groom who has been leaving cigarettes outside as nervous offerings to the aurora, and finds Oates' solidity very reassuring – and goes indeed to feed the horses with him in companionable silence, on wheat and hay chaff, the morning diet. Those of the seamen who have not darted navy-quick outdoors to fetch ice for drinking water look on with completely concealed amusement as the watchman quits his post yawning. They do not have to sit night watches. Scott has decreed this for the sake of morale: it is one of the winter's little gestures of deference towards the 'lower deck', little turnings of the world upside-down, that co-exist with the social wall of packing-cases dividing the hut in two. Every morning brings the men a spectacle of upper-class blear. And now Bowers and Wilson meet naked at the porch-end for their daily bath with a basin of snow. They grin, they grimace; and 'proceed to rub glistening limbs with this chilling substance' writes Scott, who like everybody except these two Spartans prefers washing in a rationed pint of warm water from a jug. Sounds of the weekly shave mix with the clatter as Hooper the steward sets the tables for breakfast. The ice detail, returned, report an iron-hard stillness outdoors and the moon on the rise. One by one the places fill; Clissold serves fresh bread, marmalade, porridge. Sometimes they have scrambled 'Truegg', a dehydrated yellow powder out of catering-size tins. When Nelson, the biologist, has caught some specimens of *Notothenia* in his fish trap under the sea-ice, and Atkinson has put aside the nematodes and trematodes from their guts for his parasite research, they eat those too.

The breakfasters chat amiably, reinforcing their points with the occasional wave of a fork. Griffith Taylor, the Australian geologist, is trying to get Oates' goat by advocating female suffrage: Oates' ripostes to these outrages tend to come in a slow, slow drawl. A few nights ago his voice was heard from his bunk saying, 'Poor old Griff. [Pause] Poor old Griff. [Long pause] He's not a bad fellow . . . [Very long pause] . . . but he's a bit *mouldy*.' Elsewhere around the table, someone is seeking artistic advice from Wilson. Someone else is proposing the kind of hypothetical question much valued during the winter because it keeps them all arguing for hours. They've thought of this one overnight: What would the wine-waiter at the Ritz say (and do) if you demanded a pint of bitter? Further along again, Cherry-Garrard is refusing to be drawn on the contents of the *South Polar Times*, which will be published on Midwinter Day, and is strictly secret till then, no matter how sly the approach. No, it's no *use* you asking. You'll just have to wait. No! not even a hint. Scott casts a sharp eye up the table, and is glad. Badinage; shop-talk polar and shop-talk scientific. It's a happy company. They all think so. Something pleasing has gelled from the 'diverse assortment of our company', as Scott put it in his diary a fortnight ago: 'I am very much impressed with the extraordinary and general cordiality of the relations which exist amongst our people . . . With me there is no need to draw a veil' over frictions or clashes that would be unfit for print later. The heavy-handed teasing, like the lump of lead in the keel of a toy boat, keeps conversation bobbing along upright; the gents and scientists can go to Wilson, the seamen to Bowers or Evans or Oates when the 'many rubs' of life cramped together need arbitrating or defusing. Those who are finding the constant darkness hard to bear can lean surreptitiously on the good humour for support. Scott himself finds it particularly helpful that the scientists are so willing to share their work, creating an atmosphere of amateur study among the rest that they're calling 'the University of the Antarctic'. To Scott this is the chief distinction of the 'modern style' of overwintering. It's worth working up, he thinks, when he turns his diary into a book: 'compare the interests of a winter spent by the old Arctic voyagers with our own, and look into the causes. The aspect of everything changes as our knowledge expands.' He finds it exciting to learn. He lacks scientific training (because of his naval career he missed the ordinary sort of university) but he has a sharp syllogistic mind that reasons forward unstoppably from the premises he picks up in conversation. At the thrice-weekly lectures he takes copious notes on ice physics, the aurora, physiographic techniques; and he also likes to quiz the scientific staff, mostly twenty years his junior, about their progress. Some actually find these talks rather intimidating. Scott may not know the material, but when the delight of logic grips him he is alarmingly quick at spotting a flawed deduction. Any chagrin this causes, they hide, for the key to the harmony reigning in the hut is a deliberate withdrawal from sight, on everybody's part, of disruptive emotions. Scott wants to believe the opposite. 'I do not believe there can be any life quite so demonstrative of character,' he wrote a month ago. 'Here the outward show is nothing, it is the inward purpose that counts . . . Pretence is useless.' Pretence is essential. The companionship of the winter life, the easing of the loneliness of command for Scott as he quietly communes now with Wilson at the table's head, rest on a constant demonstration by everyone to each other of truthful but partial versions of their characters. For his part Scott maintains a safety-valve by penning critical estimates of those around him. These are certainly not for publication.

On an ordinary day they would scatter now to their winter tasks; the men to sew sleeping bags and refurbish kit in a workspace lined with butter boxes, the others to lab and darkroom and typewriter and stables and meteorological post and planning session. Today is Sunday, though. The pace is easier. After breakfast comes an interval of tidying and straightening: then Scott does what ship's captains do *ex officio* on clement Sundays, whatever their beliefs, and holds a service pieced together from the Book of Common Prayer. His congregation of twenty-three stand bunched beside the piano no-one can really play. Scott's expressive voice sounds the Jacobean English of the Whitsun prayers and readings; he feels an obligation to do reverent justice, at least, to the drama of the words, and as he reads them in the wooden house on the black volcanic shore under Erebus, some passages seem to speak directly of this very gathering.

When the day of Pentecost was fully come, they were all with one accord in one place. And suddenly there came a sound from heaven, as of a rushing mighty wind, and it filled all the house . . . From all blindness of heart; from pride, vainglory, and hypocrisy; from envy, hatred, and malice, and all uncharitableness, Good Lord, deliver us . . . Thou shalt break the ships of the sea: through the east wind . . . O God, according to thy Name, so is thy praise unto the world's end.

The hymns are another matter. Wilson plinks the piano for the first note 'and I try to hit it after with doubtful success!' Next week Scott will get Cherry-Garrard 'to vamp the accompaniment', but nothing can make them any more tuneful than they were with 'Yip-I-Addy'.

Bowers sings loud. As a matter of fact, he is writing a hymn himself to celebrate the return of the sun, due in late August. When nobody is looking he will drop it into the contributions box for the *South Polar Times*. He is turning the already appropriate

> Thou, whose almighty word
> Chaos and darkness heard,
>   And took their flight;
> Hear us, we humbly pray,
> And where the Gospel-day
> Sheds not its glorious ray,
>   Let there be light!

– which is excellent for singing your head off to, especially the splendid crash you make at the end of the verse – into

> Thou whose far-reaching ray
> Heralds the dawn of day,
>   At last begun,
> Scatt'ring with glorious light
> Darkness of winter night,
> Dazzling in brilliance bright,
>   Hail mighty Sun!

Around noon a faint greyness comes into the sky, then goes, the solitary trace at present of the mighty sun; until Midwinter Day on 22 June they will still be on the year's downward slope into darkness. Some excitement: while the men are exercising the ponies outside, small black figures moving to and fro on the sea-ice at the heads of snorting duffel-clad beasts, Cherry and Bowers spot a crabeater seal flumping up from an open ice-hole near the beached bergs in the bay. Crabeaters, slim and elegant, are much less common in this area than the tubby Weddell species. They corner the seal in the moonlight and succeed in killing it. Clissold joins the scientists admiring the catch. When they've done drawing, measuring, skinning, and dissecting it, it will be his. Sometimes he feels frustrated at the unvarying raw material he has to work with. He eyes the seal: if you remove every speck of blubber, seal-meat does not taste fishy. Rissoles? Steaks? Perhaps another *galantine* . . . Scott applauded the seal soup, followed by seal steak-and-kidney pie, that Clissold conjured up last week. 'I cannot think we shall get scurvy,' he wrote.

After lunch a party of five sally out to make an experiment. Wilson, Bowers, and Cherry-Garrard will be leaving soon after Midwinter Day for their effort to reach the Cape Crozier rookery of the Emperor Penguin during the pitch-dark, sub-zero nesting season. They hope that if they can place themselves at Cape Crozier at the right time, they will be able to place in the hands of science an Emperor embryo in such an early stage of development that the link will be visible between present bird-life and its remote evolutionary ancestor, the flying saurian archaeopteryx. The embryo locked in the egg is supposed to recapitulate the primitive history of the species. The travellers will have their tent, but it would be handy if they could put more than canvas between themselves and the winter temperatures while they ornithologise. Another kind of recapitulation is in order. Along with the three directly concerned, Scott and Petty Officer Lashly choose a level patch of moonlit snow behind the hut 'to start the building of our first "igloo"'. Stamping of feet, energetic activity with a variety of competing tools. Bowers has a trowel, Wilson has a saw, Cherry has a big flat-bladed toothed knife. 'There is a good deal of difference of opinion as to the best implement with which to cut snow blocks . . . I'm inclined to think the knife will prove most effective,' writes Scott, who designed it, 'but the others don't acknowledge it *yet*.' It's hard to cut the blocks, hard to lift them, and hard to translate the mental picture of a round Eskimo home-sweet-home into architectural reality. By tea-time they have to stop. The sinking moon is casting long shadows, turning their handiwork to a confusion of light and dark planes. The igloo only stands thigh-high: they've only managed three layers of blocks. 'We must go on with this hut building till we get good at it,' writes Scott. 'I'm sure it's going to be a useful art.' Wilson is cheerfully unsanguine. He writes: 'Played at building an igloo – with no success.' At Cape Crozier the egg collectors will end up building a compromise, a hut of rock chunks with a canvas lid held down by snow slabs. Unfortunately its flapping edges will offer a little too much purchase to a blizzard, which will blow the roof off vertically; 'and ended for ever "The Age of Stone"', as a light-verse account in the *South Polar Times* will put it. The three will return from the Winter Journey pinched and dull-eyed, reminding Ponting of starved POWs. Even so, Eskimo skills do not seem specially attractive to the explorers. If they must play at being primitive, they would much rather imagine themselves as ancient Egyptians. They have a running gag about future tourists on Ross Island admiring pyramids and obelisks left behind by the expedition. Wilson paints joke pictures of stone tablets, 'Antarctic Archives', showing red cartoon people sashaying hieratically across the snow in loincloths.

Solitary excursions in safe weather, like night-watch duty, offer the opportunity for privacy. As Hooper clears away the tea things, Scott kneels in the lean-to porch to fix his ski lashings, and heads into the Antarctic night alone. Out he goes past Teddy Evans' old survey-points on the sea-ice, dubbed Sardine and Shark and other fishy S-names, towards Inaccessible Island. The ice rings sound and solid, the surface is 'the best possible', compact and smooth. Cold sorts the moisture in his breath and crystallises it in rime on his balaclava and twinkling showers when he exhales. He hears the noises of his body working but no other human sound, though sound carries in still air here over amazing distances: you can overhear conversations at miles'-range. Instead there come only the sharp cracks now and again of ice expanding on the distant Barrier, like pistols fired at random. The moon is almost down, but the sky is afire with green light, drifting and changing, blushing rose. Scott lifts his face, solemn, and drinks the aurora in. He has an endless appetite for its substanceless beauty. The twisting arches and wavering curtains of light above seem almost animated by a kind of stately life, 'and in that lies its charm', he noted a fortnight ago:

the suggestion of life, form, colour, and movement never less than evanescent, mysterious – no reality. It is the language of mystic signs and portents – the inspiration of the gods – wholly spiritual – divine signalling. Remindful of superstition, provocative of imagination. Might not the inhabitants of some other world (Mars) controlling mighty forces not thus surround our globe with fiery symbols, a golden writing which we have not the key to decipher?

Tonight there is something new: three sudden white flashes at sea level, over away by the grounded Castle Berg. Lightning? thinks Scott. Actually it is Ponting getting pictures with his flash-gun, a contrivance you load with magnesium powder and hold above your head. Ponting likes the brilliant, instantaneous smash of candlepower onto ice walls. Shadows flee into crevices, inking shapes far back for the lens. The fissured detail of the ice leaps out in deep relief. Once, though, this winter Ponting has found himself overwhelmed. He was taking the famous photograph of the sublime wall of ice. As the neon afterimage of the flash fades on his retina, and the moon reasserts itself, he gazes at the two-hundred-foot sheer edge of the Barne Glacier, enormously shattered, hugely unperturbed by tiny men with cameras, and feels 'an intense and wholly indescribable loneliness'. It's too big, too silent, too cold. It's all too much. 'Coo-ee!' shouts Ponting. Pause. Moonstruck immensity. 'Coo-ee!' replies the Barne Glacier. A perfect echo!

Among the bags and bundles festooning The Tenements are some whose contents must not be revealed till the grand Midwinter party. Bowers seizes spare evening moments to work – back turned, shoulders hunched – on a secret Christmas tree. The branches are split and jointed lengths of ski pole, the leaves are to be gull feathers. When everyone is carousing under the massed sledging banners, and the snapdragon has just been lit, he plans to have it brought forth with a flourish, hung with little satirical gifts for each man there. Oriana Wilson's sister bought them for him. He has a popgun reserved for Oates. (Who'll be delighted. 'If you want to please me very much you will fall down when I shoot you,' Oates will say, firing to left and right.)

They rejoice in festivities, which distinguish the days from one another and absorb your attention entirely in the moment, while they last. Lectures are popular for the same reason. Apart from Simpson on ice physics and Taylor on physiography, they have had Wilson on sketching, Ponting on Japan, and Meares on the bloodthirsty Lolo people of Tibet. 'Going to the pictures tonight, dearie?' says Oates. But, supper done, today closes quietly. Everybody is indoors. A comfortable fug of pipe-smoke floats over the arguments – the wine-waiter at the Ritz still has plenty of mileage left in him – and the feeble efforts at the piano. Oates re-opens his one book, Napier's *History of the Peninsula War*. Scott brings his diary up to date for another day, seated at the plan-table by his bed, surrounded by pictures of Peter and Kathleen, behind the L-shaped partition that keeps him separate from the rest. Perhaps he searches out a quotation from Browning, or the library of polar voyages presented by Sir Albert Markham and Sir Lewis Beaumont. He heads new notebooks with quotations, loads literary crannies with them, and sometimes sketches out a thought not quite expressed – about history, or the difference between courage as it is seen and as it feels – in a short assembly of borrowed words. At ten the acetylene lights go off. They settle to sleep. Wilson pads out in stockinged feet across the floor to the gramophone; selects a record, winds the handle, adjusts the horn. Though the wind is rising again, and Dines' Anemometer will wail soon, they can all hear, through the premonitory whoops of the accelerating air, and the thick crackle of the record itself, Clara Butts singing 'Abide with Me'. It is Uncle Bill 'saying goodnight to us all'.

4 October 1911
Scott's plan for reaching the pole is a baroque mechanism, like one of those whimsical clockwork devices presented to a Renaissance prince: a gilded rhinoceros model as big as a carthorse, whose horn, twisted, sets a line of silver cockerels crowing in succession along its back, until a fist-sized strawberry in red enamel drops into a tray at its back end. Scott's plan co-ordinates men, dogs, horses, and motor-sledges into a pyramid of effort, from whose apex will pop a little team of men aimed at 90° S. By now any plan he makes has to be a composite job. After

the losses of the autumn he needs to extract the maximum use from all his remaining resources. The logistics of such assorted transport have been fiendish to work out, with different loads to be pulled by different methods for different distances, each having to be factored into the equation governing the relationship between mouths to be fed and miles to be covered. And still he has no margin for error. Amundsen, starting for the pole using only one scheme of transport that he has stripped and refined and rebuilt for the task, is taking more dogs than he thinks he'll need, and far more food, just in case. The difference is not lost on Scott, who writes to Kathleen: 'I don't know what to think of Amundsen's chances. If he gets to the Pole it must be before we do, as he is bound to travel fast with dogs, and pretty certain to start early.' He does not think he is in a position to do things any other way, though. 'Any attempt to race must have wrecked my plan, besides which it doesn't appear the kind of thing one is out for.' The plan has all the defects of complexity. When Scott's faith in one of his resources wavers (as it does, up and down through this Antarctic spring, upon the news from the stables that Jehu is sickly; then that Jehu is doing better; or on the news from Day, the motor engineer, that the steel rollers have cracked; then that they can be replaced with wooden ones) his hopes slide tacitly towards another. His confidence wanes in the ponies, waxes in the motors; and vice versa, a cycle of anxiety and refuge of which he is growing heartily sick. As for the expedition's own dogs, he has decided for certain that they are an 'unpredictable element'. Before the experience with the crevasse last autumn he considered taking them to the pole. 'What a pity he didn't!', Teddy Evans will write in his memoirs – never Mr Tactful.

The plan *will* be rich in photogenic moments, dog paws whisking through the snow, caterpillar tracks crunching in a (very brief) triumph of machine over matter, faithful horses stepping on. Ponting is coming along for the first twenty-five miles to film them. But Scott cannot take him further, and there will be scenes lacking in the world's first Antarctic movie if they abide too closely by the strict rules of truth, so Ponting is seizing the opportunity of these last spring weeks before departure to mock up the missing pieces. The verb 'to pont' has taken root in the expedition. If Ponting is getting still pictures, to pont means to stand motionless in the cold, always with the interesting chance that you may fall off something if he's asked you, say, to hold a posture balanced on an iceberg. When the cinematograph comes out, pont-ing, writes Wilson, is more like 'amateur theatricals'. Today Ponting wants to capture the routine of making camp on the polar march. His camera is a slim, upright box on a tripod, with the main lens projecting out of the front and a second attached to the side as viewfinder. It attaches to the tripod like a theodolite – rigidly, with screws. Ponting cannot swivel it while he is filming. The camera must be lugged to face the subject, or else an event constructed right in front of it, on the stage of snow before the camera's eye. It looks absurdly small for its function; it's hard to believe that the world can be finessed into this repository. Ponting has no lighting, cannot in fact film indoors or anywhere the world's light does not reach. Therefore his actors today, Wilson and Scott and Petty Officer Evans and Bowers, by chance the whole party who will reach the pole bar Oates, carefully rig half a tent as backdrop. Ponting films from where the other canvas wall would be. Lens cap off, gloved hand ready for the cinematographer's even cranking of the celluloid through the gate. Action, gentlemen, please.

'We did it in sections,' reports Wilson,

first we changed our footgear and lit the primus and hung up our socks and cooked the hoosh. Second, we opened up the steaming cooker and whacked it out in the pannikins, and had our meal. Third, we packed up the cooker, tied up the provision bag, put both out of the tent and then unrolled our sleeping bags. Fourth, we had our sleeping bags out and were sitting in them writing diary, winding watch, sewing, etc., and then all got inside the bags and went to sleep!

They are giving Ponting an idealised, or maybe burlesque, record of the exact actions they will perform at each stop on the high plateau above the Beardmore Glacier, when they are propelling themselves by pure reliance on their own muscles; when there are no more dogs or ponies in view to worry about, and the punishing effects of the plan become a private matter, between themselves and their bodies. ('After all,' writes Bowers to Kathleen Scott, 'it will be a fine thing to do that plateau with man-haulage in these days of the supposed decadence of the British race.' 'I hope your little boy is as lively and strong as he appears in the many photographs of him I see round the Captain's table,' he adds.) Even Oates, who does not want to go on to the pole, who thinks Scott 'should buy a shilling book about transport', will feel a certain relaxation when his horses no longer need coaxing or slavedriving. 'I thank you, Titus,' Scott will say, the Barrier crossing accomplished and all the horseflesh depoted at Shambles Camp; and suddenly, one memorable evening, Oates will turn chatty and expansive, telling stories in the tent for hours. 'You funny old thing, you have quite come out of your shell, Soldier,' Scott will say, and throw an arm around his shoulder. Just so, then, the men in the tent will poise themselves so as not to upset the cooker, while the night's designated cook boils pemmican into hot 'hoosh'. They'll wriggle into their sleeping bags like a nest of very polite caterpillars. No matter how crowded the tent (more crowded still when Scott impulsively adds a fifth man at the last moment) they'll contrive to nestle, and to reach over each other, without forfeiting the manners which preserve privacy. Or social separation, in the case of Petty Officer Evans. They'll sleep like this through a night as white as this illusion of one, and wake every day to do the same again. Ponting's film cannot show, though, the predominant silence of the polar marches. By the time they pitch camp Scott will have paced them through a day of sticky snow surface, or *sastrugi*, himself withdrawn deep in calculation, the sole decision-maker, and they prey to the bitter little resentments that fill your mind automatically as you jerk and heave in harness, only waiting for the signal to stop. You forget, Cherry-Garrard writes, 'how the loss of a biscuit crumb left a sense of injury which lasted for a week; how the greatest friends were so much on one another's nerves that they did not speak for days for fear of quarrelling; how angry we felt when the cook ran short on the weekly bag . . .' These things vanish after sledging; seem negligible before, too. The film cannot show the way the hot food will hit their bloodstreams like a drug, replacing the sullen mood with an equally physiological flush of gaiety, during which they must get into their bags to radiate the heat that makes sleep bearable.

And they move *fast* for Ponting's camera: quick movements by well-fed men who've left the warm hut minutes ago, to be accelerated yet further, till they skitter through polar bedtime when Ponting's film gets shown in later decades at slightly too many frames-per-second. If the new medium Ponting uses yet had a technique appropriate to the antique sport of man-hauling, it would be slow-mo. Night after night the polar journey will pause on sluggish replays of these same few actions: the cooker assembled with painful concentration piece by piece, feet melting a passage inch by inch between the frost-stiffened sides of a sleeping bag.

The trick of film acting, writes Wilson, is 'to try and be absolutely natural . . . you have to completely ignore and forget the cinematograph'. Petty Officer Evans keeps his head down, never looks towards the lens. Scott finds the whole thing fascinating. Bowers and Wilson cannot help grinning.

18 January 1912

'All the day-dreams must go,' writes Scott: all the dreams predicated on the vacancy of this imaginary place. The void has let them down. The mad geometricians were right. Jules Verne was right. Poe was right. There is something at the South Pole. It is a Norwegian flag.

30 March 1912

Sometimes you wake from a dream of guilt or horror that has filled your whole sleeping mind, a dream that feels final, as if it held a truth about you that you cannot hope to evade, and the kind day dislodges it bit by bit, showing you exits where you had thought there were none, reminding you of a world where you still move among choices. Day has always done this for you. It seems unfair that it should not, today. Scott's eyes open. Green canvas wall of tent, rush of snow outside seen only as a tireless random spatter of porous dark. The canvas rustles. He has not been sleeping. He has been trying to drift, but the habit of self-command cuts him off, calls him back over and over to the realisation that it is all true. This irrevocable position *is* the whole, waking truth, and the tent is his life's last scene, beyond any possibility of alteration. He can make no effort that would change anything. If he

331

had taken Oates' advice last autumn and pushed One Ton Depot further south, he might not be lying eleven miles short of it now. If he had left different instructions about the dog-teams, even now help might be on its way, rather than receding through the Barrier blizzard as Cherry-Garrard, unknowing, drives for Cape Evans. But these are ironies that have lost their power to torment, through many repetitions. Edgar Evans is dead under a shallow mound of snow on the Beardmore: brain haemorrhage, Wilson thought. Oates 'left us the other day', as it says in Birdie's letter to his mother, neatly folded on the groundsheet. Oates is a white hummock now somewhere a little to the side of the line of march. And Wilson and Bowers lie one each side of Scott in the tent, their sleeping bags pulled over their faces. How many hours ago he does not know, the breathing first of one and then of the other turned briefly ragged and then stopped. The breath sighed out and never drew in again. Except for the silence they might be sleeping. Scott has a terrible desire that he must keep quelling, to reach and shake them, to try and summon again their company. He can imagine all too well the way the illusion of sleep would break if he did; and the moment when he asked for an answer and got none would be beyond bearing. So he must not break down and ask. He must not touch them at all. He is entirely alone, beyond all hope. For who knows what scoured and whirling distance all about, he is the only living thing. There is nothing left to do but die. But he is still here. He composes himself as best he can (it is difficult to want to stop, your mind is not adjusted to it) but nothing happens. The greater nothing which he supposes will replace this tiny green space when he goes – still unimaginable – does not arrive. His heart beats in his chest with stupid strength.

It was better when he was writing. Twelve days ago Scott's feet froze at last and crippled him. Eleven days ago, the immobilising blizzard began. Ten days ago they ran out of fuel. Eight days ago they ate the last of the food, and soon the thing became absolutely certain. Everyone wrote, though the pencil was hard to hold, and the paper glazed over with ice if you exhaled on it. Wilson wrote a letter to Oriana, a letter to his parents in Cheltenham (carefully adding the address anew on the second page in case it should be separated) and a note to his friends the Smiths. Bowers apologised to his mother that his letter should be 'such a short scribble', and for other things. 'It will be splendid however to pass with such companions as I have . . . Oh how I do feel for you when you hear all, you will know that for me the end was peaceful as it is only sleep in the cold. Your ever loving son to the end of this life and the next when God shall wipe away all tears from our eyes – H. R. Bowers.' But Scott wrote and wrote and wrote. He paid his professional debts. He told Mrs Bowers that her son had been magnificent to the end, and Mrs Wilson that her husband had the 'comfortable blue look of hope' in his eyes. He told his mother that 'the Great God has called me'. There are twelve letters by him in the tent, besides his diary and a Message to the Public. His teeth are loose in his gums from scurvy, his feet would be gangrenous if the cold were not slowing up the bacteria, his face is cracked with snow-burn and marked with unhealed red and purple sores where the frost bit at the points of the bones; but while he wrote he commanded the kingdom of words. He was *making*. He could see the story of the expedition as a parabola that descended to earth at its completion, and might be made to do so with a power and a grace that justified the whole; that gave the whole an inevitable fall, like any good story whose end is latent in its middle and beginning. He knew exactly what to do. A century and more of expectations were to hand, anonymous and virtually instinctive to him: he shaped them. Scarcely a word needed crossing out. One, inside the cover of his diary: 'Send this diary to my wife.' Correction: 'widow'. With the authority of death he insisted 'The causes of the disaster are not due to faulty organisation but to misfortune in all risks which had to be undertaken.' Into the syntax of his best sentences, he wove appeals to the practical charity of the nation, so that – like a politician on television taking care his soundbite cannot be edited into smaller units – the emotion and the appeal should be indivisible. 'These rough notes and our dead bodies must tell the tale, but surely, surely, a great rich country like ours will see that those who are dependent on us are properly provided for.' Grand sombre cadences, funeral music in words, came to him; long sentences running parallel in sound to each other, inviting a voice to work its way through the scored heights and depths of the phrasing.

We are weak, writing is difficult, but for my own sake I do not regret this journey, which has shown that Englishmen can endure hardships, help one another, and meet death with as great a fortitude as ever in the past. We took risks, we knew we took them; things have come out against us, and therefore we have no cause for complaint, but bow to the will of Providence, determined still to do our best to the last.

But he had to stop. 'It seems a pity but I do not think I can write more.' When the writing stopped, so did all that words can do to give this situation meaning. His words are exhausted. The tale is told; but he is still here, in the silence afterwards, waiting. Some people wear their roles so closely they become their skin. There is nothing left of them besides, no residue that does not fit the proper emotions of a judge, or a salesman, or an explorer. Scott is wonderfully good at his role, but he is not one of these; he has always been self-conscious. Tucked beneath him, 'I have taken my place throughout, haven't I?' says the letter to Kathleen – whether with pride, or anxiety, or final bitterness at the explorer's place and its mortal demands, he hardly knows. 'What tales you would have had for the boy, but oh, what a price to pay.' After the storied death it seems there remains all of you to die that you had only glimpsed sidelong as you subdued yourself to the part. You cannot die in a story; you have to die in your body. He wonders if the other two travelled, invisibly to him, sometime in the night hours, past the end of their belief, their belief not quite stretching all the way to the fact of death, and faced this horrible vacancy. He thinks not, and is glad. They were certain enough, so far as he could judge, that the eyes they closed here would open again elsewhere. They still looked forward, 'slept' only to wake. Sleep, sleep: all at once he hates this lulling metaphor for the disappearance of every slightest speck of forty-three years of thinking and feeling. Such a lie. It is not sleep, this formless prospect from which his mind recoils helplessly though it is imminent.

But whatever he thinks, whatever he wants, here he is still, both holding death at bay, he cannot *help* it, and wishing it would hurry. He wants to see Kathleen again. He wants the world to expand again from this narrow trap to the proportions you learn to trust, living. He thinks that he would very much like to go indoors. The tent is a feeble cone perched beneath a huge sky on a bed of ice sustained by black, black water. He left Cape Evans five months ago: for almost a hundred and fifty nights he's been in the open, or within this portable fiction of shelter. You never realise until you come out here that the world divides so absolutely into outdoors and indoors. It is almost metaphysical. It seems marvellous to him now that people take open space, and floor it and wall it and roof it, and transform it utterly. He thinks of doors opening, and himself passing through. The door at Cape Evans, of course; but also he stands on the steps by the railings in Buckingham Palace Road knocking at the coloured front door of his own house. He waits at the bigger door of the Geographical Society, and through the glass panes he can see the porter in the vestibule coming to let him in, quite unflustered by the balaclava and the drip of melting frost off his windproof smock. Thresholds: the thick metal door in the corridor of a destroyer, whose rivets are cool bulges in a skin of paint, whose foot-high sill is shiny steel in the centre where feet touch it. A screen-door in the verandah of an American house on a hot day, which has an aquarium cool you are glad of on the inside of it, and a remote buzz of insects and traffic. Doors squeaking, grating, gliding ajar with huge solidity. He thumps for entry at the doors of St Paul's, not on the little gateway inset in the greater but on the vast sculpted panels of the great door itself, which swing wide on a chessboard floor where his footsteps fall echoey yet distinct. The gates of ivory and of horn in the *Odyssey*, from whose parted leaves stream out true visions and false dreams . . . *Have the gates of death been opened unto thee? or hast thou seen the doors of the shadow of death? Hast thou perceived the breadth of the earth? declare if thou knowest it all. Where is the way where light dwelleth? and as for darkness, where is the place thereof, that thou shouldest take it to the bound thereof, and that thou shouldest know the paths to the house thereof?* . . . *Hast thou entered into the treasures of the snow? or hast thou seen the treasures of the hail . . . Out of whose womb came the ice? and the hoary frost of heaven who hath gendered it? The waters are hid as with a stone, and the face of the deep is frozen. Canst thou bind the sweet influences of Pleiades, or loose the bands of Orion?* Drift . . . Drift . . . Stop! Get a grip, man. Or, no, he supposes

335

perhaps he ought not to take hold again. But it is already done. He has tightened whatever it is in him that lashes a crumbly fear together into a block strong enough to face things. And the tent returns. The tent, the place, the two corpses, the bottle of opium tablets that would dissolve him away irresistibly if he once chose to swallow them. He is still here.

Scott kicks out suddenly, like an insomniac angry with the bedclothes. Yes, alright, but *quickly* then, without thinking. He pulls open the sleeping bag as far down as he can reach, wrenches his coat right open too, lays his arm deliberately around the cold lump of the body of his friend Edward Wilson (who is not sleeping, no, but dead) and holds tight. It is forty below in the tent. The cold comes into him. Oh how it hurts. His skin, which was the frontier of him this whole long time past, is breached: he is no longer whole: the ice is inside his chest, a spearing and dreadful presence turning the cavities of him to blue glass. His lips pull back from his teeth in an enormous snarl; but Scott has left the surface of his face, and does not know. At its tip the cold moves inside him like a key searching for a lock. An impersonal tenderness seems to be watching as it finds the latch of a box, a box of memories, and spills them out, the most private images, one by one, some that would never have been expected because they were scarcely remembered and it was never known that they had been diligently stored here all the time; one by one, each seen complete and without passion, until the last of them is reached, and flutters away, and is gone.

12 November 1912

After eight months a hand opens the tent-flaps. But it is too dark inside to see what lies on the floor: the blizzards and the great winds of the long winter, through which the three bodies lay in mineral stillness, have piled up snow upon snow until nothing shows now in the spring sunshine on the Barrier except a bamboo pole. The search party from Cape Evans burrow the tent free. Now everything is clear. Those who enter can read the macabre physical evidence of the heads, the hands, the feet. Atkinson is a doctor; Petty Officer Lashly had prophesied that scurvy would prove to have been the cause of the deaths. Cherry-Garrard writes in this diary that Wilson 'had died very quietly', and Bowers 'also quietly'. He does not care to guess how Scott died; only he will add at today's end, 'It is all too horrible – I am almost afraid to go to sleep now.' But they also see that the tent was pitched as tidily as ever; that there are rolls of photographs waiting to be developed; that the sledge buried alongside the tent carries an orderly load, part of which is made up of decayed coal specimens from the rock strata beside the Beardmore Glacier. Turn these and you can see the delicate fossils of plants in them, vestiges of the Cambrian era when Antarctica was green: just as the presence of the coal in the baggage of the dead, and the proud neatness of the final camp, are vestiges of will and intention. These speak to the discoverers as loudly as the tent's dead cargo does. While they collect up the letters and the documents they can be, they *are*, reverent as well as horrified.

And then there is Scott's diary. Atkinson takes charge of it, as Scott had instructed: 'Hour after hour, so it seemed to me,' says Cherry-Garrard, 'Atkinson sat in our tent and read.' When he has the gist of it, he summons the rest and reads aloud to them. The Message to the Public, the account of Oates' very last laconicism. The story is not alive any more than the huddled corpses are. It will be told because it makes good propaganda for the war that is coming, or because it prompts reticent passion in the passionately reticent, or because – in endless ways – it serves. The life of stories is just another metaphor. But this story has already spread to ten minds, very much as if it had been one cell eager to reproduce that Atkinson had brought out of the tent; and now they carry it northward to multiply unimaginably in the warmer world.

They collapse the tent gently. They build a cairn over it that stands black against 'sheets and sheets of iridiscent clouds'. And they turn away; so shall we.

Acknowledgements

When I first picked up Apsley Cherry-Garrard's *The Worst Journey in the World*, and met the story of Scott's last expedition for the first time, I was a student who ought urgently to have been working on something else, alone very late at night on the top storey of a tall, furnitureless house full of the smell of drying paint. All the walls looked naked and provisional. The two dark pink 1930s Penguins, fished out of a tea chest, lured me with the prospect of immersing myself in a subject utterly removed from anything I would need to think hard about.

I have incurred many debts as I discovered just how hard I needed to think – and how long. Andrew Motion first commissioned me to write this book for Faber; the Wingate Trust, with great generosity, gave me a Wingate Scholarship in 1992 that let me write Chapters 3–6 without interruption or anxiety about money. But as the timetable for the writing stretched and stretched, and I combined it with life as a freelance literary journalist, I have also relied for income on a succession of generous editors who asked for book reviews from me, and whose forbearance I frequently tried, including Jan Dalley, David Sexton, John Ryle, John Lanchester, Tom Shone, Giles Foden, Richard Gott and above all James Wood. Because polar books were steered my way, I was able to try out prototypes for some of the images, arguments and convictions in this book. I made discoveries too that I would not have done had I not had the reviewer's pipeline of unselected print flowing into my life. In return I am glad that a large part of Chapter 7 should have appeared in slightly different form as an essay in the *TLS*. Two of my friends lent me money they couldn't afford, and waited longer than they should have done to get it back. My parents twice bailed me out; I was able to finish the last chapter of the book because they bought me a month's grace. My grandmother, Mrs Nancy Spufford, decided that I was a better investment than a privatised utility. I read in the British Library, Cambridge University Library, and in the library and archive of the Scott Polar Research Institute; I would like to acknowledge the assistance of the staff at all three. I've depended on advice, assistance, encouragement and conversation from Richard Grove; Jean Grove; Antonia Byatt; Stella Martin; Edmund de Waal; Peter Spufford and Margaret Spufford; Bernice Martin and David Martin; and Marina Benjamin, with whom I've obliterated afternoons in café after café around the British Museum.

Wherever I could in the book I've patchworked in narrative devices that I've admired elsewhere, but one passage borrows so directly from another author's invention that I must acknowledge it directly: the 'concentric' fantasia on the British Empire in Chapter 9 is an expansion and embroidery on a trope in John Crowley's exquisite *Great Work of Time* (New York, 1992). At different times, different pieces of the text have been read and commented upon by Jenny Uglow, whose generous scrutiny lessened the solitude of the writing as well as making me a gift of her learning about the nineteenth century; by Ian Hunt, who swapped the news of his day with me when the news of mine was frequently a couple of paragraphs to look at; by Julian Loose at Faber and Faber, wryly tenacious even when sorely tested. I often ignored their advice completely, and all errors are mine. Above all, as I made painful progress through the later chapters of the book, my writing was sustained by the reading of Jessica Martin, who has borne the weight of the book's subject matter, manifest and latent, as an intimate presence in her life.

The writer and publisher gratefully acknowledge the permission of the Scott Polar Research Institute, Cambridge, to reproduce quotations from the manuscript diaries of Isabella Parry and Sophy Cracroft.

Selected List of Sources

Sources are in alphabetical order by chapter, and appear once only, under the heading of the first chapter that draws on them.

CHAPTER 1

Sir John Barrow, *Auto-biographical Memoir* (London, 1847)

Thomas Bewick, *History of British Birds*, 2 vols. (London, 1797, 1804)

Charlotte Brontë, *Jane Eyre* (London, 1847)

Apsley Cherry-Garrard, *The Worst Journey in the World: Antarctic 1910–1913* (London, 1922)

Charles Dickens, *Our Mutual Friend* (London, 1865)

E. R. G. R. Evans, *South with Scott* (London, 1921)

Andrew Griffin, 'Fire and Ice in *Frankenstein*', in *The Endurance of Frankenstein*, ed. George Levine and U. C. Knoepflmacher (University of California Press, 1979)

Trevor Griffiths, *Judgement Over the Dead: The Screenplay of 'The Last Place on Earth'* (London, 1986)

Roland Huntford, *Scott and Amundsen* (London, 1979; revised edn., London, 1983)

David James, *Scott of the Antarctic: The Film and Its Production* (London, 1948)

L. P. Kirwan, *The White Road* (London, 1959; reprinted as *A History of Polar Exploration*, Harmondsworth, 1962)

Edward Sabine, 'A Memoir on the Birds of Greenland', *Transactions of the Linnean Society*, vol. xii (1821)

William Scoresby, jnr., *An Account of the Arctic Regions With a History and Description of the Northern Whale-Fishery* (Edinburgh, 1820)

Grace Scott's narrative of her brother's early life, quoted and paraphrased in George Seaver, *Scott of the Antarctic: A Study in Character* (London, 1940)

Robert F. Scott, *The Voyage of the 'Discovery'* (London, 1905)

CHAPTER 2

Edmund Burke, *A Philosophical Enquiry into the Origin of our Ideas of the Sublime and Beautiful* (1757; Routledge & Kegan Paul, 1958)

- *The Early Life, Correspondence and Writings of the Rt. Hon. Edmund Burke*, ed. A. P. I. Samuels (Cambridge, 1923)

James Cook, *A Voyage Towards the South Pole and Round the World. Performed in His Majesty's Ships the* RESOLUTION *and* ADVENTURE *In the Years 1772, 1773, 1774, and 1775* (London, 1777)

Charles Darwin, *Journal of Researches into the Natural History and Geology of the Countries Visited During the Voyage of HMS 'Beagle' Round the World* (London, 1839; corrected and enlarged edn., 1845)

Terry Eagleton, *The Ideology of the Aesthetic* (Oxford, 1990)

William Hazlitt, 'Coriolanus', in *Characters of Shakespear's Plays* (London, 1817)

Richard Jeffries, 'The Great Snow', in *After London* (1885; Oxford, 1980)

Immanuel Kant, *Beobachtungen über das Gefühl des Schönen und Erhabenen* ('Observations on the Feeling of the Beautiful and Sublime'), 1763; anonymous English trans. in *Essays and Treatises on Moral, Political and Various Philosophical Subjects* (1799); trans. John Goldthwait (University of California Press, 1960)

- 'Analytic of the Sublime', in *Critique of Aesthetic Judgement*, trans. J. C. Meredith (Oxford, 1911)

Richard Payne Knight, *An Analytical Enquiry Into the Principles of Taste* (2nd edn., 1805)

M. G. Lewis, *The Monk* (London, 1796)

Longinus, *Peri Hypsous* ('On the Sublime'), trans. William Smith (1739); trans. D. A. Russell (Oxford, 1964)

Samuel H. Monk, *The Sublime: A Study of Critical Theories in Eighteenth-Century England* (Modern Languages Association of America, 1935; Ann Arbor, 1960)

Sylvia Harcstark Myers, *The Bluestocking Circle: Women, Friendship and the Life of the Mind in Eighteenth Century England* (Oxford, 1990)

Herbert G. Ponting, *The Great White South, or With Scott in the Antarctic* (London, 1921)

Anne Radcliffe, *The Romance of the Forest* (London, 1791)

Anna Seward, *Letters, Written Between the Years 1784 and 1807*, 6 vols. (Edinburgh, 1811)

– *Elegy on Captain Cook* (London, 1780)

Margaret Ashmun, *The Singing Swan* (1931)

C. J. Sullivan, narrative of Sir James Clark Ross's expedition, excerpted in 'Two Unpublished Accounts of the British Antarctic Expedition, 1839–43', in *Polar Record*, vol. 10 no. 69, pp. 587–604 (1961)

Thomas Weiskel, *The Romantic Sublime: Studies in the Structure and Psychology of Transcendence* (Baltimore, 1976)

CHAPTER 3

Ralph G. Allen, 'De Loutherbourg and Captain Cook', in *Theatre Research*, vol. IV, pp. 195–211

Samuel Taylor Coleridge, 'The Rime of the Ancient Mariner' (1797), in *Complete Poetical Works*, ed. E. H. Coleridge (Oxford, 1912)

John Livingston Lowes, *The Road to Xanadu* (1927)

William Huse, 'A Noble Savage on the Stage', in *Modern Philology*, 33 (1936)

Gordon Jackson, *The British Whaling Trade* (London, 1978)

Alan Moorehead, *The Fatal Impact: An Account of the Invasion of the South Pacific 1767–1840* (London, 1966)

John O'Keeffe, *Omai, or A Trip round the World* (1785)

– *Dramatic Works* (1798)

Sir John Pringle, 'Discourse on the Health of Mariners', delivered to the Royal Society on 30 Nov. 1776; printed as an appendix to the first edn. of James Cook, *A Voyage Towards the South Pole* (1777)

Ernest Shackleton, *South* (London, 1919)

South Georgia census 1909, in *Polar Record*, vol. 23 no. 144 (1986)

CHAPTER 4

Robert F. Almy, 'J. N. Reynolds: A Brief Biography with Particular Reference to Poe and Symmes', in *Colophon*, new series vol. II no. 2 (Winter 1937)

Sir John Barrow, *Voyages of Discovery and Research within the Arctic Regions, from . . . 1818 to the present time . . . abridged and arranged from the original narratives . . .* (John Murray, 1846)

Blackwood's Edinburgh Magazine, vol. 78 no. 481, Nov. 1855; unsigned review article, 'Modern Light Literature – Travellers' Tales'

George Gordon Lord Byron, 'A Vision of Judgement' in *The Liberal*, first number, 15 Oct. 1822; *Complete Works*, ed. Jerome J. McGann (Oxford, 1980–93)

Lewis Carroll, *The Hunting of the Snark* (1876)

P. Clark, 'The Symmes Theory of the Earth', in *Atlantic Monthly*, April 1873

Samuel Taylor Coleridge, 'Written in an Album'; Hartz mountain trip in Richard Holmes, *Coleridge: Early Visions* (London, 1989)

Wilkie Collins, *The Frozen Deep*, first performed 1857, with some rewriting by Dickens; 1866, revised by Collins for a new production; 1874, turned by Collins into a prose narrative of 218 pp., 'The Frozen Deep: A Dramatic Story in Five Scenes', and published in *The Frozen Deep and Other Stories* (London, 1905). Text of the 1857 version in *Under the Management of Mr Charles Dickens: His Production of "The Frozen Deep"*, ed. Robert Louis Brannan (Cornell University Press, 1966)

George Cruikshank, 'Landing the Treasures, or Results of the Polar Expedition!!!', 18 Jan. 1819

John Franklin, *Narrative of a Journey to the Shores of the Polar Sea in the Years 1819–20–21–22* (2 vols., London, 1823, 1824); Everyman edn., introduced by R. F. Scott, 1910

– *Narrative of a Second Expedition to the Shores of the Polar Sea in the Years 1825–27* (London, 1828)

James McBride, *Symmes's Theory of Concentric Spheres: Demonstrating that the Earth is Hollow, Habitable Within, and Widely Open About the Poles* (Cincinnati, 1826)

The North Georgia Gazette and Winter Chronicle, ed. Captain Edward Sabine (London, 1821); no. VIII, 20 Dec. 1819

W. E. Parry, *Journal of a Voyage for the Discovery of a North-West Passage from the Atlantic to the Pacific* (1821)

– *Journal of a Second Voyage for the Discovery of a North-West Passage from the Atlantic to the Pacific, in his Majesty's ships Fury and Hecla* (1824)

– *Third Voyage for the Discovery of a North-West Passage from the Atlantic to the Pacific, in his Majesty's ships Fury and Hecla* (1826)

Hesketh Pearson, *The Smith of Smiths, being The Life, Wit and Humour of Sydney Smith* (London, 1934)

Edgar Allan Poe, *The Narrative of Arthur Gordon Pym of Nantucket* (New York, 1838); Penguin English Library edn., ed. Harold Beaver (Harmondsworth, 1975)

– 'MS Found in a Bottle' (1833) and 'Hans Pfaall' in Edgar Allan Poe, *Works*, ed. James A. Harrison (New York, 1902)

Arthur Hobson Quinn, *Edgar Allan Poe: A Critical Biography* (New York, 1941)

Eleanor Porden
E. M. Gell, *John Franklin's Bride* (1930)

J. N. Reynolds, *Address, on the Subject of a Surveying and Exploring Expedition to the Pacific Ocean and South Seas. Delivered in the Hall of Representatives on the Evening of April 3, 1836* (New York, 1836)

John Ross, *A Voyage of Discovery in his Majesty's ships Isabella and Alexander for the purpose of exploring Baffin's Bay, and inquiring into the probability of a North-West Passage* (1819)

'Captain Adam Seaborn', *Symzonia; [A] Voyage of Discovery* (New York, 1820)

Mary Shelley, *Frankenstein, or, The Modern Prometheus* (London, 1818); revised edn., 1831; ed. M. J. Kennedy (Oxford, 1969)

William Veeder, *Mary Shelley and Frankenstein* (University of Chicago Press, 1986)

Marina Benjamin (ed.), *Science and Sensibility: Gender and Scientific Enquiry 1780–1945* (Oxford, 1991)

John Cleves Symmes, self-published pamphlet series: nos. 1–5, St Louis, 1818; nos. 6–8, Cincinnati, January–August 1819, including 'Arctic Memoir' and 'Light Between the Spheres'

Charles Tennyson, *Alfred Tennyson* (London, 1949)

Fanny Trollope, *Domestic Manners of the Americans* (London, 1832)

Jules Verne, *Le Sphinx des Glaces* (1897)

Edmund Wilson, *Patriotic Gore: Studies in the Literature of the American Civil War* (New York/London, 1962)

CHAPTER 5

Blackwood's Edinburgh Magazine, vol. 8 no. 44, Nov. 1820; vol. 9 no. 51, June 1821

S. T. Coleridge
– *Collected Letters of Samuel Taylor Coleridge*, ed. E. L. Griggs (Oxford, 1956–71)

Biographias Epistolaris, being the Biographical Supplement of Coleridge's Biographia Literaria, with additional letters, etc, ed. A. Turnbull (1911)

David Crantz, *The History of Greenland: including an Account of the Mission Carried On by the United Brethren in that Country* (1765); first trans. from the German 1767, 2nd revised and abridged edn., 1820

Elisha Kent Kane, *The United States Grinnell Expedition in Search of Sir John Franklin. A Personal Narrative* (1856; 2nd edn., London and Philadelphia, 1857)

The Letters of John Keats, 1814–1821, ed. H. E. Rollins (Cambridge, Mass., and CUP, 1958)

John Laing, *A Voyage to Spitzbergen* (2nd edn., 1818), p. 16, 'the *aurora borealis*, or merry-dancers'

Herman Melville, *Moby-Dick; or, The Whale* (New York, 1851); Penguin English Library edn., ed. Harold Beaver (Harmondsworth, 1972)

Howard P. Vincent, *The Trying-Out of MOBY-DICK* (Boston, 1949)

The North Georgia Gazette (London, 1821); no. XV, 7 Feb. 1820; no. XVI, 14 Feb. 1820

Frances J. Woodward, 'Joseph René Bellot, 1826–53', in *Polar Record*, vol. 5 no. 39 (1950)

CHAPTER 6

Chandos Hoskyns Abrahall, *Arctic Enterprise: A Poem in Seven Parts* (1856)

Hans Christian Andersen, *Danish Fairy Legends and Tales*, trans. Caroline Peachey (3rd edn., 1861)

J. R. Bellot, *Journal d'un voyage aux mers polaires* (1851)

Blackwood's Edinburgh Magazine, vol. 8 no. 44, Nov. 1820; vol. 9 no. 51, June 1821

Brontës

Charlotte Brontë, *Villette* (London, 1853)

– 'The History of the Year' (1829) and 'A Day at Parry's Palace', *Young Men's Magazine* for October 1830, in *Early Writings of Charlotte Brontë* vol. 1, ed. Christine Alexander (Blackwell, 1987)

Emily Brontë, *Wuthering Heights* (London, 1847)

Daniel Claustre (ed.), ' "The North-West Passage, or Voyage Finished" : A Polar Play and Musical Entertainment' (1819), in *Polar Record*, vol. 21 no. 131 (1982)

James Fenimore Cooper, *The Lost Sealers* (1849)

Cornhill Magazine

'The Search for Sir John Franklin (from the Private Journal of an Officer of the Fox)', in *The Cornhill Magazine*, no. 1 (Jan.–June 1860)

Charles Dickens, 'The Lost Arctic Voyagers, I', in *Household Words*, vol. 10 no. 245 (2 Dec. 1854); 'The Lost Arctic Voyagers, II', in *Household Words*, vol. 10 no. 246 (9 Dec. 1854)

– *The Life and Adventures of Martin Chuzzlewit* (London, 1843–4)

Jane Franklin

– 'Lady Franklin's Lament' (broadside ballad) in Cambridge University Library Madden Collection of printed ballads, 17.72

Frances J. Woodward, *Portrait of Jane* (London, 1951)

Manuscript letters of Sophy Cracroft to her mother and sisters, October 1849; Scott Polar Research Institute MS 248/247/21 and MS 248/247/15

Frank Debenham, 'The Erebus and Terror at Hobart', in *Polar Record*, vol. 3 no. 23 (1942)

Elizabeth Gaskell

– *Sylvia's Lovers* (London, 1863); OUP World's Classics edn., ed. Andrew Sanders (Oxford, 1982)

Jennifer Uglow, *Elizabeth Gaskell: A Habit of Stories* (London, 1992)

Peter Gay, *The Bourgeois Experience: Victoria to Freud. Volume I: The Education of the Senses* (OUP, New York, 1984); *Volume II: The Tender Passion* (OUP, New York, 1986)

Jean Ingelow, 'When the Sea Gives up her Dead', in *Poetical Works* (1898)

Charles Kingsley, *The Water Babies: A Fairy Tale for a Land Baby* (1863)

William H. G. Kingston, *Peter the Whaler: His Early Life, and Adventures in the Arctic Regions* (1851)

Ursula Le Guin, 'Heroes' (1986), in *Dancing at the Edge of the World: Thoughts on Words, Women, Places* (New York, 1989)

- *The Left Hand of Darkness* (New York, 1969)

- 'Sur' (1982), in *The Compass Rose* (New York, 1983)

Doris Lessing, 'Afterword' to *The Making of the Representative for Planet Eight* (London, 1982)

Leopold McClintock, *Narrative of the Discovery of the Fate of Sir John Franklin and his Companions* (London, 1859)

Robert McClure

- *M'Clure's Discovery of the North-West Passage, in HMS 'Investigator,' 1850, 1851, 1852, 1853, 1854. Edited by Commander Sherard Osborn, from the Logs and Journals of Capt. Robt. Le M. M'Clure* (London, 1856)

George MacDonald, *At the Back of the North Wind* (1871)

Jane Miller, *Women Writing About Men* (London, 1986)

H. Morley, 'Unspotted Snow', in *Household Words*, vol. 8 no. 190 (1853)

Isabella Parry

- Unpublished manuscript journal Aug. 1826–March 1827, Scott Polar Research Institute MS 438/4/1 BJ

Ann Parry, *Parry of the Arctic* (1963)

Eleanor Porden

A Brave Man and his Belongings: Being Some Passages in the Life of Sir John Franklin, RN, no author (privately printed, London, 1874); compiled for 'Sir John Franklin's grandchildren and his great nephews and nieces'

Punch cartoon

'Waiting to be Won', *Punch*, 5 June 1875; reproduced in G. Hattersley-Smith, 'The British Arctic Expedition, 1875–6', in *Polar Record*, vol. 18 no. 113 (1976)

John Rae

'The Lost Arctic Voyagers', in *Household Words*, vol. 10 no. 248 (1854)

- 'Dr Rae's Report', in *Household Words*, vol. 10 no. 249 (1854)

Robert L. Richards, *Dr John Rae* (Whitby, 1985)

Ernest Shackleton

- Letter from 'three sporty girls', in *Shackleton: His Antarctic Writings*, selected and introduced by Christopher Railing (London, 1983)

Ian R. Stone, ' "Instruction and Entertainment": Items of Polar Interest in Charles Dickens' *Household Words*', in *Polar Record*, vol. 24 no. 150 (1988)

Spiritualism

Roderic Owen, *The Fate of Franklin* (1978)

Rev. J. Henry Skewes, *Sir John Franklin: The True Secret of the Discovery of His Fate: A 'Revelation'* (1889)

Alex Owen, *The Darkened Room: Women, Power and Spiritualism in late 19th Century England* (London, 1989)

R. M. and C. R. Goldfarb, *Spiritualism and 19th Century Letters* (1978)

Alfred Tennyson, 'Sir John Franklin', in *The Times*, 31 July 1875; *The Poems of Tennyson*, ed. Christopher Ricks (London, 1972)

Emily Tennyson, *Journal*, ed. James O. Hoge (1981)

Henry D. Thoreau, *Walden* (1854)

CHAPTER 7

Owen Beattie and John Geiger, *Frozen in Time: The Fate of the Franklin Expedition* (London, 1987)

Gillian Beer, *Darwin's Plots: Evolutionary Narrative in Darwin, George Eliot and Nineteenth-Century Fiction* (London, 1983)

Frederick Blackwood, Marquess of Dufferin, *Letters from High Latitudes: Being Some Account of a Voyage in 1856 in the Schooner Yacht 'Foam' to Iceland, Jan Mayen and Spitzbergen* (London, 1856; OUP World's Classics edn., 1910)

Erasmus H. Brodie, *Euthanasia: A Poem in Four Cantos of Spenserian Metre on the Discovery of the North-West Passage by Sir John Franklin, Knight* (1866)

Frank Debenham, 'Place-Names in the Polar Regions', in *Polar Record*, vol. 3 no. 24 (1942)

Emily Dickinson

- *The Poems of Emily Dickinson*, ed. Thomas H. Johnson (Harvard, 1955)

Edward Augustus Inglefield, *A Summer Search for Sir John Franklin; With a Peep into the Polar Basin* (London, 1853)

Charles Kingsley, *Westward Ho!* (London, 1855)

Margaret Arnett Macleod and Richard Glover, 'Franklin's First Expedition as Seen By the Fur Traders', in *Polar Record*, vol. 15 no. 98 (1971)

Henry Mayhew, *London Labour and the London Poor* (1851–62)

Edgar Allan Poe, 'A Descent into the Maelstrom' (1845), in *Works*, ed. James A. Harrison (1902)

Geoffrey K. Pullum, 'The Great Eskimo Vocabulary Hoax', in *The Great Eskimo Vocabulary Hoax and Other Irreverent Essays on the Study of Language* (Chicago, 1991)

P. C. Sutherland, 'A Few Remarks on the Physical Geography', in Inglefield, *A Summer Search* (1853)

Alfred Tennyson

The Letters of Alfred Lord Tennyson ed. Cecil Y. Lang and Edgar F. Shannon, vol. 2 (1987)

- 'Tithonus', in *The Cornhill Magazine*, no. 1 (Jan.–June 1860)

- *In Memoriam A.H.H.* (1850)

CHAPTER 8

Louis Agassiz

Frank Cunningham, *James David Forbes, Pioneer Scottish Glaciologist* (Edinburgh, 1990)

Roald Amundsen, *The Northwest Passage* (London, 1908)

George Back, *Narrative of an Expedition in HMS 'Terror', undertaken with a view to Geographical Discovery on the Arctic Shores* (London, 1836)

Gillian Beer, *Can the Native Return? The Hilda Hulme Memorial Lecture* (University of London, 1989)

James Boswell

- *Boswell's London Journal: 1762–1763* (London, 1950)

- *The Life of Samuel Johnson, LL.D.* (1791)

Robert Brown, *The Races of Mankind: Being a Popular Description of the Characteristics, Manners and Customs of the Principal Varieties of the Human Family*, vol. 1 (London, 1872)

Joseph Conrad, *Heart of Darkness* (London, 1902)

Daniel Defoe, *The Life and Strange Surprizing Adventures of Robinson Crusoe, of York, Mariner* (London, 1719)

Charles Dickens, *Bleak House* (1853)

Encyclopaedia Britannica: 4th edn. (1810), 'Greenland', unsigned article; 7th edn. (1842), 'Greenland' by John Francis Smith (RRR); 8th edn. (1861), 'America' by Charles Maclaren (CM); 9th edn. (1875–89), 'Eskimo' by Robert Brown (RB); 11th edn. (1911), 'Eskimo', edited version of Brown article

John Gay, *The Beggar's Opera* (1728)

Charles Frances [*sic*] Hall, *Life with the Esquimaux* (1864)

Thomas Hardy, *The Return of the Native* (London, 1878)

Reginald Heber, 'From Greenland's icy mountains' (1811), in *Hymns Ancient and Modern Revised* (Norwich, 1972)

Matthew A. Henson

- *A Negro Explorer at the North Pole* (New York, 1912); foreword by Robert E. Peary, introduction by Booker T. Washington

Bradley Robinson, *Dark Companion* (New York, 1947)

S. Allen Counter, *North Pole Legacy: Black, White and Eskimo* (Boston, 1991)

Robert Gordon Latham, *The Natural History of the Varieties of Man* (London, 1850)

SELECTED LIST OF SOURCES

Tom Lowenstein, *Ancient Land, Sacred Whale: The Inuit Hunt and its Rituals* (London, 1993)

- *The Things That Were Said Of Them: Shaman Stories and Oral Histories of the Tikigaq People*, told by Asatchaq; translated from the Inupiaq by Tukummiq and Tom Lowenstein (Los Angeles, 1992)

John Everett Millais

J. G. Millais, *The Life and Letters of Sir John Everett Millais* (London, 1905)

Fridtjof Nansen

- *The First Crossing of Greenland*, trans. H. M. Gepp (London, 1890)

E. E. Reynolds, *Nansen* (London, 1932)

John Rae, *Narrative of an Expedition to the Shores of the Arctic Sea in 1846–7* (1850)

Rae's Arctic Correspondence, 1844–55, ed. E. E. Rich and A. M. Johnson (Hudson's Bay Record Society, (London, 1953)

No Ordinary Journey: John Rae, Arctic Explorer 1813–1893 (National Museums of Scotland, Edinburgh, 1993)

Alan Cooke, 'The Autobiography of Dr John Rae (1813–1893): A Preliminary Note', in *Polar Record*, vol. 14 no. 89 (1968)

RGS Arctic handbook

Clements Markham and others, *A Selection of Papers on Arctic Geography and Ethnology. Reprinted, and Presented to the Arctic Expedition of 1875, by the President, Council, and Fellows of the Royal Geographical Society* (London, 1875)

Henrik Rink, *Danish Greenland: Its People and Its Products*, ed. Robert Brown (first Danish edn., 1851–7; London, 1877)

- *Tales and Traditions of the Eskimo, with a Sketch of Their Habits, Religion, Language and Other Peculiarities*, ed. Robert Brown (first Danish edn., 1866; London and Edinburgh, 1875)

Edward W. Said, *Orientalism* (New York, 1978)

Vilhjalmur Stefansson, *My Life with the Eskimo* (1913)

- *The Friendly Arctic. The Story of Five Years in Polar Regions* (London, 1921)

- 'The Lost Franklin Expedition', in *Unsolved Mysteries of the Arctic* (London, 1939)

Edward Tylor, *Primitive Culture: Researches into the Development of Mythology, Philosophy, Religion, Language, Art, and Custom* (London, 1871; 3rd edn., 1891)

Joan Leopold, *Culture in Comparative and Evolutionary Perspective: E. B. Tylor and the Making of 'Primitive Culture'* (Berlin, 1980)

Richard Vaughan, *The Arctic: A History* (Gloucester, 1994)

Gino Watkins

F. Spencer Chapman, *Watkins' Last Expedition* (London, 1934)

CHAPTER 9

T. H. Baughman, *Before the Heroes Came: Antarctica in the 1890s* (Nebraska, 1994)

Hilaire Belloc, *Cautionary Tales for Children* (London, 1908)

Edmund Gosse, *Father and Son* (London, 1907)

Harry Graham, *Ruthless Rhymes for Heartless Homes* (New York, 1901; London, 1909)

Samuel Hynes, *The Edwardian Turn of Mind* (Princeton, 1968)

Rudyard Kipling, *Puck of Pook's Hill* (1906)

- *Plain Tales From the Hills* (1888)

- *Just So Stories* (1902)

- *Stalky & Co.* (1899)

- 'In the Rukh', in *Many Inventions* (1893)

Clements Markham

- *The Lands of Silence: A History of Arctic and Antarctic Exploration* (1921)

– *Antarctic Obsession: A Personal Narrative of the Origins of the British National Antarctic Expedition 1901–4*, ed. and introduced by Clive Holland (Harleston, Norfolk, 1986)

Admiral Sir Albert H. Markham, *The Life of Sir Clements Markham* (1917)

Robert K. Massie, *Dreadnought: Britain, Germany and the Coming of the Great War* (London, 1992)

Jan Morris, *Pax Britannica* (London, 1968)

Simon Nowell-Smith (ed.), *Edwardian England 1901–1914* (London, 1964)

George Orwell, 'The Art of Donald McGill' (1941), in *Critical Essays* (1946)

Eric Partridge, *A Dictionary of Historical Slang* (Penguin, 1972); abridged by Jacqueline Simpson from the 1961 edn. of his *A Dictionary of Slang and Unconventional English*

Alexander Pope, 'An Essay on Man' (1733–4)

Marcel Proust

   George D. Painter, *Marcel Proust* (London, 1959–65)

Robert Roberts, *The Classic Slum: Salford Life in the First Quarter of the Century* (Manchester, 1971)

Jonathan Rose, *The Edwardian Temperament 1895–1919* (London and Ohio, 1986)

Siegfried Sassoon, 'Blighters', in *Collected Poems 1908–1956* (London, 1961)

Elaine Showalter, *Sexual Anarchy: Gender and Culture in the Fin de Siècle* (London, 1990)

David Thomson, *Scott's Men* (London, 1977)

H. G. Wells, *History of Mr Polly* (1910)

   – *Anticipations* (1901)

   – *The War of the Worlds* (1898)

   – *The Time Machine* (1895)

White Cross League, *The Blanco Book. A Collection of Papers for Men* (1909)

355

I MAY BE SOME TIME

Edward Wilson

George Seaver, *Edward Wilson of the Antarctic: Naturalist and Friend* (1933)

CHAPTER 10

Henry Bowers: George Seaver, *'Birdie' Bowers of the Antarctic* (London, 1938)

Frank Debenham, *The Polar Regions* (London, 1930)

– *In the Antarctic: Stories of Scott's Last Expedition* (London, 1952)

Paul Fussell, *The Great War and Modern Memory* (New York and London, 1975)

William Lashly: *Under Scott's Command: Lashly's Antarctic Diaries*, ed. A. R. Ellis (London, 1969)

L. E. G. Oates

Sue Limb and Patrick Cordingley, *Captain Oates: Soldier and Explorer* (London, 1982)

Kathleen Scott, *Self-Portrait of an Artist: From the Diaries and Memoirs of Lady Kennet, Kathleen, Lady Scott* (London, 1949)

Peter Scott, *The Eye of the Wind* (London, 1961)

Robert F. Scott

– *Scott's Last Expedition*, ed. Leonard Huxley (1913)

George Seaver, *Scott of the Antarctic* (London, 1940)

Stephen Gwynn, *Captain Scott* (London, 1929)

Reginald Pound, *Scott of the Antarctic* (London, 1966)

The South Polar Times, vols. 1–3, 1902–3, 1911 (London, 1907–14)

Griffith Taylor, *With Scott: The Silver Lining* (London, 1916)

Edward Wilson

– *Diary of the 'Terra Nova' Expedition to the Antarctic, 1910–12*, ed. H. G. R. King (London, 1972)

'Yip-I-Addy', words by Will D. Cobb, music by John H. Flynn (Chappell & Co., 1908)

Wayland Young, 'On the Debunking of Captain Scott: A Critique against Myths, Errors & Distortions', in *Encounter*, vol. 54 no. 5 (1980), pp. 8–19; reply by Roland Huntford, vol. 55 no. 5 (1980), pp. 85–7.

Index